BUSINESS ethics
A REAL WORLD APPROACH

Andrew Ghillyer, Ph.D.
Vice President Academic Affairs
Argosy University, Tampa, Florida

 **Higher Education**

Boston   Burr Ridge, IL   Dubuque, IA   New York   San Francisco   St. Louis
Bangkok   Bogotá   Caracas   Kuala Lumpur   Lisbon   London   Madrid   Mexico City
Milan   Montreal   New Delhi   Santiago   Seoul   Singapore   Sydney   Taipei   Toronto

Higher Education

BUSINESS ETHICS: A REAL WORLD APPROACH

Published by McGraw-Hill, a business unit of The McGraw-Hill Companies, Inc., 1221 Avenue of the Americas, New York, NY, 10020. Copyright © 2010 by The McGraw-Hill Companies, Inc. All rights reserved. Previous edition © 2008. No part of this publication may be reproduced or distributed in any form or by any means, or stored in a database or retrieval system, without the prior written consent of The McGraw-Hill Companies, Inc., including, but not limited to, in any network or other electronic storage or transmission, or broadcast for distance learning.
Some ancillaries, including electronic and print components, may not be available to customers outside the United States.

This book is printed on acid-free paper.

2 3 4 5 6 7 8 9 0 DOW/DOW 0 9
ISBN 978-0-07-337710-0
MHID 0-07-337710-4

Vice president/Editor in chief: *Elizabeth Haefele*
Vice president/Director of marketing: *John E. Biernat*
Sponsoring editor: *Natalie J. Ruffatto*
Developmental editor: *Kristin Bradley*
Marketing manager: *Keari Green*
Lead media producer: *Damian Moshak*
Director, Editing/Design/Production: *Jess Ann Kosic*
Project manager: *Christine M. Demma*
Senior production supervisor: *Janean A. Utley*
Designer: *Anna Kinigakis*
Senior photo research coordinator: *Jeremy Cheshareck*
Photo researcher: *Jennifer Blankenship*
Media developmental editor: *William Mulford*
Media project manager: *Mark A. S. Dierker*
Cover & interior design: *Anna Kinigakis*
Typeface: *11/13 Minion*
Compositor: *Laserwords Private Limited*
Printer: *R. R. Donnelley*
Cover credit: *© Thomas Northcut/Getty Images*
Credits: The credits section for this book begins on page 346 and is considered an extension of the copyright page.

Library of Congress Cataloging-in-Publication Data
Ghillyer, Andrew.
    Business ethics: a real world approach / Andrew Ghillyer.—2nd ed.
        p. cm.
    Includes index.
    ISBN-13: 978-0-07-337710-0 (alk. paper)
    ISBN-10: 0-07-337710-4 (alk. paper)
    1. Business ethics. 2. Business ethics—Case studies. I. Title.
HF5387.G49 2010
174'.4—dc22
                                    2008053596

The Internet addresses listed in the text were accurate at the time of publication. The inclusion of a Web site does not indicate an endorsement by the authors or McGraw-Hill, and McGraw-Hill does not guarantee the accuracy of the information presented at these sites.

dedication

To my father, Norman Ghillyer, who passed away during the writing of the first edition of this book. I miss you, Dad.

about the AUTHOR

DR. ANDREW GHILLYER is the Vice President of Academic Affairs at Argosy University, Tampa, Florida. Dr. Ghillyer's past experience includes serving as chief operating officer (COO) of a civil engineering software company and director of international business relations for a global training organization. Dr. Ghillyer received his doctorate in management studies from the University of Surrey in the United Kingdom. His professional credentials span more than 25 years of operational management experience across a wide range of industries, markets, and cultures. He is a published author in the field of service quality and has an established track record of growth and achievement in both corporate and entrepreneurial environments. Dr. Ghillyer also served on the Board of Examiners for the Malcolm Baldridge National Quality Award for the 2007 Award year.

PREFACE

Business ethics has become one of the strongest news stories of the last decade. Previously renowned companies such as American Insurance Group (AIG), Bear Stearns, Enron, ImClone, Lehman Brothers, Parmalat, Tyco, and World-Com, to name a few, have been linked to a growing trend of unethical business behavior and questionable management practices. As those company executives who were accused of being responsible for the scandals faced their days in court, the public revisited each of those financial scandals. The days of the celebrity CEOs (Lee Iacocca at Chrysler, Jack Welch at General Electric) appear to have been replaced with a rogue's gallery of executives who are accused of taking multimillion-dollar salaries while misleading investors and customers about the true condition of their companies. The numbers have become too big to imagine—$63 billion at Enron, $107 billion at WorldCom—and there is an unfortunate expectation that another scandal is out there waiting to be uncovered with an even bigger number. As this second edition goes to print, the financial world is reacting to an alleged fraud involving the former chairman of the Nasdaq stock market, Bernard Madoff. Details are still unfolding, but the extent of the fraud is estimated to be $50 billion.

In response to this flood of unethical behavior and all of the negative publicity that came with it, the government tried to restore confidence and a sense of control in the form of the Sarbanes-Oxley Act of 2002, which requires CEOs, among many other things, to certify the financial statements of their organizations as true and accurate.

While Sarbanes-Oxley represents a formal attempt at an ethical framework for corporate policy makers to follow, employees who need guidance on making ethical decisions are most often referred to a company code of ethics, which is supposed to provide clear directions on "the right thing" to do. Those without a code of ethics are encouraged to use their best judgment and take care of the organization, its shareholders, customers, employees, and any other stakeholders. But here's where it gets tricky: What happens if the right thing for the customer is the wrong thing for the shareholder?

Students of business ethics are typically presented with textbooks that are directed at managers—the corporate officers responsible for maintaining the ethical reputations of their organizations—or at the senior executives responsible for the creation of their company's code of ethics. Such texts often begin with the big picture questions surrounding the relationships between business and ethics and between business and society as a whole:

- Why does an organization exist?
- Who does the organization serve?
- What are its responsibilities to its stakeholders?
- Is there a moral high ground in business?
- Does running an ethical business pay off in the long run?

Unfortunately, none of this is of any help to employees in their daily work lives. The constant pressure to deliver on increasingly challenging productivity targets or sales quotas often creates an environment in which the organization proclaims the highest standards of business ethics, but the manager provides a clearer direction: do whatever it takes to hit the target or quota. Employees' involvement with business ethics will most likely begin with an ethical dilemma: choosing between their obligation to do the right thing for their employer as a good corporate citizen and their desire to make choices and decisions that they can live with as individuals.

The objective of this book is to provide assistance to those employees by taking a journey through the challenging world of business ethics at the ground level of the organization rather than flying through the abstract concepts and philosophical arguments at the treetop level. By examining issues and scenarios that relate directly to their work environment (and their degree of autonomy in that environment), employees can develop a clearer sense of how their corporate code of ethics relates to operational decisions made on a daily basis. In addition, the material will allow them to examine their own ethical standards as individuals.

As such, students will be

1. Introduced to basic ethical definitions and situations.
2. Introduced to the ethical issues that each functional department of an organization typically faces.
3. Presented with ethical dilemmas and given the opportunity to resolve them.
4. Presented with both hypothetical and real examples of unethical behavior.
5. Left with a sense of confidence in their ability to recognize and solve ethical dilemmas.
6. Left with a sense of confidence in their ability to meet the needs of the organization's stakeholders.
7. Introduced to concepts of corporate governance and corporate social responsibility.

By equipping students of business ethics with materials and tools to help them resolve the ethical dilemmas they face in their lives, it is hoped that the predominantly negative media coverage of business ethics can be counterbalanced with the realization and firm conviction that businesses *can* operate in an ethical and honorable manner. An organization's code of ethics may bear no resemblance whatsoever to the work its employees do or the challenges they face, and their senior executives may conveniently ignore the very code they demand their people follow, but the code provides employees with the resources to take more definitive action than simply attempting to "do the right thing."

Every attempt has been made to achieve an appropriate balance between using classic case studies to convey key points and case material that is as topical as logistically possible. Organizations featured in this text include the following:

American Insurance Group (AIG)

Bank of Floyd (Virginia)

Blue Source

Boeing

Brown & Williamson Tobacco Company

Canadian Imperial Bank of Commerce (CIBC)

Coca-Cola® Company

Disney

Enron

Ford

Google™

HealthSouth®

Hewlett-Packard

Hospital Corporation of America (HCA)

ImClone Systems

Johnson & Johnson

Lehman Brothers Holdings

Malden Mills

Mattel®

Mazda

MCI

Montrose Chemical Corporation

New York Stock Exchange (NYSE)

Pacific Gas & Electric (PG&E)

Romp

Satyam Computer Services

Shell

Société Générale (SocGen)

Wal-Mart

WorldCom

Each chapter includes a variety of opportunities for students to demonstrate their comprehension of the chapter content:

- Progress Check Questions are positioned throughout the chapter to underline key points in the material.
- Cases within each chapter provide additional illustrations of the concept being reviewed.
- Discussion Exercises (with questions) allow students to apply the chapter content to other case scenarios.
- Review questions at the end of the chapter enable students to demonstrate comprehension of the material.
- Review exercises encourage further exploration of and more active participation in the material.
- Internet exercises encourage further research and introduce students to useful reference sites.
- Team exercises offer opportunities for self-reflection and debate.

To support the exploration of business ethics in both classroom and online environments, instructor materials for this text include:

- Lecture outlines reflecting key learning points for each chapter.
- Answer key for progress check questions, discussion questions, and ethical dilemmas.

- PowerPoint presentations for each chapter.
- Additional discussion cases and team exercises.
- Test bank.
- Videos.
- Web site including case study epilogues and topical case studies.

A Different Approach to Business Ethics

Business Ethics: A Real World Approach introduces the complex world of applying a code of ethics to business decisions. Unlike the other texts on the market, however, this book is written for the employee facing ethical dilemmas on a daily basis rather than managers seeking to verbalize a corporate ethics policy. By examining issues and scenarios that relate directly to the workplace, employees and future employees can develop a clearer sense of how their corporate code of ethics relates to operational decisions made on a daily basis. This text includes a variety of features that reinforce this focus on the front line.

chapter 2

Defining Business Ethics

" *A large company was hiring a new CEO. The four leading candidates worked inside the company so the board decided to ask each candidate a very basic question. The comptroller was brought in. "How much is 2 plus 2?" "This must be a trick question, but the answer is 4. It will always be 4." They brought in the head of research and development, an engineer by training. "How much is 2 plus 2?" "That depends on whether it is a positive 2 or a negative 2. It could be 4, zero, or minus 4." They brought in the head of marketing. "The way I figure it, 2 plus 2 is 22." Finally, they brought in legal counsel. "How much is 2 plus 2?" they asked. He looked furtively at each board member. "How much do you want it to be?"* "
—Tom Selleck, Commencement Speech, Pepperdine University, 2000.

Chapter Objectives

The chapter objectives introduce the concepts students should understand after reading each chapter as well as providing brief summaries describing the material to be covered.

LEARNING OBJECTIVES

After studying this chapter, you should be able to:

1. Define the term *business ethics.*
2. Identify an organization's stakeholders.
3. Discuss the position that *business ethics* is an oxymoron.
4. Summarize the history of business ethics.
5. Identify an ethical dilemma in your work environment.
6. Propose a resolution for an ethical dilemma in your work environment.

frontline focus

Just Sign the Forms

Matt, a new employee at TransWorld Industries (TWI), showed up bright and early for his first day of orientation. He was very excited. He had applied for several jobs in the area, but TWI was the one he really wanted. He had friends there and they had told him that the company seemed to be growing very quickly with lots of new products coming online. To Matt, growth meant new opportunities, and he was looking forward to applying to the management-training program as soon as he finished his 90-day probationary period.

Scott, Matt's new boss was waiting for him as soon as he reached the factory floor. "Hey, Matt, very punctual; I like that," said Scott, looking at this watch.

"Listen kid, I know HR gave you a list of things to be checked off today—payroll paperwork, training videos, parking pass, ID, and all that stuff—but we could really use an extra pair of hands around here. Your position was vacant for quite a while and we've built a nasty backlog of work that needs to get caught up ASAP.

"We could really use your help on the Morton6000—you've worked with one of those before, right?"

Matt nodded, not quite sure where this was going.

"Well, here's the deal," said Scott. "The way I see it, all those videos are going to do is tell you not to harass any of the young babes around here (which won't be difficult since none of them are young or babes), not to insult anyone's race, and not to do anything unethical, which you weren't going to do anyway, right?"

Matt nodded again, still not sure where this was going.

"So I think all that time spent watching TV would be put to better use on that backlog of work on the Morton6000. We can book the shipments, get paid by the customers that have been waiting very patiently, and you can make a good impression on your first day—sound good to you, kid?"

"But what about the videos?" asked Matt.

"Oh, don't worry about them," said Scott. "We keep them here in the office. You just sign the forms saying you watched the videos and take them up to HR after lunch when you do all your other paperwork, okay?"

1. HR requires that these training videos be viewed for a reason. What risks is Scott taking here? Review the four reasons on page XX why HR should be directly involved in any code of ethics.

2. Do you think Scott's argument for skipping the training videos is justified?

3. What should Matt do now?

Frontline Focus

Hypothetical scenarios focusing on typical ethical dilemmas that face frontline employees are featured at the beginning and end of each chapter. First, the conundrum is presented, allowing students to discuss how they would handle the situation. At the end of the chapter, the problem is resolved, and students can react to the characters' choices. This feature will spark discussion among the students with questions and references to concepts presented in the chapter.

ETHICAL dilemma

CASE 3.1 A Firm Production Date

Scott Kelly, XYZ's marketing vice president, was shouting on the telephone to Tom Evers, director of new product development in XYZ's R&D laboratories: "We're going to kick off a major ad campaign timed to make people want your new model appliance, just before we start delivering them to dealers, and I want to be sure your production date is firm and not one of those best estimates you've stuck us with in the past." Taking a quick breath, he continued: "You people in R&D don't have much credibility with marketing! You don't tell us what you're up to until it's too late for us to advise you or interact in any way. I still remember the money you spent on that water purifier we didn't want. And it didn't help your credibility when you tried to keep the project alive after we told you to kill it!"

Tom assured Scott that the schedule for starting production was absolutely firm. "We've run extensive tests, including life tests, and everything definitely indicates 'go'! We're going to do a small pilot production run and test those pilot units in employee homes. That's a purely routine confirmation, so I can assure

---

Cases

Real-life cases, presented in each chapter, provide additional illustrations of the concepts being reviewed.

☑ PROGRESS CHECK QUESTIONS

9. Explain why HR personnel might consider themselves to be the conscience of the organization.

10. Select one of the ethical transgressions listed in the HR sections and document how you would respond to that situation as the employee.

11. Why is HR's involvement in the selection of the leaders of the company so important to ethical business conduct?

12. Why have ethics policies and ethics training suddenly become so important?

Progress Questions

Progress questions are positioned through the chapter at key learning points to reinforce learning outcomes and promote retention of the material.

13. How should managers or supervisors respond to an employee who brings evidence of questionable behavior to their attention?

14. Should that employee be given any reassurances of protection for making the tough decision to come forward?

15. Do you think a hotline that guarantees the anonymity of the caller will encourage more employees to come forward?

16. Does your company have a whistle-blower hotline? How did you find out that there is (or isn't) one?

LIFEskills

Making difficult decisions

In the last chapter we talked about using your personal value system to live your life according to your own ethical standards. As you have seen in this chapter, people like Jeffrey Wigand, Sherron Watkins, Christine Casey, and David Welch may come across situations in their business lives where the behavior they observe is in direct conflict to their ethical standards, and they find themselves unable to simply look the other way.

Ask yourself what you would do in such a situation. Would you ignore it? Could you live with that decision? If you chose to speak out, either as an internal or external whistle-blower, could you live with the consequences of that decision? What if there was a negative impact on the company as a result of your actions and people lost their jobs, as they did at Enron or WorldCom? Could you live with that responsibility?

Life Skills

Life Skills boxes apply ethical concepts to scenarios that might affect students in their professional and academic lives.

End-of-Chapter Materials

Multiple activities to suit all course formats are at the end of each chapter:

[KEY TERMS]

Culpability Score (FSGO) *p.* 138

Death Penalty (FSGO) *p.* 138

Defense Industry Initiatives (DII) *p.* 136

Disclosure (FCPA) *p.* 134

Facilitation Payments (FCPA) *p.* 134

Federal Sentencing Guidelines for Organizations (FSGO) *p.* 137

Foreign Corrupt Practices Act (FCPA) *p.* 134

Prohibition (FCPA) *p.* 134

Public Company Accounting Oversight Board (PCAOB) *p.* 142

Routine Governmental Action (FCPA) *p.* 134

Sarbanes-Oxley Act (SOX) *p.* 142

REVIEW QUESTIONS

1. Which is the most effective piece of legislation for enforcing ethical business practices: FCPA, DII, FSGO, or SOX? Explain your answer.

2. "The FCPA has too many exceptions to be an effective deterrent to unethical business practices." Do you agree or disagree with this statement? Explain your answer.

3. Do you think the requirement that CEOs and CFOs sign off on their company accounts will increase investor confidence in those accounts? Why or why not?

4. Was Sarbanes-Oxley an appropriate response to the corporate misconduct that was being uncovered at the time? Why or why not?

REVIEW EXERCISE

Universal Industries. Universal Industries is in desperate need of a large contract to boost its declining U.S. revenues. The company doesn't have a lot of international exposure, despite its ambitious name, but its chief operating officer may be about to change that. By coincidence, at a recent class reunion, he ran into an old classmate who was a high-ranking federal official responsible for a lot of the bidding for large defense contracts. After several rounds of drinks, the classmate began talking about his latest projects.

Universal has done a lot of defense work as a subcontractor for the major players in the industry, and the COO was able to leverage that experience to use his insider information to get Universal added to the list for several requests for proposal (RFPs) on a large expansion of a Middle Eastern military base.

To strengthen its position in the bidding process, several key Universal operatives made unpublicized visits to the towns surrounding the base and, in return for gifts of cash and other favors to local businessmen and politicians, managed to tie up the exclusive services of several local contractors, making it almost impossible for the other contenders to meet the requirements of the RFPs. The COO was equally generous in his gift to the daughter of his classmate in recognition of his help in getting the inside information.

Unfortunately, even though the new military contracts were going to provide more than enough money to boost Universal's performance numbers, they weren't going to go into effect until the following quarter. After a behind-closed-doors discussion, the senior management team decided that Universal would adjust some of its fourth-quarter expenses in order to hit the price target that the analysts were expecting. The team fully

expected that the revenue from the military contracts would allow them to make up for the adjustments in the next financial year.

However, since Universal's annual revenue exceeded $1.4 billion, the CEO and CFO were required to put their signatures on the financial reports confirming their authenticity.

After a couple of sleepless nights, and confident that the military contracts would help them fix all this in the end, they both signed.

1. Identify the ethical transgressions in this case.

2. Which piece of legislation would apply to each transgression?

3. What would be the penalties for each transgression?

4. If Universal could prove that it had a compliance program in place, how would that affect the penalties?

INTERNET EXERCISE

Locate the Web site for Berlin-based Transparency International (TI).

1. What is the stated mission of TI?

2. Explain the Corruptions Perception Index.

3. Who are the least and most corrupt countries on the index?

4. Explain the Global Corruption Barometer.

TEAM EXERCISES

1. **Protecting your people at all costs.** Your company is a major fruit processor that maintains long-term contracts with plantation owners in Central America to guarantee supplies of high quality produce. Many of those plantations are in politically unstable areas and your U.S.-based teams travel to those regions at high personal risk. You have been contacted by a representative from one of the local groups of Freedom Fighters demanding that you make a "donation" to their cause in return for the guaranteed protection of the plantations with which you do business. The representative makes it very clear that failure to pay the donation could put your team on the ground at risk of being kidnapped and held for ransom. Your company is proud of its compliance with all aspects of the FCPA and the revised FSGO legislation. Divide into two groups and argue your case *for* and *against* paying this donation.

2. **Budgeting for bribes.** You are a midlevel manager for the government of a small African nation that relies heavily on oil revenues to run the country's budget. The recent increase in the price of oil has improved your country's budget significantly and, as a result, many new infrastructure projects are being funded with those oil dollars—roads, bridges, schools, and hospitals—which is generating lots of construction projects and very lucrative orders for materials and equipment. However, very little of this new wealth has made its way down to the lower levels of your administration. Historically, your government has always budgeted for very low salaries for government workers in recognition of the fact that their paychecks are often supplemented by payments to expedite the processing of applications and licensing paperwork. Your boss feels strongly that there is no need to raise the salaries of the lower-level government workers since the increase in infrastructure contracts will bring a corresponding

Key terms are available both as margin definitions and in list form at the end of the chapter.

Review questions demonstrate overall comprehension of the material and tie the students' understanding back to the Chapter Objectives.

Review exercises encourage further exploration of the material with more active participation.

Internet exercises promote further research and introduce students to useful reference Web sites.

Team exercises offer opportunities for self-reflection and debate.

Discussion cases with questions allow application of the chapter content to other case scenarios.

A Guided Tour—Instructor Supplements

Online Learning Center—Instructor Tools

This online content provides a number of instructional tools. These were designed specifically for instructors to use in a variety of classrooms.

Power Point Slides:

These slides help reinforce major concepts from each chapter. They are excellent for in-class lectures and supplemental learning.

Test Bank:

A comprehensive test bank is available for use in classroom assessment. The test bank includes a test table that maps all questions to Bloom's Taxonomy.

Instructor's Manual:

The Instructor's Manual provides lectures, activities, and help in accessing the text for instructors to use in conjunction with teaching.

Asset Map:

The asset map labels and organizes material for use in a multitude of learning applications.

Online Learning Center—Student Tools

The **Online Learning Center (OLC)** is a Web site that follows the text chapter-by-chapter. OLC content is ancillary and supplementary germane to the textbook; as students read the book, they can go online to review material or link to relevant Web sites. An Information Center features an overview of the text, background on the author, and the Preface and Table of Contents from the book. Instructors can access the lecture outlines, answer key, additional discussion cases and team exercises, and PowerPoint presentations. Students see case study epilogues and additional topical case studies.

Acknowledgments

Once again, I am fortunate to have been supported throughout the development of this book by a talented group of people at McGraw-Hill Higher Education who have produced a "dream team" of dedicated and experienced professionals who shepherded this author and his text through the production process with unfailing enthusiasm and support. I would like to pay special mention to my editorial team, particularly Natalie Ruffatto and Kristin Bradley. In addition, Keari Green and Megan Gates' marketing vision for this text was a creative piece to this puzzle. I would also like to say a big thank you to Christine Demma for her tireless efforts in maintaining an oftentimes challenging schedule. Last, I would like to express my appreciation to the rest of the production team, Janean Utley and Anna Kinigakis for their efforts behind the scenes.

McGraw-Hill Higher Education and Dr. Ghillyer would like to acknowledge all of the instructors who reviewed this and the first edition. Their wonderful insight and input contributed significantly to the development of this text.

2nd Edition

Cornelius Cash, *American Intercontinental University*

Kenneth W. Clapp, *Catawba College*

Mike Combe, *Eagle Gate College*

Stacey Cornett, *Central Ohio Technical College*

John Forsythe, *Utah Career College*

Richard Janowski, *Butler Business School/Sawyer Schools*

Cynthia Letsch, *Walden University*

June Maul, *IIA College*

Carol Rewers, *Davenport University*

Linda Rose, *Westwood College*

Linda-Ruth Salter, *New England Institute of Technology*

Mustafa Savliwala, *Davenport University*

Daniel Sersland, *American Intercontinental University*

Karen Smith, *Columbia Southern University*

Maria Sofia, *Bryant & Stratton*

Vicki Spivey, *Southwestern Technical College*

Harvey Weiss, *Florida National College*

1st Edition

Michelle Adams, *Bryant & Stratton*

Vicki S. Blanchard, *Bay State College*

William F. Cook, *Sanford-Brown College*

Augustine C. Emenogu, *American Intercontinental University*

Claire Kane Hall, *New England Institute of Technology*

Elizabeth D. Hall, *Tidewater Tech*

Bruce Hamby, *National American University*

William Hoffman, *Everest University*

Andrew S. Klein, *DeVry University*

Thomas M. McGovern, *Fisher College*

Susan Strucinski O'Keefe, *Moraine Valley Community College*

Michael J. Phillips, *Everest University*

Jenny L. Piper, *Thompson Institute*

Joy Richman, *American Intercontinental University*

Andrew Ghillyer
Argosy University, Tampa, Florida

brief
TABLE OF CONTENTS

table of
CONTENTS

Becoming a Transparent Organization   247
Conclusion: 250

PART

1

DEFINING BUSINESS ETHICS

>> >> We begin by exploring how people live their lives according to a standard of "right" or "wrong" behavior. Where do people look for guidance in deciding what is right or wrong or good or bad? Once they have developed a personal set of moral standards or ethical principles, how do people then interact with other members of their community or society as a whole who may or may not share the same ethical principles?

With a basic understanding of ethics, we can then examine the concept of business ethics, where employees face the dilemma of balancing their own moral standards with those of the company they work for and the supervisor or manager to whom they report on a daily basis. We examine the question of whether the business world should be viewed as an artificial environment where the rules by which you choose to live your own life don't necessarily apply. >> >>

chapter 1

Understanding Ethics

> *Ethics is about how we meet the challenge of doing the right thing when that will cost more than we want to pay.*
>
> —The Josephson Institute of Ethics

LEARNING OBJECTIVES

After studying this chapter, you should be able to:

1. Define ethics.
2. Explain the role of values in ethical decision-making.
3. Understand opposing ethical theories and their limitations.
4. Discuss *ethical relativism.*
5. Explain an *ethical dilemma.*
6. Apply a process for resolving an ethical dilemma.

Doing the Right Thing

Megan is a rental agent for the Oxford Lake apartment complex. The work is fairly boring but she's going to school in the evening, so the quiet periods give her time to catch up on her studies, plus the discounted rent is a great help to her budget. Business has been slow since two other apartment complexes opened up, and their vacancies are starting to run a little high.

The company recently appointed a new regional director to "inject some energy and creativity" into their local campaigns and generate some new rental leases. Her name is Kate Jones and, based on first impressions, Megan thinks Kate would rent her grandmother an apartment as long as she could raise the rent first.

Kate's first event is an open house, complete with free hot dogs and cokes and a clown making balloon animals for the kids. They run ads in the paper and on the radio and manage to attract a good crowd of people.

Their first applicants are Michael and Tania Wilson, an African-American couple with one young son, Tyler. Megan takes their application. They're a nice couple with a stable work history, more than enough income to cover the rent, and good references from their previous landlord. Megan advises them that they will do a background check as a standard procedure and that things "look very good" for their application.

After they leave, Kate stops by the rental office. "How did that couple look? Any issues with their application?"

"None at all," answers Megan. "I think they'll be a perfect addition to our community."

"Don't rush their application through too quickly," replies Kate. "We have time to find some more applicants and, in my experience, those people usually end up breaking their lease or skipping town with unpaid rent."

1. What would be "the right thing" to do here? How would the "Golden Rule" on page 9 relate to Megan's decision?

2. How would you resolve this ethical dilemma? Review the three-step process on page 15 for more details.

3. What should Megan do now?

What Is Ethics?

The field of **ethics** is the study of how people try to live their lives according to a standard of "right" or "wrong" behavior—in both how we think and behave towards others and how we would like them to think and behave toward us. For some, it is a conscious choice to follow a set of moral standards or ethical principles that provide guidance on how they should conduct themselves in their daily lives. For others, where the choice is not so clear, they look to the behavior of others to determine what is an acceptable standard of right and wrong or good and bad behavior. How they arrive at the definition of what's right or wrong is a result of many factors, including how they were raised, their religion, and the traditions and beliefs of their **society**.

Understanding Right and Wrong

Moral standards are principles based on religious, **cultural**, or philosophical beliefs by which judgments are made about good or bad behavior. These beliefs can come from many different sources:

- Friends
- Family
- Ethnic background
- Religion
- School
- The media—television, radio, newspapers, magazines, the Internet
- Personal role models/mentors

There's harmony and inner peace to be found in following a moral compass that points in the same direction regardless of fashion or trend.

—Ted Koppel

Your personal set of morals—your *morality*—represents a collection of all these influences as they are built up over your lifetime. A strict family upbringing or religious education would obviously have a direct impact on your personal moral standards. These standards would then provide a *moral compass* (a sense of personal direction) to guide you in the choices you make in your life.

How Should I Live?

You do not acquire your personal moral standards in the same way that you learn the alphabet. Standards of ethical behavior are absorbed by osmosis as you observe the examples (both positive and negative) set by everyone around you—parents, family members, friends, peers, and neighbors. Your adoption of those standards is ultimately unique to you as an individual. For example, you may be influenced by the teachings of your family's religious beliefs and grow to believe that behaving ethically towards others represents a demonstration of religious devotion. However, that devotion may just as easily be motivated

Beliefs come from many places. Where do your strongest beliefs come from?

either by fear of a divine punishment in the afterlife or anticipation of a reward for living a virtuous life.

Alternatively, you may choose to reject religious morality and instead base your ethical behavior on your experience of human existence rather than any abstract concepts of right and wrong as determined by a religious doctrine.

When individuals share similar standards in a community, we can use the terms *values* and *value system*. The terms *morals* and *values* are often used to mean the same thing—a set of personal principles by which you aim to live your life. When you try to formalize those principles into a code of behavior, then you are seen to be adopting a **value system**.

The Value of a Value

Just as the word *value* is used to denote the worth of an item, a person's values can be said to have a specific "worth" for them. That worth can be expressed in two ways:

1. An **intrinsic value**—where a value is a good thing in itself and is pursued for its own sake, whether anything good comes from that pursuit or not. For example, happiness, health, and self-respect can all be said to have intrinsic value.

2. An **instrumental value**—where the pursuit of that value is a good way to reach another value. For example, money is valued for what it can buy rather than for itself. As the old saying goes, "Money can't buy happiness."

Value System A set of personal principles formalized into a code of behavior.

Intrinsic Value Where a value is a good thing in itself and is pursued for its own sake, whether anything comes from that pursuit or not.

Instrumental Value Where the pursuit of that value is a good way to reach another value. For example, money is valued for what it can buy rather than for itself.

Value Conflicts

The impact of a person's or a group's value system can be seen in the extent to which their daily lives are influenced by those values. However, the greatest test of any personal value system comes when you are presented with a situation that places those values in direct conflict with an action. For example:

1. Lying is wrong—but what if you were lying to protect the life of a loved one?

2. Stealing is wrong—but what if you were stealing food for a starving child?

3. Killing is wrong—but what if you had to kill someone in self-defense to protect your own life?

How do you resolve such conflicts? Are there exceptions to these rules? Can you justify these actions based on special circumstances? Should you then start clarifying the exceptions to your value system? If so, can you really plan for every possible exception?

It is this grey area that makes the study of ethics so complex. We would like to believe that there are clearly defined rules of right and wrong and that you can live your life in direct observance of those rules. However it is more likely that situations will arise that will require exceptions to those rules. It is how you choose to respond to those situations and the specific choices you make that really define your personal value system.

Doing the Right Thing

If you asked your friends and family what *ethics* means to them, you would probably arrive at a list of four basic categories:

Superman has become a fictional representation of personal integrity. Can you find examples of individuals with personal integrity in your own life?

1. Simple truth—right and wrong or good and bad.

2. A question of someone's personal character—his or her integrity.

3. Rules of appropriate individual behavior.

4. Rules of appropriate behavior for a community or society.

The first category—a *simple truth*—also may be expressed as simply *doing the right thing*—something that most people can understand and support. It is this basic simplicity that can lead you to take ethical behavior for granted—you simply assume that everyone is committed to doing the right thing, and it's not until you are exposed to unethical behavior that you are reminded that, unfortunately, not everyone shares your interpretation of what "the right thing" is, and even if they did, they may not share your commitment to doing it.

The second category—*personal integrity,* demonstrated by someone's behavior—looks at ethics from an external rather than an internal viewpoint. All of our classic comic-book heroes—Superman, Spider-Man, Batman, and Wonder Woman, to name just a few—represent the ideal of personal integrity where a person lives a life that is true to his or her moral standards, often at the cost of considerable personal sacrifice.

Rules of appropriate individual behavior represent the idea that these moral standards we develop for ourselves impact our lives on a daily basis in our behavior and the other types of decisions we make.

Rules of appropriate behavior for a community or society remind us that we must eventually bring our personal value system into a world that is shared with people who will probably have both similar and very different value systems. Establishing an ethical ideal for a community or society allows that group of people to live with the confidence that comes from knowing they share a common standard.

Each category represents a different feature of ethics. On one level, the study of ethics seeks to understand how people make the choices they make—how they develop their own set of moral standards, how they live their lives on the basis of those standards, and how they judge the behavior of others in relation to those standards. On a second level, we then try to use that understanding to develop a set of ideals or principles by which a group of ethical individuals can combine as a community with a common understanding of how they "ought" to behave.

✓ PROGRESS CHECK QUESTIONS

1. What is the definition of *ethics*?

2. List four sources of influence for your personal moral standards.

3. Explain the difference between intrinsic and instrumental values.

4. List the four basic categories of ethics.

The Golden Rule

For some, the goal of living an ethical life is expressed by the **Golden Rule:** *Do unto others as you would have them do unto you* or *treat others as you would like to be treated.* This simple and very clear rule is shared by many different religions in the world:

> **The Golden Rule** Do unto others as you would have them do unto you.

Buddhism: "Hurt not others in ways that you yourself would find hurtful."—*Udana-Varga* 5:18

Christianity: "Therefore all things whatsoever ye would that men should do to you, do ye even so to them."—*Matthew* 7:12

Hinduism: "This is the sum of duty: do naught unto others which would cause you pain if done to you."—*Mahabharata* 5:1517

Of course, the danger with the Golden Rule is that not everyone thinks like you, acts like you, or believes in the same principles that you do, so to live your life on the assumption that your pursuit of an ethical ideal will match others' ethical ideals. could get you into trouble. For example, if you were the type of person who values honesty in your personal value system, and you found a wallet on the sidewalk, you would try to return it to its rightful owner. However, if you lost *your* wallet, could you automatically expect that the person who found it would make the same effort to return it to you?

LIFEskills

Your personal value system will guide you throughout your life, both in personal and professional matters. How often you will decide to stand by those values or deviate from them will be a matter of personal choice, but each one of those choices will contribute to the ongoing development of your values. As the work of Lawrence Kohlberg (page 17) points out, your understanding of moral complexities and ethical dilemmas grows as your life experience and education grow. For that reason, you will measure every choice you make against the value system you developed as a child from your parents, friends, society, and often your religious upbringing. The cumulative effect of all those choices is a value system that is unique to you. Of course, you will share many of the same values as your family and friends, but some of your choices will differ from theirs because your values differ.

The great benefit of having such a guide to turn to when faced with a difficult decision is that you can both step away from the emotion and pressure of a situation, and at the same time turn to a system that truly represents who you are as a person—someone with integrity who can be counted on to make a reasoned and thoughtful choice.

Ethical Theories

The subject of ethics has been a matter of philosophical debate for over 2,500 years—as far back as the Greek philosopher Socrates. Over time and with considerable debate, different schools of thought have developed as to how we should go about living an ethical life.

Ethical theories can be divided into three categories: virtue ethics, ethics for the greater good, and universal ethics.

Virtue Ethics

The Greek philosopher Aristotle's belief in individual character and integrity established a concept of living your life according to a commitment to the achievement of a clear ideal—*what sort of person would I like to become, and how do I go about becoming that person?*

Virtue Ethics A concept of living your life according to a commitment to the achievement of a clear ideal – *what sort of person would I like to become, and how do I go about becoming that person?*

The problem with **virtue ethics** is that societies can place different emphasis on different virtues. For example, Greek society at the time of Aristotle valued wisdom, courage, and justice. By contrast, Christian societies value faith, hope, and charity. So, if the virtues you hope to achieve aren't a direct reflection of the values of the society in which you live, there is a real danger of value conflict.

Ethics for the Greater Good

As the name implies, this theory is more focused on the outcome of your actions rather than the apparent virtue of the actions themselves—that is, a focus on the greatest good for the greatest number of people. Originally proposed by a Scottish philosopher named David Hume, this approach to ethics is also referred to as **utilitarianism**.

The problem with this approach to ethics is the idea that the ends justify the means. If all you focus on is doing the greatest good for the greatest number of people, no one is accountable for the actions that are taken to achieve that outcome. The 20th century witnessed one of the most extreme examples of this when Adolf Hitler and his Nazi party launched a national genocide against Jews and "defective" people on the utilitarian grounds of restoring the Aryan race.

Utilitarianism Ethical choices that offer the greatest good for the greatest number of people.

Universal Ethics

Originally attributed to a German philosopher named Immanuel Kant, **universal ethics** argues that there are certain and universal principles that should apply to *all* ethical judgments. Actions are taken out of *duty* and *obligation* to a purely moral ideal rather than based on the needs of the situation, since the universal principles are seen to apply to everyone, everywhere, all the time.

The problem with this approach is the reverse of the weakness in ethics for the greater good. If all you focus on is abiding by a universal principle, no one is accountable for the consequences of the actions taken to abide by those principles. Consider, for example, the current debate over the use of stem cells in researching a cure for Parkinson's disease. If you recognize the value of human life above all else as a universal ethical principle, how do you justify the use of a human embryo in the harvesting of stem cells? Does the potential for curing many major illnesses—Parkinson's, cancer, heart disease, kidney disease—make stem cell research ethically justifiable? If not, how do you explain that to the families who lose loved ones waiting unsuccessfully for organ transplants?

Universal Ethics Actions are taken out of *duty* and *obligation* to a purely moral ideal rather than based on the needs of the situation, since the universal principles are seen to apply to everyone, everywhere, all the time.

What if you opposed stem cell research?

Ethical Relativism

Ethical Relativism Where the traditions of your society, your personal opinions, and the circumstances of the present moment define your ethical principles.

When the limitations of each of these theories are reviewed, it becomes clear that there is no truly comprehensive theory of ethics, only a choice that is made based on your personal value system. In this context, it is easier to understand why, when faced with the requirement to select a model of how we ought to live our lives, many people choose the idea of **ethical relativism**, where the traditions of their society, their personal opinions, and the circumstances of the present moment define their ethical principles.

The idea of relativism implies some degree of flexibility as opposed to strict black-and-white rules. It also offers the comfort of being a part of the ethical majority in your community or society instead of standing by your individual beliefs as an outsider from the group. In our current society, when we talk about peer pressure among groups, we are acknowledging that the expectations of this majority can sometimes have negative consequences.

Ethical Dilemmas

Applied Ethics The study of how ethical theories are put into practice.

Ethical Dilemmas A situation in which there is no obvious right or wrong decision, but rather a right or right answer.

Up to now we have been concerned with the notion of ethical theory—how we conduct ourselves as individuals and as a community in order to live a good and moral life. However, this ethical theory represents only half of the school of philosophy we recognize as ethics. At some point, these theories have to be put into practice, and we then move into the area of **applied ethics**.

The basic assumption of ethical theory is that you as an individual or community are in control of all the factors that influence the choices that you make. In reality, your ethical principles are most likely to be tested when you face a situation in which there is no obvious right or wrong decision, but rather a right or right answer. Such situations are referred to as **ethical dilemmas**.

As we saw earlier in our review of value systems and value conflicts, any idealized set of principles or standards inevitably faces some form of challenge. For ethical theories, that challenge takes the form of a dilemma where the decision you must make requires you to make a right choice knowing full well that you are:

- Leaving an equally right choice undone.

- Likely to suffer something bad as a result of that choice.

- Contradicting a personal ethical principle in making that choice.
- Abandoning an ethical value of your community or society in making that choice.

ETHICAL dilemma

CASE 1.1 **The Overcrowded Lifeboat**

In 1842, a ship struck an iceberg and more than 30 survivors were crowded into a lifeboat intended to hold 7. As a storm threatened, it became obvious that the lifeboat would have to be lightened if anyone were to survive. The captain reasoned that the right thing to do in this situation was to force some individuals to go over the side and drown. Such an action, he reasoned, was not unjust to those thrown overboard, for they would have drowned anyway. If he did nothing, however, he would be responsible for the deaths of those whom he could have saved. Some people opposed the captain's decision. They claimed that if nothing were done and everyone died as a result, no one would be responsible for these deaths. On the other hand, if the captain attempted to save some, he could do so only by killing others and their deaths would be his responsibility; this would be worse than doing nothing and letting all die. The captain rejected this reasoning. Since the only possibility for rescue required great efforts of rowing, the captain decided that the weakest would have to be sacrificed. In this situation it would be absurd, he thought, to decide by drawing lots who should be thrown overboard. As it turned out, after days of hard rowing, the survivors were rescued and the captain was tried for his action.

1. Did the captain make the right decision? Why or why not?
2. What other choices could the captain have made?
3. If you had been on the jury, how would you have decided? Why?
4. Which ethical theory or theories could be applied here?

Source: Adapted from www.friesian.com/valley/dilemmas.htm.

CASE 1.2 **Sophie's Choice**

In the novel *Sophie's Choice,* by William Styron (Vintage Books, 1976; the 1982 movie starred Meryl Streep and Kevin Kline), a Polish woman, Sophie Zawistowska, is arrested by the Nazis and sent to the Auschwitz death camp. On arrival, she is "honored" for not being a Jew by being allowed a choice: One of her children will be spared the gas chamber if she chooses which one. In an agony of indecision, as both children are being taken away, she suddenly does choose. They can take her daughter, who is younger and smaller. Sophie hopes that her older and stronger son will be better able to survive, but she loses track of him and never does learn of his fate. Years later, haunted by the guilt of having chosen between her children, Sophie commits suicide.

Meryl Streep and
Kevin Kline.

1. Did Sophie do the right thing in choosing her son over her daughter? Why or why not?
2. Should she have felt guilty? Why or why not?
3. What other choices could Sophie have made?
4. Which ethical theory or theories could be applied here?

Source: Adapted from www.friesian.com/valley/dilemmas.htm.

CASE 1.3 Jean Valjean's Conscience

In Victor Hugo's *Les Miserables* (also recreated in the 1998 movie *Les Miserables*, with Liam Neeson, Uma Thurman, and Geoffrey Rush, and the Broadway musical), the hero, Jean Valjean, is an ex-convict living illegally under an assumed name who is wanted for breaking parole after serving 19 years for stealing a loaf of bread to feed his sister's child. Although he will be returned to prison—probably for life—if he is caught, he is a good man who does not deserve to be punished. He has established himself in a town, becoming mayor and a public benefactor. One day, Jean learns that another man, a vagabond, has been arrested for a minor crime and identified as Jean Valjean. Jean is first tempted to remain quiet, reasoning to himself that since he had nothing to do with the false identification of this vagabond, he has no obligation to save him. Perhaps this man's false identification, Jean reflects, is "an act of Providence meant to save me." Upon reflection, however, Jean judges such reasoning "monstrous and hypocritical." He now feels certain that it is his duty to reveal his identity, regardless of the disastrous personal consequences. His resolve is disturbed, however, as he reflects on the irreparable harm his return to prison will mean to so many people who depend upon him for their livelihood—especially troubling in the case of a helpless woman and her small child to whom he feels a special obligation. He now reproaches himself for being too selfish, for thinking only of his own conscience and not of others. The right thing to do, he now claims to himself, is to remain quiet, to continue making money and using it to help others. The vagabond, he comforts himself, is not a worthy person anyway. Still unconvinced and tormented by the need to decide, Jean goes to the trial and confesses.

1. Did Jean Valjean do the right thing? Why or why not?
2. Why should he feel any obligation to a vagabond he's never even met?
3. What other choices could he have made?
4. Which ethical theory or theories could be applied here?

Source: Adapted from www.friesian.com/valley/dilemmas.htm.

Resolving Ethical Dilemmas

By its very definition, an ethical dilemma cannot really be resolved in the sense that a resolution of the problem implies a satisfactory answer to the problem. Since, in reality, the "answer" to an ethical dilemma is often the lesser of two evils, it is questionable to assume that there will always be an acceptable answer—it's more a question of whether or not you can arrive at an outcome you can live with.

Joseph L. Badaracco Jr.'s book *Defining Moments* captures this notion of living with an outcome in a discussion of "sleep-test ethics"[1]:

> The sleep test . . . is supposed to tell people whether or not they have made a morally sound decision. In its literal version, a person who has made the right choice can sleep soundly afterward; someone who has made the wrong choice cannot. . . . Defined less literally and more broadly, sleep-test ethics rests on a single, fundamental belief: that we should rely on our personal insights, feelings, and instincts when we face a difficult problem. Defined this way, sleep-test ethics is the ethics of intuition. It advises us to follow our hearts, particularly when our minds are confused. It says that, if something continues to gnaw at us, it probably should.

When we review the ethical theories covered in this chapter, we can identify two distinct approaches to handling ethical dilemmas. One is to focus on the practical consequences of what we choose to do, and the other focuses on the actions themselves and the degree to which they were the right actions to take. The first school of thought argues that the ends justify the means and that if there is no harm, there is no foul. The second claims that some actions are simply wrong in and of themselves.

So, what should you do? Consider this three-step process for solving an ethical problem[2]:

Step 1. Analyze the consequences. Who will be helped by what you do? Who will be harmed? What kind of benefits and harm are we talking about? (Some are more valuable or more harmful than others: good health, someone's trust, and a clean environment are very valuable benefits, more so than a faster remote control device.) How does all of this look over the long run as well as the short run?

Step 2. Analyze the actions. Consider all of the options from a different perspective, without thinking about the consequences. How do the actions measure up against moral principles like honesty, fairness, equality, respecting the dignity of others, and people's rights? (Consider the common good.) Are any of the actions at odds with those standards? If there's a conflict between principles or between the rights of different people involved, is there a way to see one principle as more important than the others? Which option offers actions that are least problematic?

Step 3. Make a decision. Take both parts of your analysis into account and make a decision. This strategy at least gives you some basic steps you can follow.

☑ PROGRESS CHECK QUESTIONS

9. Define *ethical relativism.*

10. Define *applied ethics.*

11. What is an ethical dilemma?

12. Explain the three-step process for resolving an ethical dilemma.

If a three-step model seems too simple, Arthur Dobrin identified eight questions you should consider when resolving an ethical dilemma[3]:

1. *What are the facts?* Know the facts as best you can. If your facts are wrong, you're liable to make a bad choice.

2. *What can you guess about the facts you don't know?* Since it is impossible to know all the facts, make reasonable assumptions about the missing pieces of information.

3. *What do the facts mean?* Facts by themselves have no meaning. You need to interpret the information in light of the values that are important to you.

4. *What does the problem look like through the eyes of the people involved?* The ability to walk in another's shoes is essential. Understanding the problem through a variety of perspectives increases the possibility that you will choose wisely.

5. *What will happen if you choose one thing rather than another?* All actions have consequences. Make a reasonable guess as to what will happen if you follow a particular course of action. Decide whether you think more good or harm will come of your action.

6. *What do your feelings tell you?* Feelings are facts too. Your feelings about ethical issues may give you a clue as to parts of your decision that your rational mind may overlook.

7. *What will you think of yourself if you decide one thing or another?* Some call this your conscience. It is a form of self-appraisal. It helps you decide whether you are the kind of person you would like to be. It helps you live with yourself.

8. *Can you explain and justify your decision to others?* Your behavior shouldn't be based on a whim. Neither should it be self-centered. Ethics involves you in the life of the world around you. For this reason you must be able to justify your moral decisions in ways that seem reasonable to reasonable people. Ethical reasons can't be private reasons.

The application of these steps is based on some key assumptions: first, that there is sufficient time for the degree of contemplation that such questions require; second, that there is enough information available to you to answer the questions; and third, that the dilemma presents alternative resolutions for you to select from. Without alternatives, your analysis becomes a question of finding a palatable resolution that you can live with—much like Badaracco's sleep test—rather than the most appropriate solution.

Ethical Reasoning

When we are attempting to resolve an ethical dilemma, we follow a process of **ethical reasoning**. We look at the information available to us and draw conclusions based on that information in relation to our own ethical standards. Lawrence Kohlberg developed a framework (see Figure 1.1) that presents the argument that we develop a reasoning process over time, moving through six distinct stages (classified into three levels of moral development) as we are exposed to major influences in our lives.[4]

Ethical Reasoning Looking at the information available to us in resolving an ethical dilemma, and drawing conclusions based on that information in relation to our own ethical standards.

Level 1. Preconventional. At this lowest level of moral development, a person's response to a perception of right and wrong is initially directly linked to the expectation of punishment or reward.

- *Stage 1. Obedience and punishment orientation.* A person is focused on avoidance of punishment and deference to power and authority—that is, something is right or wrong because a recognized authority figure says it is.

- *Stage 2. Individualism, instrumentalism, and exchange.* As a more organized and advanced form of stage 1, a person is focused on satisfying his or her own needs—that is, something is right or wrong because it helps me get what I want or need.

Level 2. Conventional. At this level, a person continues to become aware of broader influences outside of the family.

- *Stage 3. "Good boy/nice girl" orientation.* At the highest stage of level 1, a person is focused on meeting the expectations of family members—that is, something is right or wrong because it pleases those family members. Stereotypical behavior is recognized and conformity to that behavior develops.

- *Stage 4. Law-and-order-orientation.* At the lowest stage of level 2, a person is increasingly aware of his or her membership in a society and the existence of codes of behavior—that is, something is right or wrong because codes of legal, religious, or social behavior dictate it.

Level	Stage	Social Orientation
Preconventional	1	Obedience and punishment
	2	Individualism, instrumentalism, and exchange
Conventional	3	"Good boy/nice girl"
	4	Law and order
Post-conventional	5	Social contract
	6	Principled conscience

FIGURE 1.1   **Lawrence Kohlberg's Stages of Ethical Reasoning**

Level 3: Post-conventional. At this highest level of ethical reasoning, a person makes a clear effort to define principles and moral values that reflect an individual value system rather than simply reflecting the group position.

- *Stage 5. Social-contract legalistic orientation.* At the highest stage of level 2, a person is focused on individual rights and the development of standards based on critical examination—that is, something is right or wrong because it has withstood scrutiny by the society in which the principle is accepted.

- *Stage 6. Universal ethical principle orientation.* At this stage, a person is focused on self-chosen ethical principles that are found to be comprehensive and consistent—that is, something is right or wrong because it reflects that person's individual value system and the conscious choices he or she makes in life. While Kohlberg always believed in the existence of stage 6, he was never able to find enough research subjects to prove the long-term stability of this stage.

Kohlberg's framework offers us a clearer view into the *process* of ethical reasoning—that is, that someone can arrive at a decision, in this case the resolution of an ethical dilemma—on the basis of a moral rationale that is built on the cumulative experience of his or her life.

Kohlberg also believed that a person could not move or jump beyond the next stage of his or her six stages. It would be impossible, he argued, for a person to comprehend the moral issues and dilemmas at a level so far beyond his or her life experience and education.

☑ PROGRESS CHECK QUESTIONS

13. What are the eight questions you should consider in resolving an ethical dilemma?

14. What assumptions are we making in the resolution of this dilemma? What should you do if you can't answer these eight questions for the dilemma you are looking to resolve?

15. What are Kohlberg's three levels of moral development?

16. What are the six stages of development in those three levels?

Now that we have reviewed the processes by which we arrive at our personal ethical principles, let's consider what happens when we take the study of ethics into the business world. What happens when the decision that is *expected* of you by your supervisor or manager goes against your personal value system? Consider these situations:

- As a salesperson, you work on a monthly quota. Your sales training outlines several techniques to "up sell" each customer—that is, to add additional features, benefits, or warranties to your product that the average customer doesn't really need. Your sales manager draws a very clear picture for you: if you don't make your quota, you don't have a job. So, if your personal value system requires that you sell customers only what they really need, are you willing to make more smaller sales to hit your quota, or do you do what the top performers do and "up sell like crazy" and make every sale count?

Doing the Right Thing—Megan Makes a Decision

Kate was right; they did receive several more applications at the open house, but each one was less attractive as a potential tenant than the Wilsons. Some had credit problems, others couldn't provide references because they had been "living with a family member," and others had short work histories or were brand-new to the area.

This left Megan with a tough choice. The Wilsons were the best applicants, but Kate had made her feelings about them very clear, so Megan's options were fairly obvious—she could follow Kate's instructions and bury the Wilsons' application in favor of another couple, or she could give the apartment to the best tenants and run the risk of making an enemy of her new boss.

The more Megan thought about the situation, the angrier she became. Not giving the apartment to the Wilsons was discriminatory and would expose all of them to legal action if the Wilsons ever found out—plus it was just plain wrong. There was nothing in their application that suggested that they would be anything other than model tenants, and just because Kate had experienced bad tenants like "those people" in the past, there was no reason to group the Wilsons in with that group.

Megan picked up the phone and started dialing. "Mrs. Wilson? Hi, this is Megan with Oxford Lake Apartments. I have some wonderful news."

1. Did Megan make the right choice here?

2. What do you think Kate's reaction will be?

3. What would have been the risks for Oxford Lake if Megan had decided *not* to rent the apartment to the Wilsons?

- You are a tech-support specialist for a small computer software manufacturer. Your supervisor informs you that a bug has been found in the software that will take several weeks to fix. You are instructed to handle all calls without admitting the existence of the bug. Specific examples are provided to divert customers' concerns with suggestions of user error, hardware issues, and conflicts with other software packages. The bug, you are told, will be fixed in a scheduled version upgrade without any admission of its existence. Could you do that?

How organizations can reach a point in their growth where such behavior can become the norm, and how employees of those organizations find a way to work in such environments, is what the field of business ethics is all about.

[KEY TERMS]

Applied Ethics *p. 12*

Culture *p. 6*

Ethical Dilemma *p. 12*

Ethical Reasoning *p. 17*

Ethical Relativism *p. 12*

Ethics *p. 6*

The Golden Rule *p. 9*

Instrumental Value *p. 7*

Intrinsic Value *p. 7*

Society *p. 6*

Universal Ethics *p. 11*

Utilitarianism *p. 11*

Value System *p. 7*

Virtue Ethics *p. 10*

[REVIEW QUESTIONS]

1. Describe the major influences in your life that contributed to your value system.

2. How would you describe your personal ethics?

3. Give an example of an ethical dilemma that you have faced and explain how you resolved it.

4. Looking back on that ethical dilemma, would you have tried to resolve it in a different way, knowing what you know now? Explain why or why not.

[REVIEW EXERCISES]

How would you act in the following situations? Why? How is your personal value system reflected in your choice?

1. You buy a candy bar at the store and pay the cashier with a $5 bill. You are mistakenly given change from a $20 bill. What do you do?

2. You are riding in a taxicab and notice a $20 bill that has obviously fallen from someone's wallet or pocketbook. What do you do?

3. You live in a small Midwestern town and have just lost your job at the local bookstore. The best-paying job you can find is at the local meatpacking plant, but you are a vegetarian and feel strongly that killing animals for food is unjust. What do you do?

4. You are having a romantic dinner with your spouse to celebrate your wedding anniversary. Suddenly, at a nearby table, a man starts yelling at the young woman he is dining with and becomes so verbally abusive that she starts to cry. What do you do?

5. You are shopping in a department store and observe a young man taking a watch from a display stand on the jewelry counter and slipping it into his pocket. What do you do?

6. You are the manager of a nonprofit orphanage. At the end of the year, a local car dealer approaches you with a proposition. He will give you a two-year-old van worth $10,000 that he has just taken as a trade-in on a new vehicle if you will provide him with a tax-deductible donation receipt for a new van worth $30,000. Your current transportation is in very bad shape and the children really enjoy the field trips they take. Do you accept his proposition?

INTERNET EXERCISE

Visit the My Code of Ethics Project (MCOE) at www.mycodeofethics.org.

1. What is the purpose of MCOE?
2. What is the organization's pledge?
3. Record three different codes/pledges/oaths from those listed on the site.
4. Write your own pledge on a topic that is important to you (a maximum of two paragraphs).

TEAM EXERCISES

1. **Take me out to the cheap seats.**[5] Divide into two groups and prepare arguments *for* and *against* the following behavior: *My dad takes me to a lot of baseball games and always buys the cheapest tickets in the park. When the game starts, he moves to better, unoccupied seats, dragging me along. It embarrasses me. Is it OK for us to sit in seats we didn't pay for?*

2. **Umbrella exchange.**[6] Divide into two groups and prepare arguments *for* and *against* the following behavior: *One rainy evening I wandered into a shop, where I left my name-brand umbrella in a basket near the door. When I was ready to leave, my umbrella was gone. There were several others in the basket, and I decided to take another name-brand umbrella. Should I have taken it, or taken a lesser-quality model, or just gotten wet?"*

3. **A gift out of the blue.** Divide into two groups and prepare arguments *for* and *against* the following behavior: *I'm a regular customer of a men's clothing magazine and they send me new catalogs about six times a year. I usually order something because the clothes are good quality with a money-back guarantee, and if the item doesn't fit or doesn't look as good on me as it did in the catalog, the return process is very easy. Last month I ordered a couple of new shirts. When the package arrived, there were three shirts in the box, all in my size, in the three colors available for that shirt. There was no note or card, and the receipt showed that my credit card had been charged for two shirts. I just assumed that someone in the shipping department was recognizing me as a valuable customer—what a nice gesture, don't you think?"*

4. **Renting a dress?** Divide into two groups and prepare arguments *for* and *against* the following behavior: *My friend works for a company that manages fundraising events for nonprofit organizations—mostly gala benefits and auctions. Since these events all take place in the same city, she often crosses paths with the same people from one event to the other. The job doesn't pay a lot, but the dress code is usually very formal. To stretch her budget and insure that she's not wearing the same dress at every event, she buys dresses, wears them once, has them professionally dry-cleaned, reattaches the label using her own label gun, and returns them to the store, claiming that they were the wrong color or not a good fit. She argues that the dry cleaning bill is just like a rental charge and she always returns them for store credit, not cash. The dress shop may have made a sale, but is this fair?*

ALL THE NEWS THAT'S FIT TO PRINT

In May 2003 an investigation by journalists from *The New York Times* found that one of their staff reporters, Jayson Blair, had committed several acts of journalistic fraud in reporting on key events for the newspaper over a period of four years with the company. The investigation revealed that at least 36 of the last 73 articles he wrote contained significant errors. Of the around 600 articles he wrote during his four years of service with the company, many contained fabricated quotes from key individuals connected with the event being reported, invented scenes that were created to build emotional intensity for the article, and material copied directly from other newspapers or news services. In addition, Mr. Blair used photographic evidence of events to write articles as if he had been there in person or interviewed people at the scene, when he had actually remained at his desk in New York.

When the extent of his unprofessional behavior was uncovered, Mr. Blair elected to resign from his position. *The New York Times* published a four-page apology to its readers including a public commitment to better journalistic integrity, and asked those readers for help in identifying any other incorrect material yet to be identified in Mr. Blair's extensive body of work. As a direct result of this fraudulent behavior, the executive editor of the paper, Howell Raines, and the managing editor, Gerald Boyd, also resigned. Jayson Blair went on to publish a memoir of his four years at The Times, called *Burning Down My Master's House*.

In her 2008 book *This Land Is Their Land*, author and columnist Barbara Ehrenreich comments that technology and the constant push for cost control in regional newspapers and news sites has prompted editors to apparently view the Jayson Blair case from a slightly different angle. Referencing the news Web site pasadenanow.com, Ehrenreich comments:

> The Web site's editor points out that he can get two Indian reporters for a mere $20,800 a year—and, no they won't be commuting from New Delhi. Since Pasadena's city council meetings can be observed on the Web, the Indian reporters will be able to cover local politics from half the planet away. And if they ever feel a need to see the potholes of Pasadena, there's always Google Earth.

So it would seem that if there is money to be saved, editors can be flexible about the location of their reporters after all. No word from Ms. Ehrenreich on whether the location of the reporters will be disclosed in the stories featured on the Web site.

Discussion Questions

1. What do Mr. Blair's actions suggest about his personal and professional ethics?

2. Mr. Blair's issues with accuracy and corrections were well known to his supervisors, prompting one of his editors to send out an email reminding all the journalists that "accuracy is all we have. . .it's what we are and what we sell." What steps should they have taken to address Mr. Blair's behavior?

3. *The New York Times* responded to the situation with a frank apology and a commitment to do better, but will that be enough to restore the confidence of readers in the accuracy and integrity of the newspaper? Why or why not?

4. Since the editors of pasadenanow.com are choosing to hire reporters they know for certain will be at a considerable distance from the stories they will be covering, does that change the ethics of the situation in comparison to the Blair story?

5. Should pasadenanow.com disclose the overseas location of its reporters? Why or why not?

6. If you were an editor for this news site, would you hire these overseas reporter as a cost control solution? Why or why not?

Source: Ehrenreich, B., "This Land is Their Land: Reports From a Divided Nation", Metropolitan Books, Henry Holt & Co., NY, 2008. Barry, D., Barstow, D., Glater, J., Liptak, A., Steinberg, J., "Times Report Who Resigned Leaves Long Trail of Deception", The New York Times, May 11, 2003. Calame, B., "Preventing a Second Jason Blair", The New York Times, June 18, 2006.

THE MAN WHO SHOCKED THE WORLD

In July 1961, a psychologist at Yale University, Dr. Stanley Milgram, a 28-year-old Harvard graduate with a Ph.D. in social psychology, began a series of experiments that were destined to shock the psychological community and reveal some disturbing insights into the capacity of the human race to inflict harm on one another. Participants in the experiments were members of the general public who had responded to a newspaper advertisement for volunteers in an experiment on punishment and learning.

The "teacher" in the experiment (one of Milgram's team of researchers) instructed the participants to inflict increasingly powerful electric shocks on a test "learner" every time the learner gave an incorrect answer to a word-matching task. The voltage level of the shocks started, in theory, at the low level of 15 volts and increased in 15-volt increments up to a potentially fatal shock of 450 volts. In reality, the voltage machine was an elaborate stage prop and the learner was an actor screaming and imitating physical discomfort as the voltage level of each shock appeared to increase. The participants were told about the deception at the end of the experience, but during the experiment they were led to believe that the voltage and the pain being inflicted were real. The teacher used no force or intimidation in the experiment other than maintaining an air of academic seriousness.

The experiment was repeated more than 20 times using hundreds of research subjects. In every case the majority of the subjects failed to stop shocking the learners, even when they believed they were inflicting a potentially fatal voltage and the learner had apparently stopped screaming with pain. Some did plead to stop the test and others argued with the teacher that the experiment was going wrong, but in the end, the majority of them obeyed the instructions of the teacher to the letter.

It's important to remind ourselves that these research participants were not criminals or psychopaths with a documented history of sadistic behavior. They were average Americans who responded to an ad and came in off the street to take part. What Milgram's research appears to tell us is that people are capable of suspending their own individual morality to someone in authority—even killing someone just because they were instructed to do it.

Milgram's research shocked the academic world and generated heated debate about the ethical conduct of the study and the value of the results in comparison to the harm inflicted on the research participants who were led to believe that it was all really happening. That debate continues to this day, even though subsequent repetitions of the study in various formats have validated Milgram's original findings. Almost 50 years later, we are faced with research data that suggest ordinary human beings are capable of performing destructive and inhumane acts without any physical threat of harm to themselves. As Thomas Bass commented, "While we would like to believe that when confronted with a moral dilemma we will act as our conscience dictates, Milgram's obedience experiments teach us that in a concrete situation with powerful social constraints, our moral senses can easily be trampled."

Discussion Questions

1. Critics of Milgram's research have argued that the physical separation between the participant and the teacher in one room and the learner in the other made it easier for the participant to inflict the shocks. Do you think that made a difference? Why or why not?

2. The treatment of the participants in the study raised as much criticism as the results the study generated. Was it ethical to mislead them into believing that they were really inflicting pain on the learners? Why?

3. The participants were introduced to the learners as equal participants in the study—that is, volunteers just like them. Do you think that made a difference in the decision to keep increasing the voltage? Why?

4. What do you think Milgram's research tells us about our individual ethical standards?

5. Would you have agreed to participate in this study? Why or why not?

6. Do you think if the study were repeated today we would get the same kind of results? Why?

Source: Cohen, A., "Four Decades After Milgram, We're Still Willing to Inflict Pain", The New York Times, December 29, 2008. Altman, A., "Why We're OK with Hurting Strangers", www.time.com, December 19, 2008.

discussion

LIFE AND DEATH

Elder Suicide or Dignified Exit? A Letter from Ohio

I'm 80. I've had a good life—mostly pretty happy, though certainly with its ups and downs. My wife died seven years ago. My children are healthy and happy, busy with their kids, careers, friends. But I know they worry about me; they feel increasingly burdened with thoughts about how to care for me when I can no longer care for myself, which—let's not kid ourselves—is coming all too soon. I live four states away from them so either they will have to uproot me and move me close to them or I'll have to go live in a nursing home. I don't relish either option. This town has been my home for nearly my whole adult life, and I don't fancy leaving. On the other hand, I do not want to live among strangers and be cared for by those who are paid minimum wage to wash urine-soaked sheets and force-feed pudding to old people.

I'm in decent health—for the moment. But things are slipping. I have prostrate cancer, like just about every other man my age. It probably won't kill me . . . but having to get up and pee four or five times a night, standing over the bowl for long minutes just hoping something will come out, this might do me in. My joints are stiff, so it doesn't really feel good to walk. I've got bits and pieces of skin cancer here and there that need to be removed. These things are all treatable, or so they say (there are pills to take and procedures to have done). But it seems to me a waste of money. Why not pass my small savings on to my grandkids, to give them a jump on college tuition?

What I don't understand is why people think that it is wrong for someone like me to just call it a day, throw in the towel. How can it be possible that I don't have a right to end my own life, when I'm ready? (But apparently I don't.)

I'm tired and I'm ready to be done with life. I'd so much rather just quietly die in my garage with the car running than eke out these last few compromised years. (Even better would be a quick shot or a small dose of powerful pills—but, alas, these are not at my disposal.)

But if I do myself in, I will be called a suicide. My death will be added to the statistics: another "elder suicide." How sad! (Doesn't the fact that so many elderly people commit suicide—and with much greater rates of success, I must say, than any other demographic group—tell you something?) Why can't this society just come up with a humane, acceptable plan for those of us ready to be finished? Why can't we old folks go to city hall and pick up our End-of-Life Packet, with the financial and legal forms to bring things into order for our children, with assistance on how to recycle all our unneeded furniture and clothes, and with a neat little pack of white pills: When ready, take all 10 pills at once, with plenty of water. Lie down quietly in a comfortable place, close your eyes, and wait.

How can choosing my own end at my own time be considered anything other than a most dignified final exit?

— Anonymous. June, 2003

Discussion Questions

1. Should people have the moral right to end their lives, if they so please?

2. Does being near the end of one's life make the decision to end it justified?

3. What might the phrase "right to die" mean?

4. Do people have the right to seek assistance in dying?

5. Do people have the right to give assistance in dying?

6. What kind of restrictions, if any, should there be on assisted suicide?

Source: Jessica Pierce, *Morality Play: Case Studies in Ethics* (New York: McGraw-Hill, 2005).

chapter 2

Defining Business Ethics

> "A large company was hiring a new CEO. The four leading candidates worked inside the company so the board decided to ask each candidate a very basic question. The comptroller was brought in. "How much is 2 plus 2?" "This must be a trick question, but the answer is 4. It will always be 4." They brought in the head of research and development, an engineer by training. "How much is 2 plus 2?" "That depends on whether it is a positive 2 or a negative 2. It could be 4, zero, or minus 4." They brought in the head of marketing. "The way I figure it, 2 plus 2 is 22." Finally, they brought in legal counsel. "How much is 2 plus 2?" they asked. He looked furtively at each board member. "How much do you want it to be?"
>
> —Tom Selleck, Commencement Speech, Pepperdine University, 2000.

LEARNING OBJECTIVES

After studying this chapter, you should be able to:

1. Define the term *business ethics*.

2. Identify an organization's stakeholders.

3. Discuss the position that *business ethics* is an oxymoron.

4. Summarize the history of business ethics.

5. Identify an ethical dilemma in your work environment.

6. Propose a resolution for an ethical dilemma in your work environment.

The Customer Is Always Right

Carol is the shift leader at a local fast food restaurant. She first started working there as a summer job for gas money for that old Honda Civic she used to drive. That was more years ago than she cared to remember and she had managed to upgrade her car to something far more reliable these days. She enjoyed working for this company. The job was hard on her feet, but when she hit the breakfast, lunch, or dinner rush, she was usually too busy to notice.

Today was an important day. Dave, the store manager, had called an "all staff meeting" to discuss the new healthy menu that the company had launched in response to public pressure for healthier lunch choices—lots of salads and new options for their side items. It was going to take a lot of work to get her staff up to speed, and Carol expected that a lot of the customers would need extra time to work through all the new options, but overall she liked the new menu and she thought that the new lower-priced items would bring in a lot of new customers who were looking for something more than burgers and fries.

The company had sent a detailed information kit on the new menu and Dave covered the material very thoroughly. As he finished the last PowerPoint slide, he asked if anyone had any questions. Since they had been in the meeting for over an hour, her team was very conscious of all the work that wasn't getting done for the lunch rush, so no one asked any questions.

As a last comment Dave said: "This new menu should hopefully bring in some new customers, but let's not forget what we're doing here. We're here to make money for our shareholders and to do that, we have to make a profit. So, we're only going to make a limited number of these new items—if they run out, offer customers something from the regular menu and don't forget to push the "upsize" menu options and ice creams for dessert—those are still our most profitable items. And if someone wants one of these new healthy salads, make sure you offer them an ice cream or shake to go with it."

Carol was amazed. The company was making a big push for this new menu and spending a ton of money on advertising and here was Dave planning to sabotage it just because he was afraid that these lower-priced items would hurt his sales (and his bonus!).

1. Look at Tables 2.1 and 2.2 and identify which stakeholders would be directly impacted by Dave's plan to sabotage the new healthy menu.

2. Describe the ethical dilemma that Carol is facing here.

3. What should Carol do now?

Defining Business Ethics

Business Ethics The application of ethical standards to business behavior.

Business ethics involves the application of standards of moral behavior to business situations. Just as we saw in our review of the basic ethical concepts of right and wrong in Chapter 1, students of business ethics can approach the topic from two distinct perspectives:

1. A *descriptive* summation of the customs, attitudes, and rules that are observed within a business. As such, we are simply documenting what *is* happening.

2. A *normative* (or *prescriptive*) evaluation of the degree to which the observed customs, attitudes, and rules can be said to be ethical. Here we are more interested in recommending what *should be* happening.

In either case, business ethics should *not* be applied as a separate set of moral standards or ethical concepts from general ethics. Ethical behavior, it is argued, should be the same both inside and outside a business situation. By recognizing the challenging environment of business, we are acknowledging the identity of the key players impacted by any potentially unethical behavior—the **stakeholders**. In addition, we can identify the troubling situation where your personal values may be placed in direct conflict with the standards of behavior you feel are expected of you by your employer.

Stakeholder Someone with a share or interest in a business enterprise.

Who Are the Stakeholders?

Table 2.1 maps out the relevant stakeholders for any organization and their respective interests in the ethical operation of that organization. Not every stakeholder will be relevant in every business situation—not all companies use wholesalers to deliver their products or services to their customers, and customers would not be involved in payroll decisions between the organization and its employees.

Stakeholders	Interest in the Organization
Stockholders or Shareholders	• Growth in the value of company stock • Dividend income
Employees	• Stable employment at a fair rate of pay • A safe and comfortable working environment
Customers	• "Fair exchange"—a product or service of acceptable value and quality for the money spent • Safe and reliable products
Suppliers/vendor partners	• Prompt payment for delivered goods • Regular orders with an acceptable profit margin
Retailers/wholesalers	• Accurate deliveries of quality products on time and at a reasonable cost • Safe and reliable products
Federal government	• Tax revenue • Operation in compliance with all relevant legislation
Creditors	• Principal and interest payments • Repayment of debt according to the agreed schedule
Community	• Employment of local residents • Economic growth • Protection of the local environment

TABLE 2.1 **Stakeholder Interests**

Stakeholders	Interest in the Organization
Stockholders or Shareholders	• False and misleading financial information on which to base investment decisions • Loss of stock value • Cancellation of dividends
Employees	• Loss of employment • Not enough money to pay severance packages or meet pension obligations
Customers	• Poor service quality (as WorldCom struggled to combine the different operating and billing systems of each company they acquired, for example)
Suppliers/vendor partners	• Delayed payment for delivered goods and services • Unpaid invoices when the company declared bankruptcy
Federal government	• Loss of tax revenue • Failure to comply with all relevant legislation
Creditors	• Loss of principal and interest payments • Failure to repay debt according to the agreed schedule
Community	• Unemployment of local residents • Economic decline

TABLE 2.2   **Stakeholder Impact from Unethical Behavior**

Of greater concern is the involvement of these stakeholders with the actions of the organization and the extent to which they would be impacted by unethical behavior. As Table 2.2 illustrates, the decision of an organization such as WorldCom to hide the extensive debt and losses they were accumulating in their aggressive pursuit of growth and market share can be seen to have impacted all of their stakeholders in different ways.

PROGRESS CHECK QUESTIONS

1. Explain the term *business ethics*.

2. Explain the difference between a *descriptive* and *prescriptive* approach to business ethics.

3. Identify six stakeholders of an organization.

4. Give four examples of how stakeholders could be negatively impacted by unethical corporate behavior.

An Ethical Crisis: Is Business Ethics an Oxymoron?

Our objective in identifying the types of unethical concerns that can arise in the business environment and the impact that such unethical behavior can have on the stakeholders of an organization is to develop the ability to anticipate such events and ultimately to put the appropriate policies and procedures in place to prevent such behavior from happening at all.

Unfortunately, over the last two decades, the ethical track record of many organizations would lead us to believe that no such policies or procedures have been in place. The standard of **corporate governance**, the extent to which the officers of a corporation are fulfilling the duties and responsibilities of their offices to the relevant stakeholders, appears to be at the lowest level in business history:

Corporate Governance The system by which business corporations are directed and controlled.

- Several prominent organizations (all former "Wall Street darlings")—Enron, HealthSouth, WorldCom—have been found to have hidden the true state of their precarious finances from their stakeholders.
- Others—Adelphia Cable, Tyco—have been found to have senior officers who appeared to regard the organization's funds as their personal bank accounts.
- Financial reports are released that are then restated at a later date.
- Products are rushed to market that have to be recalled due to safety problems at a later date.
- Organizations are being sued for monopolistic practices (Microsoft), race and gender discrimination (Wal-Mart, Texaco, Denny's), and environmental contamination (GE).
- CEO salary increases far exceed those of the employees they lead.
- CEO salaries have increased while shareholder returns have fallen. *Fast Company* magazine prints a regular column titled "CEO See-Ya" that targets CEOs who have failed to deliver at least average shareholder returns while earning lucrative compensation packages.
- CEOs continue to receive bonuses while the stocks of their companies underperform the market average (as indicated by the documented performance of the Standard & Poor's 500 Index) and thousands of employees are being laid off.

It is understandable, therefore, that many observers would believe that the business world lacks any sense of ethical behavior whatsoever. Some would even argue that the two words are as incompatible as "government efficiency," Central Intelligence Agency, or "authentic reproduction," but is "business ethics" really an **oxymoron**?

Oxymoron The combination of two contradictory terms, such as "deafening silence" or "jumbo shrimp."

It would be unfair to brand every organization as fundamentally unethical in its business dealings. There's no doubt that numerous prominent organizations that were previously held as models of aggressive business management (Enron, Global Crossing, HealthSouth, IMClone, Tyco, WorldCom) have later been proven to be fundamentally flawed in their ethical practices. This has succeeded in bringing the issue to the forefront of public awareness. However, the positive outcome from this has been increased attention to the need for third-party guarantees of ethical conduct and proactive commitments from the rest of the business world. As the Ethics and Compliance Officers Association discovered in its 2000 membership survey, of the 619 members surveyed (representing 355 organizations)[1]:

95% believe their company's commitment to ethics will increase or remain the same over the next year, including 53 percent who believe their company's commitment will increase.

99% believe their company's commitment to ethics will increase or remain the same over the next five years, including 55% who believe their company's commitment will increase.

So while these may not be the best of times for business ethics, it could be argued that the recent negative publicity has served as a wake-up call for many organizations to take a more proactive role in establishing standards of ethical conduct in their daily operations. One of they key indicators in this process has been the increased prominence of a formal **code of ethics** in an organization's public statements. The Ethics Resource Center (ERC) defines a code of ethics as[2]:

> a central guide to support day-to-day decision making at work. It clarifies the cornerstones of your organization—its mission, values and principles—helping your managers, employees and stakeholders understand how these cornerstones translate into everyday decisions, behaviors and actions. While some may believe codes are designed to limit one's actions, the best codes are actually structured to liberate and empower people to make more effective decisions with greater confidence.

Code of Ethics A company's written standards of ethical behavior that are designed to guide managers and employees in making the decisions and choices they face every day.

✓ PROGRESS CHECK QUESTIONS

5. Define the term *oxymoron* and provide three examples.

6. Is the term *business ethics* an oxymoron? Explain your answer.

7. Define the term *corporate governance*.

8. Explain the term *code of ethics*.

So the code of ethics can be seen to serve a dual function. As a message to the organization's stakeholders, the code should represent a clear corporate

How do conversations regarding ethics change when your business is closely linked to human well-being? Should ethical standards be different for a hospital or day care center?

commitment to the highest standards of ethical behavior. As an internal document, the code should represent a clear guide to managers and employees in making the decisions and choices they face every day. Unfortunately, as you will see in many of the case studies and discussion exercises in this book, a code of ethics can be easily sidestepped or ignored by any organization.

ETHICAL dilemma

CASE 2.1 The Ford Pinto

Thirty years after its production, the Ford Pinto is still remembered as a dangerous firetrap.

In the late 1960s, the baby boom generation was starting to attend college. With increasing affluence in America, demand for affordable transportation increased, and foreign carmakers captured the market with models like the Volkswagen Beetle and Toyota Corolla. Ford needed a competitive vehicle, and Lee Iacocca authorized production of the Pinto. It was to be small and inexpensive—under 2,000 pounds and under $2,000. The production schedule had it in dealers' lots in the 1971 model year, which meant that it went from planning to production in under two years. At the time, it was typical to make a prototype vehicle first and then gear up production. In this case, Ford built the machines that created the shell of the vehicle at the same time as they were designing the first model. This concurrent development shortened production time but made it harder to make modifications.

The compact design called for a so-called saddle-bag gas tank, which straddled the rear axle. In tests, rear impacts over 30 mph sometimes caused the

tank to rupture in such a way that it sprayed gas particles into the passenger compartment, somewhat like an aerosol. Canadian regulations demanded a greater safety factor, and models for export were modified with an extra buffer layer. However, the Pinto met all U.S. federal standards at the time it was made.

Ford actively campaigned against stricter safety standards throughout the production of the Pinto. The government at the time actively embraced cost/benefit analysis, and Ford's argument against further regulations hinged on the purported benefits. Under pressure, the National Highway Traffic Safety Administration came up with a figure that put a value of just over $200,000 on a human life. Using this figure, and projecting some 180 burn deaths a year, Ford argued that retrofitting the Pinto would be overly problematic.

At one point, over 2 million Pintos were on the road, so it is not surprising that they were involved in a number of crashes. However, data began to indicate that some kinds of crashes, particularly rear-end and rollover crashes, were more likely to produce fires in the Pinto than in comparable vehicles. A dramatic article in *Mother Jones* drew on internal Ford memos to show that the company was aware of the safety issue and indicted the company for selling cars "in which it knew hundreds of people would needlessly burn to death." It also claimed that installing a barrier between the tank and the passenger compartment was an inexpensive fix (less than $20). In 1978, in an almost unprecedented case in Goshen, Indiana, the state charged the company itself with the criminal reckless homicide of three young women. The company was acquitted, largely because the judge confined the evidence to the particular facts—the car was stalled and rammed at high speed by a pickup truck—but Ford was faced with hundreds of lawsuits and a severely tarnished reputation.

Under government pressure, and just before new standards were enacted, Ford recalled 1.5 million Pintos in 1978. The model was discontinued in 1980.

Lee Iacocca said that his company did not deliberately make an unsafe vehicle, that the proportion of deadly accidents was not unusually high for the model, and that the controversy was essentially a legal and public relations issue.

1. Should a manufacturer go beyond government standards if it feels there may be a potential safety hazard with its product?

2. Once the safety issue became apparent, should Ford have recalled the vehicle and paid for the retrofit? Should they have invited owners to pay for the new barrier if they so chose? If only half the owners responded to the recall, what would the company's obligation be?

3. Is there a difference for a consumer between being able to make a conscious decision about upgrading safety features (such as side airbags) and relying on the manufacturer to determine features such as the tensile strength of the gas tank?

4. Once Pintos had a poor reputation, they were often sold at a discount. Do private sellers have the same obligations as Ford if they sell a car they know may have design defects? Does the discount price absolve sellers from any responsibility for the product?

Source: K. Gibson, *Business Ethics: People, Profits, and the Planet,* (New York: McGraw-Hill, 2006), pp. 630–632.

The History of Business Ethics

Table 2.3 documents a brief history of business ethics. It illustrates several dramatic changes that have taken place in the business environment over the last four decades:

- The increased presence of an employee voice has made individual employees feel more comfortable speaking out against actions of their employers that they feel to be irresponsible or unethical. They are also more willing to seek legal resolution for such issues as unsafe working conditions, harassment, discrimination, and invasion of privacy.

- The issue of corporate social responsibility has advanced from an abstract debate to a core performance-assessment issue with clearly established legal liabilities.

- Corporate ethics has moved from the domain of legal and human resource departments into the organizational mainstream with the appointment of corporate ethics officers with clear mandates.

- Codes of ethics have matured from cosmetic public relations documents into performance-measurement documents that an increasing number of organizations are now committing to share with all their stakeholders.

- The 2002 Sarbanes-Oxley Act has introduced greater accountability for chief executive officers and boards of directors in signing off on the financial performance records of the organizations they represent.

✓ PROGRESS CHECK QUESTIONS

9. Identify a major ethical dilemma in each of the last four decades.

10. Identify a key development in business ethics in each of the last four decades.

11. Which decade saw the most development in business ethics? Why?

12. Which decade saw the most ethical dilemmas? Why?

Doing the Right Thing

So what does all this mean for the individual employee on the front lines of the organization, dealing with stakeholders on a daily basis? In most cases, the code of ethics that is displayed so prominently for all stakeholders to see (and, presumably, be reassured by) offers very little guidance when employees face ethical conflicts in the daily performance of their work responsibilities. When employees observe unethical behavior (for example, fraud, theft of company property, incentives being paid under the table to suppliers or vendor partners) or are asked to do something that conflicts with their own personal values (selling customers products or services they don't need or that don't fill their needs), the extent of the guidance available to them is often nothing more than a series of clichés:

- Consult the company code of ethics.
- Do what's right for the organization's stakeholders.
- Do what's legal.

- Do what you think is best ("use your best judgment").
- Do the right thing.

However, in many cases, the scenario the employee faces is not a clear-cut case of right and wrong, but a case of right versus right. In this scenario, the **ethical dilemma** involves a situation that requires selecting between conflicting values that are important to the employee or the organization. For example [3]:

- You have worked at the same company with your best friend for the last 10 years—in fact, he told you about the job and got you the interview. He works in the marketing department and is up for a promotion to marketing director—a position he has been wanting for a long time. You work in sales, and on your weekly conference call, the new marketing director—someone recruited from outside the company—joins you. Your boss explains that although the formal announcement hasn't been made yet, the company felt it was important to get the new director up to speed as quickly as possible. He will be joining the company in two weeks, after completing his two weeks' notice with his current employer. Should you tell your friend what happened?

- You work in a small custom metal fabrication company that is a wholly owned subsidiary of a larger conglomerate. Your parent company has announced cost-cutting initiatives that include a freeze on pay increases, citing "current market difficulties." At the same time, the CEO trades in the old company plane for a brand-new Gulfstream jet. Your colleagues are planning to strike over the unfair treatment—a strike that will cause considerable hardship for many of your customers who have come to rely on your company as a quality supplier. Do you go on strike with them?
- At a picnic given by your employer for all of the company's employees, you observe that your supervisor—who is also a friend—has had a bit too much to drink. As you're walking home after the party, she stops her car and asks if you'd like a ride home. Do you refuse her offer, perhaps jeopardizing the friendship, or take a chance on not getting home safely?

Resolving Ethical Dilemmas

Resolution of an ethical dilemma can be achieved by first recognizing the type of conflict you are dealing with:

- *Truth versus loyalty.* Do you tell the truth or remain loyal to the person or organization that is asking you not to reveal that truth?
- *Short-term versus long-term.* Does your decision have a short-term consequence or a longer-term consequence?
- *Justice versus mercy.* Do you perceive this issue as a question of dispensing justice or mercy? (Which one are you more comfortable with?)
- *Individual versus community.* Will your choice impact one individual or a wider group or community?

In the examples used above, both sides are right to some extent, but since you can't take both actions, you are required to select the better or higher right

Decade	Ethical Climate	Major Ethical Dilemmas	Business Ethics Developments
1960s	Social unrest. Antiwar sentiment. Employees have an adversarial relationship with management. Values shift away from loyalty to an employer to loyalty to ideas. Old values are cast aside.	• Environmental issues. • Increased employee–employer tension. • Civil rights issues dominate. • Honesty. • The work ethic changes. • Drug use escalates.	• Companies begin establishing codes of conduct and values statements. • Birth of social responsibility movement. • Corporations address ethics issues through legal or personnel departments.
1970s	Defense contractors and other major industries riddled by scandal. The economy suffers through recession. Unemployment escalates. There are heightened environmental concerns. The public pushes to make businesses accountable for ethical shortcomings.	• Employee militancy (employee versus management mentality). • Human rights issues surface (forced labor, substandard wages, unsafe practices). • Some firms choose to cover rather than correct dilemmas.	• Ethics Resource Center (ERC) founded (1977). • Compliance with laws highlighted. • Federal Corrupt Practices Act passed in 1977. • Values movement begins to move ethics away from compliance orientation to being "values centered."
1980s	The social contract between employers and employees is redefined. Defense contractors are required to conform to stringent rules. Corporations downsize and employees' attitudes about loyalty to the employer are eroded. Health care ethics emphasized.	• Bribes and illegal contracting practices. • Influence peddling. • Deceptive advertising. • Financial fraud (savings and loan scandal). • Transparency issues arise.	• ERC develops the U.S. Code of Ethics for Government Service (1980). • ERC forms first business ethics office at General Dynamics (1985). • Defense Industry Initiative established. • Some companies create ombudsman positions in addition to ethics officer roles. • False Claims Act (government contracting).
1990s	Global expansion brings new ethical challenges. There are major concerns about child labor, facilitation payments (bribes), and environmental issues. The emergence of the Internet challenges cultural borders. What was forbidden becomes common.	• Unsafe work practices in Third World countries. • Increased corporate liability for personal damage (cigarette companies, Dow Chemical, etc.). • Financial mismanagement and fraud.	• Federal Sentencing Guidelines (1991). • Class action lawsuits. • Global Sullivan Principles (1999). • *In re Caremark* (Delaware Chancery Court ruling re board responsibility for ethics). • IGs requiring voluntary disclosure. • ERC establishes international business ethics centers. • Royal Dutch/Shell International begins issuing annual reports on its ethical performance.
2000s		• Cyber crime. • Privacy issues (data mining). • Financial mismanagement. • International corruption. • Loss of privacy—employees versus employers. • Intellectual property theft.	• Business regulations mandate stronger ethical safeguards (Federal Sentencing Guidelines for Organizations; Sarbanes-Oxley Act of 2002). • Anticorruption efforts grow. • Shift to emphasis on corporate social responsibility and integrity management. • Formation of International ethics centers to serve the needs of global business. • OECD Convention on Bribery (1997–2000).

TABLE 2.3   **A Brief History of Business Ethics**

Source: Adapted from Ethics Resource Center, "Business Ethics Timeline." Copyright © 2002, Ethics Resource Center.

based on your own resolution process. In the first example, the two rights you are facing are

- It is right, on the one hand, to tell your friend the truth about not getting the promotion. After all, you know the truth, and what kind of world would this be if people did not honor the truth? Perhaps your friend would prefer to hear the truth from you and would be grateful for time to adjust to the idea.

- It is right, on the other hand, not to say anything to your friend because the person who told you in the first place asked you to keep it secret and you must be loyal to your promises. Also, your friend may prefer to hear the news from his supervisor and may be unhappy with you if you tell.

In this example you are faced with a truth versus loyalty conflict: do you tell your friend the truth or remain loyal to the person who swore you to secrecy?

Once you have reached a decision as to the type of conflict you are facing, three resolution principles are available to you:

- *Ends-based.* Which decision would provide the greatest good for the greatest number of people?

- *Rules-based.* What would happen if everyone made the same decision as you?

- *The Golden Rule.* Do unto others as you would have them do unto you.

None of these principles can be said to offer a perfect solution or resolution to the problem since you cannot possibly predict the reactions of the other people involved in the scenario. However, the process of resolution at least offers something more meaningful than "going with your gut feeling" or "doing what's right."

✓ PROGRESS CHECK QUESTIONS

13. Give four examples of the clichés employees often hear when faced with an ethical dilemma.

14. List the four types of ethical conflict.

15. List the three principles available to you in resolving an ethical dilemma.

16. Give an example of an ethical business dilemma you have faced in your career and explain how you resolved it, indicating the type of conflict you experienced and the resolution principle you adopted.

LIFEskills

Making tough choices

What happens when your personal values appear to directly conflict with those of your employer? Three options are open to you: leave and find another job (not as easy as it sounds); keep your head down, do what you have been asked to do, and hold on to the job; talk to someone in the company about how uncomfortable the situation is making you feel and see if you can change things. All three options represent a tough choice that you may face at some point in your career. The factors that you will have to consider in making that choice will also change as you move through your working life. Making a job change on the basis of an ethical principle may seem much less challenging to a single person with fewer responsibilities than to a midlevel manager with a family and greater financial obligations.

The important point to remember here is that while an ethical dilemma may put you in a tough situation in the present, the consequences of the choice you make may remain with you far into the future. For that reason, make the choice as objectively and unemotionally as you can. Use the checklists and other tools that are available to you in this book to work through the exact nature of the issue so that you can resolve it in a manner that you can live with.

ETHICAL dilemma

CASE 2.2 **What to Say to the Man Let Go?**

Mary worked as a secretary in a department within a branch of a large corporation. The branch director had decided that the job of her department director, Jim, would soon be discontinued. Although Mary and a few others in her department had this knowledge, Jim did not.

For a few weeks, Jim was directed to work on an array of special projects at his home office. In the meantime, an employee from a different department was told to move into Jim's office.

The branch director instructed Mary and other support staff to change Jim's voice mail, move his files out of the office, and erase his name from his assigned parking spot. Mary was told that the human resources department would call Jim to let him know what had taken place.

That week Jim called Mary because he could not get into his voice mail. He wanted to know if there were any technical problems. Mary felt torn: should she tell him the truth now or should she rely on human resources staff to tell him?

1. What kind of ethical dilemma is Mary facing?

2. Should Mary rely on the human resources staff to tell Jim? Why?

3. Could the organization have handled Jim's termination differently? How?

4. What would you do in this position? Explain your answer.

Source: Adapted from Institute for Global Ethics, "What to Say to the Man Let Go?" www.globalethics.org/dilemmas/dilemma.tmpl?id51033.

Justifying Unethical Behavior

So how do supposedly intelligent, and presumably experienced, executives and employees manage to commit acts that end up inflicting such harm on their companies, colleagues, customers, and vendor partners? Saul Gellerman identified "four commonly held rationalizations that can lead to misconduct"[4]:

1. *A belief that the activity is within reasonable ethical and legal limits—that is, that it is not "really" illegal or immoral.* Andrew Young is quoted as having said, "Nothing is illegal if a hundred businessmen decide to do it."

The notion that anything that isn't specifically labeled as wrong must be OK is an open invitation for the ethically challenged employer and employee—especially if there are explicit rewards for such creativity within those newly expanded ethical limits. The Porsches and Jaguars that became the vehicles of choice for Enron's young and aggressive employees were all the incentives needed for newly hired employees to adjust their viewpoint on the company's creative practices.

2. *A belief that the activity is in the individual's or the corporation's best interests— that the individual would somehow be expected to undertake the activity.* In a highly competitive environment, working on short-term targets, it can be easy to find justification for any act as being "in the company's best interest." If landing that big sale or beating your competitor to market with the latest product upgrades can be seen to ensure large profits, strong public relations, a healthy stock price, job security for hundreds if not thousands of employees, not to mention a healthy bonus and promotion for you, the issue of doing whatever it takes becomes a much more complex, increasingly gray ethical area.

3. *A belief that the activity is safe because it will never be found out or publicized—the classic crime-and-punishment issue of discovery.* Every unethical act that goes undiscovered reinforces this belief. Companies that rely on the deterrents of audits and spot checks make some headway in discouraging unethical behavior (or at least prompting people to think twice about it). Gellerman argues that "A trespass detected should not be dealt with discreetly. Managers should announce the misconduct and how the individuals involved were punished. Since the main deterrent to illegal or unethical behavior is the perceived probability of detection, managers should make an example of people who are detected."

4. *A belief that because the activity helps the company, the company will condone it and even protect the person who engages in it.* This belief suggests some confusion over the loyalty being demonstrated here. Companies engaged in ethical behavior—willingly or otherwise—may protect the identity of the personnel involved but only for as long as it is in the company's best interests to do so. Once that transgression is made public and regulatory bodies get involved, most cases would seem to suggest that the situation rapidly becomes one of every man for himself. As we saw with the Enron case, once the extent of the fraud became public, everyone involved suddenly became eager to distance him- or herself from both the activity and any key personnel in direct contact with that activity.

Building and Operating an Ethical Business

It is unfortunate that the media have been given so much material on unethical corporate behavior over the last decade. Unethical CEOs have become household names to the extent that the term *business ethics* seems to be more of an

The Customer Is Always Right—Carol Makes a Decision

Rachel, one of Carol's brightest team members, identified the problem that Dave had created for them right away: "So we have a new menu that's supposed to bring in new customers, but we're only going to make a few items to make sure that we sell lots of our unhealthy but more profitable items—is that it?"

"Looks like it," said Carol.

"Well, I hope I'm not working the drive-thru window when we start to run out of the new items," said Rachel. "Can you say 'bait and switch'?"

Fortunately, the new menu items wouldn't start until next week, so Carol had some time to work on this potential disaster. She couldn't believe that Dave was being so shortsighted here. She understood his concern about sales, but healthier menu items would bring in new customers, not reduce his sales to existing ones. Sure, some might switch from their Jumbo Burger to a salad once in a while, but the new sales would more than make up for that. Plus, advertising items and then deliberately running out just wasn't right. She'd run out of things before—if there had been a run on a particular item or Dave had messed up the supply order—but she had never deliberately not made items just to push customers toward more profitable items before, and she didn't plan to start now.

For the first week of the new menu items, Carol worked harder than she had done in a long time. She covered the drive-thru window through the breakfast, lunch, and dinner rushes, and when Dave made his trips to the bank for change or to their suppliers when he forgot something in the supply order, she ran in the back and made extra items to make sure they never ran out. It was a close call once or twice when she was making things to order, but the customers were never kept waiting.

At the end of the week, she had all the information she needed. Sales were up—way up—the new items were a big hit. She had been able to sell everything she had made without impacting the sales of their traditional items. Now all she had to do was confess to Dave.

1. Did Carol make the right choice here?

2. What do you think Dave's reaction will be?

3. What would the risk have been for the restaurant if they had implemented Dave's plan and deliberately run out of the new items?

oxymoron now than ever before. In such a negative environment, it is easy to forget that businesses can and do operate in an ethical manner, and that the majority of employees really are committed to doing the right thing in their time at work. The organizations that build an ethical culture based on that fundamental belief can be seen to succeed in exactly the same manner as their more "creative" counterparts, with increased revenue, profits, and market share.

However, as we will see in the following chapters, the challenge of building and operating an ethical business requires a great deal more than simply doing the right thing. The organization must devote time to the development of a detailed code of ethics that offers "guidance with traction" as opposed to traditional general platitudes that are designed to cover a multitude of scenarios with a healthy mix of inspiration and motivation.

Of greater concern is the support offered to employees when they are faced with an ethical dilemma. This involves not only the appointment of a designated corporate ethics officer with all the appropriate policies and procedures for bringing an issue to his/her attention, but also the creation and ongoing maintenance of a corporate culture of *trust*.

[KEY TERMS]

Business Ethics *p. 28*

Code of Ethics *p. 31*

Corporate Governance *p. 30*

Ethical Dilemma *p. 35*

Oxymoron *p. 30*

Stakeholder *p. 28*

[REVIEW QUESTIONS]

1. Locate the published code of ethics for the company you work for (or one you have worked for in the past). How well does that code reflect business practices you have observed in that company? Provide examples.

2. Based on the history of business ethics reviewed in this chapter, do you think the business world is becoming more or less ethical? Explain your answer.

3. Is it ever possible to justify unethical behavior? Why or why not?

4. Explain what doing the right thing means to you.

[REVIEW EXERCISE]

You are returning from a business trip. As you wait in the departure lounge for your flight to begin boarding, the gate personnel announce that the flight has been significantly overbooked and that they are offering incentives for passengers to take later flights. After several minutes, the offer is raised to a free round-trip ticket anywhere in the continental United States plus meal vouchers for dinner while you wait for your later flight. You give the offer serious consideration and realize that even though you'll get home several hours later than planned, the inconvenience will be minimal, so you give up your seat and take the free ticket and meal vouchers.

1. Since you are traveling on company time, does the free ticket belong to you or your company? Defend your choice.

2. If the later flight was actually the next day (and the airline offered you an accommodation voucher along with the meal vouchers) and you would be late getting into work, would you make the same choice? Explain your answer.

3. What if the offer only reached a $100 discount coupon on another ticket—would you still take it? If so, would you hold the same opinion about whether the coupon belonged to you or your company?

4. Should your company offer a clearly stated policy on this issue or should they trust their employees to "do the right thing"? Explain your answer.

INTERNET EXERCISE

1. Locate the Web site for the Ethics Resource Center. Does the Center offer any training programs in ethics? If so, what types of programs are available? Does the site offer links to other ethical organizations? If so, list two companies whose codes of ethics are linked from the ERC site.

2. Locate the Web site for the Ethics and Compliance Officers Association. The ECOA makes a public commitment to three key values. What are they? How does the mission of the ECOA differ from that of the ERC?

3. Locate the Web site for the Center for Business Ethics. Find the Research Publications page and identify the most recent research report released by the CBE. Briefly summarize the ethical issue discussed in the report. Do you agree or disagree with the conclusions reached in the report? Explain your answer.

TEAM EXERCISES

1. **Thanks for the training!** Divide into two groups and prepare arguments *for* and *against* the following behavior:

    You work in the IT department of a large international company. At your annual performance review, you were asked about your goals and objectives for the coming year and you stated that you would like to become MCSE (Microsoft Certified Systems Engineer) certified. You didn't get much of a pay raise (yet another cost-cutting initiative!), but your boss told you there was money in the training budget for the MCSE course—you're attending the training next week. However, after receiving the poor pay raise, you had polished your resume and applied for some other positions. You have received an attractive job offer from another company for more money, and, in the last interview, your potential new boss commented that it was a shame you didn't have your MCSE certification because that would qualify you for a higher pay grade. The new company doesn't have the training budget to put you through the MCSE training for at least two years. You tell the interviewer that you will complete the MCSE training prior to starting the new position in order to qualify for the higher pay grade. You choose not to qualify that statement with any additional information on who will be paying for the training. You successfully gain the MCSE certification and then give your two weeks' notice. You start with your new company at the higher pay grade. Is that ethical?

2. **What you do in your free time**. . . Divide into two groups and prepare arguments *for* and *against* the following behavior:

    You are attending an employee team-building retreat at a local resort. During one of the free periods in the busy agenda, you observe one of your colleagues in a passionate embrace with a young woman from another department. Since you work in HR and processed the hiring paperwork on both of them, you know that neither one of them is married, but your benefit plan provides coverage for "life partners" and both of them purchase health coverage for life partners. As you consider this revelation further, you are reminded that even if they have both ended their relationships with their respective partners, the company has a policy that expressly forbids employees from dating other employees in the company. Both you and the colleague you observed have applied for the same promotion—a promotion that carries a significant salary increase. What is your obligation here? Should you report him to your boss?

3. **Treatment or prevention?** Divide into two groups and prepare arguments for *treatment* (Group A) and *prevention* (Group B) in the following situation:

You work for a local nonprofit organization in your city that is struggling to raise funds for its programs in a very competitive grant market. Many nonprofits in your city are chasing grant funds, donations, and volunteer hours for their respective missions—homelessness, cancer awareness and treatment, orphaned children, and many more. Your organization's mission is to work with HIV/AIDS patients in your community to provide increased awareness of the condition for those at risk and also to provide treatment options for those who have already been diagnosed. Unfortunately, with such a tough financial situation, the board of directors of the nonprofit organization has determined that a more focused mission is needed. Rather than serving both the prevention and treatment goals, the organization can only do one. The debate at the last board meeting, which was open to all employees and volunteers, was very heated. Many felt that the treatment programs offered immediate relief to those in need, and therefore represented the best use of funds. Others felt that the prevention programs needed much more time to be effective and that the funds were spread over a much bigger population who might be at risk. A decision has to be reached. What do you think?

4. **Time to raise prices**. . . . Divide into two groups and prepare arguments *for* and *against* the following behavior:

You are a senior manager at a pharmaceutical company that is facing financial difficulties after failing to receive FDA approval for a new experimental drug for the treatment of Alzheimer's disease. After reviewing your test data, the FDA examiners decided that further testing was needed. Your company is now in dire financial straits. The drug has the potential to revolutionize the treatment of Alzheimer's, but the testing delay could put you out of business. The leadership team meets behind closed doors and decides the only way to keep the company afloat long enough to bring the new drug to market is to raise the prices of its existing range of drug products. However, given the financial difficulties your company is facing, some of those price increases will exceed 1,000 percent. When questions are raised about the size of the proposed increases, the chief executive officer defends the move with the following response: "Look, our drugs are still a cheaper option than surgery, even at these higher prices; the insurance companies can afford to pick up the tab, and, worst case scenario, they'll raise a few premiums to cover the increase. What choice do we have? We have to bring this new drug to market if we are going to be a player in this industry."

$2,500

Sorting through the day's mail—various catalogs, bills, and Christmas cards—I came across the letter I had been expecting from American Express. It contained a $2,500 check made out to me. Now I was faced with a dilemma I had been dreading: should I cash the check or return it?

Severances

Up until several weeks ago, I had been part of the Asian Equity Sales Group at Global Investment Banking. One morning, the managing director asked us to meet in the bank's main auditorium. Although we had heard rumors that the bank was going to close its Asian Investment Banking division, the managing director's request indicated that there might be truth to the rumors. Soon after we filed into the auditorium and took our seats, members of the human resources staff handed out severance packages in manila envelopes. Standing at the podium, the managing director announced that the bank was heading in a different direction and, as a result, drastically reducing its Asian exposure. Sitting there, I thought back to a year ago, when the same managing director had stood at the same podium and told us how excited the bank was to be expanding its presence in Asia.

The entire process of being fired took less than ten minutes. All of us from the Asian Equity sales desk were escorted up to the sales floor, told to pack our belongings, and vacate the floor within the hour. Security watched us as we packed, checking to make sure that we didn't take anything belonging to the bank. Nonetheless, while they weren't looking, I managed to place a few company note pads and pens in my bag. With my belongings and a four-month severance package in hand, I walked off the trading floor and out of the bank.

Now, in addition to my severance package, I had the $2,500 credit on my corporate American Express Card. The credit was the result of a returned Business-Class ticket to Asia that the bank had paid for and that I had recently cancelled. Normally I would have informed the human resources staff about this discrepancy and returned the money to the bank after American Express had forwarded me the check. But now, however, I felt that the bank had misled me regarding my job status.

Just four weeks before my severance, the managing director of Global Equity Sales told me that the bank would be reducing its investment-banking effort in Asia and asked if I would consider moving to the Eastern European Sales group. The managing director said that the bank valued me as an employee and would like me to consider this option. Because the bank's Eastern European division was considered strong, and I liked the managing director who ran the New York sales desk, I agreed to consider his suggestion. In the meantime, I was also interviewing with two other investment banks looking to expand their New York sales desks. In fact, one of the banks had recently offered me a job. However, after my boss asked me to move to the Eastern European Sales desk, I decided to abandon my interviews with the other banks. In short, I believed that my position at the bank was safe.

It turned out, however, that it was not only the Asian division that was being downsized. Given the turmoil in the Eastern European capital markets due to the Russian government debt default and currency devaluation, the bank was also significantly reducing its exposure in this region as well. As a result, the Eastern European sales desk job that I assumed would be mine never materialized. Since I had cut off contact with the other banks interested in hiring me, I knew resuming the interviewing process with them would take time. While the four-month severance package would get me through Christmas, I was angry that I had trusted that Global Investment Banking would retain me.

Looking down at the $2,500 check, I wondered whether I should walk down to the bank and cash it or return it to Global Investment Banking.

Discussion Questions

» »

1. Would you cash the check or return it to Global Investment Banking? What is "the right thing" to do here? Explain the reasoning behind your decision.

2. The employee feels that he was misled by his employer—is that sufficient justification for keeping the check?

3. The employee took some company notepads and pens when security wasn't looking—does that behavior suggest that he/she will most likely keep the check?

4. Is the employee's willingness to consider keeping the check really about the money or is it about the way he was treated by his employer?

5. Global Investment Banking gave the laid-off employees a four-month severance package—if they had given a six-month package, would that make a difference in this dilemma? What about a 12-month package?

6. Could Global Investment Banking have treated this employee any differently in this situation? Would that different treatment have prompted the employee to return the check without even considering the possibility of cashing it?

Source: Edward R. Freeman, Jenny Mead, and Christian Lown, "$2500," University of Virginia Darden School Foundation, 2003.

AN UNEQUIVOCAL DEDICATION TO BUSINESS ETHICS?

At a time of increasing skepticism that businesses can be both successful and ethical, one group of companies, who between them account for almost a billion dollars in global sales, have come together as the charter members of the Business Ethics Leadership Alliance (BELA). Formed in December 2008, the founding membership consists of 17 companies from a wide range of industries including retail, airlines, financial services, and computers. As you can see from the list below, some of the names may be familiar to you:

Accenture

Avaya

CACI International

Crawford

Dell

Dun & Bradstreet

Ecolab

Fluor

General Electric

Jones Lang

Lasalle

NYK Line

PepsiCo

Sempra Energy

Southern Company

The Hartford

United Airlines

Wal-Mart

Working with the Ethisphere Institute, an international think-tank that dedicates itself to "the creation, advancement and sharing of best practices in business ethics, corporate social responsibility, anti-corruption and sustainability," BELA appears to take a very clear position and invites public and private companies to join them in making an explicit pledge to four core values—Legal Compliance, Transparency, Identification of Conflicts of Interest, and Accountability.

Responding to a situation where "Through the cacophony of media stories, political finger pointing, infuriating reports of greed, and compelling stories of hardship, the business community as a whole has been characterized as a barrel full of bad apples that has the ability to spoil the global economy," the alliance members present themselves as "a growing quorum made up of some of the world's most recognizable companies joining together to affirm an unequivocal dedication to business ethics." In addition, they see it as their responsibility to "reestablish ethics as the foundation of everyday business practices."

Response to the new alliance has been mixed. Optimists appear to see this new organization as a step in the right direction, arguing that "a public so badly burned by ethical shortcomings in so many American companies will be cynical for years to come, but BELA is to be applauded for trying to turn the situation around." There are certainly some large companies getting involved here—Wal-Mart, GE, Dell, Pepsi— and they appear to be committing to specific changes in their business practices that directly correlate to many of the ethical problems identified at companies such as Enron, WorldCom, Tyco, and many others.

However, many cynics see this as just a public relations exercise for companies that have had their own business practices brought into question in the past and are now seeking redemption through a commitment to a new ethical philosophy. For example, Wal-Mart paid $11 million to the Department of Justice in settlement of a case involving the hiring of illegal immigrants by its cleaning contractors in 2005. Other class action suits are pending against the world's largest retailer. In 2006, Sempra Energy agreed to pay more than $377 million in response to allegations of manipulation of the price of natural gas during the 2001 California energy crisis.

For such a young alliance, much appears to be promised, including audits every two years and the requirement of strict compliance to the four core values, with the threat of removal from the alliance for failure to comply. It remains to be seen, however, whether such a public commitment by such well-known organizations can truly make a dent in a growing global conviction that businesses cannot really be trusted to perform in an ethical manner.

Discussion Questions

1. Visit the website for BELA at www.ethisphere.com/bela. Define the four core values in detail and explain which one you think will be the hardest for members to achieve and why.

2. Do you think it was a good idea to welcome founding members with such widely publicized ethical transgressions in their past? Why or why not?

3. BELA is a US-driven initiative at the moment. Do you think it will achieve a wider global acceptance over time? Why or why not?

4. Are the four core values—Legal Compliance, Transparency, Identification of Conflicts of Interest, and Accountability—enough to establish a credible reputation as an ethical company? What other values would you consider adding and why?

5. Cynics could argue that this is simply a public relations exercise for companies that have performed unethical business practices in the past. Optimists could argue that this is, at the very least, a step in the right direction of restoring the ethical reputation of business as a whole. What do you think?

6. According to the rules of BELA, members will be audited every two years to make sure they are in compliance with BELA standards, and can face removal from the alliance should that audit provide evidence of failure to comply. Do you think the threat of removal from the alliance will keep members in line? Why or why not?

Source: Guerrera, F and Birchall, J., "US groups in ethical standards push," *Financial Times*, December 8, 2008. Faur, P. "17 US companies form Business Ethics Leadership Alliance," www.communitelligence.com, December 10, 2008.
"Business Ethics Leadership Alliance Forms to Affirm Core Business Ethics Principles, Supply and Demand Chain Executive," www.sdcexec.com/online, December 12, 2008. MacDonald, C., Business Ethics Leadership Alliance: What's in a Promise?, www.businessethics.ca/blog/2008/12/business-ethics-leadership-alliance.html
www.ethisphere.com/bela/.

TEACHING OR SELLING?

Drug makers Worried about Conflicts of Interest Back Away from Their Sponsorship of Continuing Education

Trying to steer clear of potential conflicts of interest, two medical industry giants are distancing themselves from a little-known breed of marketing specialists. The recent steps by the drug maker Pfizer and Zimmer Holdings, a medical device manufacturer, illuminate subtle promotional tactics other companies continue to aim at doctors, despite mounting concern on the part of some physicians and ethicists.

At the center of this controversy are medical communications firms paid by pharmaceutical and device companies to produce physician-education courses. Critics say the manufacturers hire the marketing firms as intermediaries to help them influence doctors' prescriptions and procedures.

In July 2008, Pfizer announced it would no longer pay communications companies to arrange continuing medical education (CME) courses, which doctors must take to maintain their licenses. Pfizer said it would support medical education only when it's put on by hospitals and professional medical associations. Zimmer, which manufactures hip, knee, and elbow implants, has suspended funding of all CME activity. The company says it will restrict the way it funds courses in the future by identifying an independent third party, such as a professional society, to organize educational programs.

"We understand that even the appearance of conflicts in CME is damaging, and we are determined to take actions that are in the best interests of patients and physicians," Dr. Joseph M. Feczko, Pfizer's chief medical officer, said in a press release.

These moves are a blow to the marketing firms but by no means the end of their lucrative, multi-faceted roles. Hundreds of such firms in the United States design ad campaigns, hire doctors to educate colleagues about devices and medications, and produce conferences. Over the past decade, CME has become one of their most profitable businesses, as manufacturers have increasingly paid for the courses.

Industry support for CME has quadrupled since 1998, to $1.2 billion a year, according to the Accreditation Council for Continuing Medical Education (ACCME), an organization in Chicago that approves CME providers. More than half of that is funneled to marketers, with the rest going to hospitals, medical associations, and other nonprofit entities.

As industry money for continuing education proliferates, so do worries that many of the courses have become at least partly aimed at promoting products. The industry and its outside marketers say they ensure that the courses remain free of commercial influence. But some medical experts argue that when employees of communications firms are beholden to pharmaceutical and device companies, they will produce CME courses that are slanted in favor of their sponsors, even if they don't realize what they are doing. "There's not only a perception of bias, there's a reality," says Dave Davis, a vice-president of the Association of American Medical Colleges.

Discussion Questions

1. Where is the conflict of interest in this CME relationship?

2. In what way is that conflict damaging?

3. Do you think doctors would be influenced by such promotional tactics? Why or why not?

4. "Pfizer said it would support medical education only when it's put on by hospitals and professional medical associations." From a business ethics perspective, how does this decision address the conflict of interest issue?

5. If the pharmaceutical company is paying for the event, shouldn't it have the right to promote its products at the event? Why or why not? 〉〉 〉

6. Propose an alternative to canceling the CME altogether.

Source: Arlene Weintraub, "Teaching Doctors or Selling to Them," *BusinessWeek,* July 31, 2008.

THE PRACTICE OF BUSINESS ETHICS

»»   With a clearer understanding of the issues relating to business ethics and the key players involved, we can now examine how the practice of business ethics impacts an organization on a daily basis.

Chapter 3 examines how each functional department within an organization manages the challenge of building and maintaining an ethical culture.

Chapter 4 examines the topic of Corporate Social Responsibility (CSR) where we change the internal perspective of the organization to an external one and look at how an organization should interact with its stakeholders in an ethical manner.

Chapter 5 examines the challenges in maintaining an ethical culture within an organization. What policies and procedures should be put into place to ensure that the company conducts itself in an ethical manner, and what should be the consequences when evidence of unethical conduct is found?

Chapter 6 steps outside of the organizational framework and examines what legislation the government has put into place to enforce ethical conduct.

Chapter 7 examines how employees who find evidence of unethical conduct in their companies go about bringing that information to the attention of the companies' senior management or the appropriate regulatory authorities.

Chapter 8 examines the ethical debate over employee surveillance and the extent to which technology not only facilitates the prevention of unethical behavior but also jeopardizes the rights of individual employees. »»

chapter 3

Organizational Ethics

> " *I very much doubt that the Enron executives came to work one morning and said, "Let's see what sort of illegal scheme we can cook up to rip off the shareholders today." More likely, they began by setting extremely high goals for their firm . . . and for a time exceeded them. In so doing they built a reputation for themselves and a demanding expectation among their investors. Eventually, the latter could no longer be sustained. Confronting the usual judgmental decisions which one presented to executives virtually every day, and not wanting to face reality, they gradually began to lean more and more towards extreme interpretations of established accounting principles. The next thing they knew they had fallen off the bottom of the ski jump.* "
>
> —Norman R. Augustine, Retired Chairman of Lockheed Martin Corporation, in his 2004 acceptance of the Ethics Resource Center's Stanley C. Pace Leadership in Ethics award

LEARNING OBJECTIVES

After studying this chapter, you should be able to:

1. Define Organizational Ethics.

2. Explain the respective ethical challenges facing the functional departments of an organization.

3. Discuss the position that HR should be at the center of any corporate code of ethics.

4. Explain the potential ethical challenges presented by generally accepted accounting principles (GAAP).

5. Determine potential conflicts of interest within any organizational function.

6. Discuss how and why an organization's ethical culture can get off track.

Just Sign the Forms

Matt, a new employee at TransWorld Industries (TWI), showed up bright and early for his first day of orientation. He was very excited. He had applied for several jobs in the area, but TWI was the one he really wanted. He had friends there and they had told him that the company seemed to be growing very quickly with lots of new products coming online. To Matt, growth meant new opportunities, and he was looking forward to applying to the management-training program as soon as he finished his 90-day probationary period.

Scott, Matt's new boss was waiting for him as soon as he reached the factory floor. "Hey, Matt, very punctual; I like that," said Scott, looking at this watch.

"Listen kid, I know HR gave you a list of things to be checked off today—payroll paperwork, training videos, parking pass, ID, and all that stuff—but we could really use an extra pair of hands around here. Your position was vacant for quite a while and we've built a nasty backlog of work that needs to get caught up ASAP.

"We could really use your help on the Morton6000—you've worked with one of those before, right?"

Matt nodded, not quite sure where this was going.

"Well, here's the deal," said Scott. "The way I see it, all those videos are going to do is tell you not to harass any of the young babes around here (which won't be difficult since none of them are young or babes), not to insult anyone's race, and not to do anything unethical, which you weren't going to do anyway, right?"

Matt nodded again, still not sure where this was going.

"So I think all that time spent watching TV would be put to better use on that backlog of work on the Morton6000. We can book the shipments, get paid by the customers that have been waiting very patiently, and you can make a good impression on your first day—sound good to you, kid?"

"But what about the videos?" asked Matt.

"Oh, don't worry about them," said Scott. "We keep them here in the office. You just sign the forms saying you watched the videos and take them up to HR after lunch when you do all your other paperwork, okay?"

1. HR requires that these training videos be viewed for a reason. What risks is Scott taking here? Review the four reasons on page 61 why HR should be directly involved in any code of ethics.

2. Do you think Scott's argument for skipping the training videos is justified?

3. What should Matt do now?

Defining Organizational Ethics

In Chapter 2, we proposed business ethics as an area of study separate from the general subject of ethics because of two distinct issues:

1. Other parties (the stakeholders) have a vested interest in the ethical performance of an organization.

2. In a work environment, you may be placed in a situation where your personal value system may clash with the ethical standards of the organization's operating culture.

An **organization's culture** can be defined as the values, beliefs, and norms shared by all the employees of that organization. The culture represents the

> **Organizational Culture** The values, beliefs, and norms that all the employees of that organization share.

sum of all the policies and procedures—both written and informal—from each of the functional departments in the organization in addition to the policies and procedures that are established for the organization as a whole.

In this chapter, we can begin to examine individual departments within an organization and the ethical dilemmas that members of those departments face each day. To simplify this examination, we will consider an organization in terms of its functional areas within a **value chain** (see Figure 3.1).

A value chain is composed of the key functional inputs that an organization provides in the transformation of raw materials into a delivered product or service. Traditionally, these key functions are identified as:

Value Chain The key functional inputs that an organization provides in the transformation of raw materials into a delivered product or service.

1. Research and development (R&D), which develops and creates new product designs.

2. Manufacturing, which sources the components and builds the product.

3. Marketing (and advertising).

4. Sales.

5. Customer service.

Supporting each of these functional areas are the line functions:

1. Human resource management (HRM), which coordinates the recruitment, training, and development of personnel for all aspects of the organization.

2. Finance, which can include internal accounting personnel, external accounting personnel, and external auditors who are called upon to certify the accuracy of a company's financial statements.

3. Information systems (IS or IT), which maintain the technology backbone of the organization—data transfer and security, e-mail communications, internal and external Web sites, as well as the individual hardware and software needs that are specific to the organization and its line of business.

4. Management, the supervisory role that oversees all operational functions.

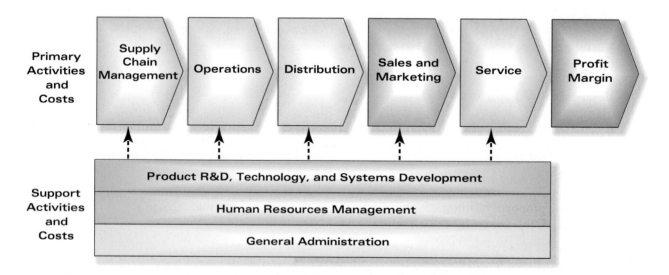

FIGURE 3.1 A Representative Company Value Chain

Source: Adapted with permission of the Free Press, a division of Simon & Schuster Adult Publishing Group, from *Competitive Advantage: Creating and Sustaining Superior Performance,* by Michael Porter, Copyright © 1995, 1998 by Michael E. Porter. All rights reserved. From A. A. Thompson Jr. and A. I. Strickland III, *Crafting & Executing Strategy: The Quest for Competitive Advantage: Concepts and Cases,* 14th ed. (New York: Irwin McGraw-Hill, 2005), p. 99.

Each of these functional line areas can represent a significant commitment of resources—personnel, dollars, and technology. From an ethical perspective, employees in each of these areas can face ethical challenges and dilemmas that can be both unique to their departmental responsibilities and common to the organization as a whole.

The functional areas of sales, customer service, information technology, and management typically have operational policies that reflect the overall ethical culture of the organization. They will be addressed in subsequent chapters in this text. In this chapter, we will focus on five specific organizational areas: R&D, manufacturing, marketing (including advertising), human resources (HR), and finance (including accounting and auditing).

✓ PROGRESS CHECK QUESTIONS

1. Explain the term *organizational culture*.

2. Define the term *value chain*.

3. List the five key functional areas within an organization.

4. List the four primary line functions.

The Ethics of Research and Development (R&D)

R&D professionals carry the responsibility for the future growth of the organization. Without new products to sell, organizations can lose their customers to competitors who are offering better, faster, and/or cheaper products. R&D teams incorporate customer feedback from market research, competitive feedback from closely monitoring their competition, and strategic input from the organization's senior management team to develop a product design that, hopefully, will allow the organization to capture and maintain a leading position in their market.

However, alongside this responsibility comes an equally critical commitment to the consumer in the provision of a product that is of the highest quality, safety, and reliability. Defective products not only put consumers at risk, they also generate negative press coverage (damaging the organization's reputation) and very expensive lawsuits that can put the organization at risk of bankruptcy.

When we consider these opposing objectives, the potential for ethical dilemmas is considerable. As professionals in their respective fields of science,

Have you ever purchased a product that you thought might have been rushed through research and development? What did the experience do to your perception of the company?

engineering, and design, R&D teams are tasked with making a complex set of risk assessments and technical judgments in order to deliver a product design. However, if the delivery of that design does not match the manufacturing cost figures that are needed to sell the product at a required profit margin, then some tough decisions have to be made.

If "better, cheaper, faster" is the ideal, then compromises have to be made in functionality or manufacturing to meet a targeted cost figure. If too many features are taken out, marketing and advertising won't have a story to tell, and the salespeople will face difficulties in selling the product against stiff competition. If too few changes are made, the company won't be able to generate a profit on each unit and meet its obligations to shareholders who expect the company to be run efficiently and to grow over the long term.

For the R&D team, the real ethical dilemmas come when decisions are made about product quality. Do we use the best materials available or the second best to save some money? Do we run a full battery of tests or convince ourselves that the computer simulations will give us all the information we need?

ETHICAL dilemma

CASE 3.1 A Firm Production Date

Scott Kelly, XYZ's marketing vice president, was shouting on the telephone to Tom Evers, director of new product development in XYZ's R&D laboratories: "We're going to kick off a major ad campaign timed to make people want your new model appliance, just before we start delivering them to dealers, and I want to be sure your production date is firm and not one of those best estimates you've stuck us with in the past." Taking a quick breath, he continued: "You people in R&D don't have much credibility with marketing! You don't tell us what you're up to until it's too late for us to advise you or interact in any way. I still remember the money you spent on that water purifier we didn't want. And it didn't help your credibility when you tried to keep the project alive after we told you to kill it!"

Tom assured Scott that the schedule for starting production was absolutely firm. "We've run extensive tests, including life tests, and everything definitely indicates 'go'! We're going to do a small pilot production run and test those pilot units in employee homes. That's a purely routine confirmation, so I can assure you that the production date is locked in. Go ahead with your ad campaign—we're giving you a sure winner this time."

But Tom was wrong. A glitch appeared near the end of the pilot test and very close to the production date. In a hastily called engineering meeting, to which marketing was *not* invited, a quick-fix design change was approved. Another short pilot production run would be made and the revised units would again be tested in employee homes. A delay of one to two months, perhaps longer, for start of production was indicated. With this schedule set, Tom arranged a meeting with marketing to apprise them of the problem and the new production schedule.

Scott exploded as soon as Tom began his account of the production delay. "You gave me a firm production date! We've got a major ad campaign under way and its timing is critical. We'll have customers asking for these new models and the dealers won't have them. We'll look silly to our customers and our dealers will be upset."

"Now wait," Tom interrupted, "I didn't give you the production date as absolutely firm. I remember cautioning you that a problem could develop in the pilot run and suggested you allow for it in kicking off the ad campaign. I told you we'd do our best to make the date but that there's always an element of chance with a new machine. We're better off having customers asking dealers where the new models are than being out there with a big quality problem."

1. Tom was obviously overconfident in the final stages of the testing process, but was his behavior unethical? Why or why not?

2. Given Scott's concerns over R&D's credibility, should he have taken Tom's production date as being absolutely firm?

3. In fact, Scott was so skeptical of Tom's production date that he recorded their original conversation without Tom's knowledge and then produced the recording when Tom denied giving a firm production date. Tom responded: "You taped my conversation without telling me! That's unethical." Was it?

4. Has Scott's behavior damaged future relations between marketing and R&D? In what way? How could this situation have been avoided?

Source: Adapted from W. Gale Cutler, "When R&D Talks, Marketing Listens—on Tape," *Research Technology Management* 37, no. 4 (July/August 1994), p. 56.

Ethics in Manufacturing

The relationship between R&D and manufacturing is often a challenging one. Managers complain about designs being thrown "'over the wall" to manufacturing with the implication that the product design may meet all the required specifications, but now it falls to the manufacturing team to actually get the thing built.

The pressures here are very similar to those in the R&D function as manufacturers face the ethical question of "do you want it built fast, or do you want it built right?" Obviously, from an organizational perspective, you want both, especially if you know that your biggest competitor also is racing to put a new product on the market (and if they get there before you do, all of your sales projections for your product will be worthless).

Here again, you face the ethical challenges inherent in arriving at a compromise—which corners can be cut and by how much. You want to build the product to the precise design specifications, but what if there is a supply problem? Do you wait and hold up delivery, or do you go with an alternative (and less reliable) supplier? Can you be sure of the quality that alternative supplier will give you?

Ethics in Marketing

Once the manufacturing department delivers a finished product, it must be sold. The marketing process (which includes advertising, public relations, and sales) is responsible for ensuring that the product

If the final product is not compromised, are there still risks associated with poor ethics in manufacturing?

reaches the hands of a satisfied customer. If the marketers did their research correctly and communicated the data to the R&D team accurately, and assuming the finished product meets the original design specifications and the competition hasn't beaten you to market with their new product, this should be a slam dunk, but with all these assumptions, a great deal can go wrong.

Opinions on the marketing process vary greatly in relation to how close you are to the process itself. Marketers see themselves as providing products (or services) to customers who have already expressed a need for and a desire to purchase those products. In this respect, marketers are simply communicating information to their customers about the functionality and availability of the product, and then communicating back to the organization the feedback they receive from those customers.

Utilitarianism Ethical choices that offer the greatest good for the greatest number of people.

Critics of marketing tend to see it as a more manipulative process whereby unsuspecting customers are induced by slick and entertaining commercials and advertisements in several different media—magazines, radio, television, the Internet, and so forth—to buy products they don't really need and could quite easily live without.

From an ethical standpoint, these opposing arguments can be seen to line up with distinct ethical theories. Marketers emphasize customer service and argue that since their customers are satisfied, the good outcome justifies the methods used to achieve that outcome no matter how misleading the message or how unnecessary the product sold. As we reviewed in Chapter 1, this represents a view of ethics called **utilitarianism**. Critics argue that the process itself is wrong irrespective of the outcome achieved—that is, how can you be proud of an outcome when the customer never needed that product to begin with and was manipulated, or at the very least influenced, by a slick ad campaign into feelings of envy,

What role does marketing play in the perception that coffee brewed at Starbucks® is superior to coffee brewed at home?

inadequacy, or inequality if he or she didn't rush out and buy it? On this side of the debate we are considering **universal ethics**.

These opposing positions become more complex when you consider the responsibility of a corporation to generate profits for its stockholders. Long-term profits come from sales growth, which means selling more of what you have or bringing new products or services to the market to increase your overall sales revenue. To do that, you must find ways to sell more to your existing customer base and, ideally, find more customers for your products and services. Unless you are selling a basic commodity in a developing country that has a desperate need for your product, at some point you reach a place where customers can survive without your product or service, and marketing must now move from informing customers and prospects about the product or service to persuading or influencing them that their lives will be better with this product or service and, more importantly, they will be better with your company's version.

Marketing professionals abide by a code of ethics adapted by the American Marketing Association (AMA). (For additional information, please refer to the Appendix 2). That code speaks eloquently about doing no harm, fostering trust, and improving "customer confidence in the integrity of the marketing exchange system," and establishes clear ethical values of honesty, responsibility, fairness, respect, openness, and citizenship. These are all honorable standards for any profession, but the question remains as to whether or not encouraging people to buy things they don't need is truly an ethical process.

Philip Kotler explored this debate further in his classic article: "Is Marketing Ethics an Oxymoron?" (2004). His concern over the pressures of expanding consumption (the constant growth we discussed earlier in this section) was further complicated by the issue of reducing the side effects of that consumption, specifically in products that are perceived as harmful to the body—cigarettes, alcohol, junk food—as well as to the environment—nonrecyclable packaging or products that leach chemicals into landfills such as batteries or electrical equipment.

In response to these pressures, Kotler makes the following observation[1]:

> As professional marketers, we are hired by . . . companies to use our marketing toolkit to help them sell more of their products and services. Through our research, we can discover which consumer groups are the most susceptible to increasing their consumption. We can use the research to assemble the best 30-second TV commercials, print ads, and sales incentives to persuade them that these products will deliver great satisfaction. And we can create price discounts to tempt them to consume even more of the product than would normally be healthy or safe to consume. But, as professional marketers, we should have the same ambivalence as nuclear scientists who help build nuclear bombs or pilots who spray DDT over crops from the airplane. Some of us, in fact, are independent enough to tell these clients that we will not work for them to find ways to sell more of what hurts people. We can tell them that we're willing to use our marketing toolkit to help them build new businesses around substitute products that are much healthier and safer. But, even if these companies moved toward these healthier and safer products, they'll probably continue to push their current "cash-cows." At that point, marketers will have to decide whether to work for these companies, help them reshape their offerings, avoid these companies altogether, or even work to oppose these company offerings.

5. Identify the three functional components of the marketing process.

6. Explain why marketers feel that their involvement in the production and delivery of goods and services is an ethical one.

7. Explain the opposing argument that marketing is an unethical process.

8. Which argument do you support? Provide an example to explain your answer.

Ethics in Human Resources

The human resources function within an organization should ideally be directly involved in the relationship between the company and the employee throughout that employee's contract with the company:

- The creation of the job description for the position.
- The recruitment and selection of the right candidate for the position.
- The orientation of the newly hired employee.
- The efficient management of payroll and benefits for the (hopefully) happy and productive employee.
- The documentation of periodic performance reviews.
- The documentation of disciplinary behavior and remedial training, if needed.
- The creation of a career development program for the employee.

Finally, if the employee and the company eventually part ways, the HR department should coordinate the final paperwork, including any severance benefits, and should host an exit interview to ensure that anything that the organization can learn from the departure of this employee is fed back into the company's strategic plan for future growth and development.

Every step of the life cycle of that company–employee contract has the potential for ethical transgressions. Most HR professionals see their direct involvement in this contract as acting as the conscience of the organization in many ways. If the right people are hired in the first place, it is believed, many other problems are avoided down the road. It's when organizations fail to plan ahead for vacancies and promotions that the pressure to hire someone who was needed yesterday can lead to the gradual relaxation of what may be clearly established codes of ethics.

What ethical issues might arise for a human resource professional when privy to an employee's personal and professional history?

Consider the following ethical transgressions[2]:

- You are behind schedule on a building project and your boss decides to hire some illegal immigrants to help get the project back on track. They are paid in cash "under the table" and your boss justifies the decision as being "a 'one-off'—besides, the INS [Immigration and Naturalization Service] has bigger fish to fry than a few undocumented workers on a building site! If we get caught, we'll pay the fine—it will be less than the penalty we would owe our client for missing our deadline on the project."

- Your company has hired a new regional vice president. As the HR specialist for her region, you are asked to process her payroll and benefits paperwork. Your boss instructs you to waive the standard one-year waiting period for benefits entitlement and enroll the new VP in the retirement and employee bonus plan immediately. When you raise the concern that this is illegal, your boss informs you that this new VP is a close friend of the company president and advises you that, in the interests of your job security, you should "just do it and don't ask questions!"

- On your first day as the new HR specialist, you mention to your boss that the company appears to be out of employee handbooks and both the minimum wage and OSHA (Occupational Safety and Health Administration) posters that are legally required to be posted in the employee break room. Your boss laughs and says, "we've been meaning to get around to that for years—trust me, there will always be some other crisis to take priority over all that administrative stuff."

In each of these scenarios, accountability for the transgression would ultimately end with the HR department as the corporate function that is legally responsible for ensuring that such things don't happen.

For this reason, many advocates of ethical business conduct argue that HR should be at the center of any corporate code of ethics—not as the sole creator of the code, since it is a document that should represent the entire organization, but certainly as the voice of reason in ensuring that all the critical areas are addressed[3]:

1. *HR professionals must help ensure that ethics is a top organizational priority.* The recent business scandals have shown that simply relying on the presence of an ethical monitor will not prevent unethical behavior. HR should be the ethical champion in the organization, including hiring a formal ethics officer if necessary.

2. *HR must ensure that the leadership selection and development processes include an ethics component.* The terrible metaphor of a fish rotting from the head is relevant here. HR must be involved in hiring leaders who not only endorse and support but also model the ethical standards needed to keep the company out of danger. The biggest challenge here is convincing the leadership team that it's not just the rank-and-file employees who should be put through ethics training.

3. *HR is responsible for ensuring that the right programs and policies are in place.* As we will learn in future chapters in this book, financial penalties for unethical behavior are now directly connected to evidence of efforts to actively prevent unethical conduct. The absence of appropriate policies and training programs can now increase the fines that are levied for unethical behavior.

4. *HR must stay abreast of ethics issues (and in particular the changing legislation and sentencing guidelines for unethical conduct).* Response to the recent corporate scandals has been swift and frustratingly bureaucratic. Organizations now face reams of documentation that are designed to regulate ethical behavior in the face of overwhelming evidence that organizations cannot, it would seem, be trusted to do it on their own.

☑ PROGRESS CHECK QUESTIONS

9. Explain why HR personnel might consider themselves to be the conscience of the organization.

10. Select one of the ethical transgressions listed in the HR sections and document how you would respond to that situation as the employee.

11. Why is HR's involvement in the selection of the leaders of the company so important to ethical business conduct?

12. Why have ethics policies and ethics training suddenly become so important?

Ethics in Finance

The finance function of an organization can be divided into three distinct areas: financial transactions, the **accounting function**, and the **auditing function**:

1. The financial transactions—the process by which the flow of money through an organization is handled—involve receiving money from customers and using that money to pay employees, suppliers, and all other creditors (taxes and the like), with hopefully enough left over to create a profit that can be either reinvested back into the business or paid out to owners/shareholders. Part of this function may be outsourced to specialists such as Paychex or ADP, for example.

2. The accounting function keeps track of all those financial transactions by documenting the money coming in (credits) and money going out (debits) and balancing the accounts at the end of the period (daily, weekly, monthly, quarterly, annually). The accounting function can be handled by accounting professionals that are hired by the company, outside accounting firms that are contracted by the company, or usually a combination of the two.

3. When an organization's financial statements, or books, have been balanced, they must then be reported to numerous interested parties. For small businesses, the most important customers are government agencies—state income, and sales taxes and federal taxes the IRS collects on the profits generated by the business. In addition, lenders and creditors will want to see financial statements that have been certified as accurate by an impartial third-party professional. That certification is offered by auditors—typically certified professional accountants and/or auditing specialists.

> **Accounting Function** The function that keeps track of all the company's financial transactions by documenting the money coming in (credits) and money going out (debits) and balancing the accounts at the end of the period (daily, weekly, monthly, quarterly, annually).

> **Auditing Function** The certification of an organization's financial statements, or "books" as being accurate by an impartial third-party professional. An organization can be large enough to have internal auditors on staff as well as using external professionals—typically certified professional accountants and/or auditing specialists.

As an organization grows and eventually goes public by selling stock in the organization on a public stock exchange, the need for certified financial documents becomes even greater. Existing and potential investors will make the decision to invest in the shares of that organization based on the information presented in those certified financial statements—specifically, the profit and loss statement and the balance sheet. Investors look to those documents for evidence of financial stability, operational efficiency, and the potential for future growth. Many organizations are large enough to maintain their own internal auditors to monitor the accuracy of their financial functions.

All in a Day's Work: Internal Auditors' Roles

According to the Institute of Internal Auditors[4]:

internal auditors are grounded in professionalism, integrity, and efficiency. They make objective assessments of operations and share ideas for best practices; provide counsel for improving controls, processes and procedures, performance, and risk management; suggest ways for reducing costs, enhancing revenues, and improving profits; and deliver competent consulting, assurance, and facilitation services.

Internal auditors are well disciplined in their craft and subscribe to a professional code of ethics. They are diverse and innovative. They are committed to growing and enhancing their skills. They are continually on the lookout for emerging risks and trends in the profession. They are good thinkers. And to effectively fulfill all their roles, internal auditors must be excellent communicators who listen attentively, speak effectively, and write clearly.

Sitting on the right side of management, modern-day internal auditors are consulted on all aspects of the organization and must be prepared for just about anything. They are coaches, internal and external stakeholder advocates, risk managers, controls experts, efficiency specialists, and problem-solving partners. They are the organization's safety net.

It's certainly not easy, but for these skilled and competent professionals, it's all in a day's work.

ETHICAL dilemma

CASE 3.2 "Ethics, Schmethics"—Enron's Code of Ethics

In July 2000, Enron Corporation published an internal code of ethics document that ran 64 pages in length (see the Appendix 1). Page 12 of the document proudly announced the company's position on business ethics:

Employees of Enron Corp., its subsidiaries, and its affiliated companies (collectively the "Company") are charged with conducting their business affairs in accordance with the highest ethical standards. An employee shall not conduct himself or herself in a manner which directly or indirectly would be detrimental to the best interests of the Company or in a manner which would bring to the employee financial gain separately derived as a direct consequence of his or her employment with the Company. Moral as well as legal obligations will be fulfilled openly, promptly, and in a manner which will reflect pride on the Company's name.

Products and services of the Company will be of the highest quality and as represented. Advertising and promotion will be truthful, not exaggerated or misleading.

Agreements, whether contractual or verbal, will be honored. No bribes, bonuses, kickbacks, lavish entertainment, or gifts will be given or received in exchange for special position, price or privilege . . . Relations with the Company's many publics—customers, stockholders, governments, employees, suppliers, press, and bankers—will be conducted in honesty, candor, and fairness."

Subsequent investigations into the inner workings of Enron Corp. revealed that the only time this code of ethics received formal attention (other than, presumably, when it was created and formally accepted) was when the board of directors voted to waive key provisions of the code in order to allow the off-balance-sheet partnerships that Chief Financial Officer Andy Fastow ultimately used to hide over half a billion dollars of debt from analysts and investors.

A more realistic picture of the apparent flexibility of Enron's ethical culture can be found in the extreme conflict of interest represented in its relationship with Arthur Andersen. Andersen provided both consulting and auditing services for fees running into millions of dollars—money that became so critical to Andersen's continued growth that its employees were encouraged to sign off on off-balance-sheet transactions—transactions that were not shown on Enron's publicly-reported balance sheet—that stretched the limits of generally accepted accounting principles (GAAP) to their furthest edges. In addition, Enron hired former Andersen employees to manage the affairs of their former colleagues, which further strengthened the conflict of interest in a relationship that was supposed, at the very least, to be at arm's length, and, at best, above reproach.

1. What is the purpose of a code of ethics?

2. Do you think the employees of Enron Corp. were told about the vote to put aside key elements of the code of ethics? If not, why not? If they had been told about the decision, what do you think their reaction would have been?

3. Do you think that the employees of Enron Corp. were planning to defraud investors all along? If not, why not?

4. Explain the conflict of interest in Enron's relationship with Arthur Andersen.

Source: Enron Code of Ethics, www.smokinggun.com.

Ethical Challenges

For internal employees in the finance, accounting, and auditing departments, the ethical obligations are no different from those of any other employee of the organization. As such, they are expected to maintain the reputation of the organization and abide by the code of ethics. Within their specific job tasks, this would include not falsifying documents, stealing money from the organization, or undertaking any other form of fraudulent activity related to the management of the organization's finances.

However, once we involve third-party professionals who are contracted to work for the company, the potential for ethical challenges and dilemmas increases dramatically.

GAAP

GAAP The generally accepted accounting principles that govern the accounting profession—not a set of laws and established legal precedents, but rather a set of standard operating procedures within the profession.

The accounting profession is governed not by a set of laws and established legal precedents, but rather by a set of generally accepted accounting principles, typically referred to as **GAAP** (*gap*). These principles are accepted as standard operating procedures within the industry, but, like any operating standard, they are open to interpretation and abuse. The taxation rates that Uncle Sam expects you to pay on generated profits may be very clear, but the exact process by which you arrive at that profit figure is far from clear and places considerable pressure on accountants to manage the expectations of their clients.

Creative Bookkeeping Techniques

Corporations try to manage their expansion at a steady rate of growth. If they grow too slowly or too erratically from year to year, investors may see them as unstable or in danger of falling behind their competition. If they grow too quickly, investors may develop unrealistic expectations of their future growth. This inflated outlook can have a devastating effect on your stock price when you miss your quarterly numbers for the first time. Investors have shown a pattern of overreacting to bad news and dumping their stock.

It is legal to defer receipts from one quarter to the next to manage your tax liability. However, accountants face ethical challenges when requests are made for far more illegal practices such as falsifying accounts, underreporting income, overvaluing assets, and taking questionable deductions.

These pressures are further compounded by competitive tension as accounting firms compete for client business in a cutthroat market. Unrealistic delivery deadlines, reduced fees, and fees that are contingent on providing numbers that are satisfactory to the client are just some examples of the ethical challenges modern accounting firms face.

A set of accurate financial statements that present an organization as financially stable, operationally efficient, and positioned for strong future growth can do a great

What are the long term benefits of GAAP for employees? Consumers?

deal to enhance the reputation and goodwill of an organization. The fact that those statements have been certified by an objective third party to be "clean" only adds to that. However, that certification is meant to be for the public's benefit rather than the corporation's. This presents a very clear ethical predicament. The accounting/auditing firm is paid by the corporation, but it really serves the general public, who are in search of an impartial and objective review.

The situation can become even more complex when the accounting firm has a separate consulting relationship with the client—as was the case with Arthur Andersen and their infamous client Enron. Anderson's consulting business generated millions of dollars in fees from Enron alone. If the auditing side of their business chose to stand up to Enron's requests for creative bookkeeping policies, those millions of dollars of consulting fees, as well as additional millions of dollars in auditing fees, would be placed in serious jeopardy. As we now know, the senior partners on the Enron account chose not to stand up to Enron, and their decision eventually sank Arthur Andersen entirely.

With so many ethical pressures facing the accounting profession, and a guidebook of operating standards that is open to such abuse, the last resort for ethical guidance and leadership is the Code of Conduct issued by the American Institute of Certified Public Accountants (AICPA). For additional information, please refer to the Appendix 3.

LIFEskills

Being socially responsible

Review the company value chain in Figure 3.1 on page 54. Consider the company you currently work for, or one that you hope to work for in the future. The department in which you work holds a specific place and function in that value chain, and the extent to which you interact with the other departments on that chain in a professional and ethical manner has a great deal to do with the long-term growth and success of the organization.

Of course, that's easy to say but a lot harder to do. Balancing departmental goals and objectives (to which you are held accountable) with larger company performance targets can be a challenge when resources are tight and you are balancing fierce competition in a tough economy. In that kind of environment, an organization's commitment to ethical conduct can be tested as the pressure to close deals and hit sales targets increases. Ethical dilemmas develop here when business decisions have to be made that will negatively affect one department or another. In addition, you may face your own dilemmas when you are tasked with obligations or responsibilities that conflict with your own value system.

In those situations, remain aware of the bigger picture and consider the results for all the stakeholders involved in the decision—whether it's your colleagues at work or your family members and friends. You may be the one making the decision, but others will share the consequences.

✓ PROGRESS CHECK QUESTIONS

13. List the three primary areas of the finance function in an organization.

14. Explain how the accounting profession is governed by GAAP.

15. Why would audited accounts be regarded as being "clean"?

16. What key decision brought about the demise of Arthur Andersen?

Conflicts of Interest

The obligation that an auditing firm has to a paying client, while at the same time owing an objective, third-party assessment of that client's financial stability to stakeholders and potential investors, represents a potentially significant **conflict of interest**. We will examine the government's response to this conflict of interest in more detail in Chapter 6 when we review the Sarbanes-Oxley Act of 2002 and the impact that legislation has attempted to have on the legal enforcement of ethical business practices.

Conflict of Interest A situation where one relationship or obligation places you in direct conflict with an existing relationship or obligation.

However, as the value chain model we reviewed at the beginning of this chapter shows us, the potential for conflicts of interest within an organization can go far beyond the finance department:

- At the most basic level, simply meeting the needs of your organization's stakeholders can present conflicts of interest when you consider the possibility that what is best for your shareholders (increased profits) may not be best for your employees and the community if the most efficient means to achieve those increased profits is to close your factory and move production overseas.

- Selling a product that has the potential to be harmful to your customers represents an equally significant conflict of interest. The convenience of fast food carries with it the negative consequences of far more calories than you need to consume in an average day. McDonald's®, for example, has responded with increased menu choices to include salads and alternatives to french fries and soda—but the Big Mac® continues to be one of its best-selling items.

- Selling a product that has the potential to be harmful to the environment also carries a conflict of interest. Computer manufacturers such as Dell and Hewlett-Packard now offer plans to recycle your old computer equipment rather than throwing it into the landfill. Fast food companies like McDonald's® have changed their packaging to move away from clamshell boxes for their burgers. Beverage companies such as Nestlé are now producing bottles for their bottled water that use less plastic to minimize the impact on landfills.

Conflicts of interest do not just happen in large corporations. What are the potential conflicts that arise by this employee informing her friend that a sale next week will save her 30 percent, but not informing other customers?

These attempts to address conflicts of interest all have one thing in common. Whether they were prompted by internal strategic policy decisions or aggressive campaigns by customers and special interest groups, the decisions had to come from the top of the organization. Changing the way an organization does business can sometimes begin with a groundswell of support from the front line of the organization (where employees interact with customers), but eventually the key decisions on corporate policy and (where appropriate) capital expenditure have to come from the senior leadership of the organization. Without that endorsement, any attempts to make significant changes tend to remain as departmental projects rather than organizationwide initiatives.

So When Does It Start to Go Wrong?

The Ethics Resource Center (ERC), a nonprofit U.S. organization devoted to the advancement of organizational ethics surveyed more than 3,000 American workers in its 2005 National Business Ethics Survey (NBES). The findings showed that more than half of U.S. employees have observed at least one example of workplace ethical misconduct in the past year, and 36 percent have observed two or more. This represents a slight increase from the results of the 2003 survey. During the same period, willingness to report observed misconduct at work to management declined to 55 percent, a decrease of 10 percentage points since 2003. Types of misconduct employees observed most include[5]:

- Abusive or intimidating behavior toward employees (21 percent).

- Lying to employees, customers, vendors, or the public (19 percent).

- Situations that placed employee interests over organizational interests (18 percent).

- Violations of safety regulations (16 percent).
- Misreporting of actual time worked (16 percent).

Behavior such as the Ethics Resource Center documented in the NBES represents the real organizational culture more than any corporate statements or policy manuals. Employees learn very quickly about "the rules of the game" in any work environment, and make the choice to "go with the flow" or if the rules are unacceptable to their personal value systems, to look for employment elsewhere.

Of greater importance for the organization as a whole is the fact that any unethical behavior is allowed to persist for the long term. Explanations for the behavior (or for the failure to address the behavior) are plentiful:

- "That's common practice in this industry."
- "It's a tough market out there and you have to be willing to bend the rules."
- "They're not in my department."
- "I don't have time to watch their every move—head office gives me too much to do to babysit my people."
- "If I fire them for a policy violation, the union rep would be on my back in a heartbeat."
- "If I fire them for a policy violation, I'd be one short—do you know how long it would take me to find a replacement and train him?"
- "The bosses know they do it—if they turn a blind eye, why shouldn't I?"
- "They don't pay me to be a company spy—I've got my own work to do."

So, if bending the rules, stretching the truth, breaking the rules, and even blatantly lying have become a depressingly regular occurrence in your workplace, the question must be asked as to where the pressure or performance expectation comes from to make this behavior necessary. The answer can be captured in one word: *profit*.

This doesn't mean that nonprofit organizations don't also face problems with unethical behavior or that the pursuit of profit is unethical. What it means is that the obligation to deliver profits to owners or shareholders has created a convenient "get out of jail free" card, where all kinds of behavior can be justified in the name of meeting your obligations to your shareholders. You, as an individual, wouldn't normally do this, but you have a deadline or quota or sales target to meet, and your boss isn't the type to listen to explanations or excuses, so maybe just this once if you (insert ethical transgression here), you can get over this hurdle—just this once. Unfortunately, that's how it started for the folks at Enron, and that's how it could start for you. They fudged the numbers for one quarter and managed to get away with it, but all that did was raise investor expectations for the next quarter, and they found themselves on a train they couldn't get off.

As we shall see in the next chapters, if the organization doesn't set the ethical standard, employees will perform to the ethical standards of the person who controls their continued employment with the company—their boss.

How well companies set ethical standards can be measured by the extensive legislation that now exists to legally enforce (or at least attempt to enforce) ethical behavior in business.

Just Sign the Forms—Matt Makes a Decision

Matt really wanted this job, and he really wanted to make a good first impression with Scott. Plus, Scott was right; he wasn't going to harass anyone or insult others based on their race, and he certainly wasn't going to risk his chances at the management training program by doing anything unethical. What's the worst that could happen? If anyone from HR ever found out that he didn't watch the training videos, he could show them how the company had benefited from his making up the backlog on the Morton6000, and he was sure that Scott would back him up.

Matt signed the forms and got to work.

Three months later, Matt finished his probationary period and met with the HR director to review his performance and, Matt hoped, discuss his application for the management training program. The HR director was very friendly and complimentary about Matt's performance over the last 90 days. But he had one question for Matt: "The production log for the Morton6000 shows that you made a big dent in our backlog on your first morning here. I'm curious how you managed to do that when your paperwork shows that you spent three hours watching training videos as part of your new employee orientation."

1. What should Matt tell the HR director?

2. What do you think the HR director's reaction will be?

3. What are Matt's chances of joining the management training program now?

[KEY TERMS]

[REVIEW QUESTIONS]

1. Provide three examples of unethical behavior that you have observed at the company you work for (or a company you have worked for in the past). What were the outcomes of this behavior?

2. Should the HR department be the ethics champion in the organization? Why or why not?

3. What are "creative bookkeeping techniques"? Provide three examples.

4. Would you leave your position with a company if you saw evidence of unethical business practices? Why or why not? What factors would you consider in making that decision?

REVIEW EXERCISE

Ambush Marketing. As billboards, radio commercials, print ads, and 30-second or 60-second TV spots become increasingly lost in the blurred onslaught of advertising, the larger advertising companies are increasingly turning to more creative means to get the name of their product or service in front of the increasingly overloaded attention span of Joe Public.

Consider the following:

- "Imagine you're at [the Washington Monument] when a young couple with a camera approaches and kindly asks if you'll take their picture. They seem nice enough, so you grab the camera. As you're lining up the shot, the gentleman explains it's the newest model, he got it for only $400 and it does this, that and the other. Cool. You take the picture and walk away. It's nice to help people."

- "The New York bar is crowded, with a line of people three deep. Just as you manage to flag [the bartender's] attention, a neighboring patron tries to latch on to your good luck. 'Say, buddy, I see you're about to order a couple of drinks,' your neighbor says. 'If I give you a ten-spot, could you get me a Peach Royale?' The request seems harmless. Why not?"[6]

- A colorful cardboard box plastered with a well-known logo of a certain computer maker sits in the lobby of your building for several days. Not only does the trademark get noticed, but residents may also assume a neighbor has made the purchase. So the computer company gets a warm association in the minds of certain consumers.[7]

All perfectly reasonable and innocent everyday occurrences, right? But how would you feel if the couple at the Washington Monument raving about their new camera were really a pair of actors planted in targeted locations to praise the virtues of digital cameras to an unsuspecting public? Your innocent neighbor in the bar was actually performing a "lean-over"—a paid commercial for Peach Royale; and the computer box was left in the lobby of your building deliberately at the minimal cost of a "contribution" to the building's doorman.

So now you get really paranoid. You've heard of product placement, where movies offer lingering shots on specific products (funny how the actors always drink Coke or Heineken® beer; and didn't Halle Berry look great in that Coral-colored Ford Thunderbird in the James Bond movie *Die Another Day*—did you know you could buy a Thunderbird in that exact color?). But what if that group of commuters on your morning train discussing a new movie or TV show or book was planted there deliberately? What if the friendly woman with the cute six-year-old at the playground who was talking about how her son loves his new video game was also an actress?

Such tactics take the concept of target marketing to a whole new level. Advertisers plant seemingly average folks in the middle of a demographically desirable crowd and begin to sing the praises of a new product or service while conveniently failing to mention that they have been hired to do so, and may have never even heard of the product or service before they took the gig.

1. Is this unethical marketing? Explain why or why not.

2. Critics argue that such campaigns "blur the lines between consumerism and con artistry." Is that a fair assessment? Why or why not?

3. How would you feel if you were involved in such an ambush?

4. If the majority of consumers are already skeptical about most advertising they are exposed to, how do you think the general public would feel about such marketing campaigns?

5. Supporters of these campaigns argue that our economy is built on consumerism and that if you don't find more effective ways to reach consumers, the entire economy will suffer. Does that make the

practice OK? Should we just accept it as a nuisance and a necessary evil like solicitation calls during dinner?

6. Would your opinion change if the advertisers were more obvious in their campaigns—such as admitting after each skit that the raving fans were really actors?

INTERNET EXERCISE

Locate the Web site for the Institute of Internal Auditors.

1. What is the stated mission of the IIA?
2. What are the two essential components of the IIA's code of ethics?
3. Why did Cynthia Cooper become one of the IIA's most well-known members?

TEAM EXERCISES

1. **Is it ethical to ambush?** Divide into two teams. One team must prepare a presentation advocating the use of the ambush marketing tactics described in the Review Exercise. The other team must prepare a presentation explaining the ethical dilemmas those tactics present.

2. **In search of an ethical department.** Divide into groups of three or four. Each group must select one of the organizational departments featured in this chapter (HR, R&D, marketing, sales, and finance) and document the potential areas for unethical behavior in that department. Prepare a presentation outlining an example of an ethical dilemma in that department and propose a solution for resolving it.

3. **An isolated incident?** Divide into two groups and prepare arguments *for* and *against* the following behavior: You are the regional production manager for a tire company that has invested many millions of dollars in a new retreading process that will allow you to purchase used tires, replace the tread, and sell them at a significantly lower cost (with a very healthy profit margin for your company). Initial product testing has gone well and expectations for this very lucrative new project are very high. Promotion prospects for those managers associated with the project are also very good. The company chose to go with a "soft" launch of the new tires, introducing them into the Malaysian market with little marketing or advertising to draw attention to the new product line. Once demand and supply is thoroughly tested, the plan is to launch the new line worldwide with a big media blitz. Sales so far have been very strong based on the low price. However, this morning, your local contact in Malaysia sent news of a bus accident in which two schoolchildren were killed. The cause of the accident was the front left tire on the bus, which lost its tread at high speed and caused the bus to roll over. You are only three days away from your next progress report meeting, and only two weeks from the big worldwide launch. You decide to categorize the accident as an isolated incident and move forward with your plans for the introduction of your discount retread tires to the world market.

4. **The sole remaining supplier.** Divide into two groups and prepare arguments *for* and *against* the following behavior: Back in the mid-1970s heart pacemakers ran on transistors before advances in technology replaced them with the silicon computer chips we are all familiar with today. Your company has found itself in a situation where it is the last remaining supplier of a particular transistor for the current models of heart pacemakers on the market. Your competitors have all chosen to get out of the business, claiming that the risks of lawsuits related to malfunctioning pacemakers was simply too great to make the business worthwhile. Your management team has now arrived at the same conclusion. The chief executive officer defends the decision by arguing that as a business-to-business supplier to other manufacturers, you have no say in how the transistors are used, so why should the fact that they are used in life-saving equipment factor into the decision? Your responsibility is to your shareholders, not to the patients who depend on these pacemakers. You are not responsible for all the other manufacturers getting out of the business.

BOOSTING YOUR RÉSUMÉ

"Everybody has stretched the truth a little on their résumés at one time or another, right?" That's the question that people who are about to give their own résumés a little boost ask themselves as a way of dealing with the twinge of guilt they are probably feeling as they adjust their job title or make that six months of unemployment magically disappear by claiming a consulting project. In the harsh light of day, résumé inflation is not only unethical, but if you transfer those untruths onto a job application form, which is a legal document, then the act becomes illegal. Consider the outcomes for these former occupants of high-ranking (and high-paying) positions:

- Marilee Jones, Dean of Admissions for the Massachusetts Institute of Technology (MIT), claimed to hold degrees in biology from Rensselaer Polytechnic Institute and Albany Medical College and to hold a doctorate degree. She resigned in April 2007 after officials at MIT discovered the truth.

- George O'Leary resigned just five days after being hired as Notre Dame's football coach in 2001 when it was revealed that he did not hold a master's degree in education from New York University, nor had he ever played football for the school (both of which he had claimed on his résumé).

- Ronald Zarrella, former CEO of Bausch and Lomb, the eye care company, was required to give up $1.1 million of a planned $1.65 million bonus when it was discovered that although he had attended New York University's Stern School of Business, he had never earned the MBA that he claimed to have on his résumé. Interestingly, the board of directors of Bausch & Lomb, a company recognized by Standard & Poor's as an example of good corporate governance, chose not to fire Mr. Zarrella, claiming that he brought too much value to the company and its shareholders to dismiss him.

So if the risks are so high, why do people continue to embellish the details on a document that is supposed to accurately reflect their skills and work experience? Pressure! Getting hired by a company is a competitive process and you need to make the best sales pitch you can to attract the attention of the HR person assigned to screen the applications for a particular position (or, at least, the applications that make it through the software program that screens résumés for keywords related to the open position). In such a pressured environment, justifying an action on the basis of an assumption that everyone else is probably doing it starts to make sense. So, changing dates, job titles, responsibilities, certifications, and/or academic degrees can now be classified as "little white lies"; but as you can see from our three examples in this case, those little white lies can come back to haunt you.

Discussion Questions

1. Does the competitive pressure to get hired justify the decision to boost your résumé? Why?

2. Do you think the board of directors of Bausch & Lomb made the right decision in choosing not to fire Mr. Zarrella? Why or why not?

3. What steps should companies take during the hiring process to insure that such bad hires do not happen?

4. Can you polish your résumé without resorting to little white lies? Provide some examples of how you might do that.

5. If someone who has been unemployed for two years decides to boost his or her résumé, to compete in a very tough job market, does the two years make the decision any less unethical? Why or why not?

6. If you discovered that a colleague at work had lied on her résumé, what would you do?

Source: Stroud, J, "Six people who were caught lying on their resumes", www.therecruiterslounge, October 11, 2007.

WORLDCOM'S CREATIVE ACCOUNTING

In 1996 Betty Vinson landed a midlevel accounting position at WorldCom, a small long-distance telephone company in Jackson, Mississippi. During the next few years, the company grew very rapidly via acquisitions of companies such as Brooks Fiber, a high-speed telecom services company; MCI, the number-two long-distance carrier; Skytel, a leading paging firm; and UUNet, a major owner of Internet backbone. Two years after joining WorldCom, Vinson was promoted to a senior manager in the firm's corporate accounting division, reporting to Buford Yates, Director of General Accounting. She and her staff of 10 compiled quarterly reports and analyzed company operating expenses and loss reserves. The reserves were set aside to cover specific kinds of expenses.

WorldCom's profits grew rapidly until the middle of 2000 when the telecommunications industry entered a protracted slump. The company's line costs, lease fees paid to other telephone companies to use portions of their networks, began to increase as a percentage of the firm's revenue.

This ratio was closely watched by Wall Street as an indicator of the firm's health. The company's CEO, Bernard Ebbers, and CFO, Scott Sullivan, warned Wall Street that earnings for the second half of the year would fall below expectations. During the third quarter, due to the failure of some of its small customers, WorldCom was saddled with $685 million in unpaid bills.

Vinson, Yates, and Troy Normand, the accountant in charge of monitoring the firm's fixed expenses, searched for ways to cover the shortfall in preparation of the release of the third-quarter report. They were able to locate $50 million that could be applied to the unpaid bills, but that was a far cry from $685 million. In October Yates met with Vinson and Normand and told them that Sullivan and David Myers, the firm's controller, directed him to take $828 million out of the reserve account designated to cover line costs and other items for the telecommunications unit and use it to cover other expenses. That would reduce reported expenses and increase earnings.

Vinson, Normand, and Yates were concerned that the adjustment was not an approved accounting transaction. Accounting rules state that reserves can be established only if there is an expectation that a loss will occur in the unit where the reserve is established. The reserve can be depleted only if there is a good business reason for doing so. Because no business reason existed for dipping into the reserve account, Vinson and Normand told Yates that doing so was not following good accounting practices. Yates replied that he was not pleased with the action, but he was assured that this was a one-time transaction and would never happen again; thus, he had agreed to go along with the transfer. On that basis Vinson and Normand agreed to make the transfer.

The company's third-quarter results were reported on October 26. On that day, Vinson told Yates that she was planning to resign. Normand expressed similar inclinations. Ebbers got wind of the unrest in the accounting department and told Myers that the accountants would never again be placed in such an untenable position. Myers and Sullivan met with Vinson and Normand several days later. Sullivan explained that he was working on the firm's financial problems. He appealed to them to stay until he was able to get things under control and then they could leave if they wanted to, but he needed them to right the ship.

Normand stated that he was concerned that he would be held liable for making the accounting changes. Sullivan told the two that nothing they had done was illegal and that he would assume all responsibility for their actions. He further stated that the profit projections for the coming quarter had been cut in half and an accounting manipulation would not be needed. Following the meeting, Vinson's resolve to find another position weakened. She told her husband about the meeting and her concerns over the accounting irregularities, and he urged her to quit. But she was the chief breadwinner of the family earning more than her husband's $40,000 a year, and her job provided the family health insurance. She was

ORGANIZATIONAL ETHICS 73

also worried about finding a new position because she was a middle-aged woman.

Vinson rationalized that because Sullivan was considered one of the top CFOs in the country and had approved the transaction, it must be all right. After talking with Normand about how difficult it would be to find another job, both decided to stay. During the first quarter of 2001, things got worse. There were no reserves to tap and the funds gap was $771 million.

Sullivan ordered that the amount of line costs be transferred from an operating expense account to a capital expense account. That moved them from a direct expense against income to a depreciable expense, thus increasing short-term "profitability." Vinson was shocked with this directive. She knew that line costs were operating costs that could not legally be counted as a capital expense.

In fact, Yates had balked at the plan when Myers had told him about it, and Myers had told Sullivan that the transfer could not be justified when he was given the order. However, Sullivan told Myers that the transfer was WorldCom's only way out of its financial troubles. Vinson felt trapped. The threat to resign had already been used and she was afraid to quit her job before she had another one. Vinson, Normand, and Yates met to discuss the order but did not resolve the issue. Vinson decided to update her résumé and begin looking for another job.

Vinson, Normand, and Yates finally went along with the order to transfer the expenses. To do so, they had to decide which of five capital expense accounts to transfer the expenses to. Meyers met with them during this process and they all expressed how unhappy they were with the transaction. But they felt they had to do it to save the company. Vinson executed the entries to transfer the $771 million, changing dates of numerous transactions in the computer. The same process took place during the following three quarters: $560 million for the second quarter, $743 million for the third quarter, and $941 million for the fourth quarter. Early the next year, Vinson was promoted from senior manager to Director of Management Reporting, and Normand was promoted to Director of Legal Entity Accounting.

Discussion Questions

1. Who are the stakeholders in the case?

2. What actions should Vinson have taken and when? What prevented her from taking such actions?

3. What actions should Vinson's colleagues have taken?

4. Who is ultimately responsible for the accounting regularities?

5. Who is legally responsible for the accounting irregularities?

6. Who is morally responsible for the accounting irregularities?

Sources: Michael E. Kanell, "Ebbers Building a WorldCom Empire Fearless: CEO Not Expected to Let Up on Acquisitions, a Key to Firm's Stunning Success," *The Atlanta Journal–Constitution*, May 21, 2000, p. G1; Susan Pulliam, "A Staffer Ordered to Commit Fraud Balked, Then Caved," *The Wall Street Journal* 141, no. 121 (June 23, 2003), pp. A1, A6; *Securities and Exchange Commission v. Betty L. Vinson and Troy M. Normand*, 02 CV 8083 (JSR) Complaint (Securities Fraud), United States District Court for the Southern District of New York.

D. J. Fritzsche, *Business Ethics: A Global and Managerial Perspective*, 2nd ed. (New York: McGraw-Hill, 2005), pp. 197–99.

JOHNSON & JOHNSON AND THE TYLENOL® POISONINGS

A bottle of Tylenol® is a common feature of any medicine cabinet as a safe and reliable painkiller, but in the fall of 1982, this household brand was driven to the point of near-extinction along with the fortunes of parent company Johnson & Johnson as a result of a product-tampering case that has never been solved. On September 29, 1982, seven people in the Chicago area died after taking Extra-Strength Tylenol® capsules that had been laced with cyanide. Investigators later determined that the bottles of Tylenol® had been purchased or shoplifted from seven or eight drug stores and supermarkets and then replaced on shelves after the capsules in the bottle had been removed, emptied of their acetaminophen powder, and filled with cyanide.

The motive for the killings was never established, although a grudge against Johnson & Johnson or the retail chains selling the brand was suspected. A man called James Lewis attempted to profit from the event by sending an extortion letter to Johnson & Johnson, presumably inspired by the $100,000 reward the company had posted, but the police dismissed him as a serious suspect. He was jailed for 13 years for the extortion but never charged with the murders.

The response of Johnson & Johnson to the potential destruction of their most profitable product line has since become business legend and is taught today as a classic case study in crisis management at universities all over the world.

Company chairman James E. Burke, and other senior executives, were initially advised to only pull bottles from the Midwest region surrounding the Chicago area where the deaths had occurred. The decision they made was to order the immediate removal and destruction of more than 31 million bottles of the product nationwide, at an estimated cost to the company of more than $100 million. At the time, Tylenol® held a 35 per cent share of the painkiller market. This attack on the brand quickly reduced that share to less than 7 percent.

Why would the company make such an expensive decision when there were cheaper and more acceptable options open to it? To answer that question, we need to look at the company's "Credo"—the corporate philosophy statement that has guided the company since its founder, General Robert Wood Johnson, wrote the first version in 1943.

The opening line of the Credo explains why the decision to incur such a large cost in responding to the Tylenol® deaths was such an obvious one for the company to make: "We believe our first responsibility is to the doctors, nurses and patients, to mothers and fathers' and all others who use our products and services." That responsibility prompted the company to invest millions in developing tamper-proof bottles for their number one brand and a further $100 million to win back the confidence of their customers.

The actions appeared to pay-off. In less than a year, Tylenol® had regained a market share of more than 28 percent. Whether that dramatic recovery was due to savvy marketing or the selfless response of company executives in attempting to do "the right thing" for their customers remains a topic of debate over a quarter of a century later.

Discussion Questions

1. Although Johnson & Johnson took a massive short-term loss as a result of its actions, it was cushioned by the relative wealth of the company. Should it have acted the same way if the survival of the firm were at stake?

2. James E. Burke reportedly said that he felt that there was no other decision he could have made. Do you agree? Could he, for example, have recalled Tylenol® only in the Midwest? Was there a moral imperative to recall all Tylenol®?

« «

3. What was the moral minimum required of the company in this case? Would it favor some stakeholders more than others? How would you defend balancing the interests of some stakeholders more than others?

4. Imagine that a Third-World country volunteers to take the recalled product. Its representatives make assurances that all the tablets will be visually inspected and random samples taken before distribution. Would that be appropriate in these circumstances? Would it have been a better solution than destroying all remaining Tylenol® capsules?

5. Apparently no relatives of any of the victims sued Johnson & Johnson. Would they have had a moral case if they had? Should the company have foreseen a risk and done something about it?

6. How well do you think a general credo works in guiding action? Would you prefer a typical mission statement or a clear set of policy outlines, for example? Do you see any way in which the Johnson & Johnson credo could be improved or modified?

Source: Tifft, S., Griggs, L., "Poison Madness in the Midwest", www.Time.com, October 11, 1982. Molotsky, I., "Tylenol Maker Hopeful on Solving Poisoning Case," *The New York Times*, February 20, 1986. Rudolph, B., "Coping with Catastrophe", www.Time.com, February 24, 1986. Johnson & Johnson Credo: www.jnj.com/connect/about-jnj/jnj-credo/

chapter 4

Corporate Social Responsibility

> *Years ago William Jennings Bryan once described big business as "nothing but a collection of organized appetites."*
>
> —Daniel Patrick Moynihan, 1986

LEARNING OBJECTIVES

After studying this chapter, you should be able to:

1. Describe and explain *corporate social responsibility* (CSR).

2. Distinguish between *instrumental* and *social contract* approaches to corporate management.

3. Summarize the five driving forces behind CSR.

4. Distinguish between the three types of CSR.

5. Understand the challenges of a CSR initiative.

6. Apply the key components of a successful CSR initiative.

frontline focus

A Stocking Error

Claire is a management trainee at MegaDrug, a national retail pharmacy. She has only been there a month, which the store manager, Mr. Jones, seems to think requires that she must still learn every task from the ground up. So today, Claire is developing her management skills by restocking some shelves in the allergy section.

Claire doesn't really mind. She knows that when she's running her own store, she'll have to stock shelves on some days, especially if someone calls in sick, so it's good practice—plus, you get to help customers who are looking for items and they're usually very grateful for your help.

As she's stocking the shelves, Claire notices that the quantities of name brand allergy medicines are much smaller than the company's own-label brand. She immediately brings it to Mr. Jones' attention, fully expecting him to tell her to put out more of the name brands to balance out the shelves equally.

However, Mr. Jones's response catches Claire by surprise.

"Oh, really? There must have been a stocking error in the storeroom—somebody didn't fill the order requisition correctly," said Mr. Jones. "The good news is, the company makes a lot more money on our own-label brand, so maybe running out of the name brands will encourage customers to give us a try."

"Not to worry," he continued, "I'd rather have one or two customers complain about an unavailable item than lose profitable sales of our house brand. Leave the shelf stocked as it is."

1. MegaDrug advertises that it is a socially responsible organization that puts its stakeholders first. Is Mr. Jones being ethically responsible to his customers here? Read the definition of ethical corporate social responsibility (CSR) on page 89 for more details.

2. Mr. Jones would rather have one or two customers complain about an unavailable item than lose profitable sales of MegaDrug's own brand. Is denying customers a choice of products a valid solution?

3. What should Claire do now?

Corporate Social Responsibility

Corporate Social Responsibility (CSR) The actions of an organization that are targeted toward achieving a social benefit over and above maximizing profits for its shareholders and meeting all its legal obligations.

Corporate Citizenship An alternative term for corporate social responsibility, implying that the organization is a responsible citizen in meeting all its obligations.

Corporate Conscience An alternative term for corporate social responsibility, implying that the organization is run with an awareness of its obligations to society.

The New Lemonade Stand . . .

Consider that age-old icon of childhood endeavors: THE LEMONADE STAND. Within a CSR context, it's as if today's thirsty public wants much more than a cool, refreshing drink for a quarter. They're demanding said beverage be made of juice squeezed from lemons not sprayed with insecticides toxic to the environment, prepared by persons of appropriate age in kitchen conditions which pose no hazard to those workers. It must be offered in biodegradable paper cups and sold at a price which generates a fair, livable wage to the workers—who, some might argue, are far too young to be toiling away making lemonade for profit anyway. It's enough to drive young entrepreneurs . . . straight back to the sandbox.[1]

Corporate social responsibility (CSR)—also referred to as **corporate citizenship** or **corporate conscience**—may be defined as the actions of an organization that are targeted toward achieving a social benefit over and above maximizing profits for its shareholders and meeting all its legal obligations.

This definition assumes that the corporation is operating in a competitive environment and that the managers of the corporation are committed to an aggressive growth strategy while complying with all federal, state, and local legal obligations. These obligations include payment of all taxes related to the profitable operation of the business, payment of all employer contributions for its workforce, and compliance with all legal industry standards in operating a safe working environment for its employees and delivering safe products to its customers.

However, the definition only scratches the surface of a complex and often-elusive topic that has gained increased attention in the aftermath of corporate scandals that have presented many organizations as being the image of unchecked greed. While CSR may be growing in prominence, much of that prominence has come at the expense of organizations that found themselves facing boycotts and focused media attention on issues that previously were not considered as part of a traditional strategic plan. As Porter and Kramer (2006) point out[2]:

> Many companies awoke to (CSR) only after being surprised by public responses to issues they had not previously thought were part of their business responsibilities. Nike, for example, faced an extensive consumer boycott after *The New York Times* and other media outlets reported abusive labor practices at some of its Indonesian suppliers in the early 1990s. Shell Oil's decision to sink the *Brent Spar,* an obsolete oil rig, in the North Sea led to Greenpeace protests in 1995 and to international headlines. Pharmaceutical companies discovered that they were expected to respond to the AIDS pandemic in Africa even though it was far removed from their primary product lines and markets. Fast-food and packaged food companies are now being held responsible for obesity and poor nutrition.

> Activists of all kinds . . . have grown much more aggressive and effective in bringing public pressure to bear on corporations. Activists may target the most visible or successful companies merely to draw attention to an issue, even if those corporations actually have had little impact on the problem at hand. Nestlé, for example, the world's largest purveyor of bottled water, has become a major target in the global debate about access to fresh water, despite the fact that Nestlé's bottled water sales consume just 0.0008% of the world's fresh water supply. The inefficiency of agricultural irrigation, which uses 70% of the world's supply annually, is a far more pressing issue, but it offers no equally convenient multinational corporation to target.

Whether the organization's discovery of the significance of CSR was intentional or as a result of unexpected media attention, once CSR becomes part of its strategic plan, choices have to be made as to how the company will address this new element of corporate management. Many take an **instrumental approach** to CSR and argue that the only obligation of a corporation is to make profits for its shareholders in providing goods and services that meet the needs of its customers. The most famous advocate of this "classical" model is the Nobel Prize–winning economist Milton Friedman, who argued that[3]:

> The view has been gaining widespread acceptance that corporate officials . . . have a social responsibility

Is McDonald's® more culpable for childhood obesity than a local burger joint since it sells to a much wider audience? Should your local restaurants be held to similar standards?

that goes beyond serving the interests of their stockholders. . . This view shows a fundamental misconception of the character and nature of a free economy. In such an economy, there is one and only one social responsibility of business—to use its resources and engage in activities designed to increase its profits so long as it stays within the rules of the game, which is to say, engages in open and free competition, without deception or fraud. . . Few trends could so thoroughly undermine the very foundations of our free society as the acceptance by corporate officials of a social responsibility other than to make as much money for their stockholders as possible.

From an ethical perspective, Friedman argues that it would be unethical for a corporation to do anything other than deliver the profits for which its investors have entrusted it with their funds in the purchase of shares in the corporation. He also stipulates that those profits should be earned "without deception or fraud." In addition, Friedman argues that, as an employee of the corporation, the manager has an ethical obligation to fulfill his role in delivering on the expectations of his employers[4]:

> In a free-enterprise, private-property system, a corporate executive is an employee of the owners of the business. He has direct responsibility to his employers. That responsibility is to conduct the business in accordance with their desires, which generally will be to make as much money as possible while conforming to the basic rules of the society, both those embodied in law and those embodied in ethical custom. . . The key point is that, in his capacity as a corporate executive, the manager is the agent of the individuals who own the corporation . . . and his primary responsibility is to them.

This article is quoted in full in Appendix 4.

☑ PROGRESS CHECK QUESTIONS

1. Define *corporate social responsibility*.

2. Name two other terms that may be used for socially aware corporate behavior.

3. Give four examples of a corporation's legal obligations.

4. Do you agree or disagree with Friedman's argument? Why?

Management without Conscience

Friedman's view of the corporate world supports the rights of individuals to make money with their investments (provided it is done honestly) and it recognizes the clear legality of the employment contract—as a manager, you work for me, the owner (or us, the shareholders), and you are expected to make as much profit as possible to make our investment in the company a success. This position does not prevent the organization from demonstrating some form of social conscience—donating to local charities or sponsoring a local Little League team, for example—but it restricts such charitable acts to the discretion of the owners (presumably in good times rather than bad), rather than recognizing any formal obligation on the part of the corporation and its management team.

This very simplistic model focuses on the internal world of the corporation itself and assumes that there are no external consequences to the actions of the corporation and its managers. Once we acknowledge that there is a world outside that is impacted by the actions of the corporation, we can consider the **social contract approach** to corporate management.

In recent years, the notion of a social contract between corporations and society has undergone a subtle shift. Originally, the primary focus of the social contract was an economic one, assuming that continued economic growth would bring an equal advancement in quality of life. However, the rapid growth of U.S. businesses in size and power in the 1960s, '70s, and '80s changed that focus. Continued corporate growth was not matched by an improved quality of life. Growth at the expense of rising costs, wages growing at a lower rate than inflation, and the increasing presence of substantial layoffs to control costs were seen as evidence that the old social contract was no longer working.

> **social contract approach** The perspective that a corporation has an obligation to society over and above the expectations of its shareholders.

The growing realization that corporate actions had the potential to impact tens of thousands of citizens led to a clear opinion shift. Fueled by special interest groups including environmentalists and consumer advocates, consumers began to question some fundamental corporate assumptions: Do we really need 200 types of breakfast cereal or 50 types of laundry soap just so we can deliver aggressive earnings growth to investors? What is this constant growth really costing us?

The modern social contract approach argues that since the corporation depends on society for its existence and continued growth, there is an obligation for the corporation to meet the demands of that society rather than just the demands of a targeted group of customers. As such, corporations should be recognized as social institutions as well as economic enterprises. By recognizing all their stakeholders (customers, employees, shareholders, vendor partners, and their community partners) rather than just their shareholders, corporations, it is argued, must maintain a longer-term perspective than just the delivery of quarterly earnings numbers.

PROGRESS CHECK QUESTIONS

5. Do investors *always* invest money in companies to make a profit?

6. What is the *instrumental* model of corporate management?

7. What is the *social contract* model of corporate management?

8. Do you agree or disagree with the social contract model? Why?

Management by Inclusion

Corporations do not operate in an isolated environment. As far back as 1969, Henry Ford II recognized that[5]:

> The terms of the contract between industry and society are changing. . . Now we are being asked to serve a wider range of human values and to accept an obligation to members of the public with whom we have no commercial transactions.

Their actions impact their customers, their employees, their suppliers, and the communities in which they produce and deliver their goods and services. Depending on the actions taken by the corporation, some of these groups will be positively impacted and others will be negatively impacted. For example, if a corporation is operating unprofitably in a very competitive market, it is unlikely that it could raise prices to increase profits. Therefore, the logical choice would be to lower costs—most commonly by laying off its employees, since giving an employee a pink slip takes him or her off your payroll immediately.

While those laid-off employees are obviously hardest hit by this decision, it also has other far-reaching consequences. The communities in which those employees reside have now lost the spending power of those employees, who, presumably, no longer have as much money to spend in the local market until they find alternative employment. If the corporation chooses to shut down an entire factory, the community also loses property tax revenue from that factory, which negatively impacts the services it can provide to its residents—schools, roads, police force, and so forth. In addition, those local suppliers who made deliveries to that factory also have lost business and may have to make their own tough choices as a result.

What about the corporation's customers and shareholders? Presumably the layoffs will help the corporation remain competitive and continue to offer low prices to its customers, and the more cost-effective operation will hopefully improve the profitability of the corporation. So there are, at least on paper, winners *and* losers in these situations.

Recognizing the interrelationship of all these groups leads us far beyond the world of the almighty bottom line, and those organizations that do demonstrate a "conscience" that goes beyond generating profit inevitably attract a lot of attention. As Jim Roberts, professor of marketing at the Hankamer School of Business, points out[6]:

I like to think of corporate social responsibility as doing well by doing good. Doing what's in the best long-term interest of the customer is ultimately doing what's best for the company. Doing good for the customer is just good business.

Look at the tobacco industry. Serving only the short-term desires of their customers has led to government intervention and a multi-billion dollar lawsuit against the industry because of the industry's denial of the consequences of smoking. On the other hand, alcohol manufacturers realized that by at least showing an interest in their consumers' well-being ("don't drink and drive," "Drink Responsibly," "Choose a Designated Driver") they have been able to escape much of the wrath felt by the tobacco industry. It pays to take a long-term perspective.

"Doing well by doing good" seems, on the face of it, to be an easy policy to adopt, and many organizations have started down that road by making charitable donations, underwriting projects in their local communities, sponsoring local events, and engaging in productive conversations with special interest groups about

In Canada, cigarette packaging is required to have a graphic label that details the potential health risks of smoking. How do you think consumers in the United States would respond to the government's help to be good corporate citizens?

earth-friendly packaging materials and the use of more recyclable materials. However, mistrust and cynicism remain among their customers and citizens of their local communities. Many still see these initiatives as public relations exercises with no real evidence of dramatic changes in the core operating philosophies of these companies. Consider the media coverage devoted to Aaron Feuerstein and his response to a devastating fire.

ETHICAL dilemma

CASE 4.1 Malden Mills

Lawrence, Massachusetts, is 25 miles north of Boston. In the mid-1800s it was one of several planned industrial sites that developed the local textile industry based on the waterpower derived from the nearby Merrimack River. By 1900 the town had a population of over 95,000 and mills that worked day and night.

In 1906, Henry Feuerstein founded Malden Mills in nearby Lowell and Feuerstein's son, Samuel, relocated it to Lawrence in 1956. It has traditionally been a closely held private firm. The company survived a number of boom and bust cycles and watched the exodus of other manufacturers to the American South and overseas.

In 1981 the firm developed Polar Tec, a lightweight versatile fleece fabric that has become synonymous with outdoor gear, and its future seemed secure. However, on a bitterly cold night in December 1995, a devastating fire burned most of the plant to the ground.

The CEO, Aaron Feuerstein, could have accepted an insurance settlement and closed the factory or moved operations overseas. Instead, he spent $15 million of his own money keeping all 3,000 employees on the payroll, with benefits, for three months while the factory was rebuilt. Feuerstein said,

> I have a responsibility to the worker. . . I have an equal responsibility to the community. It would have been unconscionable to put 3,000 people on the streets and deliver a deathblow to the cities of Lawrence and Methuen.

Maybe on paper our company is worth less to Wall Street, but I can tell you it is worth more.

While the factory was being rebuilt, the human resources division used federal and state funding to give many of the displaced workers additional training, especially on computers. Feuerstein was lionized in the press and given a number of national and international awards for his stance. The new plant is environmentally sensitive, and reportedly individual productivity increased significantly.

Nevertheless, Malden Mills again hit hard times. Faced with financial difficulties that stemmed largely from financing the debt for rebuilding, it filed Chapter 11 bankruptcy in November 2001.

In October 2003, the firm successfully emerged from Chapter 11. Aaron Feuerstein has been replaced as CEO, and there are six new directors on the board. Recent orders from the U.S. armed forces have given Malden Mills a significant boost.

1. How would you describe Feuerstein's approach to helping his workers and the community when the factory burned?

2. Do you think the employees should have been expected to deal with the consequences of the fire without his help?

3. Could Feuerstein have done anything more for his workers?

4. What do you think most organizations would have done in this situation?

Source: K. Gibson, *Business Ethics: People, Profits, and the Planet* (New York: McGraw-Hill, 2006), pp. 645–47.

The Driving Forces behind Corporate Social Responsibility

Joseph F. Keefe of NewCircle Communications asserts that there are five major trends behind the CSR phenomenon[7]:

1. *Transparency:* We live in an information-driven economy where business practices have become increasingly transparent. Companies can no longer sweep things under the rug—whatever they do (for good or ill) will be known, almost immediately, around the world.

2. *Knowledge:* The transition to an information-based economy also means that consumers and investors have more information at their disposal than at any time in history. They can be more discerning, and can wield more influence. Consumers visiting a clothing store can now choose one brand over another based upon those companies' respective environmental records or involvement in sweatshop practices overseas.

3. *Sustainability:* The earth's natural systems are in serious and accelerating decline, while global population is rising precipitously. In the last 30 years alone, one-third of the planet's resources—the earth's "natural wealth"—have been consumed. . . We are fast approaching or have already crossed the sustainable yield thresholds of many natural systems (fresh water, oceanic fisheries, forests, rangelands), which cannot keep pace with projected population growth. . . As a result, corporations are

under increasing pressure from diverse stakeholder constituencies to demonstrate that business plans and strategies are environmentally sound and contribute to sustainable development.

4. *Globalization:* The greatest periods of reform in U.S. history . . . produced child labor laws, the minimum wage, the eight-hour day, workers' compensation laws, unemployment insurance, antitrust and securities regulations, Social Security, Medicare, the Community Reinvestment Act, the Clean Air Act, Clean Water Act, Environmental Protection Agency, and so forth. All of these reforms constituted governmental efforts to intervene in the economy in order to (improve) the worst excesses of market capitalism. Globalization represents a new stage of capitalist development, this time without . . . public institutions [in place] to protect society by balancing private corporate interests against broader public interests.

5. *The Failure of the Public Sector:* Many if not most developing countries are governed by dysfunctional regimes ranging from the [unfortunate] and disorganized to the brutal and corrupt. Yet it is not developing countries alone that suffer from [dilapidated] public sectors. In the United States and other developed nations, citizens arguably expect less of government than they used to, having lost confidence in the public sector as the best or most appropriate venue for addressing a growing list of social problems.

Even with these major trends driving CSR, many organizations have found it difficult to make the transition from CSR as a theoretical concept to CSR as an operational policy. Ironically, it's not the ethical action itself that causes the problem; it's how to promote those acts to your stakeholders as proof of your new corporate conscience without appearing to be manipulative or scheming to generate press coverage for policies that could easily be dismissed as feel-good initiatives that are simply chasing customer favor.

In addition, many CSR initiatives do not generate immediate financial gains to the organization. Cynical customers may decide to wait and see if this is real or just a temporary project to win new customers in a tough economic climate. This delayed response tests the commitment of those organizations that are inclined to dispense with experimental initiatives when the going gets tough.

Corporations that choose to experiment with CSR initiatives run the risk of creating adverse results and ending up worse off than when they started:

- Employees feel that they are working for an insincere, uncaring organization.
- The public sees little more than a token action concerned with publicity rather than community.
- The organization does not perceive much benefit from CSR and so sees no need to develop the concept.

✓ PROGRESS CHECK QUESTIONS

9. List the five major trends driving CSR.

10. Which one do you think is the most important? Why?

11. Explain why organizations are struggling to adopt CSR initiatives.

12. Why would customers be cynical of CSR initiatives?

For those organizations that doubt the momentum of these trends, consider an example of the problems Coca-Cola® faced in the United States as a result of their business practices in Asia and South America.

ETHICAL dilemma

CASE 4.2 Banning the Real Thing

In 1999, following a campaign by a student group known as Students Organizing for Labor and Economic Equality (SOLE), the University of Michigan instituted a Vendor Code of Conduct that specified key performance criteria from all university vendors. The code included the following:

General Principles

The University of Michigan has a longstanding commitment to sound, ethical, and socially responsible practices. In aligning its purchasing policies with its core values and practices, the University seeks to recognize and promote basic human rights, appropriate labor standards for employees, and a safe, healthful, and sustainable environment for workers and the general public. . . In addition, the University shall make every reasonable effort to contract only with vendors meeting the primary standards prescribed by this Code of Conduct.

Primary Standards

- Nondiscrimination
- Affirmative Action
- Freedom of Association and Collective Bargaining
- Labor Standards: Wages, Hours, Leaves, and Child Labor
- Health and Safety
- Forced Labor
- Harassment or Abuse

Preferential Standards

- Living Wage
- International Human Rights
- Environmental Protection
- Foreign Law

Compliance Procedures

University–Vendor Partnership. The ideal University–vendor relationship is in the nature of a partnership, seeking mutually agreeable and important goals. Recognizing our mutual interdependence, it is in the best interest of the University to find a resolution when responding to charges or questions about a vendor's compliance with the provisions of the Code.

On November 30, 2004, SOLE submitted formal complaints against one specific university vendor—the Coca-Cola® Company—with whom the university held 12 direct and indirect contracts totaling just under $1.3 million in FY 2004. The complaints against Coke were as follows:

- Bio-solid waste disposal in India. The complaint alleged that bottling plant sludge containing cadmium and other contaminants has been distributed to local farmers as fertilizer.

- Use of groundwater in India. The complaint alleged that Coca-Cola® is drawing down the water table/aquifer by using deep bore wells; water quality has declined; shallow wells used by local farmers have gone dry; and poor crop harvests near bottling plants have resulted from lack of sufficient irrigation water.

- Pesticides in the product in India. Studies have found that pesticides have been detected in Coca-Cola® products in India that are in excess of local and international standards.

- Labor practices in Colombia. Data showing a steep decline in SIALTRAINAL, a Colombian bottler's union (from approximately 2,300 to 650 in the past decade); SOLE claims repeated incidents with paramilitary groups threatening and harming union leaders and potential members, including allegations of kidnapping and murder. SOLE is also concerned about working conditions within the bottling plants.

The Vendor Code of Conduct Dispute Review Board met in June 2005 to review the complaints and recommended that Coca-Cola® agree in writing no later than September 30, 2005, to a third-party independent audit to review the complaints. An independent auditor satisfactory to both parties had to be selected by December 31, 2005. The audit had to be completed by March 2006, with the findings to be received by the university no later than April 30, 2006. Coca-Cola® would then be expected to put a corrective action plan in place by May 31, 2006. Since one of the 12 contracts was scheduled to expire on June 30, 2005, with another 7 expiring between July and November 2005, Coca-Cola® was formally placed on probation until August 2006 pending further investigation of the SOLE complaints. The board also recommended that the University not enter into new contracts or renew any expiring contracts during this period, and that it agree only to short-term conditional extensions with reassessment at each of the established deadlines to determine if Coca-Cola® has made satisfactory progress toward demonstrating its compliance with the Vendor Code of Conduct.

The situation got progressively worse for Coca-Cola®. By December 2005, at least a dozen institutions worldwide had divested from the Coca-Cola® Company on the grounds of alleged human rights violations in Asia and South America. On December 8th, New York University began pulling all Coke products from its campus after Coke refused to submit to an independent investigation by that day's deadline.

On December 30, 2005, the University of Michigan suspended sales of Coke products on its three campuses beginning January 1, 2006, affecting vending machines, residence halls, cafeterias, and campus restaurants. Kari Bjorhus, a spokesperson for the Coca-Cola® Company, told the *Detroit News,* "The University of Michigan is an important school, and I respect the way they worked with us on this issue. We are continuing to try hard to work with the university to address concerns and assure them about our business practices."

1. Which ethical standards are being violated here?
2. Is the university being unreasonable in the high standards demanded in its Vendor Code of Conduct?
3. Do you think the university would have developed the Vendor Code of Conduct without the aggressive campaign put forward by SOLE?
4. How should Coca-Cola® respond in order to keep the University of Michigan contracts?

Source: University of Michigan, www.umich.edu; Associated Press, December 30, 2005; *The Michigan Daily,* September 29, 2005; University of Michigan News Service, June 17, 2005.

The Triple Bottom Line

Organizations pursue operational efficiency through detailed monitoring of their bottom line—that is, how much money is left over after all the bills have been paid from the revenue generated from the sale of their product or service. As a testament to how seriously companies are now taking CSR, many have now adapted their annual reports to reflect a triple bottom-line approach, where they provide social and environmental updates alongside their primary bottom-line financial performance. The phrase has been attributed to John Elkington, co-founder of the business consultancy SustainAbility, in his 1998 book *Cannibals with Forks: The Triple Bottom Line of 21st Century Business.* As further evidence that this notion has hit the business mainstream, there is now a trendy acronym "3BL" for you to use to prove, supposedly, that you are on the "cutting edge" of this new trend. (For a more detailed critique of 3BL, please review the 2003 article by Wayne Norman and Chris MacDonald in Appendix 5.)

To some degree, 3BL is like the children's story, "The Emperor's New Clothes." While it may be easy to support the idea of organizations pursuing social and environmental goals in addition to their financial goals, there has been no real evidence of *how* to measure such achievements and no one has yet volunteered to play the part of the little boy who tells the emperor he is naked.

If you subscribe to the old management saying that "if you can't measure it, you can't manage it," the challenges of delivering on any 3BL goals become apparent. Wayne and MacDonald present the following scenario[8]:

. . . Imagine a firm reporting that:

(a) 20 percent of its directors were women,

(b) 7 percent of its senior management were members of "visible" minorities,

(c) It donated 1.2 percent of its profits to charity,

(d) The annual turnover rate among its hourly workers was 4%, and

(e) It had been fined twice this year for toxic emissions.

Now, out of context (e.g. without knowing how large the firm is, where it is operating, and what the averages are in its industrial sector) it is difficult to say how good or bad these figures are. Of course, in the case of each indicator we often have a sense of whether a higher or lower number would generally be better, from the perspective of social/ethical performance. The conceptual point, however, is that these are quite simply not the sort of data that can be fed into an income-statement-like calculation to produce a final net sum.

So, if you can't measure it, can you really arrive at a "bottom line" for it? It would appear that many organizations are taking a fairly opportunistic approach in adopting the terminology without following through on the delivery of a consistent methodology. Could the "feel good" terminology associated with 3BL help you make a convincing case if you are seeking to make amends for prior transgressions? Consider the following from Coca-Cola's® 2004 Citizenship Report[9]:

Our Company has always endeavored to conduct business responsibly and ethically. We have long been committed to enriching the workplace, preserving and protecting the environment, and strengthening the communities where we operate. These objectives are all consistent with—indeed essential to—our principal goal of refreshing the marketplace with high-quality beverages.

If we compare this commitment to the accusations made by students at the University of Michigan in Case 4.2, we can see how challenging CSR can be. It may be easy to make a public commitment to CSR, but actually delivering on that commitment to the satisfaction of your customers can be much harder to achieve.

Jumping on the CSR Bandwagon

This same triple perspective can be applied to the opportunistic way in which many companies have jumped on the CSR bandwagon by adapting the concept for their own purposes. On the basis of this behavior, we can identify three distinct types of CSR: *Ethical, Altruistic,* and *Strategic.*

Ethical CSR represents the purest or most legitimate type of CSR in which organizations pursue a clearly defined sense of social conscience in managing their financial responsibilities to shareholders, their legal responsibilities to their local community and society as a whole, and their ethical responsibilities to do the right thing for all their stakeholders.

Organizations in this category have typically incorporated their beliefs into their core operating philosophies. Companies such as The Body Shop, Ben & Jerry's® Homemade Ice Cream, and Tom's of Maine were founded on

Ethical CSR Organizations pursue a clearly defined sense of social conscience in managing their financial responsibilities to shareholders, their legal responsibilities to their local community and society as a whole, and their ethical responsibilities to "do the right thing" for all their stakeholders.

the belief that the relationship between companies and their consumers did not have to be an adversarial one, and that corporations should honor a social contract with the communities in which they operate and the citizens they serve.

Altruistic CSR takes a philanthropic approach by underwriting specific initiatives to give back to the company's local community or to designated national or international programs. In ethical terms, this giving back is done with funds that rightly belong to shareholders but, it is unlikely that McDonald's® shareholders, for example, would file a motion at the next annual general meeting for the return of the funds that McDonald's® gives to the support of its Ronald McDonald® houses.

Altruistic CSR Organizations take a philanthropic approach by underwriting specific initiatives to give back to the company's local community or to designated national or international programs.

Of greater concern is that the choice of charitable giving is at the discretion of the corporation, which places the individual shareholders in the awkward position of unwittingly supporting causes they may not support on their own, such as the pro-life and gun control movements. Critics have argued that, from an ethical perspective, this type of CSR is immoral since it represents a violation of shareholder rights if they are not given the opportunity to vote on the initiatives launched in the name of corporate social responsibility.

The relative legitimacy of altruistic CSR is based on the argument that the philanthropic initiatives are authorized without concern for the corporation's overall profitability. Arguing in *utilitarian* terms, corporations are merely doing the greatest good for the greatest number.

Examples of altruistic CSR often occur during crises or situations of widespread need. Consider the following:

- In the 1980s, Richard Branson's Virgin Group launched Mates Condoms in response to growing concern over the spread of HIV/AIDS. The company operated on the philosophy that the need for the availability of the product far outweighed the need to make a profit.

- Southwest Airlines supports the Ronald McDonald Houses with donations of both dollars and employee-donated volunteer hours. The company considers giving back to the communities in which it operates an appropriate part of its mission.

- Shell Oil Corporation responded to the devastation of the tsunami disaster in Asia in December 2004 with donations of fuel for transportation rescue and water tanks for relief aid, in addition to financial commitments of several million dollars for disaster relief. Shell employees matched many of the company's donations.

- In September 2005 the home improvement retail giant Home Depot announced a direct cash donation of $1.5 million to support the relief and rebuilding efforts in areas devastated by Hurricane Katrina. In addition, the company announced a corporate month of service, donating 300,000 volunteer hours to communities across the country and over $200,000 in materials to support the activities of 90 stores in recovery, cleanup, and rebuilding efforts in their local communities.

Strategic CSR Philanthropic activities are targeted toward programs that will generate the most positive publicity or goodwill for the organization.

Strategic CSR runs the greatest risk of being perceived as self-serving behavior on the part of the organization. This type of philanthropic activity targets programs that will generate the most positive publicity or goodwill for the organization. By supporting these programs, companies achieve the best of both worlds: they can claim to be doing the right thing and, on the assumption that good publicity brings more sales, they also can meet their fiduciary obligations to their shareholders.

Volunteer work as corporate policy is not limited to major corporations. What are some smaller scale examples of altruistic efforts that companies can engage in?

Compared to the alleged immorality of altruistic CSR, critics can argue that strategic CSR is ethically commendable because these initiatives benefit stakeholders while meeting fiduciary obligations to the company's shareholders. However, the question remains: Without a win–win payoff, would such CSR initiatives be authorized?

The danger in this case lies in how actions are perceived. Consider for example, two initiatives launched by the Ford Motor Corporation:

- Ford spent millions on an ad campaign to raise awareness of the need for booster seats for children over 40 pounds and under 4'9" (most four- to eight-year-olds) and gave away almost a million seats as part of the campaign.

- During the PR battle with Firestone Tires over who was to blame for the rollover problems with the Ford Explorer, Ford's CEO at the time, Jacques Nasser, made a public commitment to spend up to $3 billion to replace 13 million Firestone Wilderness AT tires for free on Ford Explorers because he saw them as an "unacceptable risk to our customers."

If we attribute motive to each campaign, the booster seat campaign could be interpreted as a way to position Ford as the auto manufacturer that cares about the safety of its passengers as much as its drivers. The tire exchange could be interpreted the same way, but given the design flaws with the Ford Explorer alleged by Firestone, couldn't it also be seen as a diversionary tactic?

13. Explain the term *triple bottom line*.

14. Explain the term *Ethical CSR*.

15. Explain the term *Altruistic CSR*.

16. Explain the term *Strategic CSR*.

LIFEskills

Being socially responsible

Consider how important your beliefs about corporate social responsibility (CSR) and sustainability are in your daily life. Do you spend your hard-earned money at stores that promote environmental awareness and "green" capitalism? Or does your budget force you to find the best prices and not think about the damage done to achieve the lowest possible cost?

How will those beliefs impact your life choices in the future? Will you focus your employment search on companies with good CSR records? Or will the need to pay the bills outweigh that element and force you to take the highest-paying job you can find? It is important to remember that the paycheck may not be enough to address a poor cultural fit or a direct conflict between your values and those of your employer. It's better to extend your search for a while, if necessary, to find a company that you are proud to work for rather than taking the first opportunity that comes along only to find yourself at odds with many of the company's policies and philosophies.

One of the newest and increasingly questionable practices in the world of CSR is the notion of making your operations "carbon neutral" in such a way as to offset whatever damage you are doing to the environment through your greenhouse gas emissions by purchasing credits from "carbon positive" projects to balance out your emissions. Initially developed as a solution for those industries that face significant challenges in reducing their emissions (airlines or automobile companies for example), the concept has quickly spawned a diverse collection of vendors who can assist you in achieving carbon neutrality, along with a few markets in which emissions credits can now be bought and sold.

Carbon Offset Credits

Do you know what your carbon footprint is? At www.carboncounter.org, you can calculate the carbon dioxide emissions from your home, your car, and any air travel you do, and then calculate your total emissions on an annual basis. The result is your footprint. You can then purchase credits to offset your emissions and render yourself carbon neutral. If you have sufficient funds, you can purchase more credits than you need to achieve neutrality and then join the enviable ranks of carbon positive people who actually take more carbon dioxide out of the cycle than they produce. That, of course, is a technicality since you aren't driving less or driving a hybrid, nor are you being more energy conscious in how you heat or cool your home. You are doing nothing more than buying credits from other projects around the world, such as tree planting in indigenous forests, wind farms, or even outfitting African farmers with energy-efficient stoves, and using those positive emissions to counterbalance your negative ones. Companies such as Dell Computer, British Airways, Expedia® Travel, and BP have experimented with programs where customers can pay a fee to offset the emissions spent in manufacturing their products or using their services.

If this sounds just a little strange, consider that this issue of offsetting is serious enough to have been ratified by the Kyoto Protocol—an agreement between 160 countries that became effective in 2005 (and which the USA has yet to sign). The protocol requires developed nations to reduce their greenhouse gas emissions not only by modifying their domestic industries (coal, steel, automobiles, etc.) but also by funding projects in developing countries in return for carbon credits. It didn't take long for an entire infrastructure to develop in order to facilitate the trading of these credits so that organizations with high emissions (and consequently a larger demand for offset credits) could purchase credits in greater volumes than most individual projects would provide. In the first nine months of 2006, the United Nations estimated that over $22 billion of carbon was traded.

As with any frontier market, the early results for this new industry have been questionable to say the least. Examples of unethical practices include:

- Inflated market prices for credits—priced per ton of carbon dioxide—varying from $3.50 to $27 a ton, which explains why some traders are able to generate profit margins of 50 percent.

- The sale of credits from projects that don't even exist.

- Selling the same credits from one project over and over again to different buyers who are unable to verify the effectiveness of the project since they are typically set up in remote geographical areas.

- Claiming offset credits on projects that are profitable in their own right (see Case 4.3).

As these questionable practices gain more media attention, some of the larger players in this new industry—companies such as Morgan Stanley and Deutsche Bank, which have multibillion-dollar investments in the credit trading arena—are demanding that commonly accepted codes of conduct be established in order to clean up the market and offer greater incentives for customers to trade their credits. In November 2006, Deutsche Bank teamed up with more than a dozen investment banks and five carbon-trading organizations in Europe to create the European Carbon Investors and Services Association (ECIS) to promote the standardization of carbon trading on a global scale.

ETHICAL dilemma

CASE 4.3 Blue Source

Blue Source is a United States–based carbon-offsetting company, committed to providing an effective solution for organizations seeking to deal with their greenhouse gas (GHG) emission problems and make their operations carbon neutral by purchasing enough offset credits to match their own emissions. Founded in 2001, the company is organized into two business units—the Portfolio Development Group, which designs, develops, and operates the offset projects for the company; and the Portfolio Group, which is responsible for "aggregating, marketing, and managing all the climate change offset portfolio" projects and also sourcing new projects for the long-term sustainability of the fund. Aggregation involves collecting offsets from multiple projects amounting to "hundreds of millions of offsets," which can then be sold to large corporations seeking to make themselves carbon neutral in their business operations.

Credits are captured from multiple project types, but one of the most successful has been enhanced oil recovery, where carbon dioxide is pumped into depleted oil wells to bring up the remaining oil. This achieves two positive outcomes—the removal of the carbon dioxide from the atmosphere and the retrieval of oil that would normally be abandoned in favor of drilling a new well somewhere else. However, the recent increases in the price of oil have meant that the barrels of oil salvaged from these depleted wells can be sold for enough money to make the project profitable without the inclusion of revenue from the sale of offset credits. As Harvey and Fidler point out. "There is nothing illegal in these practices. However, some companies that are offsetting their emissions have avoided such projects because customers may find them controversial."

1. Visit the Blue Source Web site at www.bluesource.com and explain how the Blue Source business model works.

2. Does pumping carbon dioxide into oil wells meet the definition of CSR? Why or why not?

3. The rising price of oil has made many of Blue Source's projects financially viable without the addition of carbon offset credits. Should the credits then be taken away? Why or why not?

4. If you were responsible for making your company carbon neutral, would you use Blue Source? Why or why not?

Source: Fiona Harvey and Stephen Fidler, "Industry Caught in 'Carbon Credit' Smokescreen," *Financial Times,* April 26, 2007.

So, if there is nothing ethically wrong in "doing well by doing good," why isn't everyone doing it? The key concern here must be customer perception. If an organization commits to CSR initiatives, then they must be real commitments rather than short-term experiments. You may be able to gamble on the short-term memory of your customers, but the majority will expect you to deliver on your commitment and to provide progress reports on those initiatives that you publicized so widely.

But what about some of the more well-known CSR players? When we consider Ben & Jerry's® Homemade Ice Cream or The Body Shop, for example, both organizations made the concept of a corporate social conscience a part of their core philosophies before CSR was ever anointed as a management buzzword. As such, their good intent garnered vast amounts of goodwill: Investors admired their financial performance and customers felt good about shopping there. However, if the quality of their products had not lived up to customer expectations, would they have prospered over the long term? Would customers have continued to shop there if they didn't like the products? "Doing well by doing good" will only get you so far.

In this context, it is unfair to accuse companies with CSR initiatives of abandoning their moral responsibilities to their stakeholders. Even if you are leveraging the maximum possible publicity from your efforts, that will only get the people in the door. If the product or service doesn't live up to expectations, they won't be back. Customers will not settle for second-rate service or product quality just because a charitable cause is involved. Therefore, your product or service must meet and ideally exceed the expectations of your customers, and if you continue to do that for the long term (assuming you have a reasonably competent management team), the needs of your stakeholders should be well taken care of.

What remains to be seen, however, is just how broadly or, more specifically, how quickly the notion of 3BL will become part of standard business practice and reach some common terminology that will allow consumers and investors to accurately assess the extent of a company's social responsibility. As long as annual reports simply present glossy pictures of the company's good deeds around the world, it will be difficult for any stakeholder to determine whether a change has taken place in that company's core business philosophy, or whether it's just another example of opportunistic targeted marketing.

Without a doubt, the financial incentive (or threat, depending on how you look at it) is now very real, and has the potential to significantly impact an organization's financial future. Consider these two recent examples:

- In April 2003, the California Public Employees Retirement System (CALPERS), which manages almost $750 million dollars for 1.5 million current and retired employees of the State of California, publicly urged pharmaceutical company GlaxoSmithKline to review its policy of charging for AIDS drugs in developing countries. In March 2008, CALPERS went even further and listed five American companies on its 2008 Focus List to highlight the pension fund's concerns about stock and financial underperformance and corporate governance practices (which we'll learn more about in the next chapter). The companies listed were the Cheesecake Factory®, Hilb Rogal & Hobbs® (an insurance brokerage firm), Ivacare (a health care equipment provider), La-Z-Boy, and Standard Pacific (a homebuilding company).

- In June 2006, the government of Norway, which manages a pension fund from oil revenues for its citizens of over $200 billion notified Wal-Mart and Freeport (a United States–based mining company) that they were being excluded as investments for the pension fund on the grounds that the companies have been responsible for either environmental damage or the violation of human rights in their business practices.

With such financial clout now being put behind CSR issues, the question of adoption of some form of social responsibility plan for a corporation should no longer be if but when.

A Stocking Error—Claire Makes a Decision

Claire decides to follow Mr. Jones's instructions and leave the shelves stocked with much more of Mega-Drug's own brand than the name brands that many customers use exclusively.

As the day progresses, the allergy medicines continue to be a top-selling item because it is the middle of allergy season, and by noon the stocks of name brands are getting low. Now Claire has a choice to make. Does she follow Mr. Jones's instructions and encourage customers to try MegaDrug's own brand? Or does she simply apologize for the item being out of stock, with the risk that upset customers will ask to speak to the manager?

After a few minutes, Claire hits upon a solution—rain checks! She'll work the register for the rest of the day (Mr. Jones was only going to have her do paperwork anyway) and anyone who complains about the name brand being out of stock will be issued a rain check with a sincere apology.

By closing time, 24 rain checks had been issued. Claire provided Mr. Jones with the numbers and suggested that a more even balance of brand name and store brand items be placed on the shelves. The good news was that the store would have a new delivery by tomorrow afternoon.

1. Did Claire do the right thing here?

2. What would the consequences have been for MegaDrug if Claire had not done this?

3. What do you think Mr. Jones will do when he finds out?

[KEY TERMS]

[REVIEW QUESTIONS]

1. Review the CSR policies of a company of your choice. Would you classify their policies as ethical, altruistic, strategic, or a combination of all three? Provide examples to support your answer.

2. Would the CSR policies of an organization influence your decision to use their products or services? Why or why not?

3. Both Ben & Jerry's® and The Body Shop have been purchased by larger companies—Ben & Jerry's® by Unilever in 2000 for $326 million and The Body Shop by L'Oreal for $1.14 billion in March 2006. Do you think this will impact their CSR policies? How and why?

4. Consider the company you currently work for (or one you have worked for in the past). What initiatives could they start to be more socially responsible? How would you propose such changes?

[REVIEW EXERCISE]

In the past five years, as part of its strategic resource development program, Global Oil Inc.[10] has made strategic capital investments in African countries with historically unstable government regimes and highly sensitive tribal relationships in order to tie up future oil reserves. With each investment, Global Oil has placed considerable emphasis (and PR attention) on its role as a "partner" or "good neighbor" in each region, making very public donations to local infrastructure projects, schools, and health care initiatives.

Jon Bennett had risen through the ranks in his 15-year career with Global Oil to the position of Director of Corporate Social Responsibility for the African Region. In this role, Bennett's responsibilities could be summarized in one phrase: *keep the locals happy* at each one of Global's project sites. With enough funds in the CSR budget to support a few strategically placed projects, this goal had been easy to achieve and Bennett had received his fair share of coverage in the local media as he promoted all of Global's community projects. However, in the last nine months, one particular area had begun to show up on Bennett's daily incident reports with increasing regularity.

The Odone people were the first to admit that Global's presence on their land (and the few community projects they funded) had brought some improvement to the welfare of their citizens—there was some preventive health care now, an improved water supply, a couple of schools for the children, and regular work for an increasing number of men drawn away from their traditional farming work to the higher-paying oil crew jobs. However, with all those benefits had come substantial profits for Global Oil and many negatives for the Odone people: Global had experienced several oil spills that had damaged the coastal waters of the region and there were increasing reports of accidents and threats to any employees who considered discussing Global's business activities with local journalists. The frequent positive press coverage of Global's good neighbor programs in the region provided a constant reminder of the disparity between perception and reality.

The Odone's discontent started to express itself through picketing outside the refinery gates and small acts of property damage. Slowly their case began to gather a higher media profile until it reached the attention of an environmental and human rights organization that began to spread the Odone story to its worldwide membership. With this higher profile came an increase in momentum. The picketing became more vocal and the property damage more expensive. It was obvious that tempers were beginning to rise.

Two weeks later, one of the leading members of the human rights organization was found badly beaten in a remote area of Odone land. He never recovered from his injuries and died a week later. The media response was immediate and extremely negative, accusing Global Oil (without any proof) of either direct or indirect involvement depending on the angle of the story.

Suddenly Jon Bennett's reputation in the region came under extreme scrutiny. The good neighbor was suddenly the corporate bully, and the environmental and human rights organizations quickly built support for boycotts of Global products and any Global customers or suppliers. Bennett's bosses at Global Oil HQ wanted answers and action—quickly!

Bennett stuck with what he knew best—his media contacts. Responding to the obvious urgency of the situation, he launched a new initiative—"A Plan of Action for the Odone People"—in which he pledged, as a corporate officer of Global Oil, to clean up all the oil spills, address any threats to local employees, and further increase Global's community projects in the area. In short, Bennett committed to addressing all the complaints on the Odone's list of grievances, though in true corporate fashion, the pledges came without specific performance deadlines. In the interests of saving time and getting the greatest PR bang for his buck, Bennett announced his new initiative at a press conference from Global's regional headquarters. No one from the Odone was informed of the new initiative before the press conference, nor was anyone from the Odone people invited to attend.

The Environmental and Human Rights activists claimed an immediate victory and switched their attentions to other corporate wrongdoers elsewhere in the world. Bennett kept his job. But the next morning, the picket line outside the refinery was larger and louder than ever.

1. What ethical violations did Global Oil commit here?
2. What ethical violations did Jon Bennett commit?
3. Were Global's community projects examples of Ethical, Altruistic, or Strategic CSR? Explain your answer.
4. How could Global Oil have handled things differently?

INTERNET EXERCISES

1. Locate the Web site for Business for Social Responsibility. What is the stated mission of the BSR? What does the BSR do? List four benefits that BSR claims corporations can achieve through CSR programs. List four well-known companies that are members of BSR.

2. Locate the Web site for IdealsWork. What is the goal of the IdealsWork organization? What services does the organization offer? How does the mission of the BSR differ from that of IdealsWork?

3. Locate the Web site for the corporate social responsibility newswire CSRWire. What does CSRWire do? List four CSRWire members and explain the services they receive from CSRWire. Find the CSR Events page and identify the next scheduled event. Briefly summarize the location and planned agenda for the event. If the event has a Web site, visit the site and record the name of one of the keynote speakers.

TEAM EXERCISES

1. **Instrumental or social contract?** Divide into two teams. One team must prepare a presentation advocating for the *instrumental* model of corporate management. The other team must prepare a presentation arguing for the *social contract* model of corporate management.

2. **Ethical, Altruistic, or Strategic?** Divide into three groups. Each group must select *one* of the following types of CSR: Ethical CSR, Altruistic CSR, or Strategic CSR. Prepare a presentation arguing for the respective merits of each approach and offer examples of initiatives that your company could engage in to adopt this strategy.

3. **Closing down a factory:** Divide into two groups and prepare arguments *for* and *against* the following behavior: Your company is managing to maintain a good profit margin on the computer parts you manufacture in a very tough economy. Recently, an opportunity has come along to move your production capacity overseas. The move will reduce manufacturing costs significantly as a result of tax incentives and lower labor costs, resulting in an anticipated 15 percent increase in profits for the company. However, the costs associated with shutting down your United States–based operations would mean that you wouldn't see those increased profits for a minimum of three years. Your U.S. factory is the largest employer in the surrounding town, and shutting it down will result in the loss of over 800 jobs. The loss of those jobs is expected to devastate the economy of the local community.

4. **A limited campaign:** Divide into two groups and prepare arguments *for* and *against* the following behavior: You work in the marketing department of a large dairy products company. The company has launched a "revolutionary" yogurt product with ingredients that promote healthy digestion. As a promotion to launch the new product, the company is offering to donate 10 cents to the American Heart Association (AHA) for every foil top from the yogurt pots that is returned to the manufacturer. To support this campaign, the company has invested millions of dollars in a broad "media spend" on television, radio, Web, and print outlets, as well as the product packaging itself. In very small print on the packaging and advertising is a clarification sentence that specifies that the maximum donation for the campaign will be $10,000. Your marketing analyst colleagues have forecast that first-year sales of this new product will reach 10 million units, with an anticipated participation of 2 million units in the pot-top return campaign (a potential donation of $200,000 without the $10,000 limit). Focus groups that were tested about the new product indicated clearly that participants in the pot-top return campaign attach positive feelings about their purchase to the added bonus of the donation to the AHA.

WAL-MART

By most accounts Wal-Mart is among the most successful companies in the world. Its revenues for 2007 were $379 billion, more than five times larger than the next largest retailer, Target. For comparison, in the same year Saudi Arabia was ranked by the World Bank as the 24th largest economy in the world with an estimated Gross Domestic Product (GDP) of $381 billion and Switzerland was ranked 22nd with a GDP of $415 billion. Wal-Mart operates almost 7,300 stores, and over 4,000 of them are in the United States. It is estimated that 200 million people shop at Wal-Mart each week. Worldwide, Wal-Mart employs 2 million people. It is the largest private employer in the United States and the single largest employer in 25 separate U.S. states.

Wal-Mart was founded in the early 1960s by Sam Walton in Rogers, Arkansas. Walton's original marketing strategy was to emphasize low prices, and this strategy continues today as reflected in its marketing campaign of "everyday low prices." Wal-Mart is able to achieve low retail prices by leveraging its buying power as the world's largest retailer and by controlling labor costs. Wal-Mart sells more socks, toothpaste, dog food, sporting goods, guns, diamonds, and groceries than any other business in the world. Alone, it accounts for the sale of 30 percent of all household goods (laundry detergent, soap, paper towels) and 15 percent of all CDs, as well as 28 percent of Dial soap's total sales, 24 percent of Del Monte Foods', 23 percent of Clorox's, and 23 percent of Revlon's. Wal-Mart is the single largest importer from China, accounting for almost 10 percent of all Chinese imports to the United States, worth an estimated $12 billion in 2002.

At first glance, Wal-Mart's success promotes a number of values. Stockholders have received significant financial benefits from Wal-Mart. Consumers also receive financial benefits in the form of low prices, employees benefit from having jobs, many businesses benefit from supplying Wal-Mart with goods and services, and communities benefit from tax-paying corporate citizens.

Wal-Mart cites several other values that it promotes in its own self-description. Wal-Mart describes itself as a business that "was built upon a foundation of honesty, respect, fairness and integrity." What is described as the "Wal-Mart culture" is based on three basic beliefs attributed to founder Sam Walton: respect for individuals, service to customers, and striving for excellence.

Despite this, not everyone agrees that Wal-Mart lives up to high ethical standards. Critics portray Wal-Mart as among the least admired corporations in the world. Ethical criticisms have been raised against Wal-Mart on behalf of every major constituency—customers, employees, suppliers, competitors, communities—with whom Wal-Mart interacts. For example, some critics charge that Wal-Mart's low-priced goods, and even their placement within stores, are a ploy to entice customers to purchase more and higher-priced goods. Such critics charge Wal-Mart with deceptive and manipulative pricing and marketing.

Perhaps the greatest ethical criticisms of Wal-Mart have involved treatment of workers. Wal-Mart is well-known for its aggressive practices aimed at controlling labor costs. Wal-Mart argues that this is part of their strategy to offer the lowest possible prices to consumers. By controlling labor costs through wages, minimum work hours, and high productivity, and by keeping unions away, Wal-Mart is able to offer consumers the lowest everyday prices.

Wal-Mart has also been accused of illegally requiring employees to work overtime without pay and to work off the clock. Employees in Wisconsin, Michigan, Missouri, Kansas, Ohio, Washington, Illinois, West Virginia, and Iowa have filed lawsuits alleging such illegal labor practices. Wal-Mart has also been accused of obstructing employees' attempts to organize unions. The National Labor Relations Board filed suit against Wal-Mart stores in Pennsylvania and Texas charging illegal antiunion activities. Maine's Department of Labor fined Wal-Mart for violating child labor laws, finding 1,436 child labor law infractions in some 20 different Wal-Mart stores. Wal-Mart has also been sued in Missouri, California, Arkansas, and Arizona for violating the Americans with Disabilities Act.

Discussion Questions

1. How would you describe the managerial philosophy of Wal-Mart? What principles are involved? What are the overriding aims, values, and goals of Wal-Mart?

2. Evaluate the management philosophy of Wal-Mart from the point of view of stockholders, employees, customers, the local community, and suppliers.

3. Should business management always seek the lowest prices for its customers and the highest rate of return on investment? What reasons might there be for seeking something less for customers and stockholders?

4. Economists define costs in terms of opportunities forgone. What opportunities are forgone by Wal-Mart's "everyday low price" marketing strategy? Who pays the costs of Wal-Mart's low prices?

5. Wal-Mart's wages are above the legally required minimum wage, and health benefits are not legally mandated. Are there reasons for a business to take actions not required by law that might reduce profits?

6. Does Wal-Mart have any responsibilities to its suppliers other than those specified in their contracts?

Source: Joseph R. DesJardins, *An Introduction to Business Ethics,* 2nd ed., New York: McGraw-Hill, 2006, pp. 49–52.

CORPORATE SOCIAL IRRESPONSIBILITY

Despite PR posturing, corporate philanthropy is down from 25 years ago. To be taken seriously, companies should pledge 1% of pretax earnings, say Leo Hindery Jr. and Curt Weeden.

When companies forsake their broadly defined social responsibilities or use spin to construct a deliberately over-inflated image of their corporate citizenship, the end result is a private sector and a civil society out of balance.

Too prevalent today are heavily promoted, self-generated snippets designed to show how businesses are meeting their obligations to society. Paid advertisements that wave banners about how companies address global warming, curb health-care costs, or improve public education often are smoke screens to hide a troubling trend: the significant falloff in corporate charitable contributions.

Anemic Generosity

Twenty-five years ago, businesses allocated about 2%, on average, of their pretax profits for gifts and grants, according to a report by the Giving USA Foundation and Indiana University Center on Philanthropy. Today, companies are only about one-third as generous. Based on a recent analysis of IRS tax returns—which are, of course, devoid of hype—business charitable deductions now average only about 0.7 percent of pretax earnings. (These figures don't take into account employee volunteer hours, as the IRS does not allow deductions for employee volunteer time, even if it is time off with pay.)

Granted, measuring overall corporate responsibility requires more than just analyzing a company's philanthropic donations. Fair treatment of employees, making or selling safe products, paying taxes, and complying with environmental standards are all ingredients that should be in the social responsibility mix. However important these things are, though, they are not more important than a corporation wide commitment to use an appropriate percentage of a company's pretax resources to address critical issues that affect employees, communities, the nation, and the planet.

Badly needed is a meaningful voluntary commitment by the business community to "ante up" a minimum budget for corporate philanthropy. A reasonable requirement for any company that wants to call itself a good corporate citizen ought to be to spend at least 1% of its previous year's pretax profit for philanthropic purposes.

Nonfinancial Returns

Convincing senior management to increase rather than cut back a company's philanthropy budget may seem a daunting, if not impossible, task, particularly at a time when the overall corporate profit picture has become so fuzzy. But if executives understand that an effectively managed contribution program can deliver strong returns to a corporation, then 1% of pretax earnings should take on the look and feel of an investment, not a handout.

Rather than a self-imposed tax, a contribution can actually be managed in a way that makes it a powerful business tool. That happens when, to the extent practicable, company donations are directed to nonprofit groups closely aligned with the interests of the corporation's employees, communities, and business objectives. At the same time, a corporate contribution shouldn't be solely about advancing the interests of the company. If contributions are designed only to bolster the bottom line, if they are used to support pet projects of senior managers or board members, or if they are purely selfish in their intent, we believe they fall short of the definition of what it takes to be considered the proper conduct of a good corporate citizen.

This ante-up proposal is intended to be the bottom rung of the corporate citizenship ladder. Businesses that are "best in class" in the corporate philanthropy field also need to manage contributions strategically that go well beyond the recommended pretax minimum of 1%. Some companies are already clearing this higher bar. In Minneapolis–St. Paul, for example, more than 150 companies—including such large corporations as Target and General Mills—are every year donating at least 5% of their pretax earnings. (Disclosure: In 1998, the year before Tele-Communications, where I was then CEO, merged into AT&T, TCI contributed a bit more than 1% of its operating cash flow to charity. Like our counterparts in the cable industry, TCI in those years had substantial pretax losses because of significant depreciation and amortization.)

To reverse the downward trend in corporate giving, we need a cadre of self-motivated and sensitive CEOs to lead the way. We need men and women who will match actions with words by carrying out combined corporate contributions and community-relations initiatives that are supported by adequate resources and time, rather than by more chest-beating ad campaigns and press releases.

Discussion Questions

1. Why would companies choose to inflate the image of their corporate citizenship?

2. Is it ethical to direct company donations to "nonprofit groups closely aligned with the interests of the corporation's employees, communities, and business objectives"? Why or why not?

3. Is it ethical to direct company donations to support "pet projects of senior managers or board members"? Why or why not?

4. Why would budgeting a fixed percentage of pretax profits for corporate philanthropy be seen as a more convincing commitment to CSR than just funding a variety of projects?

5. The authors of this article claim that "an effectively managed contribution program can deliver strong returns to a corporation." What might those returns be?

6. Does the fact that Target and General Mills donate five times more than the minimum 1 percent make them five times more socially responsible? Why or why not?

Source: Leo Hindery, Jr., 8 Curt Weeden, "Corporate Social Irresponsibility" *BusinessWeek Viewpoint* (July 8, 2008). Hindey is a contributor to the *BusinessWeek* column Outside Shot. He is a managing partner of InterMedia Partners, former CEO of Tele-Communications Inc., its successor AT&T Broadband, and the YES Network. Curt Weeden is President of Business & Nonprofit Strategies, Inc. and former CEO of the Association of Corporate Contributions Professionals. He is the author of *Corporate Social Investing* (Berrett-Koehler, 1998).

discussion
EXERCISE 4.3

THE PESTICIDE DDT

In 1939 Paul Muller, a Swiss chemist working for J. R. Geigy, was looking for a way to protect woolens against moths. His quest led him to a white crystalline powder called dichloro diphenyl trichloroethane that had a devastating effect on flies. The powder, subsequently known as DDT, would become the first modern synthetic pesticide and earn Muller the 1948 Nobel Prize for chemistry. In 1942 Geigy sent some of the powder to its New York office. Victor Froelicher, a Geigy chemist in the New York office, translated the document describing the powder and its amazing attributes into English and gave a sample of the powder to the Department of Agriculture.

The U.S. Army had tasked the Department of Agriculture with finding a way to protect its soldiers from insect-borne diseases. In some of the military units, up to 80 percent of the soldiers were out sick with malaria. After testing thousands of compounds, the Department's research station in Orlando, Florida, found DDT to be most effective. It was subsequently used by the armed forces in Europe and Asia to battle typhus, malaria, and other diseases that held the potential to devastate the allied fighting forces. It proved extremely effective and is credited with shortening the war.

At that time malaria was common in Asia, the Caribbean, Europe, and the southern part of the United States. Millions of people died from malaria each year. With the effectiveness of the pesticide proven in the war years, DDT became the insecticide of choice around the world. It was effective on a wide range of insect pests, it did not break down rapidly so it did not have to be reapplied often, and it was not water soluble and thus was not washed off when it rained. Farmers and homeowners used DDT to protect crops and kill nuisance insects and pests that spread disease. Countries used it to protect their populations. In 1931–32 more than 22,000 people died from malaria in South Africa's KwaZulu-Natal province. By 1973 the deaths had dropped to 331 for the whole country and by 1977 there was only one death from malaria in South Africa.

Chemical manufacturers were turning out DDT in record volumes. Montrose Chemical Corporation in Montrose, California, was one of the largest, beginning production in 1942. However, clouds had been building on the horizon. In 1962 Rachel Carson published a book entitled *Silent Spring* that exposed a link between the mass use of DDT and the death of birds and fish. DDT was found to be toxic to fish and indirectly toxic to birds due to its persistence in the environment. It tended to accumulate in fatty tissue, and it became more concentrated as it moved up the food chain. Birds of prey started failing to reproduce because their eggshells became so thin they could not survive the incubation period. DDT began showing up in human breast milk. Some sources claimed DDT causes cancer, but the experts disagree regarding that claim. Concern about the effects of DDT grew until the Environmental Protection Agency banned its use in the United States at the end of 1972, 10 years after the publication of *Silent Spring*. However, DDT could still be produced and sold abroad. Montrose continued to export DDT to Africa, India, and other countries until 1982. DDT was banned in Cuba in 1970, in Poland in 1976, in Canada and Chile in 1985, and in Korea, Liechtenstein, and Switzerland in 1986. The product has also been banned in the European Union, Mexico, Panama, Sri Lanka, Sweden, and Togo, among other countries. The persistence of the chemical is evidenced by traces of it still found in the Great Lakes 30 years after application stopped.

Discussion Questions

1. Did the Montrose Chemical Corporation violate any ethical standards in manufacturing and selling DDT to the public?

2. What should they have done differently?

3. Was it ethical to manufacture and sell DDT to other countries after the Environmental Protection Agency (EPA) banned its use in the United States due to its harmful effects?

4. Did the EPA make the right decision when it banned DDT?

5. Should Muller's Nobel Prize be taken away now that DDT has been found to be harmful?

6. Is the ability to save lives worth the risk to the environment?

Sources: Dan Chapman, "A Father & Son Story: Dusting Off DDT's Image/Long-Maligned Pesticide May Be Regaining Favor as Mosquito Menace Grows," *The Atlanta Journal-Constitution* (September 9, 2001), p. D1; Malcolm Gladwell, *The New Yorker* 77, 17 (July 2, 2001), p. 42; P. S. Thampi, "India among Top DDT Users; Need Early Ban," *The Indian Express* (August 10, 1998); Edmund P. Russell III, "The Strange Career of DDT: Experts, Federal Capacity, and Environmentalism in World War II," *Technology and Culture* 40, 4 (October 1999), pp. 770–796; Michael Satchell and Don L. Boroughs, "Rocks and Hard Places DDT: Dangerous Scourge or Last Resort; South Africa," *U.S. News & World Report* 129, 23 (December 11, 2000), p. 64; Deborah Schoch, "Regional Report SOUTH BAY Chemical Reaction Discovery of DDT in the Back Yards of Two Local Homes Has Rekindled Concern and Fear," *The Los Angeles Times* (June 9, 1994), p. 22. D. J. Fritzsche, *Business Ethics: A Global and Managerial Perspective,* 2nd ed. (New York: McGraw-Hill, 2005), pp. 176–78.

chapter 5

Corporate Governance

> *Earnings can be as pliable as putty when a charlatan heads the company reporting them.*
>
> —Warren Buffet

LEARNING OBJECTIVES

After studying this chapter, you should be able to:

1. Explain the term *corporate governance.*

2. Explain the respective roles of the Chief Executive Officer (CEO), Chief Financial Officer (CFO), and Chief Operating Officer (COO).

3. Understand the responsibilities of the Board of Directors.

4. Explain the responsibilities of the major governance committees.

5. Explain the differences between the following two governance methodologies: "comply or explain" and "comply or else."

6. Identify an appropriate corporate governance model for an organization.

"Incriminating Evidence"

Marco is a paralegal for a large regional law firm. His company has just landed a new and very important client—Chemco Industries, one of the largest employers in the area.

Marco's prospects with his firm appear to have taken a major leap, as he has been assigned to support one of the senior partners of the law firm, David Collins, as he prepares to defend Chemco in a lawsuit brought by a group of Chemco shareholders.

The lawsuit claims that the senior management of Chemco knew that the firm's financial performance for the second quarter of the year was way below Wall Street expectations. They also knew that the likely reaction to that news would be a dramatic reduction in the price of Chemco shares. In addition, the lawsuit claims that since the stock price would most likely go below the price of the stock options that the board of directors had granted to senior management, those options would be worthless. So, rather than let that happen, the Chemco shareholders argued, senior management "massaged the numbers" on the company's true financial performance while selling their own shares in the company, and they kept massaging the numbers until they were able to exercise all their stock options.

Marco is well aware of the significance of this case and is excited at the prospect of working with David Collins. His first assignment is to review all the correspondence relating to stock transactions by senior management in order to document exactly when they exercised their stock options and sold their stock. The review is expected to take several days of intensive work.

On the third day, Marco comes across a paper copy of an e-mail from David Collins to the CEO of Chemco. Since this would have no relevance to the sale of stock, Marco assumes that the e-mail was misfiled and starts to place the sheet of paper in a separate pile for refiling later. As he does so, one word that is bolded and underlined in the e-mail catches his eye—"problematic." As he reads the e-mail in full, Marco realizes that David Collins is advising the CEO to "ensure that any e-mails or written documentation that could be 'problematic' for their case be removed immediately."

1. Which committee would have granted stock options to the senior management of Chemco Industries? Review Figure 5.1 on page 110 for more information on this.

2. The e-mail suggests that the CEO was well aware of what was going on at Chemco Industries. Do you think the board of directors was aware of the activities of senior management? Which committee would be responsible for monitoring ethical practices at Chemco?

3. What should Marco do now?

Corporate Governance

The business world has seen an increasing number of scandals in recent years, and numerous organizations have been exposed for poor management practices and fraudulent financial reporting. When we review those scandals, several questions come to mind:

- Who was minding the store?
- How were these senior executives allowed to get away with this?

- Aren't companies supposed to have a system of checks and balances to prevent such behavior?
- When did the CEO of an organization suddenly become answerable to no one?

In seeking answers to these questions, we come to the issue of who really carries the authority in an organization—that is, who has the final say? In other words, are corporations governed in the same manner as our society? And if they're not, are these examples of unethical corporate behavior evidence that they should be?

Corporate governance is the process by which organizations are directed and controlled. However, when we examine who is controlling the corporation, and for whom, the situation gets a little more complicated. Before the development of large corporations, which are separate legal entities, managers and owners of organizations were the same people. As the organizations grew, wealthy owners started to hire professional managers to run the businesses on their behalf, which raised some interesting questions:

Corporate Governance The system by which business corporations are directed and controlled.

- Could the managers be trusted to run the businesses in the best interests of the owners?
- How would they be held accountable for their actions?
- How would absentee owners keep control over these managers?

The development of a separate corporate entity allowed organizations to raise funds from individual shareholders to grow their operations. The involvement of these individual shareholders diluted the ownership of the original owners and also brought in a new group to which the managers of the business would now be accountable. As the corporations grew in size, and pension funds and other institutional investors purchased larger blocks of shares, the potential impact of the individual shareholder was greatly diminished, and the managers were presented with a far more powerful "owner" to whom they were now accountable.

As we discussed in Chapter 4, in addition to the interests of their owners, some argue that managers are accountable to the *public* interest—or, more specifically, to their stakeholders: their customers, their vendor partners, state and local entities, and the communities in which they conduct their business operations.

So, corporate governance is concerned with how well organizations meet their obligations to all these people. Ideally, mechanisms are in place to hold them accountable for that performance and to introduce corrective action if they fail to live up to that performance expectation.[1]

Corporate governance is about the way in which boards oversee the running of a company by its managers, and how board members are in turn accountable to shareholders and the company. This has implications for company behavior towards employees, shareholders, customers, and banks. Good corporate governance plays a vital role in underpinning the integrity and efficiency of financial markets. Poor corporate governance weakens a company's potential and at worst can pave the way for financial difficulties and even fraud. If companies are well governed, they will usually outperform other companies and will be able to attract investors whose support can finance further growth.

What Does Corporate Governance Look Like?

The *owners* of the corporation (at the top of Figure 5.1) supply equity or risk capital to the company by purchasing shares in the corporation. They are typically a fragmented group, including individual public shareholders, large blocks of private holders, private and public institutional investors, employees, managers, and other companies.

The **board of directors,** in theory, is elected by the owners to represent their interests in the effective running of the corporation. Elections take place at annual shareholders' meetings, and directors are appointed to serve for specific periods of time. The board is typically made up of inside and outside members—inside members hold management positions in the company, whereas outside members do not. The term *outside director* can be misleading because some outside members may have direct connections to the company as creditors, suppliers, customers, or professional consultants.

The **audit committee** is staffed by members of the board of directors. The primary responsibilities of the audit committee are to oversee the financial reporting process, monitor internal controls (such as how much spending authority an executive has), monitor the choice of accounting policies and procedures, and oversee the hiring and performance of external auditors in producing the company's financial statements.

The **compensation committee** is also staffed by members of the board of directors. The primary responsibility of the compensation committee is to oversee compensation packages for the senior executives of the corporation (such as salaries, bonuses, stock options, and other benefits such as, in extreme cases, personal use of company jets). Compensation policies for the employees of the corporation are left to the management team to oversee.

The corporate governance committee represents a more public demonstration of the organization's commitment to ethical business practices. The committee (staffed by board members and specialists) monitors the ethical performance of the corporation and oversees compliance with the company's internal code of ethics as well as any federal and state regulations on corporate conduct.

Board of Directors A group of individuals hired to oversee governance of an organization. Elected by vote of the shareholders at the annual general meeting (AGM), the true power of the board can vary from institution to institution from a powerful unit that closely monitors the management of the organization, to a body that merely rubber-stamps the decisions of the chief executive officer (CEO) and executive team.

Audit Committee An operating committee staffed by members of the board of directors plus independent or outside directors. The committee is responsible for monitoring the financial policies and procedures of the organization—specifically the accounting policies, internal controls, and the hiring of external auditors.

Compensation Committee An operating committee staffed by members of the board of directors plus independent or outside directors. The committee is responsible for setting the compensation for the CEO and other senior executives. Typically, this compensation will consist of a base salary, performance bonus, stock options, and other perks.

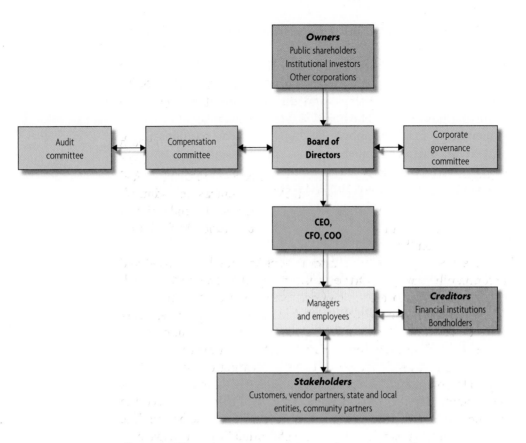

FIGURE 5.1 **Governance of the Modern Corporation**

Source: Adapted from Fred R. Kaen, A Blueprint for Corporate Governance, New York: AMACOM, 2003.

✓ PROGRESS CHECK QUESTIONS

1. Define *corporate governance*.

2. Explain the roles of the CEO, CFO, and COO.

3. Explain the role of the board of directors.

4. What is an *outside director*?

In Pursuit of Corporate Governance

While the issue of corporate governance has reached new heights of media attention in the wake of recent corporate scandals, the topic itself has been receiving increasing attention for over a decade.

In 1992 Sir Adrian Cadbury led a committee in Great Britain to address "Financial Aspects of Corporate Governance" in response to public concerns over directors' compensation at several high-profile companies in Great Britain. The subsequent financial scandals surrounding BCCI (Bank of Credit and Commerce International) and the activities of publishing magnate Sir Robert Maxwell generated more attention for the committee's report than was originally anticipated. In the executive summary of the report, Cadbury outlined the committee's position on the newly topical issue of corporate governance:[2]

At the heart of the Committee's recommendations is a Code of Best Practice designed to achieve the necessary high standards of corporate behaviour. . . . By adhering to the Code, listed companies will strengthen both their control over their businesses and their public accountability. In so doing they will be striking the right balance between meeting the standards of corporate governance now expected of them and retaining the essential spirit of enterprise.

Two years after the release of the Cadbury Report, attention shifted to South Africa, where Mervyn King, a corporate lawyer, former High Court judge, and the current Governor of the Bank of England, led a committee that published the "King Report on Corporate Governance" in 1994. In contrast to Cadbury's focus on internal governance, the King Report "incorporated a code of corporate practices and conduct that looked beyond the corporation itself, taking into account its impact on the larger community."[3]

"King I," as the 1994 report became known, went beyond the financial and regulatory accountability upon which the Cadbury Report had focused and took a more integrated approach to the topic of corporate governance, recognizing the involvement of all of the corporation's stakeholders—the shareholders, customers, employees, vendor partners, and the community in which the corporation operates—in the efficient and appropriate operation of the organization.[4]

Even though King I was widely recognized as advocating the highest standards for corporate governance, the committee released a second report eight years later—inevitably referred to as "King II," which formally recognized the need to move the stakeholder model forward and consider a triple bottom line as opposed to the traditional single bottom line of profitability. The triple bottom line recognizes the economic, environmental, and social aspects of a company's activities. In the words of the King II report, companies must "comply or explain" or "comply or else."[5]

Although it was released in Great Britain, the King I report impacted business across the globe.

According to King II,

> successful governance in the world in the 21st century requires companies to adopt an inclusive and not exclusive approach. The company must be open to institutional activism and there must be greater emphasis on the sustainable or non-financial aspects of its performance. Boards must apply the test of fairness, accountability, responsibility and transparency to all acts or omissions and be accountable to the company but also responsive and responsible towards the company's identified stakeholders. The correct balance between conformance with governance principles and performance in an entrepreneurial market economy must be found, but this will be specific to each company.[6]

Two Governance Methodologies: "Comply or Explain" or "Comply or Else"?

"Comply or Explain" A set of guidelines that require companies to abide by a set of operating standards or explain why they choose not to.

"Comply or Else" A set of guidelines that require companies to abide by a set of operating standards or face stiff financial penalties.

The Cadbury report argued for a guideline of **comply or explain,** which gave companies the flexibility to comply with governance standards or explain why they do not in their corporate documents (annual reports, for example). The vagueness of what would constitute an acceptable explanation for not complying, combined with the ease with which such explanations could be buried in the footnotes of an annual report (if they were even there at all), raised concerns that comply or explain really wouldn't do much for corporate governance.

The string of financial scandals that followed the report led many critics to argue that comply or explain obviously offered no real deterrent to corporations. The answer, they argued, was to move to a more aggressive approach of **comply or else,** where failure to comply results in stiff financial penalties. The Sarbanes-Oxley Act of 2002 (see Chapter 6) incorporates this approach.

✓ PROGRESS CHECK QUESTIONS

5. Which two scandals greatly increased the attention paid to the 1992 Cadbury Report?

6. Explain the "right balance" that Cadbury encourages companies to pursue.

7. Explain the difference between the King I and King II reports.

8. Explain the difference between "comply or explain" and "comply or else".

"In the Know" or "In the Dark"?

With the exception, perhaps, of corporate governance committees, each of the corporations that have faced charges for corporate misconduct in recent years used the governance model shown in Figure 5.1. When questioned, the boards of these corporations all shared similar stories of being "ambushed" or kept in the dark about the massive frauds the senior executives of their corporations allegedly carried out.

What does this mean for investors seeking to put their retirement funds in dependable companies that are well run? What about employees seeking reassurance that those senior corporate officers in the executive suites can be counted on to steer the company to a promising future rather than run it aground?

If all these companies had a governance model in place, where was the oversight? Is it the model that's at fault or the people filling the assigned roles in that model? Consider the different interpretations of just how much authority rests with these official overseers illustrated in Cases 5.1 and 5.2.

> *One cannot say that the checks and balances against excessive power within the old WorldCom didn't work adequately. Rather, the sad fact is that there were no checks and balances.*
>
> —R. C. Breedon[7]

E T H I C A L dilemma

CASE 5.1 A Tale of Two Boards

In the shadows of the corporate scandals that have dominated the media over the last few years (Enron, WorldCom, Tyco, and others), two examples of boardroom dramas in the United States shine an unflattering light on corporate governance in practice. The Boeing Corporation seemed to stumble from one crisis to another, ending with the departure of the promised savior of the corporation for his own ethical indiscretions. The Disney organization delivered a classic power struggle between "right" and "might" as disgruntled directors challenged the activities of a CEO whose 20-year performance record appeared to give him absolute power.

Source: "A Tale of Two Boards," *The Economist*, December 4, 2003.

Disney

The principal lesson from Disney appears to be that, with someone as clever and overbearing as [Michael] Eisner at the top, the most brilliantly designed governance rules in the world can sometimes mean zilch. Eisner's approach can be identified in his relationships to directors:

- "Although Disney's corporate bylaws require that the board of directors hire the president, neither the compensation committee nor the full Disney board reviewed or approved the agreement (between Michael Eisner and Michael Ovitz)."

- "By the time [Michael] Ovitz was fired, stock options had made Eisner the company's second largest individual shareholder, eclipsing even Roy and other members of the Disney family. Only the Bass [family] held a bigger stake."

- At the same time that his ownership was growing, Eisner had consolidated power by isolating board members, compromising their independence, and stripping them of any real oversight function.

Michael Eisner is still a controversial figure in the Disney Corporation. What actions did he take that might be considered harmful to the company?

- "Disney maintained that the other 12 directors were 'independent' in the sense that they didn't work for the company. But that was defining 'independent' so narrowly as to be meaningless."

- "Irwin Russell, Eisner's personal lawyer, negotiated Eisner's lucrative contract and had a professional duty of loyalty to Eisner simultaneous to his duty to shareholders. Yet Russell was also the chairman of Disney's compensation committee. (Incredibly, during the Eisner contract negotiations, Russell represented Eisner, and Ray Watson stepped in for Disney). Everyone on the board seemed to think that Russell was an inherently fair-minded and decent person, and so no one appears to have raised any questions about such blatant conflict of interest."

- Director Robert Stern was Eisner's personal architect and was beholden to Eisner for an immense amount of work from Disney, including designing the new animation building.

- Reveta Bowers was the principal of the prestigious Center for Early Education in West Hollywood, a school attended by Eisner's sons and the children of other Disney executives, who also gave the school donations.

- Eisner had named Leo O'Donovan, a Jesuit priest and president of Georgetown University, to the board after Eisner's son Breck graduated from Georgetown. He gave Georgetown $1 million and his foundation financed a school scholarship.

- George Mitchell earned a $50,000 consulting fee in addition to his board stipend, and his law firm earned hundreds of thousands of dollars in legal fees representing Disney on various matters.

- The Council of Institutional Investors urged shareholders to withhold approval of Eisner's new contract in February, but only 12 percent of votes were withheld and the contract was approved. Later that year, Eisner exercised Disney stock options, then worth $565 million before taxes, once again earning the title of America's highest-paid executive.

- Eisner was dismissive of critics: "Most CEO's don't understand the entertainment business. They don't understand our problems. If they have so much time to spend on our company, what are they doing at their company? I don't see that as an asset. I'd rather have my kindergarten school teacher who taught my kids telling me about our products."

Sources: James B. Stewart. *The Disney* War, Simon & Schuster, NY, 2005.

Boeing

For Boeing, the presence of good governance policies and a tough, independent board did not prevent the company from stumbling from one fiasco to another. Even with a board that was packed with redoubtable figures such as John Shalikashvili, a former chairman of the Joint Chiefs of Staff, and James McNerney, the boss of 3M™, and a reasonably good reputation among governance experts and activist shareholders, the company still committed one ethical breach after another:

Like Disney, Boeing is a cautionary tale. How might things have been different with a change in leadership?

- In the summer of 2003, it was revealed that Boeing had held on to 25,000 documents belonging to a rival, Lockheed Martin, for several years after it dismissed two former Lockheed employees for stealing them. The two employees were charged and the Department of Justice conducted a wider inquiry. The Pentagon canceled Boeing contracts worth over $1 billion.

- Mike Sears, CFO, was fired for misconduct in November 2003 after "violating company policies by communicating with a government official about future employment at Boeing while she [Darleen Druyun] was still dealing with purchases of tanker aircraft from Boeing." Ms. Druyun had gone on to join Boeing and was fired along with Mr. Sears.

- On December 1, 2003, Phil Condit resigned as chairman and chief executive officer of Boeing, explaining that "accountability begins at the top." Since his designated successor, Mike Sears, had been fired earlier in 2003, the board invited Harry Stonecipher, a 67-year-old former vice chairman of Boeing, back to run the company. Mr. Stonecipher, who had run McDonnell Douglas before the two companies merged in 1997, was seen as a man who "could schmooze the Pentagon's top brass while taking hard-nosed decisions within Boeing."

- In March 2005, Stonecipher was forced to resign after Boeing's board of directors was informed of an affair between Mr. Stonecipher and a female employee "who did not report directly to him." Evidence of the affair had apparently been discovered by the company's surveillance software, which was designed to "flag" e-mails using specific keywords.

1. How did Michael Eisner manage to exert so much power at Disney?
2. Was it in the shareholders' best interests to have so much power resting in the hands of the CEO? Explain your answer.
3. Boeing's corporate governance policies seemed to be of little use in these cases—why?
4. Was Phil Condit's decision to resign as chairman and CEO the right thing to do? Explain your answer.

Source: "Where's Boeing Going?" *The Economist*, Nov. 27, 2003; "Tanked Up," *The Economist*, December 4, 2003; "The End of the Office Affair," *The Economist*, March 10, 2005.

The Chairman and the CEO

If the model of corporate structure shown at the beginning of this chapter is followed, the stockholders of a corporation should elect members of the board of directors. In turn, that board of directors should elect a chairman. As we have seen from cases such as Michael Eisner's kinglike approach to governance at Disney, however, the model is typically ignored.

The first step in a policy of disregarding the corporate governance model is the decision to merge the roles of chief executive officer (CEO) and chairman of the board into one individual. In this situation, the oversight that the board of directors is supposed to provide has been lost and the operational focus of the company has switched from long term (to the extent that board members serve a two-year contract) to short term, where the CEO is focusing on the numbers for the next quarter.

The argument in favor of merging the two roles is one of efficiency—by putting the leadership of the board of directors and the senior management team in the hands of the same person, the potential for conflict is minimized and, it is argued, the board is given the benefit of leadership from someone who is in touch with the inner workings of the organization rather than an outsider who needs time to get up to speed.

The argument against merging the two roles is an ethical one. Governance of the corporation is now in the hands of one person, which eliminates the checks and balances process that the board was created for in the first place. As time passes, as we have seen with the Disney example, the CEO slowly populates the board with friends who are less critical of the CEO's policies and more willing to vote larger and larger salary and benefits packages—how else do you become the highest-paid CEO in the country? With a rubber-stamp board in place to authorize his every wish, the CEO now becomes a law unto himself. The independence of the board is compromised, and the power of the stockholders is minimized. The CEO can pursue policies that are focused on maintaining a high share price in the short term (to maximize the price he will get when he cashes in all the share options that his friends on the board gave him in the last contract) without any concern for the long-term stability of the organization—after all, there will probably be another CEO by then.

☑ PROGRESS CHECK QUESTIONS

9. What is the argument in favor of merging the roles of chairman and CEO?

10. What is the argument against merging the roles of chairman and CEO?

11. Explain the difference between a short-term and long-term view in the governance of a corporation.

12. Is it unethical to populate your board of directors with friends and business acquaintances? Why or why not?

Effective Corporate Governance

To be considered effectively governed, organizations must have mechanisms in place that oversee both the long-term strategy of the company and the appointment of those personnel tasked with the responsibility of delivering that strategy. The appointment of those critical personnel inevitably includes their selection, ongoing performance evaluation, and compensation.

Delivering on these responsibilities requires more than just job descriptions and formal bylaws that govern the respective responsibilities and authority of various committees. To be truly effective, boards should follow these six steps:[8]

1. *Create a climate of trust and candor.* The board of directors and the senior executives should be working in partnership toward the successful achievement of organizational goals rather than developing an adversarial relationship where the board is seen as an obstacle to the realization of the CEO's strategic vision.

2. *Foster a culture of open dissent.* Proposals should be open for frank discussion and review rather than subject to the kind of alleged rubber-stamping that came to characterize Michael Eisner's tenure at Disney. Dissent ensures that all aspects of proposals are reviewed and discussed thoroughly.

3. *Mix up roles.* Rotation of assignments can avoid typecasting, and a conscious effort to switch between "good cop" and "bad cop" supporting and dissenting roles can ensure positive debate of all key proposals brought before the board.

4. *Ensure individual accountability.* Rubber-stamping generates collective indifference—how can you consider yourself accountable if you were only voting with a clearly established majority? If there is significant fallout from a major strategic initiative, all members should consider themselves accountable. This approach would address any pretense of being ambushed or in the dark.

5. *Let the board assess leadership talent.* The board members should actively meet with future leaders in their current positions within the organization rather than simply waiting for them to be presented when a vacancy arises.

6. *Evaluate the board's performance.* Many critics consider board seats as the U.S. equivalent of life peerages in Great Britain—that is, you win the title of "Lord" on the basis of what you have done in your career or whom you know, without any further assessment of your contribution or performance. Effective corporate governance demands superior performance from everyone involved in the process.

Twenty-Two Questions for Diagnosing Your Board

Walter Salmon, a longtime director with over 30 years of boardroom experience, took this prescriptive approach even further in a 1993 *Harvard Business Review* article by recommending a checklist of 22 questions to assess the quality of your board. If you answer yes to all 22 questions, you have an exemplary board.[9]

1. Are there three or more outside directors for every insider?
2. Are the insiders limited to the CEO, the COO, and the CFO?

3. Do your directors routinely speak to senior managers who are not represented on the board?

4. Is your board the right size (8 to 15 members)?

5. Does your audit committee, not management, have the authority to approve the partner in charge of auditing the company?

6. Does your audit committee routinely review high-exposure areas?

7. Do compensation consultants report to your compensation committee rather than to the company's human resources officers?

8. Has your compensation committee shown the courage to establish formulas for CEO compensation based on long-term results—even if formulas differ from industry norms?

9. Are the activities of your executive committee sufficiently contained to prevent the emergence of a two-tier board?

10. Do outside directors annually review succession plans for senior management?

11. Do outside directors formally evaluate your CEO's strengths, weaknesses, objectives, personal plans and performance every year?

12. Does your nominating committee rather than the CEO direct the search for new board members and invite candidates to stand for election?

13. Is there a way for outside directors to alter the meeting agenda set by your CEO?

14. Does the company help directors prepare for meetings by sending relevant routine information, as well as analyses of key agendas ahead of time?

15. Is there sufficient meeting time for thoughtful discussion in addition to management monologues?

16. Do the outside directors meet without management on a regular basis?

17. Is your board actively involved in formulating long-range business strategy from the start of the planning cycle?

18. Does your board, rather than the incumbent CEO, select the new chief executive—in fact as well as in theory?

19. Is at least some of the director's pay linked to corporate performance?

20. Is the performance of each of your directors periodically reviewed?

21. Are directors who are no longer pulling their weight discouraged from standing for reelection?

22. Do you take the right measures to build trust among directors?

Even with a board that passes all the tests and meets all the established criteria, ethical misconduct can still come down to the individual personalities involved. Consider the media storm surrounding the compensation package for Richard Grasso, the former Chairman and CEO of the New York Stock Exchange (NYSE).

ETHICAL dilemma

CASE 5.2 Richard Grasso and the NYSE

In 2000, at the beginning of the new millennium, 57-year-old Richard A. Grasso of the New York Stock Exchange had everything a Wall Street chief executive could ask for: a board of directors with the unconditional devotion of puppies, market dominance aided by favorable regulations, and above all, a nice salary. But as word emerged of his mind-boggling $188 million pay package, not even Grasso's obedient board—or a giveback of $48 million—could save him. Under mounting public pressure, Grasso stepped down on September 17, 2002.

Grasso was, in a sense, the ultimate victim of the NYSE's secretive corporate culture and Stone Age governance practices. If the Big Board had a less malleable board, Grasso's greed might not have been allowed to run rampant. In the end, Grasso was paid so grotesquely that he antagonized even his most faithful constituents, the traders on the NYSE floor.

Richard Grasso

Now that he's gone, the Big Board will have a tougher time than ever maintaining its strong competitive position. His interim successor, former Citigroup Chairman John S. Reed, has put in place an independent board, separated NYSE regulators from the Big Board's management, selected a separate CEO, and is preparing to demand repayment of a sizeable portion of Grasso's pay package. If the governance changes work, that could mean serious reform of the floor trading system that Grasso had so effectively defended—and a new era for the NYSE.

Grasso [later] filed suit . . . against his former employer and current Chairman John Reed for breach of contract and the $50 million in back pay he says the NYSE still owes him. Grasso . . . also personally [sued] Reed for defamation of character . . . Grasso's actions were in response to a lawsuit filed by New York Attorney General Eliot Spitzer on May 24 [2003] demanding that the former Big Board chief return more than $100 million of the $139.5 million he received as head of the NYSE in 2002. Spitzer sued under the state's Not-for-Profit Corporation Law, which mandates that the compensation scheme for a nonprofit, such as the NYSE, must be "reasonable."

The Grasso countersuit was filed in federal court in the Southern District of New York on July 20. Grasso charged that the NYSE "breached its contract . . . by maliciously disparaging him through Mr. Reed's false and defamatory statements. The exchange and Mr. Reed must be held accountable for their shameful conduct and the injury that they have caused Mr. Grasso."

Legal experts speculate that Grasso's countersuit may be more legal posturing than an effort to get back his money (Grasso says whatever he gets will be donated to charity). And winning defamation suits is no easy feat, says First Amendment specialist Victor A. Kovner, senior partner with Davis Wright Tremaine in New York. "Grasso is a public figure, therefore any claim for defamation based on Reed's statement . . . would have to show they were [made] with actual malice or that there were serious doubts about the truth" of those statements, says Kovner. "It is remote that they'll be able to show that."

Missing Claims

Grasso claims in his suit that Reed told the public and the press that Grasso's compensation was the result of "impropriety," a word that Kovner says shows an opinion, not a statement of fact. "A word of opinion, it seems to me, is not unlawful," he says. He adds that when Reed made these statements, plenty of public criticism and questions were already being raised about Grasso's pay.

In July 2008, the Appellate Division of New York State Supreme Court (a midlevel New York appeals court) dismissed the claims against Grasso, concluding that the state attorney general's case (initiated by Eliot Spitzer) to pursue the claims lapsed when the stock exchange changed from a nonprofit to a for-profit organization in 2005 by merging with an all-electronic trading rival, Archipelago Holdings. Spitzer's case had been based on an alleged violation of New York nonprofit corporate law that required compensation for executives to be *reasonable*.

1. Which stakeholders are impacted by this case?

2. Where were the failures in corporate governance in this case?

3. If Richard Grasso had made $139.5 million working for a for-profit company instead of a nonprofit, would that have made his compensation package more ethical? Explain your answer.

4. Does the fact that Grasso stated that he would donate the $50 million in back pay that he sued for make him more or less unethical? Explain your answer.

Source: "Dick Grasso Comes Back Swinging," Mara Der Hovanesian, *BusinessWeek*, July 21, 2004. "The Best and Worst Managers of 2003," *BusinessWeek* Online, January 12, 2004.

The Dangers of a Corporate Governance Checklist

There is more to effective corporate governance than simply maintaining a checklist of items to be monitored on a regular basis. Simply having the mechanisms in place will not, in itself, guarantee good governance. Enron, for example, had all its governance boxes checked:[10]

- Enron separated the roles of Chairman (Kenneth Lay) and Chief Executive Officer (Jeffrey Skilling)—at least until Skilling's surprise resignation.

- The company maintained a roster of independent directors with flawless résumés.

- It maintained an audit committee consisting exclusively of nonexecutives.

However, once you scratched beneath the surface of this model exterior, the true picture was a lot less appealing:

- Many of the so-called independent directors were affiliated with organizations that benefited directly from Enron's operations.

- The directors enjoyed substantial "benefits" that continued to grow as Enron's fortunes grew.

- Their role as directors of Enron, a Wall Street darling, guaranteed them positions as directors for other companies—a career package that would be jeopardized if they chose to ask too many awkward questions and gain reputations as troublemakers.

A Fiduciary Responsibility

While media coverage of corporate scandals have tended to concentrate on the personalities involved—Kenneth Lay and Jeffrey Skilling at Enron, Bernard Ebbers at WorldCom, Richard Scrushy at HealthSouth, John Rigas at Adelphia Cable, and Dennis Kozlowski at Tyco—we cannot lose sight of the fact that corporate governance is about managers fulfilling a fiduciary responsibility to the owners of their companies. A fiduciary responsibility is ultimately based on trust, which is a difficult trait to test when you are hiring a manager or to enforce once that manager is in place. Enforcement only becomes an option when that trust has been broken. In the meantime, organizations must depend on oversight and the development of processes and mechanisms to support that oversight—the famous checks and balances.

The payoff for such diligence is that "a commitment to good corporate governance . . .make[s] a company both more attractive to investors and lenders, and more profitable. Simply put, it pays to promote good corporate governance."[11] For example,

- A Deutsche Bank study of Standard & Poor 500 firms showed that companies with strong or improving corporate governance outperformed those with poor or deteriorating governance practices by about 19 percent over a two-year period.

- A Harvard/Wharton study showed that if an investor purchased shares in U.S. firms with the strongest shareholder rights and sold shares in the ones with the weakest shareholder rights, the investor would have earned abnormal returns of 8.5 percent per year.

- The same study also found that U.S.-based firms with better governance have faster sales growth and were more profitable than their peers.

- In a 2002 McKinsey survey, institutional investors said they would pay premiums to own well-governed companies. Premiums averaged 30 percent in Eastern Europe and Africa and 22 percent in Asia and Latin America.

✓ PROGRESS CHECK QUESTIONS

13. What are the six steps to effective corporate governance?

14. Select your top six from Walter Salmon's "22 Questions for Diagnosing Your Board" and defend your selection.

15. Provide three examples of how Enron "had its governance boxes checked."

16. Provide three examples of evidence that good corporate governance can pay off for organizations.

So, having the right model in place will not take you far if that model is eventually overrun by a corporate culture of greed and success at all costs. Even organizations that have been publicly exposed for their lack of corporate governance still appear to have lessons to learn. Tyco, for example, made a very public commitment to clean house under the direction of Edward Breen, "but it has refused to replace the audit firm that failed to uncover massive abuses by its former chief executive or to give up its Bermuda domicile [formal offshore residence for tax purposes], which insulates it from shareholder litigation and so genuine accountability." In addition, "at WorldCom (now MCI), where Michael Capellas was brought in to clean up the mess left by Bernie Ebbers, the bankruptcy court vetoed his proposed compensation package as "grossly excessive."[12]

No system of corporate governance can completely defend against fraud or incompetence. The test is how far such aberrations can be discouraged and how quickly they can be brought to light. The risks can be reduced by making the participants in the governance process as effectively accountable as possible. The key safeguards are properly constituted boards, separation of the functions of chairman and of chief executive, audit committees, vigilant shareholders, and financial reporting and auditing systems that provide full and timely disclosure.[13]

LIFEskills

Governing your career

In this chapter we have reviewed the importance of organizational oversight through a corporate governance structure. Give some thought to the oversight of your career in the future. As you have read, an organization's board of directors is designed to be both an advisory group and a governing body. Do you have a team of people you can count on for advice or guidance? Do you work with a mentor who is willing to share his or her experience and advice with you to help you make important decisions in your life?

Many successful businesspeople acknowledge that developing a dream team of advisors has been critical to their business and personal success in life. Being willing to reach out to others and seek their advice and guidance on a regular basis, they believe, has helped them prepare for important decisions and plan for long-term career choices. Making those decisions is ultimately your responsibility, but the more insight and information you have available to you, the more confident you may be in the final choice that you make.

Why would people agree to serve on your dream team? Perhaps they want to give something back in recognition of the success they have earned or to share in the joy of watching someone they regard as having tremendous potential move on to bigger and better career opportunities. Then, as you progress in your business career, you, in turn, can give something back by agreeing to mentor a young student with strong potential or to serve on the dream team of several promising students to help them succeed in their lives.

"Incriminating Evidence"— Marco Makes a Decision

Marco broke into a cold sweat as soon as he finished reading the e-mail. He realized that if it were made public, it would mean the end for the CEO of Chemco, the senior managers, David Collins, and probably anyone assigned to the Chemco case. What the heck was he supposed to do now? Tell David Collins? Pretend he hadn't found it and shred it? Should he go public with it or send it anonymously to the lawyers for the Chemco shareholders?

He started imagining what the consequences would be for each of those actions and decided that anything that involved him looking for a new paralegal position wasn't a good choice. He also thought about the Enron case and how long it had taken to get the two senior officers, Ken Lay and Jeff Skilling, into court, with no money left at the end of it all to return to shareholders who had lost their life savings when the company collapsed.

"It's just not worth it," Marco thought. "And anyway, who would pay attention to a rookie paralegal"? With that, he took the piece of paper and placed it into the shredder.

1. What could Marco have done differently here?

2. What do you think will happen now?

3. What will be the consequences for Marco, David Collins, and Chemco Industries?

[KEY TERMS]

Audit Committee *p. 109*

Board of Directors *p. 109*

Compensation Committee *p. 109*

"Comply or Else" *p. 112*

"Comply or Explain" *p. 112*

Corporate Governance *p. 108*

REVIEW QUESTIONS

1. Outline the corporate governance structure of the company you work for (or one you have worked for in the past).

2. Do you think corporate governance should be enforced through the "comply and explain" model or the "comply or else" model? Explain your answer.

3. If you were an employee of the Disney Corporation, how would you have felt about Michael Eisner holding so much power as chairman and CEO?

4. If you were an employee of Boeing, how would you have felt about Phil Condit's resignation as a demonstration that "accountability begins at the top"? Would you have felt more reassured by his departure? Explain your answer.

REVIEW EXERCISE

GlobalMutual was, by all accounts, a model insurance company. Profits were strong and had been for several years in a row. The company carried the highest ratings in its industry, and it had recently been voted one of the top 100 companies to work for in the United States in recognition of its very employee-focused work environment. GlobalMutual offered very generous benefits: free lunches in the cafeteria, onsite daycare facilities, and even free Starbucks Coffee in the employee break rooms. In an industry that was still struggling with the massive claims after a succession of hurricanes in the United States, GlobalMutual was financially stable and positioned to become one of the major insurance companies in the nation.[14]

So, why were the CEO, William Brown; the CFO, Anne Johnson; and the COO, Peter Brooking, all fired on the same day with no explanation other than that the terminations were related to issues of conduct?

1. Who would most likely have intervened to terminate the senior team over issues of conduct?

2. Give some examples of the kind of ethical misconduct that could have led to the termination of the entire senior leadership of GlobalMutual.

3. Was it a good idea to fire them all at the same time with no detailed explanation?

4. How are the stakeholders of GlobalMutual likely to react to this news? Explain your answer.

INTERNET EXERCISE

Locate the Web site of the World Council for Corporate Governance.

1. What are the mission, vision and objectives of the WCFCG?

2. What was the 2005 London Declaration?

3. Explain the acronym PREEMPTIVE.

TEAM EXERCISES

1. **Chairman and/or CEO.** Divide into two teams. One team must prepare a presentation advocating for the separation of the roles of chairman and CEO. The other team must prepare a presentation arguing for the continued practice of allowing one corporate executive to be both chairman and CEO.

2. **Compensation.** You serve on your organization's compensation committee, and you are meeting to negotiate the retirement package for your CEO who is retiring after a very successful 40-year career with your organization—the last 20 as CEO, during which time the company's revenues grew more than fourfold and gross profits increased by over 300 percent. Divide into two teams, arguing *for* and *against* the following compensation package being proposed by the CEO's representative:

   - Unlimited access to the company's New York apartment.
   - Unlimited use of the corporate jet and company limousine service.
   - Courtside tickets to New York Knicks games.
   - Box seats at Yankee Stadium.
   - VIP seats at the French Open, U.S. Open, and Wimbledon tennis tournaments.
   - A lucrative annual consulting contract of $80,000 for the first five days and an additional $17,500 per day thereafter.
   - Reimbursement for all professional services—legal, financial, secretarial, and IT support.
   - Stock options amounting to $200 million.

3. **An appropriate response.** You sit on the Board of Directors of a major airline that just experienced a horrendous customer service event. A severe snowstorm stranded several of your planes and caused a ripple effect throughout your flight schedule, stranding thousands of passengers at airports across the country and keeping dozens of passengers as virtual hostages on planes for several hours as they waited for departure slots at their airport. The press has covered this fiasco at length and is already calling for a passenger bill of rights that will be based primarily on all the things your airline didn't do to take care of its' passengers in this situation. Your CEO is the founder of the airline, and he has been featured in many of your commercials raving about the high level of customer service you deliver. The board is meeting to review his continued employment with the company. Divide into two teams and argue the case *for* and *against* terminating his employment as a first step in restoring the reputation of your airline.

4. **Ideal corporate governance.** Divide into groups of three or four. Each group must map out its ideal model for corporate governance of an organization—for example, the number of people on the board of directors; separate roles of chairman and CEO, inside and outside directors, and employee representation on the board. Prepare a presentation arguing for the respective merits of each model and offer evidence of how each model represents the best interests of all the organization's stakeholders.

HEWLETT-PACKARD: PRETEXTING

On January 23, 2006, journalists Dawn Kawamoto and Tom Krazit, from the technology news organization CNET, published an article on computer maker Hewlett Packard's (HP) strategic plans that prompted the HP board of directors, led by Chairwoman Patricia Dunn, to launch an ill-fated investigation into what they saw as a serious breach of corporate security through leaks to the media—apparently from one of their own board members. CNET's source was former director George Keyworth, but before that information could be uncovered, the HP board would choose to pursue a path of unprecedented corporate arrogance and highly questionable business practices.

Dunn's response to the leaks was to launch a detailed investigation into the activities of the other members of her board, several key employees at HP, and nine business reporters who were suspected of being the recipients of the sensitive corporate information that was being leaked from inside the boardroom. Private investigators were hired to spy on these identified individuals, and those detectives were allegedly encouraged to use all means necessary to identify the source of the leaks, including taking the unbelievable step of hiring contractors to **pretext** cell phone records of the individuals they were investigating. This involved calling the cell phone company and pretending to be the account holder in order to access the private account information and phone records. Pretexting is illegal in California (home of HP's Palo Alto headquarters) and other states, which immediately prompted the involvement of the California Attorney General's Office, the Justice Department, and the Securities and Exchange Commission (SEC) when the activities of the HP board came to light.

With so much state and federal firepower involved in the case, it was inevitable that Congress would become involved, and when called to appear before the congressional committee to explain the actions of her board, Patricia Dunn defended her position by arguing that everything the board did had been cleared by their legal advisors. The questionable ethics of the behavior were apparently not reviewed, but as far as Dunn was concerned, legality was a nonissue since her legal team had given it the green light. This decision to check in advance appeared, from her perspective, to clear her of all wrongdoing.

Further testimony established that several of Dunn's fellow board members did not endorse the pretexting tactics, nor did they support blocking George Keyworth's reelection to the board once his role in the leaks had been established. Directors Dick Hackborn, Tom Perkins, and George Keyworth had all been close associates of the founding partners of the company, Bill Hewlett and Dave Packard, and just as Dunn felt that HP's high standards warranted the aggressive investigation, the trio believed that HP's legacy—referred to as "The HP Way," made such activities unacceptable. Dunn allegedly chose to keep vital information on the investigation from her fellow directors, including "which investigation firm had been hired, whether HP people would be involved, or what methods would be used."

The probe of the leaks was finally discussed in detail at a board meeting on May 18, at which time the use of pretexting was revealed. Several of the board members expressed concern over the use of tactics that they had not authorized, and Director Tom Perkins was prompted to contact AT&T to review the pretexting issue in detail.

Once indicted by the Justice Department, Dunn was hastily dismissed and replaced by Mark Hurd, the CEO of HP, who had been hired from NCR to replace Carly Fiorina. This represented an interesting choice for HP, since it was now endowing the roles of Chairman and CEO in the same person, after only recently making an explicit decision to separate the roles in the interests of greater corporate oversight.

Discussion Questions

1. Was the CNET story sufficient justification for the HP board's actions? Why or why not?

2. HP Chairwoman Patricia Dunn defended the actions of the board by arguing that HP's higher standards of corporate integrity justified such aggressive actions as pretexting. Do their higher standards make the behavior of the board more or less ethical? Explain.

3. Does the fact that HP's legal advisors approved the actions of Dunn and her board beforehand clear them of all responsibility in this case? Why or why not?

4. Does pretexting match the founding principles of "The HP Way?"

5. The board voted to dismiss Patricia Dunn in light of her indictment—was that the right decision? Why or why not?

6. How can CEO Mark Hurd restore the reputation of HP after this?

Sources: Lorraine Woellert, "HP Leak: Let's Turn to the Evidence," *Businessweek,* September 27, 2006; David H. Holtzman, "Hubris at HP–and Beyond," *Businessweek,* October 12, 2006; and Lorraine Woellert and Robert D. Hof, "Ganging up on Hewlett-Packard" *Businessweek,* September 12, 2006.

EXERCISE 5.2

SOCGEN

In 1995, Barings Bank PLC, which proudly boasted of its position as banker to the Queen of England, collapsed after announcing trading losses of £827 million. The majority of those losses (greater than $1 billion) were attributed to one trader, Nick Leeson, who had been promoted from a back office clerical role to a position as a futures trader. Leeson had used his knowledge of back office procedures to hide the size of the trades he was placing on the Japanese stock market. The reward for his efforts was a six-year jail sentence. Fortunately, Barings' clients were in no danger because the losses involved only Barings' own trading accounts. The Dutch bank Internationale Nederland Groep NV (ING) subsequently purchased the assets of the collapsed bank.

In January 2008, history repeated itself on a much grander scale when Société Générale (SocGen), one of France's largest banks, revealed that a rogue trader, Jérôme Kerviel, had placed a series of bad bets on European futures to the tune of a €4.9 billion ($7.9 billion) loss for SocGen.

Kerviel's activities sent a shockwave through world financial markets that were already reeling from large trading losses from the U.S. mortgage crisis, not only because of the sheer size of SocGen's losses that were allegedly attributable to one trader, but also because of the apparent lack of controls in place over transactions amounting to billions of dollars.

Investigations into the exact methods by which Kerviel was able to conceal his activities revealed significant gaps in both SocGen's risk management systems (the extent to which the bank is exposed to risky trades), and financial controls (the functional department responsible for ensuring that all trades—purchases and sales—are balanced at the end of a trading period):

- How could an inexperienced midlevel trader earning a modest €100,000 a year (a low salary by the standards of his fellow traders) be allowed to run up a trading position with a risk exposure to the bank of as much as €50 billion?
- Investigations revealed that Kerviel had been engaging in unauthorized trades since 2005 and

that the European exchange on which he placed those trades had raised concerns about his activities in November 2007. Some suggested that the profits Kerviel's trading activity for that year earned—€55 million ($81 million)—factored into SocGen's decision not to investigate Kerviel's activities in any detail.

- Kerviel's profits in 2007 appeared to convince him that he had discovered a new and highly lucrative system for futures trading. Investigators could find no other motive for his actions than simply a desire to increase his remuneration at the bank through a year-end bonus for strong financial performance. They found no evidence of any intent to embezzle funds, and they noted an apparently naïve belief in his trading skills.
- While there were changes in personnel in the aftermath of the disastrous trading activities, including the head of the equity futures division and the head of Information Technology, the board of directors of SocGen refused to accept the resignation of chief executive officer Daniel Bouton, and he, in turn, declined to accept the resignation of Jean-Pierre Mustier, the chief executive of SocGen's corporate and investment banking division.
- Critics of SocGen's leadership team argued that a takeover of the bank would be the inevitable outcome of this event. One analyst was quoted as stating: "The management has lost its credibility and that is the first barrier to any takeover bid. There is likely to be a lot of interest from around Europe."
- Kerviel was arrested at the end of January and charged with breach of trust, falsifying and using falsified documents, and breaching IT control access codes.
- In contrast, Kerviel has also become something of an Internet celebrity, with many French sites hailing him as a modern-day Robin Hood or the Che Guevara of finance. One enterprising Web merchant quickly produced a range of T-shirts

in support of Mr. Kerviel, including one that reads "Jérôme Kerviel's girlfriend," and another that reads, "Jérôme Kerviel, €4,900,000,000, Respect."

- SocGen's biggest rival in France, BNP Paribas, had tried unsuccessfully to acquire SocGen back in 1999 in a hostile takeover bid. The rival was therefore the most logical choice to come after SocGen in such an obvious moment of defenselessness. However, after considering the option of another takeover bid, BNP chose not to pursue the opportunity. SocGen has been able to avoid the same fate as Barings Bank by raising an $8 billion rescue fund from private equity investors.

SocGen's clear lack of risk management and financial controls inevitably caught the attention of France's finance minister, Christine Lagarde. Her initial report on the incident, produced within eight days of the event while many simultaneous investigations were still ongoing, raised several key questions including the ease with which Kerviel appeared to avoid detection, even though his trades amounted to billions of dollars; the extent to which the losses caused broader market problems, and what needed to be done to ensure the event never happened again. Her report ended with a call on the French government to give more power to punish those who fail to follow established best practices.

Discussion Questions

1. Who are the stakeholders in this case?

2. What did Kerviel do wrong?

3. What did SocGen do wrong?

4. Identify the ethical violations that occurred in this case.

5. Would the outcome have been different if Kerviel's trades in European futures had worked out?

6. What actions could SocGen have taken to prevent such large losses?

Sources: BBC, "Nick Leeson and Barings Bank," www.bbc.co.uk/crime/caseclosed/nickleeson.shtml; Marcus W. Brauchli, Nicholas Bray, and Michael R. Sesit, "Barings PLC Officials May Have Been Aware of Trader's Position," *The Wall Street Journal* 132, 44 (March 6, 1995), pp. A1, A6; Nicholas Bray and Michael R. Sesit, "Barings Was Warned Controls Were Lax but Didn't Make Reforms in Singapore," *The Wall Street Journal* 132, 42 (March 2, 1995), p. A3; Paula Dwyer, William Glasgall, Dean Foust, and Greg Burns, "The Lessons from Barings' Straits," *BusinessWeek,* 3415 (March 13, 1995), pp. 30–33; Alexander MacLeod, "Youthful Trader Sinks Britain's Oldest Bank," *The Christian Science Monitor* 87, 64 (February 28, 1995), pp. 1, 8; Peter Thal Larsen, "SocGen Rogue Trade: Six Sleepless Nights Reveal the Full Impact of Scandal," *Financial Times,* January 25, 2008, pp. 16–17; Martin Arnold and Lina Saigol, "Doubts Cast on Bouton's Position," *Financial Times,* January 25, 2008, p. 17; Pan Kwan Luk, "From 'le Rogue' to the Che of Our Times," *Financial Times,* January 31, 2008, p. 19; Peggy Hollinger, "Hard-hitting Lagarde Points up SocGen's Lack of Control," *Financial Times,* February 5, 2008, p. 6.

discussion

HEALTHSOUTH

HealthSouth is America's largest provider of outpatient surgery and rehabilitation services. It owns or operates over 1,800 facilities across the country and serves 70 percent of the rehabilitation market. It was founded in 1984 by Richard Scrushy, a former respiratory therapist who believed that efficient one-stop shopping could be applied to the health care industry. From the time it went public in 1986, the Birmingham, Alabama, firm exceeded Wall Street expectations, a pattern that would continue for the next 15 years. In 1992 Scrushy aggressively began to acquire other clinics, and HealthSouth stock soared 31 percent annually between 1987 and 1997.

Scrushy cut a charismatic figure; the headquarters housed a museum dedicated to his achievements. He flew his own jet, mingled with celebrities, and sang with a band. For his third wedding in 1997 he chartered a plane to fly 150 guests to Jamaica. His workers knew him as King Richard.

His management style impressed many analysts. *Fortune* magazine described him in 1999 as executing his ideas brilliantly and said he was a taskmaster and a micromanager. Scrushy honed his technique, centralizing every piece of data imaginable. Every Friday a stack of printouts detailing the performance of each facility landed on his desk; when any one of them had a problem, Scrushy pounced. HealthSouth managed everything out of Birmingham: construction, purchasing, billing, even personnel. While this kind of top-down management may sound impossibly bureaucratic, Scrushy's troops made it work efficiently. Needed supplies and authorizations arrived within 30 days. Administrators who couldn't hit budget targets were fired. Says Scrushy, "We can call 'em and tell 'em, 'Jump through hoops! Stand on your head!' "

However, behind the scenes was a pattern of institutionalized fraud. By the third quarter of 2002, the $8 billion company had overstated its assets by $800 million. According to testimony, the fraud began shortly after the company went public when Scrushy wanted to impress Wall Street. If the results were not what he expected, Scrushy would allegedly tell his staff to "fix it." They would then convene in what came to be known as a "family meeting" to adjust the figures, a process they called "filling the gap." The internal accountants kept two sets of books—one with the true figures and one that they presented to the outside world.

HealthSouth was able to keep up the deception in a number of ingenious ways that systematically fooled outside auditors. One scheme involved what are known as contractual adjustments. Sometimes the government or insurer would not fully reimburse a facility for the amount charged to a patient. This amount would be subtracted from gross revenues. In typical double entry accounting, any loss of revenue has to be balanced by an increase in liabilities. HealthSouth simply failed to enter the liability amount. Its accountants also posted regular expenses as long-term capital expenditures and billed group therapies as single-person sessions. They routinely inflated the value of their assets. The practices were pervasive but individually so small that they rarely met the threshold levels that would trigger review by an outside auditor. The inside accountants were careful to make sure the adjustments were uneven and dispersed around the country so they appeared realistic.

Five HealthSouth accounting employees have been convicted of fraud. Four did not receive prison sentences, though. Their lawyers argued that they were obeying orders, subject to constant intimidation, and relatively low on the organizational chart. The judge declared at sentencing that although three held the rank of vice president, "These four were essentially data entry clerks, regardless of their job titles."

Scrushy was fired by the board on March 31, 2003. On November 4, 2003, Scrushy was indicted for securities fraud, money laundering, and other charges. He had maintained throughout that he was unaware of the illegal accounting practices. He was secretly recorded saying that he was worried about signing "fixed up" financials. As part of the Sarbanes-Oxley Act of 2002, an executive has to certify the company's financial reports. In August of that year, Scrushy signed that he had reviewed and endorsed

HealthSouth's 2001 annual report and the second quarter report for 2002. He claimed on CBS's *60 Minutes* program in October 2003 that he had signed because he trusted the five chief financial officers who prepared the figures. In June 2005, an Alabama jury cleared Scrushy of all charges, although the Securities and Exchange Commission (SEC) reached a settlement of $81 million with him in April 2007 consisting of a payback of $52 million of bonuses and interest as a result of an Alabama lawsuit, $17 million in a similar Delaware lawsuit, $1.5 million to settle a lawsuit brought by former HealthSouth employees, and other forfeitures and fines. Scrushy was also prohibited from serving as an officer or director of a publicly traded company for at least five years under the terms of the settlement.

Discussion Questions

1. Is it fair to hold a CEO responsible for any and all actions of a company? Consider that Scrushy was not an accountant and that the outside auditors, Ernst & Young, did not detect the fraud. If he were not involved, should he still be held accountable?

2. Would it have been appropriate for employees to blow the whistle in this case? Was there imminent harm to people? What would be an appropriate motive for whistle-blowing, and how much proof do you believe the employee would have needed to be credible?

3. From your research and reading, what dynamics set the moral tone at HealthSouth? Do you feel that employees were influenced by the corporate culture?

4. There seems to have been a significant amount of wrongdoing at HealthSouth. A number of executives were involved in fraud, but there also appears to have been a great deal of complicity on the part of more rank-and-file workers. How would you assign moral culpability in a case like this?

5. Derek Parfit describes a case called the Harmless Torturers. He says that in the bad old days, one torturer gave a jolt of 1,000 volts to a victim, but nowadays 1,000 operators each flip a switch carrying 1 volt. Any individual contribution to the overall effect is negligible, and therefore each one believes he has not personally done any significant harm. Would the same logic apply in the HealthSouth case? What, if anything, is wrong with the reasoning involved?

6. For a long time, HealthSouth posted profits, and Scrushy was a darling of Wall Street analysts. At what point, if any, should there have been greater regulatory oversight? Do you believe the outside auditors or the board should have acted more like bloodhounds than watchdogs?

Source: Gibson, K., "Business Ethics: People, Profits, and the Planet," (2006), McGraw-Hill, New York, NY. pp.634–636. The New York Times, April 24, 2007.

chapter 6

The Role of Government

> *People who enjoy eating sausage and obey the law should not watch either being made.*
>
> —Otto von Bismarck, (1815–1898), Chancellor of Germany

LEARNING OBJECTIVES

After studying this chapter, you should be able to:

1. Identify the five key pieces of U.S. legislation designed to discourage, if not prevent, illegal conduct within organizations.

2. Understand the purpose and significance of the Foreign Corrupt Practices Act (FCPA).

3. Categorize the six key principles of the Defense Industry Initiatives (DII).

4. Calculate monetary fines under the three-step process of the U.S. Federal Sentencing Guidelines for Organizations (FSGO).

5. Compare and contrast the relative advantages and disadvantages of the Sarbanes-Oxley Act (SOX).

Too Much Trouble

Susan is a junior accounting assistant with one of the largest auditing firms in the Midwest. Since the Enron fraud case and the passing of the Sarbanes-Oxley Act, her company has been very busy—in fact, they have so much business, they are starting to turn clients down.

For Susan, so much business means great opportunities. Each completed audit takes her one step closer to running her own auditing team and finally to leading her own audit. The work is hard and the hours are often long, but Susan loves the attention to detail and the excitement of discovering errors and then getting them corrected. Also, knowing that their clients are releasing financial reports that are clean and accurate makes her feel that she is doing her part to restore the reputation of the financial markets one client at a time.

One morning, her boss, Steven Thompson, comes into her office carrying a thick manila folder. "Hi, Susan, what are you working on right now?" he asks.

"Typical Thompson," Susan thinks. "Straight to the point with no time for small talk."

"We should be finished with the Jones audit by the end of the day, why?" Susan replied.

"I need a small favor," Thompson continued. "We've had this new small-business client show up out of the blue after being dropped by his previous auditor. It really couldn't have happened at a worse time. We've got so many large audits in the pipeline that I can't spare anyone to work on this, but I don't want to start turning business away in case word gets out that we're not keeping up with a growing client base—who knows when the next big fish will come along?"

"I'm not sure I follow you, Steven," answered Susan, confused.

"I don't want to turn this guy away, but we don't want his business either—too small to be a real money-maker. So, just take a quick look at his file and then quote him a price for our services—and here's where I need the favor. Make the quote high enough that he will want to go somewhere else—can you do that?"

1. The Sarbanes-Oxley Act created an oversight board for all auditing firms. Look at the outline of the act on page 142 for more information on the Public Company Accounting Oversight Board (PCAOB). Would the PCAOB endorse trying to dump a prospective client in this manner?

2. Is being too busy with other clients a justification for deliberately driving this customer away?

3. What should Susan do now?

Key Legislation

For those organizations that have demonstrated that they are unable to keep their own house in order by maintaining a strong ethical culture, the last line of defense has been a legal and regulatory framework that offers financial incentives to promote ethical behavior and imposes penalties for those that choose not to adopt such behavior. Since the 1970s, there have been five key attempts at behavior modification to discourage, if not prevent, illegal conduct within organizations:

- The Foreign Corrupt Practices Act (1977).
- The Defense Industry Initiatives (1986).
- The U.S. Federal Sentencing Guidelines for Organizations (1991).

Foreign Corrupt Practices Act (FCPA) Legislation introduced to control bribery and other less-obvious forms of payment to foreign officials and politicians by American publicly traded companies.

Disclosure (FCPA) The FCPA requires corporations to fully disclose any and all transactions conducted with foreign officials and politicians.

Prohibition (FCPA) The FCPA incorporated the wording of the Bank Secrecy Act and the Mail Fraud Act to prohibit the movement of funds overseas for the express purpose of conducting a fraudulent scheme.

Facilitation payments (FCPA) Payments that are acceptable (legal) provided they expedite or secure the performance of a routine governmental action.

Routine governmental action (FCPA) Any regular administrative process or procedure, excluding any action taken by a foreign official in the decision to award new or continuing business.

- The Sarbanes-Oxley Act (2002).
- The Revised Federal Sentencing Guidelines for Organizations (2004).

The FCPA

The **Foreign Corrupt Practices Act (FCPA)** was introduced to more effectively control bribery and other less-obvious forms of payment to foreign officials and politicians by American publicly traded companies as they pursued international growth. Prior to the passing of this law, the illegality of this behavior was punishable only through "secondary" sources of legislation:

1. The Securities and Exchange Commission (SEC) could fine companies for failing to disclose such payments under their securities rules.
2. The Bank Secrecy Act also required full disclosure of funds that were taken out of or brought into the United States.
3. The Mail Fraud Act made the use of the U.S. mail or wire communications to transact a fraudulent scheme illegal.

By passing the FCPA, Congress was attempting to send a clear message that the competitiveness of U.S. corporations in overseas markets should be based on price and product quality rather than the extent to which companies had paid off foreign officials and political leaders. To give the legislation some weight, the U.S. Department of Justice (DOJ) and the Securities and Exchange Commission (SEC) jointly enforce the FCPA.

The act encompasses all the secondary measures that were currently in use to prohibit such behavior by focusing on two distinct areas:

- **Disclosure.** The act requires corporations to fully disclose any and all transactions conducted with foreign officials and politicians, in line with the SEC provisions.
- **Prohibition.** The act incorporates the wording of the Bank Secrecy Act and the Mail Fraud Act to prohibit the movement of funds overseas for the express purpose of conducting a fraudulent scheme.

A Bark Worse Than Its Bite

Even with the apparent success of consolidating three pieces of secondary legislation into one primary tool for the prohibition of bribery, the FCPA was still criticized for lacking any real teeth because of its formal recognition of **facilitation payments,** which would otherwise be acknowledged as bribes. The FCPA finds these payments acceptable provided they expedite or secure the performance of a **routine governmental action.**

Examples of Routine Governmental Action include:

- Providing permits, licenses, or other official documents to qualify a person to do business in a foreign country.
- Processing governmental papers, such as visas and work orders.

- Providing police protection, mail pickup and delivery, or scheduling inspections associated with contract performance or inspections related to transit of goods across a country.

- Providing phone service, power, and water supply; loading and unloading cargo; or protecting perishable products or commodities from deterioration.

- Performing actions of a similar nature.

The key distinction in identifying bribes was the exclusion of any action taken by a foreign official in the decision to award new or continuing business. Such decisions, being the primary target of most questionable payments, were not deemed to be routine governmental action.[1]

FCPA in Action

Chiquita Brands International Inc.[2] According to the September 14, 2004, edition of *The Wall Street Journal*, Chiquita Brands International Inc. disclosed to the DOJ and the SEC that its Greek unit made improper payments as part of a local tax audit settlement. Chiquita also disclosed that the payments, totaling $18,021, were similar to payments that its Colombian subsidiary made in 1996 and 1997, which were previously disclosed to the SEC.

Monsanto Corporation According to the May 27, 2004, edition of *The Wall Street Journal,* Monsanto Corp. began cooperating with an investigation regarding allegations that it bribed an Indonesian official to influence the repeal of a decree likely to adversely affect the company. The government claimed that in 2002 a senior Monsanto manager based in the United States authorized and directed an Indonesian consulting firm to make an illegal payment of $50,000 to a senior Indonesian Ministry of Environment official in order to repeal an unfavorable decree that could affect the company's operations. However, the decree was not repealed, which highlights the fact that a company can still be found in violation of the FCPA even if a bribe is unsuccessful.

Making Sense of FCPA

Table 6.1 summarizes the fine lines between legality and illegality in some of the prohibited behaviors and approved exceptions in the FCPA provisions.

The Department of Justice can enforce criminal penalties of up to $2 million per violation for corporations and other business entities. Officers, directors, stockholders, employees, and agents are subject to a fine of up to $250,000 per violation and imprisonment for up to five years. The SEC may bring a civil fine of up to $10,000 per violation. Penalties under the books and recordkeeping provisions can reach up to $5 million and 20 years' imprisonment for individuals and up to $25 million for organizations.

✓ PROGRESS CHECK QUESTIONS

1. What was the primary purpose of the FCPA?

2. What was the maximum fine for a U.S. corporation under the FCPA?

3. Which two distinct areas did the FCPA focus on?

4. List four examples of routine governmental action.

Illegal	Legal
Bribes: • Payments of money or anything else of value to influence or induce any foreign official to act in a manner that would be in violation of his or her lawful duty. • Payments, authorizations, promises, or offers to any other person if there is knowledge that any portion of the payment is to be passed along to a foreign official or foreign political party, official, or candidate for a prohibited purpose under the act. Note that knowledge is defined very broadly and is present when one knows an event is certain or likely to occur; even purposely failing to take note of an event or being willfully blind can constitute knowledge.	**Grease payments:** • Facilitating payments to foreign officials in order to expedite or secure the performance of a routine governmental action. For example, routine governmental action could include obtaining permits, licenses, or other official documents; expediting lawful customs clearances; obtaining the issuance of entry or exit visas; providing police protection, mail pick-up and delivery, and phone service; and performing actions that are wholly unconnected to the award of new business or the continuation of prior business.
Recordkeeping and accounting provisions: • Books, records, and accounts must be kept in reasonable detail to accurately and fairly reflect transactions and dispositions of assets. • A system of internal accounting controls is devised to provide reasonable assurances that transactions are executed in accordance with management's authorization.	**Marketing expenses:** • Payments to foreign officials made in connection with the promotion or demonstration of company products or services (e.g., demonstration or tour of a pharmaceutical plant) or in connection with the execution of a particular contract with a foreign government.
	Payments lawful under foreign laws: • Payments may (very rarely) be made to foreign officials when the payment is "lawful under the written laws of the foreign country."
	Political contributions: • Unlike in the United States, where foreign nationals are prohibited from making political contributions to U.S. political parties and candidates, it may occasionally be appropriate for a U.S. company's overseas operations to make a political contribution on behalf of the company. Contributions not only include checks to political parties or candidates, but also payments for fundraising dinners and similar events. This would be an example of a payment that could violate the FCPA were it not for written local law. **Donations to foreign charities:** • U.S. companies may make donations to bona fide charitable organizations provided that the donation will not be used to circumvent the FCPA and that the contribution does not violate local laws, rules, or regulations.

TABLE 6.1   Illegal versus Legal Behaviors under the FCPA

Defense Industry Initiatives (DII)

Defense Industry Initiatives (DII)
Six principles that "were intended to promote sound management practices, to ensure that companies were in compliance with complex regulations, and to restore public confidence in the defense industry."

The full title of this document is the **Defense Industry Initiatives (DII)** on Business Ethics and Conduct. Consisting of six key principles, which were ratified by several defense contractors in 1986 in response to a series of recommendations by an Independent Blue Ribbon Commission on Defense Management. The committee had been convened to address growing public concern over "procurement irregularities" in the performance of business contracts by major defense contractors.[3]

It agreed upon these ideals:

1. Each company will have and adhere to a written code of business ethics and conduct.

2. The company's code will establish the high values expected of its employees and the standards by which they must judge their own

conduct and that of their organization; each company will train its employees concerning their personal responsibilities under the code.

3. Each company will create a free and open atmosphere that allows and encourages employees to report violations of its code to the company without fear of retribution for such reporting.

4. Each company will have the obligation to self-govern by monitoring compliance with federal procurement laws and adopting procedures for voluntary disclosure of violations of federal procurement laws and corrective actions taken.

5. Each company will have the responsibility to each of the other companies in the industry to live by standards of conduct that preserve the integrity of the defense industry.

6. Each company must have public accountability for its commitment to these principles.

In June 1986, 24 defense contractors pledged to promote ethical business conduct through the implementation of policies, procedures, and programs. The DII has since grown to 48 member firms, including virtually all of the top 25 defense contractors.[4]

The U.S. Federal Sentencing Guidelines for Organizations (FSGO) (1991)

The U.S. Federal Sentencing Commission was established in 1984 by the Comprehensive Crime Control Act and was charged with developing uniform sentencing guidelines for offenders convicted of federal crimes. The guidelines became effective on November 1, 1987. At that time, they consisted of seven chapters and applied only to individuals convicted of federal offenses.

In 1991, an eighth chapter was added to the guidelines. Chapter 8 is more commonly referred to as the **Federal Sentencing Guidelines for Organizations (FSGO).** It applies to organizations and holds them liable for the criminal acts of their employees and agents.

Federal Sentencing Guidelines for Organizations (FSGO) Hold businesses liable for the criminal acts of their employees and agents.

FSGO takes the same approach as the DII in requiring organizations to police themselves by preventing and detecting the criminal activity of their employees and agents.

In its mission to promote ethical organizational behavior and increase the costs of unethical behavior, the FSGO establishes a definition of an organization that is so broad as to prompt the assessment that "no business enterprise is exempt." In addition, the FSGO includes such an exhaustive list of covered business crimes that it appears frighteningly easy for an organization to run afoul of federal crime laws and become subject to FSGO penalties.

Penalties under FSGO include monetary fines, organizational probation, and the implementation of an operational program to bring the organization into compliance with FSGO standards.

Monetary Fines under the FGSO

If an organization is sentenced under FSGO, a fine is calculated through a three-step process:

Step 1: Determination of the "Base Fine" The base fine will normally be the greatest of:

- The monetary gain to the organization from the offense.
- The monetary loss from the offense caused by the organization, to the extent the loss was caused knowingly, intentionally, or recklessly.
- The amount determined by a judge based upon an FSGO table.

The table factors in both the nature of the crime and the amount of the loss suffered by the victim. Fraud, for example, is a level 6 offense; a fraud causing harm in excess of $5 million is increased by 14 levels to a level 20 offense. Evidence of extensive preplanning to commit the offense can raise that two more levels to level 22. To put these levels in dollar terms, crimes at level 6 or lower involve a base fine of $5,000; offense levels of 38 or higher involve a base fine of $72.5 million.

Culpability Score (FSGO) The calculation of a degree of blame or guilt that is used as a multiplier of up to four times the base fine. The culpability score can be adjusted according to aggravating or mitigating factors.

Death Penalty (FSGO) Where the fine is set high enough to match all the organization's assets—and basically put the organization out of business. This is warranted where the organization was operating primarily for a criminal purpose.

Step 2: The Culpability Score Once the base fine has been calculated, the judge will compute a corresponding degree of blame or guilt known as the **culpability score.** This score is simply a multiplier with a maximum of four, so the worst-case scenario would be a fine of four times the maximum base fine of $72.5 million, for a grand total of $290 million. The culpability score can be increased (aggravated) or decreased (mitigated) according to predetermined factors.

Aggravating factors:

- High-level personnel were involved in or tolerated the criminal activity.
- The organization willfully obstructed justice.
- The organization had a prior history of similar misconduct.
- The current offense violated a judicial order, injunction, or condition of probation.

Mitigating Factors:

- The organization had an effective program to prevent and detect violations of law.
- The organization self-reported the offense to appropriate governmental authorities, fully cooperated in the investigation, and accepted responsibility for the criminal conduct.

Step 3: Determining the Total Fine Amount The base fine multiplied by the culpability score gives the total fine amount. In certain cases, however, the judge has the discretion to impose a so-called **death penalty,** where the fine is set high enough to match all the organization's assets. This is warranted where the organization was operating primarily for a criminal purpose.

Is the fraud that this employee is committing somehow less wrong because it is only a few thousand dollars and produces a handful of victims?

Organizational Probation

In addition to monetary fines, organizations also can be sentenced to probation for up to five years. The status of probation can include the following requirements:

- Reporting the business's financial condition to the court on a periodic basis.
- Remaining subject to unannounced examinations of all financial records by a designated probation officer and/or court-appointed experts.
- Reporting progress in the implementation of a compliance program.
- Being subject to unannounced examinations to confirm that the compliance program is in place and is working.

Compliance Program

Obviously the best way to minimize your culpability score is to make sure that you have some form of program in place that can effectively detect and prevent violations of law—a compliance program. The FSGO prescribes seven steps for an effective compliance program:

1. Management oversight. A high-level official (corporate ethics officer) must be in charge of and accountable for the compliance program.
2. Corporate policies. Policies and procedures designed to reduce the likelihood of criminal conduct in the organization must be in place.
3. Communication of standards and procedures. These ethics policies must be effectively communicated to every stakeholder of the organization.
4. Compliance with standards and procedures. Evidence of active implementation of these policies must be provided through appropriate monitoring and reporting (including a system for employees to report suspected criminal conduct without fear of retribution).
5. Delegation of substantial discretionary authority. No individuals should be granted excessive discretionary authority that would increase the risk of criminal conduct.
6. Consistent discipline. The organization must implement penalties for criminal conduct and for failing to address criminal misconduct in a consistent manner.
7. Response and corrective action. Criminal offenses, whether actual or suspected, must generate an appropriate response, analysis, and corrective action.

If all of this seems like an enormous administrative burden, consider the following example: A $25,000 bribe has been paid to a city official to ensure an award of a cable television franchise. This is a level 18 offense with a base penalty of a $350,000 fine. Based on a variety of factors (e.g., culpability, multipliers), that penalty is now increased to $1.4 million. The minimum fine with mitigating circumstances (for example, the company has a compliance plan and there was no high-level involvement in the bribery) would have placed this fine in the $17,500 to $70,000 range instead of $1.4 million.

If that doesn't discourage you, consider the additional risk of negative publicity to your organization, which could result in a significant loss of sales, additional scrutiny from vendors, and even a drop in your stock price.[5]

Revised Federal Sentencing Guidelines for Organizations (2004)

In May 2004, the U.S. Sentencing Commission proposed to Congress that there should be modifications to the 1991 guidelines to bring about key changes in corporate compliance programs. The revised guidelines, which Congress formally adopted in November 2004, made three key changes:

- They required companies to periodically evaluate the effectiveness of their compliance programs on the assumption of a substantial risk that any program is capable of failing. They also expected the results of these risk assessments to be incorporated back into the next version of the compliance program.

- The revised guidelines required evidence of actively promoting ethical conduct rather than just complying with legal obligations. For the first time, the concept of an ethical culture was recognized as a foundational component of an effective compliance program.

- The guidelines defined accountability more clearly. Corporate officers are expected to be knowledgeable about all aspects of the compliance program, and they are required to receive formal training as it relates to their roles and responsibilities within the organization.

ETHICAL dilemma

CASE 6.1 The Bribery Gap

In 1997, 35 countries signed the Organization for Economic Cooperation and Development (OECD)'s convention to make it a crime to bribe foreign officials. However, in the last half of 2004:

- Bristol-Myers Squibb revealed that the Securities and Exchange Commission launched an investigation into some of the company's German units for possible violations of the FCPA.

- Three former Lucent Corp. employees were alleged to have bribed Saudi Arabia's former telecommunications minister with cash and gifts worth up to $21 million.

- Halliburton Corp., under investigation by both the Department of Justice and the SEC, disclosed that it may have bribed Nigerian officials to secure favorable tax treatment for a liquefied natural gas facility.

- The SEC hit the U.S. unit of Swiss-based ABB Ltd. with a $16.4 million judgment reflecting information on bribery and . . . accounting improprieties. The charges, which [ABB] settled without admitting or denying guilt, were that ABB's U.S. and foreign units paid $1.1 billion in bribes to officials in Nigeria, Angola, and Kazakhstan between 1998 and 2003 . . . In one instance, the SEC alleged, ABB's country manager for Angola gave out $21,000 in a paper bag to five officials of the state-owned oil company.

American companies operating under increasing federal and regulatory scrutiny face real consequences from trying to do business in a global business environment in which foreign business seems to function on the basis of "gifts" at every stage of the transaction:

- During the 12 months ended April 30, 2004, according to a U.S. Commerce Department report, competition for 47 contracts worth $18 billion may have been affected by bribes that foreign firms paid to foreign officials. Because U.S. companies wouldn't participate in the tainted deals, the department estimates, at least 8 of those contracts, worth $3 billion, were lost to them.

- For Lockheed Martin Corp., a $2.4 billion merger agreement with Titan Corp. eventually fell through in 2004 after what Titan [documents] described as "allegations that improper payments were made, or items of value were provided by consultants for Titan or its subsidiaries."

1. Is it ethical for U.S. regulations to put U.S. companies at an apparent disadvantage to their foreign competitors? Explain why or why not.

2. If foreign companies pay bribes, does that make it OK for U.S. companies to do the same? Explain why or why not.

3. If you could prove that new jobs, new construction, and valuable tax revenue would come to the United States if the bribe were paid, would that change your position? Explain your answer.

4. It would seem that the playing field will never be level—someone will always be looking for a bribe, and someone will always be willing to pay it if they want the business badly enough. If that's true, why bother to put legislation in place at all?

Source: David M. Katz, "The Bribery Gap," *CFO* 21, no. 1 (January 2005), p. 59.

☑ PROGRESS CHECK QUESTIONS

9. Explain the seven steps of an effective compliance program.

10. What are *aggravating* and *mitigating* factors?

11. Explain the risk assessments required in the 2004 Revised FSGO.

12. What were the three key components of the 2004 Revised FSGO?

LIFEskills

Governing your own ethical behavior

Does the fact that we appear to need government legislation to enforce ethical business practices both here and overseas suggest that we are unable to self-govern our individual ethical behavior? Can we be trusted to act in an ethical manner both in our personal and professional lives? Or do we need a regulatory framework and a clearly defined system of punishment to force people to act ethically or face the consequences?

As we discussed in Chapter 1, your personal value system represents the cumulative effect of a series of influences in your life—your upbringing, religious beliefs, community influences, and peer influences from your friends. As such, your ethical standards already represent a framework of influences that have made you the person you are today. However, where you take that value system in the future depends entirely on you. State and federal bodies may put punitive legislation in place to enforce an ideal model of personal and professional behavior, but whether or not you abide by that legislation comes down to the decisions you make on a daily basis. Can you stay true to your personal value system and live your life according to your own ethical standards? Or are you the type of person who is swayed by peer pressure and social norms to the point where you find yourself doing things you wouldn't normally do?

Developing a clear sense of your personal values is as much about knowing what you aren't willing to do as it is about knowing what you are willing to do. Understanding the difference allows you to remain grounded and focused while those around you sway in the wind in search of someone to help them make a decision. It's when that someone is not acting in their best interests that poor decisions are made and things can start to go wrong.

The Sarbanes-Oxley Act (2002)

Sarbanes-Oxley Act (SOX) A legislative response to the corporate accounting scandals of the early 2000s that covers the financial management of businesses.

The **Sarbanes-Oxley Act (SOX)**[6] became law on July 30, 2003. It was a legislative response to a series of corporate accounting scandals that had begun to dominate the financial markets and mass media since 2001.

Launched during a period of extreme investor unrest and agitation, SOX was hailed by some as "one of the most important pieces of legislation governing the behavior of accounting firms and financial markets since (the SEC) legislation in the 1930s."

However, supporters of this law were equally matched by its critics, leaving no doubt that SOX may be regarded as one of the most controversial pieces of corporate legislation in recent history.

The act contains 11 sections, or titles, and almost 70 subsections covering every aspect of the financial management of businesses. Each of the 11 sections can be seen to relate directly to prominent examples of corporate wrongdoing that preceded the establishment of the legislation—the Enron scandal in particular.

Title I: Public Company Accounting Oversight Board (PCAOB)

Public Company Accounting Oversight Board (PCAOB) An independent oversight body for auditing companies.

The series of financial collapses of publicly traded companies that the financial community had previously recommended as "strong buys" or "Wall Street darlings" had the greatest negative impact on investor confidence—especially since the accounts of all these companies had supposedly been audited as accurate by established and highly regarded auditing firms.

The creation of the **Public Company Accounting Oversight Board (PCAOB)** as an independent oversight body was an attempt to reestablish the perceived independence of auditing companies that the conflict of interest in Arthur Andersen's auditing and consulting relationship with Enron had called into question. In addition, as an oversight board, the PCAOB was charged with maintaining compliance with established standards and enforcing rules and disciplinary procedures for those organizations that found themselves out of compliance. Any public accounting firms that audited the records of publicly traded companies were required to register with the board and to abide by any operational standards set by that board.

Title II: Auditor Independence

In addition to establishing the PCAOB, SOX introduced several key directives to further enforce the independence of auditors and hopefully restore public confidence in independent audit reports. It:

1. Prohibits specific "nonaudit" services of public accounting firms as violations of auditor independence.

2. Prohibits public accounting firms from providing audit services to any company whose senior officers (Chief Executive Officer, Chief Financial Officer, Controller) were employed by that accounting firm within the previous 12 months.

3. Requires senior auditors to rotate off an account every five years, and junior auditors every seven years.

4. Requires the external auditor to report to the client's audit committee on specific topics.

5. Requires auditors to disclose all other written communications between management and themselves.

Titles III through XI

Here are some highlights of Titles III through XI.

Title III: Corporate Responsibility

- Requires audit committees to be independent and undertake specified oversight responsibilities.

- Requires CEOs and CFOs to certify quarterly and annual reports to the SEC, including making representations about the effectiveness of their control systems.

- Provides rules of conduct for companies and their officers regarding pension blackout periods—a direct response to the Enron situation where corporate executives were accused of selling their stock while employees had their company stock locked in their pension accounts.

Title IV: Enhanced Financial Disclosures

- Requires companies to provide enhanced disclosures, including a report on the effectiveness of internal controls and procedures for financial reporting (along with external auditor sign-off on that report), and disclosures covering off-balance-sheet transactions—most of the debt Enron hid from analysts and investors was placed in off-balance-sheet accounts and hidden in the smallest footnotes in their financial statements.

Title V: Analyst Conflicts of Interest

- Requires the SEC to adopt rules to address conflicts of interest that can arise when securities analysts recommend securities in research reports and public appearances—each of the "rogue's gallery" of companies in the 2001–2002 scandals had been highly promoted as growth stocks by analysts.

Title VI: Commission Resources and Authority

- Provides additional funding and authority to the SEC to follow through on all the new responsibilities outlined in the act.

Title VII: Studies and Reports

- Directs federal regulatory bodies to conduct studies regarding consolidation of accounting firms, credit rating agencies, and certain roles of investment banks and financial advisors.

Title VIII: Corporate and Criminal Fraud Accountability

- Provides tougher criminal penalties for altering documents, defrauding shareholders, and certain other forms of obstruction of justice and securities fraud. Arthur Andersen's activities in shredding Enron documents directly relates to this topic.
- Protects employees of companies who provide evidence of fraud. Enron and WorldCom were both exposed by the actions of individual employees (see Chapter 7, "Blowing the Whistle").

Title IX: White-Collar Crime Penalty Enhancements

- Provides that any person who attempts to commit white-collar crimes will be treated under the law as if the person had committed the crime.
- Requires CEOs and CFOs to certify their periodic reports and imposes penalties for certifying a misleading or fraudulent report.

Title X: Corporate Tax Returns

- Conveys the sense of the Senate that the CEO should sign a company's federal income tax return.

Title XI: Corporate Fraud and Accountability

- Provides additional authority to regulatory bodies and courts to take various actions, including fines or imprisonment, with regard to tampering with records, impeding official proceedings, taking extraordinary payments, retaliating against corporate whistleblowers, and certain other matters involving corporate fraud.

ETHICAL dilemma

CASE 6.2 An Unethical Way to Fix Corporate Ethics?

Foxes Guarding the Henhouse?

The Sarbanes-Oxley Act, which the United States enacted in an atmosphere of extraordinary agitation in 2002, is one of the most influential—and controversial—pieces of corporate legislation ever to have hit a statute book. Its original aim, on the face of it, was modest: to improve the accountability of managers to shareholders, and [then] calm the raging crisis of confidence in American capitalism aroused by scandals at Enron, WorldCom, and other companies. The law's methods, however, were anything but modest, and its implications . . . are going to be far-reaching.

The cost of all this [new oversight] is steep. A survey by the FEI, an association of top financial executives, found that companies paid an average of $2.4 million more for their audits [in 2004] than they had anticipated (and far more than the statute's designers had envisaged). . . . This result underlines a notable and unintended consequence of the legislation: it has provided a bonanza for accountants and auditors—a profession thought to be much at fault in the scandals that inspired the law, and which the statute sought to rein in and supervise.

Already reduced in number by consolidation and the demise of Arthur Andersen, the big accounting firms are now known more often as the Final Four than the Big Four, since any further reduction is thought unlikely.

Who's Looking Out for the Little Guy?

Smaller companies without access to the internal resources (or funds to pay for external resources) to comply with Sarbanes-Oxley are being particularly hard-hit by the legislation, even though the transgressions that prompted the statute in the first place came from large, publicly traded organizations. This is not to suggest that smaller firms don't face their own ethical problems—it just seems that they are expected to carry an administrative burden that is equal to that of their much larger counterparts.

Not Very Neighborly

Sarbanes-Oxley applies to all companies that issue securities under U.S. federal securities statutes, whether headquartered within the United States or not. Thus, in addition to U.S.-based firms, approximately 1,300 foreign firms from 59 countries fall under the law's jurisdiction.

Reactions to SOX from this quarter were swift. Some foreign companies that had previously contemplated offering securities in the U.S. market reconsidered in light of the conflicts they believe SOX created. For example, in October 2002, Porsche AG announced it would not list its shares on the New York Stock Exchange.

Too Much Trouble— Susan Makes a Decision

Susan was beginning to realize that the Sarbanes-Oxley Act was a mixed blessing. Greater scrutiny of corporate financial reports was meant to reassure investors and it was certainly bringing her firm plenty of business, but now she was faced with this "small favor" to her boss. On the face of it, she couldn't really understand why they just didn't tell this guy that they only worked with clients worth a dollar figure that was higher than his company's valuation and be done with it, but Thompson was so paranoid about their reputation and he was convinced that the next big client was always just around the corner.

Susan spent a couple of hours reviewing the file. Thompson's assessment had been accurate—this was a simple audit with no real earning potential for the company. If they weren't so busy, they could probably assign a junior team—her team perhaps—and knock this out in a few days, but Thompson had bigger fish to fry.

Susan thought for a moment about asking Thompson to let her put a small team together to do this one, but then she realized that by not delivering on the "small favor" he had asked, she could be ruining her chances for getting assigned to some of the bigger audits down the road. So she ran the numbers, multiplied them by four, and submitted the price quotation.

Unfortunately, the quotation was so outrageous that the small business client complained to the PCAOB, which promptly wrote a letter demanding a full explanation of Susan's company's pricing schedule. . . .

1. What could Susan have done differently here?

2. What do you think will happen now?

3. What will be the consequences for Susan, Steven Thompson, and their auditing firm?

A company press release identified the passage of SOX as the "critical factor" for this decision and singled out CEO and CFO certification of financial statements for criticism. After recounting the process Porsche uses to prepare, review, and approve its financial reports, the release concluded that "any special treatment of the Chairman of the Board of Management (i.e., Porsche's CEO) and the Director of Finance would be illogical because of the intricate network within which the decision-making process exists; it would be irreconcilable with German law."

1. SOX has introduced sweeping changes in the name of enforcing corporate ethics. Is it really a "fair" piece of legislation? Explain your answer.

2. Do U.S. ethical problems give us the right to demand ethical controls from international companies based outside the United States?

3. Does the decision to increase auditing requirements seem to be an ethical solution to the problem of questionable audits? Explain your requirements.

4. If there were more than four large accounting firms in the marketplace, would that make the decision more ethical? Explain your answer.

Source: "A Price Worth Paying?" *The Economist*, May 19, 2005.

Section 404 of the Sarbanes-Oxley Act (listed as Title IV in this chapter) is estimated to have generated auditing fees in the hundreds of millions of dollars—all in the hope of enforcing ethical conduct in U.S. organizations. The

13. Explain the role of the PCAOB.

14. Which title requires CEOs and CFOs to certify quarterly and annual reports to the SEC?

15. Which title protects employees of companies who provide evidence of fraud?

16. What are the five key requirements for auditor independence?

legislation was swift and wide-ranging and was specifically designed to restore investor confidence in what, for a brief period, appeared to be financial markets that were run with two primary goals: corruption and greed.

The danger with such a rapid response is that key issues have a tendency to be overlooked in the eagerness to demonstrate responsiveness and decisiveness. In this case, the question of whether you can really legislate ethics was never answered.

What SOX delivers is a collection of tools and penalties to punish offenders with enough severity to put others off the idea of bending or breaking the rules in the future, and enough policies and procedures to ensure that any future corporate criminals are going to have to work a lot harder to earn their money than the folks at Enron, WorldCom, and the rest—there are a lot more people watching now.

However, SOX does not help you to create an ethical corporate culture or to hire an effective and ethical board of directors—you still have to do that for yourself. Just be sure to remember that there are now a lot more penalties and people waiting to catch you if you don't.

Dispatch 2008

In September and October 2008, financial markets around the world suffered a severe crash as the consequences of aggressive lending to subprime borrowers in a deregulated environment came back to haunt companies that, as recently as a few months earlier, had reported record earnings based on these questionable lending practices. Some companies, such as JP Morgan Chase (which purchased the assets of Bear Stearns and Washington Mutual at fire sale prices) and Wells Fargo (which purchased Wachovia Bank at an equally discounted price), were able to benefit from this downturn, but two companies in particular came to exemplify a new round of corporate arrogance and questionable ethics that earned them a place in the rogue's gallery previously occupied by such infamous companies as Enron, World-Com, and HealthSouth.

AIG (American Insurance Group), formerly one of the world's largest insurance companies, received a

The financial crisis that began in fall 2008 had an impact that will likely affect markets for some time.

lifeline loan of $85 billion from the U.S. government in September 2008, followed by an additional $ 37.8 billion in October 2008. The need for the rescue funding (which AIG was expected to repay by selling pieces of its global business) followed the company's descent into near-bankruptcy after it invested extensively in complicated financial contracts used to underwrite mortgage-backed securities.

Intervening to rescue a venerable name in the finance industry could be justified on the basis of a need to restore stability at a time of extreme global instability, but when two senior executives for AIG—Chief Executive Martin J. Sullivan and Chairman Robert Willumstad—appeared before the House Oversight and Government Reform Committee, questions focused less on the company's recovery strategy and more on the lack of oversight and poor financial judgment that got them into the mess in the first place.

The decision to proceed with a celebratory sales meeting in California for the top sales agents of AIG's life insurance subsidiary, with a budget for the event of $440,000, only one week after the government came forward with the $85 billion bailout loan, drew particular criticism from members of the committee. In addition, Mr. Sullivan's positive comments, recorded in December 2007, reassuring investors of AIG's financial health only days after receiving warnings from company auditors about the company's exposure to these risky mortgage contracts drew severe criticism from the committee.

In November 2008, the Federal Reserve and the Treasury Department coordinated an even larger deal for AIG that raised the overall cost of the rescue to $152.5 billion, after the company petitioned that the sale of assets to repay the loan would take longer than originally anticipated. After announcing a $25 billion loss for the third quarter of 2008, AIG was able to negotiate a reduction in the original bailout loan from $85 billion to only $60 billion, along with a reduction in the interest rate on that loan. The additional $37.8 billion loan was replaced by an outright purchase of $40 billion of AIG stock as part of the Treasury's $700 billion bailout package—the so-called Troubled Asset Relief Program (TARP). In addition, the Federal Reserve purchased $22.5 billion of the company's mortgage-backed securities and added an additional $30 billion to underwrite the complicated financial contracts that had led to AIG's near collapse.

Lehman Brothers Holdings, an investment house that had historically been held in the same high regard as AIG, did not fare as well in this financial crisis. For reasons known only to the government, Lehman did not receive a bailout loan like AIG's and collapsed in the summer of 2008. When Chief Executive Richard S. Fuld, Jr., appeared before the House Oversight and Government Reform Committee in October 2008, questions focused on the same issue of reassurances of financial health in the face of audited reports indicating extreme risk exposures, and, in particular, Mr. Fuld's highly lucrative compensation package with Lehman—a total of almost $500 million in salary and bonus payments over the last eight years of his employment with the company.

It is ironic and alarming that the enactment of the Sarbanes-Oxley Act, supposedly to prevent the recurrence of the type of corporate malfeasance that Enron and WorldCom came to exemplify, should be followed so quickly by evidence that the lessons from the days of Enron remain unlearned. At the time of writing, it remains unclear as to whether calls for prosecution of the chief executives of AIG and Lehman under the Sarbanes-Oxley legislation will be answered. There appears to be evidence that the requirement that CEOs and CFOs be personally accountable for the accuracy of any and all financial reports was not met in either case, but whether the government will choose to place a priority on this point in the face of a more pressing need to restore confidence in an unstable global financial market remains to be seen.

[KEY TERMS]

[REVIEW QUESTIONS]

1. Which is the most effective piece of legislation for enforcing ethical business practices: FCPA, DII, FSGO, or SOX? Explain your answer.

2. "The FCPA has too many exceptions to be an effective deterrent to unethical business practices." Do you agree or disagree with this statement? Explain your answer.

3. Do you think the requirement that CEOs and CFOs sign off on their company accounts will increase investor confidence in those accounts? Why or why not?

4. Was Sarbanes-Oxley an appropriate response to the corporate misconduct that was being uncovered at the time? Why or why not?

[REVIEW EXERCISE]

Universal Industries. Universal Industries is in desperate need of a large contract to boost its declining U.S. revenues. The company doesn't have a lot of international exposure, despite its ambitious name, but its chief operating officer may be about to change that. By coincidence, at a recent class reunion, he ran into an old classmate who was a high-ranking federal official responsible for a lot of the bidding for large defense contracts. After several rounds of drinks, the classmate began talking about his latest projects.

Universal has done a lot of defense work as a subcontractor for the major players in the industry, and the COO was able to leverage that experience to use his insider information to get Universal added to the list for several requests for proposal (RFPs) on a large expansion of a Middle Eastern military base.

To strengthen its position in the bidding process, several key Universal operatives made unpublicized visits to the towns surrounding the base and, in return for gifts of cash and other favors to local businessmen and politicians, managed to tie up the exclusive services of several local contractors, making it almost impossible for the other contenders to meet the requirements of the RFPs. The COO was equally generous in his gift to the daughter of his classmate in recognition of his help in getting the inside information.

Unfortunately, even though the new military contracts were going to provide more than enough money to boost Universal's performance numbers, they weren't going to go into effect until the following quarter. After a behind-closed-doors discussion, the senior management team decided that Universal would adjust some of its fourth-quarter expenses in order to hit the price target that the analysts were expecting. The team fully expected that the revenue from the military contracts would allow them to make up for the adjustments in the next financial year.

However, since Universal's annual revenue exceeded $1.4 billion, the CEO and CFO were required to put their signatures on the financial reports confirming their authenticity.

After a couple of sleepless nights, and confident that the military contracts would help them fix all this in the end, they both signed.

1. Identify the ethical transgressions in this case.
2. Which piece of legislation would apply to each transgression?
3. What would be the penalties for each transgression?
4. If Universal could prove that it had a compliance program in place, how would that affect the penalties?

INTERNET EXERCISE

Locate the Web site for Berlin-based Transparency International (TI).

1. What is the stated mission of TI?
2. Explain the Corruptions Perception Index.
3. Who are the least and most corrupt countries on the index?
4. Explain the Global Corruption Barometer.

TEAM EXERCISES

1. **Protecting your people at all costs.** Your company is a major fruit processor that maintains long-term contracts with plantation owners in Central America to guarantee supplies of high quality produce. Many of those plantations are in politically unstable areas and your U.S.-based teams travel to those regions at high personal risk. You have been contacted by a representative from one of the local groups of Freedom Fighters demanding that you make a "donation" to their cause in return for the guaranteed protection of the plantations with which you do business. The representative makes it very clear that failure to pay the donation could put your team on the ground at risk of being kidnapped and held for ransom. Your company is proud of its compliance with all aspects of the FCPA and the revised FSGO legislation. Divide into two groups and argue your case *for* and *against* paying this donation.

2. **Budgeting for bribes.** You are a midlevel manager for the government of a small African nation that relies heavily on oil revenues to run the country's budget. The recent increase in the price of oil has improved your country's budget significantly and, as a result, many new infrastructure projects are being funded with those oil dollars—roads, bridges, schools, and hospitals—which is generating lots of construction projects and very lucrative orders for materials and equipment. However, very little of this new wealth has made its way down to the lower levels of your administration. Historically, your government has always budgeted for very low salaries for government workers in recognition of the fact that their paychecks are often supplemented by payments to expedite the processing of applications and licensing paperwork. Your boss feels strongly that there is no need to raise the salaries of the lower-level government workers since the increase in infrastructure contracts will bring a corresponding

increase in payments to those workers, and, as he pointed out, "companies that want our business will be happy to make those payments." Divide into two groups and argue *for* and *against* the continuation of this arrangement.

3. **The pros and cons of SOX.** Divide into two teams. One team must defend the introduction of Sarbanes-Oxley as a federal deterrent to corporate malfeasance. The other team must criticize the legislation as being ineffective and an administrative burden.

4. **The key components of SOX.** Divide into groups of three or four. Distribute the 11 sections of SOX reviewed in this chapter. Each group must prepare a brief presentation outlining the relative importance of their section to the overall impact of SOX and the prohibition of unethical business practices.

discussion EXERCISE 6.1

PONZI SCHEMES

The practice of providing old (or early) investors above-average returns on their investment with funds raised from new (or late) investors, in the absence of any real business operation to generate profits is illegal, unethical, and, regrettably, not a new idea. It used to be referred to as "robbing Peter to pay Paul". In 1899, a New York scam artist named William Miller promised investors returns as high as 520 percent in one year based on his supposed insider information on profitable businesses. He scammed people out of almost $25 million in today's money before being exposed and jailed for 10 years.

In 1920 the practice was given a new name —Ponzi scheme—in "honor" of Charles Ponzi, an Italian immigrant who, after numerous failed business ventures, began to promote the spectacular returns to be made by buying International Reply Coupons (IRC)—coupons that could be used to purchase stamps in order to reply to a letter, like an international self-addressed envelope—in local currencies, and cashing them in at US currency rates. For example: "a person could buy 66 International Reply Coupons in Rome for the equivalent of $1. Those same 66 coupons would cost $3.30 in Boston," where Ponzi was based. It is debatable whether or not Ponzi genuinely believed that he had stumbled across a real business opportunity—a simplified version of currency trading in a way—but his response was immediate, promising investors returns of 50% on their original investment in just 90 days. However, the opportunity attracted so much money so quickly—as much as $1 million poured into his office in one day—that Ponzi was either unable or unwilling to actually buy the IRCs. Had he tried to do so, he would have realized that there were not enough IRCs in existence to deliver the kinds of returns he was promising his investors. Instead, Ponzi chose to use the funds coming in from new investors to pay out the promised returns to older investors—robbing Peter to pay Paul.

It was only a matter of time before the funds coming in would be insufficient to meet the demands of older investors with their original capital and their 50% return. Ponzi was able to keep the scheme going by encouraging those older investors to keep "rolling over" their investment, but once rumors began to surface about the questionable nature of the Ponzi enterprise, fewer and fewer people opted to rollover, choosing instead to take their money out. At that point the whole system collapsed and Ponzi's business enterprise was exposed as fraudulent. For his brief encounter with fame and fortune, Charles Ponzi eventually served 12 years in prison, and was deported back to Italy. He later emigrated to Brazil, still presumably in search of fame and fortune. He died in 1949 in the charity ward of a Rio de Janeiro hospital with only enough money to his name to cover his burial expenses. His name, however, lives on—the practice of "robbing Peter to pay Paul" was forever replaced with the name "Ponzi scheme".

In subsequent decades, Ponzi has inspired many imitators:

- In 1985, a San Diego currency trader, David Dominelli, convinced more than 1,000 investors to part with $80 million in a classic Ponzi scheme.
- In the 1990s, a Florida church—Greater Ministries International—scammed nearly 20,000 people out of $500 million on the basis of a promise that God would double the money of truly pious investors.
- Lou Pearlman, the theatrical impresario and businessman who launched the screams of thousands of teenage girls with the boy-band N'Sync, stole over $300 million from investors over two decades.
- As recently as January 2009, the Securities and Exchange Commission (SEC) charged an 82-year-old man, Richard Piccoli, with operating a Ponzi scheme that scammed investors out of $17 million over 5 years by promising "safe" returns of only 7% based on real estate investments that were never made.

In December 2008, a formerly highly respected Wall Street money manager, Bernard Madoff, was accused of masterminding a Ponzi scheme on such a grand scale that the practice may well be replaced with the name "Madoff scheme" from this point onwards. The amount of money involved in Madoff's alleged scam is staggering—an estimated total of $50 billion stolen over decades. The story is still unfolding as this case study is being written, with extensive investigations underway by the SEC, and numerous lawsuits are already pending, but what has been established so far presents a story that reveals as much about the wealthy investors who trusted their money to Madoff as it does about the man himself.

Bernard Madoff, a low-profile investment professional, former chairman of the NASDAQ stock exchange, and an occasional consultant to the SEC on matters of investment regulation, became a multimillionaire in the early days of computer-based stock trading before he became attracted to the more lucrative business of managing other people's money. He built a reputation of sure and steady returns for his clients, earning the affectionate nickname "T-Bill Bernie" to reflect the same security as investing in government-backed treasury bills. Madoff's success wasn't based on spectacular returns from year to year (he averaged between 10 and 18 percent per year), but rather on consistent solid performance year after year. He didn't market his services aggressively, preferring instead to allow satisfied clients to bring in family members and friends. He generated an aura of exclusivity, often declining to accept investments, which only served to make those potential investors want to invest with him even more.

This perceived exclusivity and a strategic marketing plan that targeted wealthy investors in places like Palm Beach, Florida allowed Madoff to build a solid reputation over decades, attracting high profile investors and large investments from global banks in the hundreds of millions of dollars along the way. However, the financial meltdown at the end of 2008 prompted investors to start withdrawing their funds to meet other obligations, and when Madoff was faced with withdrawal requests totaling almost $7 billion, the carefully constructed scam fell apart in a matter of hours.

In the early emotional days of this exposed and still alleged scandal, one of the primary concerns is the appointment of blame. Who knew what, when, and could this have been prevented? The SEC has come under considerable scrutiny for its role in this. Madoff's operation was examined on 4 separate occasions since 1999, with two detailed investigations launched in 1992 and 2006. No evidence of fraud was uncovered and Madoff received only a mild reprimand for irregularities in paperwork. Now that $50 billion appears to have disappeared, with no trading records available to track the money, there are many questions to be answered.

Boston-based money manager Harry Markopoulos wrote an 18-page letter to the SEC in 2005 identifying 29 different "red flags" about Madoff's operation, basically questioning both the mathematical improbability of such solid returns year after year, and suggesting that the only way to achieve those returns was to either trade on insider information or create a totally fictitious trading record.

Supposedly "sophisticated" investors, who gave Madoff large sums to invest from pension funds, family trusts, and endowments, have been wiped out. Even worse, many individual investors who entrusted their savings to other money managers who then invested that money with Madoff, have also lost substantial amounts in an investment they never even knew they had.

Much will be written about Madoff's psychological state of mind in allegedly masterminding such a complex scam over decades, and, more importantly, fooling so many of the elite of Wall Street and the regulatory mechanisms that are supposed to be in place to prevent such a scam from ever taking place. It remains to be seen whether this information will produce any dramatic changes in the regulatory framework of the financial markets to ensure that a Ponzi scheme on such a staggering scale never occurs again.

Discussion Questions

1. Why was Madoff occasionally referred to as "T-Bill Bernie"?

2. Charles Ponzi was a working-class Italian immigrant who was eager to find success in America. Bernard Madoff was already a multimillionaire before he started his alleged scheme. Does that make one more unethical than the other? Why or why not?

3. Explain how a Ponzi scheme works.

4. Does the fact that Madoff offered less outrageous returns (10–18% per year) on investments compared to Ponzi's promise of a 50% return in only 90 days, make Madoff any less unethical? Why or why not?

5. Can the investors who put their money in Madoff's funds without any due diligence, often on the basis of a tip from a friend or a "friend-of-a-friend," really be considered victims in this case? Why or why not?

6. What should investors with Bernard Madoff have done differently here?

Source: Altman, A., "Ponzi Schemes," *Time.com*, December 15, 2008. Gapper, J., "Wall Street insiders and fools' gold," *The Financial Times*, December 17, 2008. Sloan, A., "Commentary: The real lesson of the Madoff case," *CNN.com*, January 9, 2009. Zuckoff, M., "What Madoff could learn from Ponzi," *CNNmoney.com*, January 13, 2009. Chew, R., "Bernie Madoff's Victims: Why Some Have No Recourse," *Time.com*, January 12, 2009.

INDIA'S ENRON

In December 2008, one of the largest players in India's outsourcing and information technology sectors, Satyam Computer Services, fell from grace with such force and speed that the reverberations are being felt around the globe. Ironically, the name 'Satyam' means "truth" in Sanskrit, but the company, founded by brothers Ramalinga and Ramu Raju, now has a new nickname: India's Enron.

Founded in 1987, Satyam was positioned to take full advantage of the capabilities of satellite-based broadband communications, allowing them to serve clients across the globe from its offices in Hyderabad. The rising demand for computer programmers to fix code in software programs in advance of Y2K fueled an aggressive growth plan for the company. It was listed on the Bombay Stock Exchange in 1991, and achieved a listing on the New York Stock Exchange in May 2001. By 2006, Satyam had about 23,000 employees and was reporting annual revenues of $1 billion. Growth continued as the company served expanding needs for outsourced services from American companies looking to control and preferably reduce operating costs. By 2008, Satyam was reporting over $2 billion in revenue with 53,000 employees in 63 countries worldwide. This made the company the fourth-largest software services provider alongside such competitors as WiPro Technologies, Infosys, and HCL. It was serving almost 700 clients, including 185 Fortune 500 companies, generating more than half of its revenue from the United States. Satyam's client roster included such names as General Electric, Cisco, Ford Motor Company, Nestlé, and the United States Government.

Prominence in the software services sector brought with it increased attention and a growing reputation. In 2007, Ramalinga Raju was the recipient of Ernst & Young's "Entrepreneur of the Year" award. In September 2008 the company received the Golden Peacock Award for Corporate Governance from the World Council for Corporate Governance, which endorsed Satyam as a leader in ethical management practices.

Signs that there were problems at Satyam first appeared in October 2008 when it was revealed that the World Bank had banned the company from pursuing any service contracts after evidence was uncovered that Satyam employees had offered "improper benefits to bank staff" and "failed to account for all fees charged" to the World Bank. WiPro Technologies had also been banned by the World Bank in 2007 for "offering shares of its 2000 initial public offering to World Bank employees," so Satyam appeared to have some company in the arena of questionable business practices in the software solutions sector.

However, the situation escalated in December 2008 after Satyam's board voted against a proposed deal for Satyam to buy two construction companies for $1.6 billion. The Raju brothers held ownership stakes in both companies, and they were run by Ramalinga Raju's sons. Four directors resigned in response to the proposed deal, and Satyam stock was punished by investors, forcing the brothers to sell their own stock as the falling share price sparked margin calls on their investment accounts. Apparently the dire financial situation prompted Ramalinga Raju to confess in a four-and-a-half-page letter to the board of Satyam Computer Services that the company had been overstating profits for several years and that $1.6 billion in assets simply did not exist. It did not take long for investors to piece the information together that the proposed $1.6 billion purchase of the construction companies would have, conveniently, filled the $1.6 billion hole in Satyam's accounts.

In his confession, Raju attempted to address accusations of a premeditated fraud by stating that "What started as a marginal gap between actual operating profit and the one reflected in the books of accounts continued to grow over the years. It has attained unmanageable proportions as the size of the company operations grew," he wrote. "It was like riding a tiger, not knowing how to get off without being eaten."

The analogy of being eaten by a tiger certainly seems appropriate. The scandal has had repercussions for the software services sector as a whole, casting shadows on Satyam's competitors, and also on India's corporate governance framework. As with Enron's collapse, attention has immediately turned to the role of the accounting company responsible for auditing Satyam's accounts and, allegedly, failing to notice that $1.6 billion in assets did not exist. For Enron it was Arthur Andersen, and the accounting firm did not survive. For Satyam it is Pricewaterhouse Coopers, which appears to have certified that Satyam had $1.1 billion in cash in its accounts, when the company really had only $78 million.

The response of Indian authorities has been immediate—jail for the founders of Satyam, and the swift appointment of an interim board of more reputable businessmen as the country scrambles to restore its reputation and reassure investors and customers alike that Satyam was a regrettable exception rather than a common example of unethical business practices in the face of competitive pressures in a global market.

Much remains to be uncovered. How have Satyam's clients been affected by this? Cisco is already on record as stating that it did not expect any "material impact." For Satyam's competitors, the future is a little less clear. Reassuring investors that they have better financial controls than Satyam will help them win clients away from Satyam in the long term, but for now, the entire software services industry is under considerable scrutiny, as is India's control over its corporations that have risen to global prominence in less than two decades.

Discussion Questions

1. Does Ramalinga Raju's assertion that this fraud only "started as a marginal gap," change the ethical question here? Would the situation be different if there was evidence that there had been a deliberate intent to deceive investors from the beginning?

2. The analogy of riding a tiger suggests that the situation got out of control for the Raju brothers, but the ban by the World Bank implies that there were other questionable business practices at Satyam. What do you think about the company? Is it fair to call it "India's Enron"?

3. Why do you think Satyam's board of directors refused to support the proposed purchase of the construction companies?

4. Outline the similarities between the Enron scandal and Satyam Computer Services' situation.

5. Do you think Pricewaterhouse Coopers will suffer the same fate as Arthur Andersen did after the Enron scandal? Why or why not?

6. America responded to Enron with the Sarbanes-Oxley Act. Do you think the Indian Government will have a similar response? Explain.

Source: Timmons, H., "Financial Scandal at Outsourcing Company Rattles a Developing Country," *The New York Times*, January 8, 2009. Corcoran, E., "The Seeds of the Satyam Scandal," *Forbes*, January 8, 2009. Balachandran, S.V., "The Satyam Scandal," *Forbes*, January 7, 2009. Kahn, J, Timmons, H, Wassener, B., "Board Tries to Chart Path for Outsourcer Hit by Scandal," *The New York Times*, January 13, 2009.

MARTHA STEWART AND IMCLONE SYSTEMS

At the end of December 2001, design guru Martha Stewart, chief executive of Martha Stewart Living Omnimedia, reportedly sold 3,928 shares of stock in a drug company called ImClone Systems. The 3,928 shares represented her entire holding in ImClone, and the sale fetched over $227,000 for Stewart, based on an average selling price of around $58 per share—not a large transaction by Wall Street standards. In fact, such an average sale, out of the millions of transactions that took place that day, should not have drawn any undue attention, until it was revealed that Stewart had a long-standing relationship with the chief executive of ImClone Systems, Dr. Sam Waksal, and that within a day or two of her sale, the Food and Drug Administration (FDA) would announce an unfavorable ruling on ImClone's new cancer drug, Erbitux, which sent the stock plummeting from a high of $75 per share to an eventual low of only $5.24 per share in September 2002.

Further investigation revealed that members of Waksal's immediate family also sold blocks of shares in the two days preceding the FDA announcement. One of his daughters sold a block of shares worth $2.5 million, and his other daughter, along with her husband, sold shares worth $300,000. Waksal was unable to complete the sale of almost 80,000 of his own shares in the company. The fact that Waksal had dated Stewart's daughter for years added a further complication to what was rapidly becoming a very questionable business arrangement.

The Erbitux drug was believed to hold tremendous potential as a cancer treatment—so much so that Bristol-Myers Squibb had agreed to pay $2 billion in 2001 for the rights to the drug, prompting the increase in the share price to $70. The subsequent collapse in the share price also impacted shares in Stewart's own company—after Waksal was arrested on accusations of insider trading in his own company's shares, the shares of Martha Stewart Living Omnimedia fell by 12 percent.

At the time of Waksal's arrest, Stewart, who had yet to be accused of any wrongdoing, offered a defense to the media that she had an arms' length relationship to the sale of the stock—in other words she had an existing order with her broker to sell the stock if it went below $60 per share, and so this transaction was automatic rather than an event prompted by insider information from her friend Sam Waksal. However, further investigation revealed that even though the stock price had fallen below $60 on other occasions in the months preceding the sale, there was no automatic sale of the shares as Stewart had claimed. In addition, it was revealed that Stewart had placed a call to her broker, Peter Bacanovic, during a refueling stop on a flight to Mexico on her private jet. She made a call to Waksal during that same stop, and, by coincidence, Bacanovic was also the broker for Waksal and his two daughters. He was subsequently suspended by Merrill Lynch.

After numerous attempts by her legal team to fight on her behalf, Stewart was required to deliver more than 1,000 pages of documents—including email messages from her laptop and phone records—to the congressional committee investigating the sale of her ImClone stock in August 2002. She was eventually indicted, not for the sale of the stock based on insider trading, but for obstruction of justice for lying to federal regulators under oath about the details surrounding the transaction. She served a five-month prison sentence and an additional five months under house arrest. Bacanovic also served a five-month sentence for crimes related to the sale of the stock on behalf of Stewart and members of the Waksal family; he was banned from the securities industry and paid a $75,000 fine to the Securities and Exchange Commission (SEC) to settle insider trading charges. Waksal himself was sentenced to an 87-month prison sentence, and he settled the SEC insider trading case against him and his father for more than $5 million.

Ironically, Erbitux proved to be more persistent than many had imagined. After being rejected by the FDA in 2001 on the basis of "shoddy data from ImClone", the drug received formal approval in February 2004. The impact on ImClone's share price was immediate, and by July 2008, more than six years after the now infamous sale of Stewart's shares, the price of ImClone was once again back above $60 per share. The original transaction saved Stewart about $45,000 in losses by selling before the FDA rejection was announced. In retrospect, the cost to her company, her investors, and, some would argue, to her reputation, was much higher.

Discussion Questions

1. Identify the ethical transgressions that took place in this case.

2. When the connection between ImClone Systems and Martha Stewart was first revealed, analysts speculated that she would emerge relatively unscathed from any investigation, "forced at worst to return any profit she made from selling ImClone." Does her subsequent jail sentence imply that she was targeted as a high profile test case of insider trading? Why or why not?

3. Does the size of Stewart's transaction (3,928 shares for about $227,000) make her behavior any more or less ethical than that of Dr. Waksal's daughter who sold $2.5 million in ImClone shares at the same time as Stewart? Explain your answer.

4. What would prompt a highly regarded public figure such as Martha Stewart to obstruct the course of justice by failing to reveal the true nature of her sales transaction with the ImClone stock?

5. What do you think would have happened if Stewart had cooperated with federal investigators?

6. If Martha Stewart's sale of ImClone stock really was a high-profile test case, what message do you think it sent to other high-profile investors?

Sources: Andrew Pollack, "Martha Stewart Said to Sell Shares before FDA Ruling," *The New York Times*, June 7, 2002; Constance L. Hays, "ImClone Case Drags Martha Stewart Shares Down," *The New York Times*, June 13, 2002; Andrew Pollack, "ImClone Cancer Drug behind Martha Stewart Trial Approved by FDA," *The New York Times*, February 13, 2004; Jenny Anderson, "Two Are Charged over Trading in ImClone," *The New York Times*, March 10, 2005; Landon Thomas, Jr., "The Broker Who Fell to Earth," *The New York Times*, October 13, 2006.

chapter 7

Blowing the Whistle

> *The word whistle-blower suggests that you're a tattletale or that you're somehow disloyal . . . But I wasn't disloyal in the least bit. People were dying. I was loyal to a higher order of ethical responsibility.*
>
> —Dr. Jeffrey Wigand, The Insider

LEARNING OBJECTIVES

After studying this chapter, you should be able to:

1. Explain the term *whistle-blower*.

2. Explain the difference between internal and external whistle-blowing.

3. Understand the different motivations of a whistle-blower.

4. Evaluate the possible consequences of ignoring the concerns of a whistle-blower.

5. Recommend how to build internal policies to address the needs of whistle-blowers.

6. Analyze the possible risks to oneself in becoming a whistle-blower.

frontline focus

Good Money

Ben is a sales team leader at a large chain of tire stores. The company is aggressive and is opening new stores every month. Ben is very ambitious and sees plenty of opportunities to move up in the organization—especially if he is able to make a name for himself as a star salesman.

As with any retail organization, Ben's company is driven by sales, and it is constantly experimenting with new sales campaigns and incentive programs for its salespeople. Ben didn't expect this morning's sales meeting to be any different—a new incentive tied to a new campaign, supported by a big media campaign in the local area.

Ben's boss, John, didn't waste any time in getting to the point of the meeting:

"OK guys, I have some big news. Rather than simply negotiating short-term incentives on specific brands to generate sales, the company has signed an exclusive contract with Benfield Tires to take every tire produced in the new Voyager line. That exclusive contract comes with a huge discount based on serious volume. In other words, the more tires we sell, the more money we'll make—and I'm talking about good money for the company and very good bonus money for you—so put everybody into these tires. If we do well in this first contract with Benfield, there could be other exclusives down the road. This could be the beginning of something big for us."

John then laid out the details on the sales incentive and showed Ben and his fellow team leaders how they could earn thousands of dollars in bonuses over the next couple of months if they pushed the new Benfield Voyagers.

Ben could certainly use the money, but he was concerned about pushing a new tire model so aggressively when it was an unknown in the marketplace. He decided to talk to their most experienced tire mechanic, Rick. Rick had worked for the company for over 25 years—so long that many of the younger guys joked that he either had tire rubber in his veins or had apprenticed on Henry Ford's Model T.

"So, Rick, what do you think about these new Benfield Voyagers?" asked Ben. "Are they really such a good deal for our customers or are they just a moneymaker for us?"

Rick was very direct in his response: "I took a look at some of the specs on them and they don't look good. I think Benfield is sacrificing quality to cut costs. By the standards of some of our other suppliers, these tires would qualify as 'seconds'—and pretty bad ones too. You couldn't pay me to put them on my car—they're good for 15,000 miles at the most. We're taking a big risk promoting these tires as our top model."

1. If Ben decides to raise concerns about the product quality of the Benfield Voyagers, he will become a whistle-blower. The difference between internal and external whistle-blowing is explained on page 162. Which approach should Ben follow if he does decide to raise his concerns?

2. The five conditions that must exist for whistle-blowing to be ethical are outlined on page 163. Has Rick given Ben enough information to be concerned about the Benfield Voyagers?

3. What should Ben do now?

Blowing the Whistle

In August 2001, Sherron Watkins, an accountant in the finance department of Enron, sent an email to Chairman and CEO Kenneth Lay warning of potential problems with the company's accounting practices. By the end of December 2001, Enron had filed for bankruptcy; its stock, which had once traded as high as $90 a share, was worthless; and more than 4,000 employees had lost not only their jobs, but also their retirement funds, which had been invested primarily in Enron stock.

Watkins' anonymous memo to Lay after the departure of Enron CEO Jeffrey Skilling read as follows:

Dear Mr. Lay,

Has Enron become a risky place to work? For those of us who didn't get rich over the last few years, can we afford to stay? . . . I am incredibly nervous that we will implode in a wave of accounting scandals. My eight years of Enron work history will be worth nothing on my résumé, the business world will consider the past successes as nothing but an elaborate accounting hoax. (Jeffrey) Skilling is resigning now for "personal reasons" but I think he wasn't having fun, looked down the road and knew this stuff was unfixable and would rather abandon ship now than resign in shame in 2 years. . . . We are under too much scrutiny and there are probably one or two disgruntled "redeployed" employees who know enough about the "funny" accounting to get us in trouble.

Sherron Watkins' follow-up memo to Ken Lay and others, after her responsibility for the first anonymous memo had been revealed expanded upon her original message:

One of the overriding basic principles of accounting is that if you explain the "accounting treatment" to a man on the street, would you influence his investing decisions? Would he sell or buy the stock based on a thorough understanding of the facts? If so, you best present it correctly and/or change the accounting. . . . My concern is that the footnotes don't adequately explain the transactions.

I firmly believe that executive management of the company must have a clear and precise knowledge of these transactions and they must have the transactions reviewed by objective experts in the fields of securities laws and accounting. I believe Ken Lay deserves the right to judge for himself what he believes the probabilities of discovery to be and the estimated damages to the company from those discoveries and decide one of two courses of action:

1. The probability of discovery is low enough and the estimated damage too great; therefore we find a way to quietly and quickly reverse, unwind, write down these positions/transactions.
2. The probability of discovery is too great, the estimated damage to the company too great; therefore we must quantify, develop damage containment plans, and disclose.

I firmly believe that the probability of discovery significantly increased with (Jeffrey) Skilling's shocking departure. Too many people are looking for a smoking gun.

What Is Whistle-Blowing?

When an employee discovers evidence of malpractice or misconduct in an organization, he or she faces an ethical dilemma. On the one hand, the employee must consider the "rightness" of his or her actions in raising concerns about this misconduct, and the extent to which such actions will benefit both the organization and the public good. On the other hand, the employee must balance a public duty with a corresponding duty to his or her employer to honor the trust and loyalty placed in him or her by the organization.

So, some serious choices have to be made here. First, the employee can choose to "let it slide" or "turn a blind eye"—a choice that will relate directly to the corporate culture under which the organization operates. An open and trusting culture would encourage employees to speak out for the greater good of the company and their fellow employees. A closed and autocratic culture, on the other hand, would lead employees to believe that it would be wiser not to draw attention to themselves, to simply keep their mouths shut. However, if an employee's personal value system prompts him or her to speak out on the misconduct, the employee immediately takes on the role of a **whistle-blower.**

The employee then faces a second and equally important choice. One option is to bring the misconduct to the attention of a manager or supervisor and take the complaint through appropriate channels within the organization. We refer to this option as **internal whistle-blowing.** If the employee chooses to go outside the organization and bring the misconduct to the attention of law-enforcement officials or the media, we refer to this decision as **external whistle-blowing.**

Whistle-Blower An employee who discovers corporate misconduct and chooses to bring it to the attention of others.

Internal Whistle-Blowing When an employee discovers corporate misconduct and brings it to the attention of his or her supervisor, who then follows established procedures to address the misconduct within the organization.

External Whistle-Blowing When an employee discovers corporate misconduct and chooses to bring it to the attention of law-enforcement agencies and/or the media.

The Ethics of Whistle-Blowing

It may be argued that whistle-blowers provide an invaluable service to their organizations and the general public. The discovery of illegal activities before the situation is revealed in the media could potentially save organizations millions of dollars in fines and lost revenue from the inevitable damage to their corporate reputation. The discovery of potential harm to consumers (from pollution or product-safety issues, for example) offers immeasurable benefit to the general public. From this perspective, it is easy to see why the media often applauds whistle-blowers as models of honor and integrity at a time when integrity in the business world seems to be in very short supply.

However, in contrast to the general perception that whistle-blowers are brave men and women putting their careers and personal lives at risk to do the right thing, some argue that such actions are not brave at all—they are, it is argued, actions motivated by money or by the personal egos of "loose cannons" and "troublemakers" who challenge the policies and practices of their employers while claiming to act as the corporate conscience. In addition, rather than being viewed as performing a praiseworthy act, whistle-blowers are often severely criticized as informers, 'sneaks,' spies, or 'squealers' who have in some way breached the trust and loyalty they owe to their employers.

☑ PROGRESS CHECK QUESTIONS

1. What is a whistle-blower?

2. What is internal whistle-blowing?

3. What is external whistle-blowing?

4. Is whistle-blowing a good thing?

When Is Whistle-Blowing Ethical?

Whistle-blowing is appropriate—ethical—under five conditions[1]:

1. When the company, through a product or decision, will cause serious and considerable harm to the public (as consumers or bystanders), or break existing laws, the employee should report the organization.

2. When the employee identifies a serious threat of harm, he or she should report it and state his or her moral concern.

3. When the employee's immediate supervisor does not act, the employee should exhaust the internal procedures and chain of command to the board of directors.

4. The employee must have documented evidence that is convincing to a reasonable, impartial observer that his or her view of the situation is accurate, and evidence that the firm's practice, product, or policy seriously threatens and puts in danger the public or product user.

5. The employee must have valid reasons to believe that revealing the wrongdoing to the public will result in the changes necessary to remedy the situation. The chance of succeeding must be equal to the risk and danger the employee takes to blow the whistle.

When Is Whistle-Blowing Unethical?

If there is evidence that the employee is motivated by the opportunity for financial gain or media attention, or that the employee is carrying out an individual vendetta against the company, then the legitimacy of the act of whistle-blowing must be questioned.

The potential for financial gain in some areas of corporate whistle-blowing can be considerable:

- On November 30, 2005, New York City's Beth Israel Hospital agreed to pay $72.9 million to resolve allegations from a former hospital executive that it falsified Medicare cost reports from 1992 to 2001. The case stemmed from a 2001 whistle-blower lawsuit filed in the U.S. District Court in New York City by former Beth Israel vice president of financial services, Najmuddin Pervez. Mr. Pervez is expected to receive 20 percent of the recovery amount, around $15 million.[2]

- Douglas Durand, former vice president of sales for TAP Pharmaceutical Products, received a $126 million settlement from the U.S. government after filing suit against his employer and a TAP

Douglas Durand

rival, the former Zeneca, Inc., accusing both companies of overcharging the federal government's Medicare program by tens of millions of dollars.[3]

Whether the motivation to speak out and reveal the questionable behavior comes from a personal ethical decision or the potential for a substantial financial windfall will probably never be completely verified, but the threat of losing your job or becoming alienated from colleagues by speaking out against your employer must be diminished by the knowledge that some financial security will likely result. Whether the choice is based on ethical or financial considerations, the key point is that you had better be very sure of your facts and your evidence had better be irrefutable before crossing that line.

✓ PROGRESS CHECK QUESTIONS

5. List five conditions for whistle-blowing to be considered ethical.

6. Under what condition could whistle-blowing be considered unethical?

7. If you blow the whistle on a company for a personal vendetta against another employee but receive no financial reward, is that more or less ethical than doing it just for the money?

8. Would the lack of any financial reward make you more or less willing to consider being a whistle-blower? Why?

The Year of the Whistle-Blower

Since examples of internal whistle-blowing rarely receive media attention, it is impossible to track the history of such actions. However, external whistle-blowing is a 20th-century phenomenon. One of the first instances of the use of the term *whistle-blower* occurred in 1963 when Otto Otopeka was dismissed from the U.S. State Department after giving classified documents on security risks to the chief counsel of the Senate Subcommittee on Internal Security. In the 1970s, the Watergate scandal broke after former Marine commander Daniel Ellsberg leaked over 7,000 pages of confidential Pentagon documents on government misconduct in the Vietnam conflict to the press, risking life imprisonment to do so; and an anonymous source named Deep Throat (only recently revealed to be Mark Felt, former assistant director of the FBI during the Nixon administration) helped *Washington Post* journalists Bob Woodward and Carl Bernstein expose the extent of government misconduct in attempting to track down Ellsberg.

Public awareness of whistle-blowers reached a peak in 2002 when *Time* magazine awarded its Person of the Year award to three women "of ordinary demeanor but exceptional guts and sense"[4]:

Sherron Watkins, the vice president at Enron Corporation, who, in the summer of 2001, wrote two key emails (quoted at the beginning of this chapter) warning Enron Chairman Ken Lay that it was only a matter of time before the company's creative "accounting treatment" would be discovered and bring the entire organization down.

Coleen Rowley, an FBI staff attorney, who rose to public prominence in May 2002 when she made public a memo to Director Robert Mueller about the frustration and dismissive behavior she faced from the FBI when her Minneapolis, Minnesota, field office argued for the investigation of a suspected terrorist, Zacarias Moussaoui, who was later indicted as a co-conspirator in the September 11, 2001, attacks.

Cynthia Cooper, whose internal auditing team first uncovered questionable accounting practices at WorldCom. Her team's initial estimates placed the discrepancy at $3.8 billion; the final balance was nearer to $11 billion.

ETHICAL dilemma

CASE 7.1 The Insider

With their classic portrayals of good guys against the corporate bad guys, movie portrayals of whistle-blowers are by no means a new idea. Films such as *The China Syndrome, Silkwood,* and *The Insider* have documented the risks and challenges whistle-blowers face in bringing the information they uncover to the general public.

The movie *The Insider* documents the case of Dr. Jeffrey Wigand and his decision to go public with information alleging that his employer, the tobacco

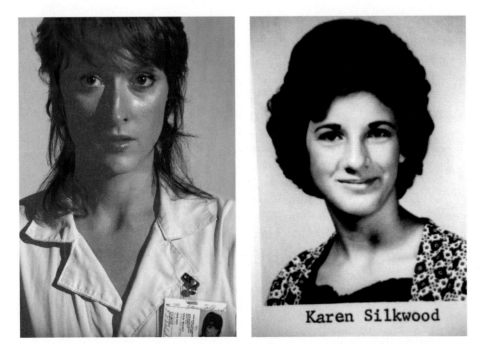

In the 1983 film *Silkwood,* Meryl Streep portrayed Karen Silkwood, a nuclear plant employee who blew the whistle on unsafe practices. The real Karen Silkwood died in an auto accident under mysterious circumstances.

company Brown & Williamson (B&W), was actively manipulating the nicotine content of its cigarettes. Wigand was portrayed by Russell Crowe, and the part of Lowell Bergman, the CBS *60 Minutes* producer who helped Wigand go public, was portrayed by Al Pacino.

The movie captures several key issues that are common to many whistle-blower cases:

- Wigand was initially reticent to speak out about the information—partly out of fear of the impact on his family if he lost his severance package and health benefits under the terms of his confidentiality agreement with B&W, and partly because of his strong sense of integrity in honoring any contracts he had signed. It was only after B&W had chosen to modify the confidentiality agreement after firing Wigand (allegedly for "poor communication skills") that Wigand, angered by B&W's apparent belief that he wouldn't honor the confidentiality agreement he had signed, chose to go public.

- B&W's response was immediate and aggressive. They won a restraining (gag) order against Wigand to prevent him from giving evidence as an expert witness in a case against tobacco companies brought by the State of Mississippi, but he testified anyway. B&W then proceeded to undertake a detailed disclosure of Wigand's background in order to undermine his reputation, eventually releasing a thick report titled "The Misconduct of Jeffrey S. Wigand Available in the Public Record." The extent to which the findings of this investigation were exaggerated was later documented in a *New York Times* newspaper article. The movie portrays Bergman as providing the material for a *New York Times* journalist to refute the B&W claims against Wigand.

- Wigand's testimony was extremely damaging for B&W. He not only accused the CEO of B&W, Thomas Sanderfur, of misrepresentation in stating before congressional hearings tin 1994 that he believed that nicotine was not addictive, but Wigand also claimed that cigarettes were merely "a delivery system for nicotine."

- Even though Wigand's credibility as a witness had been verified, CBS initially chose not to run Wigand's interview with CBS reporter Mike Wallace in fear of a lawsuit from B&W for "tortious interference" (defined as action by a third party in coming between two parties in a contractual relationship—that is, CBS would be held liable for intervening between Wigand and B&W in the confidentiality agreement Wigand had signed). The fact that CBS's parent company was in the final stages of negotiations to sell CBS to the Westinghouse Corporation was seen as evidence of CBS's highly questionable motivation in avoiding the danger of "tortious interference." In reality, the fear of litigation was probably well founded. After ABC had run an equally controversial segment on its *Day One* show accusing Philip Morris of raising nicotine levels in their cigarettes, Philip Morris, along with another tobacco company, R. J. Reynolds, launched a $10 billion lawsuit against ABC, which was forced to apologize and pay the tobacco companies' legal fees (estimated at over $15 million).

- In November 1998, B&W subsequently joined with three other tobacco giants—Philip Morris, R. J. Reynolds, and Lorillard—in signing the Tobacco Master Settlement Agreement (MSA), settling state lawsuits against them in 46 states for recovery of the medical costs of treating smoking-related illnesses. The settlement totaled $206 billion and included provisions that forbade marketing directly or indirectly to children and banned or restricted the use of cartoons, billboards, product placement, or event sponsorship in the marketing of tobacco products.

- As vice president for research and development for B&W, Wigand was a corporate officer for the company and, therefore, the highest-ranking insider ever to turn whistle-blower at the time. His reward for speaking out was that he never reached the $300,000 salary level he held at B&W again. At the time his story went public, he had found employment as a teacher in Louisville, Kentucky, teaching chemistry and Japanese for $30,000 a year—a profession he proudly and happily maintains to this day. His marriage didn't survive the intense media scrutiny and B&W's attempts to discredit him.

- Six years later, Wigand was interviewed by *Fast Company* magazine and he shared his unhappiness with the title of whistle-blower:

"The word whistle-blower suggests that you're a tattletale or that you're somehow disloyal," he says. "But I wasn't disloyal in the least bit. People were dying. I was loyal to a higher order of ethical responsibility."

1. Dr. Wigand was initially unwilling to go public with his information. What caused him to change his mind?
2. Did CBS pursue Wigand's story because it was the right thing to do or because it was a good story?
3. Since CBS played such a large part in bringing Dr. Wigand's story to the public, do you think the network also had an obligation to support him once the story broke? Explain why or why not.
4. Was CBS's decision not to run the interview driven by any ethical concerns?

Source: Elizabeth Gleick, "Where There's Smoke," *Time* 147 (February 12, 1996), p. 54; Ron Scherer, "One Man's Crusade against Tobacco Firms," *Christian Science Monitor* 88, no. 4 (November 30, 1995), p. 3. "Jeffrey Wigand: The Whistle-Blower," *Fast Company*, March 2002.

The Duty to Respond

Whether you believe whistle-blowers to be heroes who face considerable personal hardship to bring the harsh light of media attention to unethical behavior, or you take the opposing view that they are breaking the oath of loyalty to their employer, the fact remains that employees are becoming increasingly willing to respond to any questionable behavior they observe in the workplace. The choice for an employer is to ignore them and face public embarrassment and potentially ruinous financial penalties, or to create an internal system that allows whistle-blowers to be heard and responded to *before* the issue escalates to an external whistle-blowing case. Obviously, responding to whistle-blowers in this context means addressing their concerns, and not, as many employers have decided, firing them.

Prior to 2002, legal protection for whistle-blowers existed only through legislation that encouraged the moral behavior of employees who felt themselves compelled to speak out, without offering any safeguards against retaliation aimed at them. As far back as the False Claims Act of 1863, designed to prevent profiteering from the Civil War, the government has been willing to split up to 50 percent of the recovered amount with the person filing the petition—a potentially lucrative bargain—but it offered no specific prohibitions against retaliatory behavior.

The Whistleblower Protection Act of 1989 finally addressed the issue of retaliation against federal employees who bring accusations of unethical behavior. The act imposed specific performance deadlines in processing whistle-blower complaints and guaranteed the anonymity of the whistle-blower unless revealing the name would prevent criminal activity or protect public safety. The act also required prompt payment of any portion of the settlement to which the whistle-blower would be entitled, even if the case were still working its way through the appeals process.

ETHICAL dilemma

CASE 7.2 **The Cold, Hard Reality**

The media's attention to Jeffrey Wigand, Sherron Watkins, Coleen Rowley, and Cynthia Cooper could lead you to believe that doing the right thing and speaking out against the perceived wrongdoings of your employer will guarantee you public support as an honorable and ethical person, putting the needs of your fellow human beings before your own. In reality, the majority of whistle-blowers face the opposite situation. They are branded as traitors, shunned by their former colleagues, and often singled out to the extent that they never find work in their respective industries again. Consider the cases of the following two individuals who made the same tough ethical choices as their more-famous counterparts with far more negative outcomes.

Christine Casey joined the toymaker Mattel in 1994. In 1997 she was assigned to develop a system to more efficiently allocate production among Mattel's factories. Future production was based on sales forecasts, and it was these forecast figures that led to Casey's ethical crisis with her employer. She quickly discovered that the factory managers regarded the official sales forecasts as being so high that they usually ignored them and worked toward production quotas on the basis of what their fellow managers were using—often keeping two sets of figures to hide their actions. The inflation of sales figures was a key problem for Mattel's most profitable item—Barbie dolls.

In February 1999, Casey made her concerns known to a Mattel director, Ned Mansour, and proposed a new approach to sales forecasting that would address the inflated figures that the CEO of Mattel, Jill Barad, had been sharing with financial analysts through 1997, 1998, and into 1999. Casey believed that her new approach would ensure that profits could be forecasted more accurately based on more realistic sales and production figures. She documented that the initial response from Mr. Mansour was friendly, but her position and reputation within Mattel began to decline very rapidly. In August 1999, she received her first-ever negative performance review since joining Mattel. She was then stripped of most of her job duties and relocated to a cubicle next to a pile of packing boxes.

In October 1999, she expressed concerns that "misrepresentation of earnings projections has made the company vulnerable to shareholder litigation" in a letter to Mattel's former Chief Financial Officer, Harry Pierce. Her concerns went unheeded, and after declining a monetary offer from Mattel to waive her legal rights, Casey resigned in November 1999.

After Casey filed suit against Mattel in November 2000, the company hired John Quinn, a top corporate attorney with an established winning record for his corporate clients. In September 2002, the judge ruled in favor of Mattel and against Casey, arguing that she was not eligible for protection under whistle-blower laws because she had made constructive proposals to senior management rather than filing explicit complaints. An appeal is pending.

Jill Barad, former CEO of Mattel, left the company with a severance package of $50 million in February 2000, and the company settled $122 million of shareholder lawsuits without admitting any wrongdoing in accusations of inflated sales forecasts.

David Welch became the Chief Financial Officer at the Bank of Floyd (Virginia) in 1999 after working for the bank's outside auditing firm. The bank, a unit of Cardinal Bancshares, was just shy of 50 years old with a slow and steady growth record and six local branches. Two years into his contract, Welch began noticing financial irregularities in how the bank was being operated. Specifically, these irregularities included the following:

1. Bank officials had been inflating Cardinal's reported income.

2. CEO R. Leon Moore had engaged in insider trading (trading stock on the basis of access to privileged information).

3. The bank had been holding cash reserves in separate accounts to manipulate earnings in future quarters.

4. The bank had allowed charge-offs (bad debts written off) that exceeded their internal control policies.

Welch raised his concerns within the organization, but he was ignored and in October 2002 he was fired. Two months later, he filed for whistle-blower protection under the Sarbanes-Oxley Act. In reviewing the case, the judge ruled that "Welch's whistle-blowing made him vulnerable to 'adverse and discriminatory employment action'" and awarded him $38,327 in back pay and $26,505 in special damages, and specified that Welch would be eligible for back pay until he was reinstated. Cardinal insisted that the judge "simply didn't understand the case" and appealed.

Legal documentation gathered in support of the appeal includes a bank examiner's report that allegedly found a number of errors in Welch's work performance to the extent that Cardinal Bancshares has "concerns about the quality of his work as CFO." In addition, several Cardinal employees have allegedly threatened to quit if Welch is reinstated.

To date, it is estimated that Welch has incurred almost $125,000 in legal fees fighting the case, compared to Cardinal Bancshares' legal bill of around $500,000. The CEO of the Bank of Floyd, R. Leon Moore, remains convinced that Welch's actions were motivated solely by money and refuses to settle the case until the bank is vindicated. In the meantime, despite two legal orders to reinstate him "with the same seniority, status and benefits he would have had but for (Cardinal's) unlawful discrimination," Welch remains unemployed and is convinced that "my worst fears were realized. I can't get a job in this industry."

1. Who took the greater risk here: Christine Casey or David Welch?

2. Was the alleged behavior at Mattel more or less unethical than the behavior at the Bank of Floyd?

3. Do you think Casey and Welch regret their decisions to go public with their information? Why or why not?

4. Do you think their behavior changed anything at either company?

Source: "Christine Casey: Whistleblower," *The Economist*, January 18–24, 2003, p. 62. Karen Krebsbach, "The Long, Lonely Battle of David E. Welch," *US Banker* 115, no. 30 (August 2005), pp. 30–34; Duncan Adams, "Whistle-Blower's Case Blazes Trail," *Knight Ridder Tribune Business News*, September 7, 2005, p. 1.

The Whistleblower Protection Act of 1989 applied only to federal employees. Not until the Sarbanes-Oxley Act of 2002 (also known as the Corporate and Criminal Fraud Accountability Act, and most commonly abbreviated to SOX) did Congress take an integrated approach to the matter of whistle-blowing by both prohibiting retaliation against whistleblowers and encouraging the act of whistle-blowing itself[5]:

> The statute requires public companies not only to adopt a code of business ethics, but also to set up an internal apparatus to receive, review, and solicit employee reports concerning fraud and/or ethical violations. The teeth of the statute can be found in an enforcement scheme that includes administrative, civil, **and** criminal enforcement mechanisms and provides for both corporate **and** individual liability. . . . Interestingly, [SOX] does not protect employee complaints to the news media. Such reports, by themselves, do not constitute whistle-blowing under [SOX].
>
> Employees who prevail in whistle-blower cases . . . are entitled to damages, which may include:
>
> 1. Reinstatement to the same seniority status that the employee would have had but for the adverse employment action.
> 2. Back pay.
> 3. Interest.
> 4. All compensatory damages to make the employee whole.
> 5. "Special Damages," including litigation costs, reasonable attorney fees and costs, expert witness fees, and "all relief necessary to make the employee whole."
>
> [SOX] does not provide for punitive damages.

✓ PROGRESS CHECK QUESTIONS

9. If an employee blows the whistle on an organization on the basis of a rumor, is that ethical?

10. If that information turns out to be false, should the employee be liable for damages? Explain your answer.

11. Compensation to "make the employee whole" under SOX isn't as clear as a percentage of the funds recovered for a government whistle-blower. Does that make it less likely that we'll see more whistle-blowing under SOX?

12. Under SOX, complaining to the media isn't recognized as whistle-blowing. Is that ethical?

Given this new legal environment surrounding whistle-blowers, all employers would be wise to put the following mechanisms in place:

1. A well-defined process to document how such complaints are handled—a nominated contact person, clearly identified authority to respond to the complaints, firm assurances of confidentiality, and nonretaliation against the employee.

2. An employee hotline to file such complaints, again with firm assurances of confidentiality and nonretaliation to the employee.

3. A prompt and thorough investigation of all complaints.

4. A detailed report of all investigations, documenting all corporate officers involved and all action taken.

Above all, employers must have a commitment to follow through on any and all reports whether or not those reports end up being substantiated. For a **whistle-blower hotline** to work, *trust* must be established between employees and their employer—trust that the information can be given anonymously and without fear of retaliation, even if the identity of the whistle-blower is ultimately revealed during the investigation.

> **Whistle-Blower Hotline** A telephone line where employees can leave messages to alert a company of suspected misconduct without revealing their identity.

The organization can make all the promises in the world, but until that first report is investigated through to a full conclusion, the hotline may never ring again. If the investigation is perceived to be half-hearted, or there is even the remotest suggestion of a cover-up, then the hotline will definitely never ring again.

✔ PROGRESS CHECK QUESTIONS

13. How should managers or supervisors respond to an employee who brings evidence of questionable behavior to their attention?

14. Should that employee be given any reassurances of protection for making the tough decision to come forward?

15. Do you think a hotline that guarantees the anonymity of the caller will encourage more employees to come forward?

16. Does your company have a whistle-blower hotline? How did you find out that there is (or isn't) one?

LIFEskills

Making difficult decisions

In the last chapter we talked about using your personal value system to live your life according to your own ethical standards. As you have seen in this chapter, people like Jeffrey Wigand, Sherron Watkins, Christine Casey, and David Welch may come across situations in their business lives where the behavior they observe is in direct conflict to their ethical standards, and they find themselves unable to simply look the other way.

Ask yourself what you would do in such a situation. Would you ignore it? Could you live with that decision? If you chose to speak out, either as an internal or external whistle-blower, could you live with the consequences of that decision? What if there was a negative impact on the company as a result of your actions and people lost their jobs, as they did at Enron or WorldCom? Could you live with that responsibility?

Speaking out in response to your own ethical standards is only one part of the decision. The consequences for you, your immediate family, your co-workers, and all the other stakeholders in the organization represent an equally important part of that decision. You can see why whistle-blowers face such emotional turmoil before, during, and after what is probably one of the toughest decisions of their lives.

If you find yourself in such a situation, don't make the decision alone. Talk to people you can trust and let them help you review all the issues and all the potential consequences of the decision you are about to make.

Whistle-Blowing as a Last Resort

The perceived bravery and honor in doing the right thing by speaking out against corporate wrongdoing at personal risk to your own career and financial stability adds a gloss to the act of whistle-blowing that is undeserved. The fact that an employee is left with no option but to go public with information should be seen as evidence that the organization has failed to address the situation internally for the long-term improvement of the corporation and all its stakeholders. Becoming a whistle-blower and taking your story public should be seen as the last resort rather than the first. The fallout of unceasing media attention and the often terminal damage to the reputation and long-term economic viability of the organization should be enough of a threat to force even the most stubborn executive team to the table with a commitment to fix whatever has been broken. Regrettably, the majority of executives appear to be willing to take a third option to Sherron Watkins' proposal of either an internal or external fix—they choose to either bury the information and hire the biggest legal gunslinger they can find to discredit the evidence or, as in the case of Jeffrey Wigand, the employers tie their employees in such restrictive confidentiality agreements that speaking out exposes the employee to extreme financial risk, which managers no doubt hope will prompt the employee to "keep his mouth shut."

As Peter Rost explains[6]:

A study of 233 whistle-blowers by Donald Soeken of St. Elizabeth's Hospital in Washington, DC, found that the average whistle-blower was a man in his forties with a strong conscience and high moral values.

After blowing the whistle on fraud, 90 percent of the whistle-blowers were fired or demoted, 27 percent faced lawsuits, 26 percent had to seek psychiatric or physical care, 25 percent suffered alcohol abuse, 17 percent lost their homes, 15 percent got divorced, 10 percent attempted suicide, and 8 percent were bankrupted. But in spite of all this, only 16 percent said they wouldn't blow the whistle again.

For an example of a whistle-blower policy, review the policy for The World Wildlife Fund in Appendix 6.

Good Money— Ben Makes a Decision

Ben lost a lot of sleep that night. He trusted Rick as his most experienced tire mechanic, but he had never seen him be so negative about one particular tire model—and it wasn't as if he had anything to gain by trashing the reputation of a tire that the company wanted to sell so aggressively.

The company had sold seconds before—heck, they even sold "used" tires for those customers looking to save a few bucks. How was this any different? Plus, Rick didn't have to deal with the sales pressure that John placed on his team leaders—you had to hit your quota every week or else—and if the company was pushing Benfield Voyagers, then John expected to see him sell Benfield Voyagers by the dozen.

But what if Rick was right? What if Benfield had cut corners to save on costs? They could end up with another Firestone disaster on their hands. What was Ben supposed to do with this information? If Rick was so concerned, why wasn't he speaking up? The company advertised its employee hotline for everyone to use if they had concerns about any business practices. Why was it Ben's job to say something? He needed this job. He had bills to pay just like the other guys in the store—in fact, the bills were getting pretty high and that bonus money would really help right now.

Ben tossed and turned for a few more hours before reaching a decision. Rick might be right to be concerned, but he was only one guy. The guys at corporate looked at the same specs as Rick did, and if they could live with them, then so could Ben. He wasn't going to put his neck on the block just on the basis of Rick's concerns. If the company was putting its faith in Benfield Voyagers, then Ben was going to sell more of them than anyone else in the company.

Two weeks later, there was a fatal crash involving a minivan with three passengers—a husband and wife and their young son. The minivan had been fitted with Benfield Voyagers at Ben's tire store just one week earlier.

1. What do you think will happen now?

2. What will be the consequences for Ben, Rick, their tire store, and Benfield?

3. Should Ben have spoken out against the Voyager tires?

[KEY TERMS]

Whistle-blower *p. 171*

External Whistle-Blowing *p. 162*

Internal Whistle-Blowing *p. 162*

Whistle-Blower *p. 162*

[REVIEW QUESTIONS]

1. You work for a meatpacking company. You have discovered credible evidence that your company's delivery drivers have been stealing cuts of meat and replacing them with ice to ensure that the delivery meets the stated weight on the delivery invoice. The company has 12 drivers and, as far as you can tell, they are *all* in on this scheme. Your company has a well-advertised whistle-blower hotline. What do you do?

2. What would you do if your company did *not* have a whistle-blower policy?

3. You later discover that one of the drivers was not a part of the scheme but was fired anyway when the information was made public. What do you do?

4. Should the driver get his job back? Why or why not?

[REVIEW EXERCISE]

Amalgamated Forest Products.[7] Amalgamated Forest Products, Inc., operates three major pulp mills in some of the more remote regions of the Upper Peninsula. The firm has been facing difficult financial times due to the recession, and this has caused substantial hardship in the three small communities where the mills are located. In addition, the company has been required to take the lead among the five pulp and paper companies in the region in developing a response to new government proposals to put effluent controls on the discharge of wastewater from pulp and paper mills in environmentally sensitive areas of the region.

The report, entitled "Endangered Species: The Pulp and Paper Industry in the Upper Peninsula," was prepared by Tina Pacquette, the manager of financial analysis. Frank Wilson, the manager of corporate reporting, led the data collection team that compiled the majority of the data Tina used in her report. The data that Frank's team had collected did not support everyone's fears. The primary requirement from the new proposals was the construction of a lagoon for wastewater treatment. The data indicated that this new cost element would only increase average operating costs by 8–10 percent, which, according to market forecasts, would be offset by a corresponding increase of at least 10 percent in customer demand for paper in the region. Frank's team had held a celebratory dinner when the data collection project was finished, and they had discussed how compliance with these new standards would put Amalgamated at the leading edge of the industry in the region—for once their employees would have something to be happy about.

Amalgamated's CEO, Jean Letourneau, was scheduled to present the findings of Tina's report before a congressional committee next week and the sales team was already planning for an aggressive campaign once the news of Amalgamated's compliance to the new proposals was made public.

On the Thursday morning before the committee hearings, Frank stopped by Tina's office to make sure that the report needed no last-minute adjustments. Tina was in a meeting, but her assistant Susan was busy making hard copies of the report for distribution to the board of directors, who were meeting that afternoon to review the final version of the report before the committee hearings next week. Frank decided to wait for Tina to return, and as Susan rushed to her desk to answer the phone, Frank started leafing through the final version of the report. As he reached the fourth page of the report, Frank gave an audible gasp and ran off to find his boss, Jim McIntosh.

"Jim, we have a serious problem with this report—the data are all wrong!" yelled Frank as he burst into McIntosh's office without knocking. Fortunately Jim didn't have anyone in with him, but the expression on his face conveyed his immediate anger that Frank had burst in without knocking—although when Frank revisited the events in the coming days, it occurred to him that the one emotion Jim didn't convey was surprise.

Jim remained calm, asked Frank to close the office door, and then asked him to start from the beginning. After five minutes of point-by-point review just of the one page Frank had read in Tina's office, the reality of the situation suddenly hit Frank. The report wasn't wrong as the result of a typing error; the data had been deliberately changed—there were too many changes, all of which conveyed a much bleaker future for Amalgamated, for this to be anything but a deliberate act.

Frank looked across at Jim McIntosh, who realized that Frank had figured things out. "For heaven's sake, Frank, wake up and smell the coffee! You're about to damage all the important things in your life: your career, your friendships, and your company!"

"I'm sorry, Jim," Frank replied softly, "I know you and I have worked together for a long time, but you can't seriously be willing to let this report go forward. We both know these numbers are bogus, and our CEO is about to testify on their accuracy in front of a congressional committee hearing next week. We need to see Letourneau—now!"

"Well, Frank, your stubbornness is about to cause a real problem for a lot of people," said Jim, his face purple with barely subdued rage. "Wait here! I'll get Letourneau, and we'll see what he thinks about all this!" Jim exited the office and slammed the door.

A few moments later, the door opened abruptly and Jim entered with the company CEO. Jean Letourneau was a distinguished man of approximately 60 years of age. He had a long history with Amalgamated and a solid reputation in the pulp and paper industry. "What's the problem, Frank?" Letourneau's voice broke into the silence. "Jim tells me that you have a few concerns about the report that we're submitting to the committee."

"Well, Mr. Letourneau, I think we—the company—have some major problems here. The report indicates that we'll have severe financial problems if we're forced into building that lagoon for wastewater treatment. In fact, the report says we will most likely be pushed into bankruptcy if the legislation is passed. But these cost estimates are highly inflated. There's no way that our operating costs would rise by 30 percent. The data my team collected, which I double-checked personally, show an increase of only 8–10 percent. The other cost estimates are all just as highly inflated, and the prediction of our product demand forecasts a further deepening of the recession, when we've been planning for a 10 percent increase in demand. Sir, you are scheduled to testify to the accuracy of these numbers in front of a Congressional Committee next week!"

"Slow down, son," Letourneau's calm voice broke in, "we have to use different figures for different purposes. When we report to our shareholders, we give them numbers that are substantially altered from our internal documents, right?" We do that for two reasons—one, because our shareholders don't all have the financial knowledge to read the reports anyway; and two, because we can't go making all our proprietary information available to anyone who wants to read it. In this case, we have to make those dunderheads in the government see what all this regulation is going to do to us. Besides, they know we're going to use the most effective numbers to justify our position—that's common practice."

"But this isn't simply a matter of different figures," Frank sputtered. "These numbers have been totally fabricated. And they don't take into account the damage we're doing to the Wanawashee River. The same stuff we're dumping was cleaned up by our competition years ago. The towns and villages downstream are still drinking this garbage. We're going to be subject to a huge lawsuit if they ever trace it to us. Then, where will we be? If this all blows up, we could all go to jail!"

"We'll cross that bridge when we come to it," McIntosh interjected. "You've got to remember what's at stake here. These communities are totally dependent on Amalgamated for their economic survival. As the mill goes, so goes the town. It's your buddies you'd be threatening to put out of work, Frank. This legislation may not bankrupt us, but it will certainly put a squeeze on profits. If profits are gone, there'll be no more reinvestment by corporate. They're putting a lot of pressure on us to improve the bottom line since the merger last year. They're talking about cutting all of that new production line equipment we requested."

"The bottom line is this, Frank," Letourneau said softly. "You're an important part of our team—your guys did a great job in pulling all the original data together. We see a great future for you here at Amalgamated, and we'd hate to see you go because of this small difference of opinion. However, we need to have everyone on the same page here. Besides, Jim tells me this isn't even your responsibility—all your team had to do was gather the data. If you hadn't picked up a copy of the report in Tina's office, we wouldn't have even involved you. Now, take the rest of the day off, go home to Cheryl and the kids, and take out that new speedboat of yours. Think the problem through, and I'm sure you'll see the long-term benefit of what we're doing here. This pollution problem is a local problem that we can resolve here, not in some fancy legislature in Washington. Besides, we've had the problem for as far back as I can remember, so a few extra years certainly won't hurt."

1. What should Frank do now?
2. Considering the stakeholder model, who will be impacted by Letourneau's bogus figures?
3. If Frank goes public with the real figures, what do you think the likely consequences will be for all the parties involved?
4. The senior team at Amalgamated obviously feels that their financial hardships justify their actions. Is that a valid argument? Why or why not?
5. How could Letourneau and his team have handled this in a more ethical manner?
6. Letourneau and McIntosh feel that Frank is the troublemaker here. Is that a fair assessment?

INTERNET EXERCISE

Visit the Government Accountability Project (GAP) at www.whistleblower.org.

1. What is the mission of GAP?
2. How is GAP funded?
3. What kind of assistance is available through GAP for someone thinking about becoming a whistle-blower?

TEAM EXERCISES

1. **Guilt by Omission.** Divide into two groups and prepare arguments *for* and *against* the following behavior: You work for a large retail clothing company that spends a large amount of its advertising budget emphasizing that its clothes are "Made in America." You discover that only 15 percent of its garments are actually "made" in America. The other 85 percent are actually either cut from patterns overseas and assembled here in the United States, or cut and assembled overseas and imported as completed garments. Your hometown depends on this clothing company as the largest local employer. Several of your friends and family work at the local garment assembly factory. Should you go public with this information?

2. **"Tortious Interference."** Divide into two groups and prepare arguments *for* and *against* the following behavior: In the case of Dr. Jeffrey Wigand and the Brown & Williamson Tobacco Company, the CBS Broadcasting Company chose not to air Dr. Wigand's *60 Minutes* interview with Mike Wallace under threat of legal action for "tortious interference" between B&W and Dr. Wigand. There were suspicions that CBS was more concerned about avoiding any potential legal action that could derail its pending sale to the Westinghouse Corporation. Was CBS behaving ethically in putting the welfare of its stakeholders in the Westinghouse deal ahead of its obligation to support Dr. Wigand?

3. **A New Approach to Freshness.** Divide into two groups and prepare arguments *for* and *against* the following behavior: You work in the meat department of store #2795 of a large retail grocery chain. The company recently announced a change in the meat-handling protocols from the primary supplier. Starting in January 2009, the meat will be gassed with carbon monoxide before packaging. This retains a brighter color for the meat and delays the discoloration that usually occurs as the meat begins to spoil. You understand from the memo that there will be no information on the product label to indicate this protocol change and that the company has no plans to notify customers of this new process. Should you speak out about the procedure?

4. **California Organic.** Divide into two groups and prepare arguments *for* and *against* the following behavior: You work in the accounting department of a family-owned mushroom grower based in California that sells premium organic mushrooms to local restaurants and high-end retail grocery stores. The company's product range includes both fresh and dried mushrooms. Your organic certification allows you to charge top dollar for your product, but you notice from invoices that operating costs are increasing significantly without any increase in revenues. The market won't absorb a price increase, so the company has to absorb the higher costs and accept lower profits. One day you notice invoices for the purchase of dried mushrooms from a Japanese supplier. The dried mushrooms are not listed as being organic, but they are apparently being added to your company's dried mushrooms, which are labeled organic and California-grown. Should you speak out about this?

WHISTLE-BLOWING AND THE PROFESSIONAL

This case describes an actual situation in which a public employee blew the whistle on wrongdoing in a state agency. The names have been changed, but the facts are as stated below.

Barbara Reznik joined the Department of Transportation as an architect in 1982. In 1988, after six years on the job, Reznik told her superiors about what she regarded as fraud and corruption in the department's purchasing and leasing practices. Reznik claimed that officials were accepting kickbacks for awarding contracts to certain companies and contractors. She noted that this practice was costing the taxpayers millions of dollars.

Reznik waited several months for a response to her charges, but none was forthcoming. Finally, she approached her superiors once again, informing them that she intended to report the problems to outside authorities. Within one month, the department began an investigation of Reznik's long-distance telephone use over a two-year period. Investigators found one improper 13-cent phone call among the thousands of calls and referred the violation to the county district attorney. The next month, the department began investigating Reznik's use of sick leave. An audit found that she failed to attend a therapy session for a leg injury she suffered on the job. Reznik said she missed the appointment because her car brakes failed and that she had called her supervisor from the repair shop to explain the problem. Reznik was subsequently fired from her job and indicted.

Barbara Reznik decided to sue under the state's Whistleblower Act. The law prohibits retaliation against public employees who exercise good faith in reporting official wrongdoing. The state's supreme court has ruled that "whistle-blowers act in good faith as long as they truly believe that something illegal is going on and that their belief was reasonable in light of the employee's training and experience."

A public employee who reports a violation of law and is retaliated against or experiences discrimination can file a suit against the governmental body for actual and punitive damages and/or reinstatement, lost wages, court costs, and legal fees. A supervisor who has wrongfully fired or suspended a whistle-blower from a public agency can be fined up to $1,000. The burden of proof in such cases is on the whistle-blower who sues the government.

Shortly after Reznik initiated legal action, the district attorney offered to drop the criminal proceedings against her if Reznik would drop her lawsuit. She refused to do so. Ultimately, the charges against Reznik were dismissed.

Reznik was successful in her lawsuit and was awarded $3.5 million in personal damages, $10 million in punitive damages, and $160,000 in attorney fees. That was in 1991. The state appealed the decision at both the appellate and the Supreme Court levels, and lost each time. Now, four years after the initial decision, the state owes Reznik $20.4 million, because interest accrues at the rate of about $4,800 per day.

Reznik has not been able to collect her award from the state, however, because the Whistleblower Act requires that the legislature first fund the amount in its budget. The legislature has been reluctant to do so since most members view the award as excessive. The position of many of the legislators seems to be that it is not in the public interest to divert such a large amount of money from funds available to meet the needs of the public. However, a compromise was eventually reached between those legislators supporting payment and those against it. The offer is to pay Reznik only the $3.5 million awarded for personal damages. Reznik refuses, stating that, as a matter of principle, she believes that the legislature should pay the full $20.4 million.

Reznik has now been unemployed for four years. She has received one or two low-level clerical job offers, but has been unable to secure a position similar in responsibility to the one she had at the Department of Transportation. She has turned down the clerical job offers, knowing that she would only accept such employment temporarily—that is, until she receives payment from the state. At that time, she would once again seek a more suitable position or simply retire.

Reznik owes $4.6 million to her lawyers for services performed after the initial lawsuit. She also borrowed $1 million from a financier. She is currently living in a trailer and often has to rely on friends for meals and other financial support.

Discussion Questions

1. Do you think that Barbara Reznik has a right to expect the state to pay the full $20.4 million? How does the public interest enter into your assessment of the appropriateness of the state's offer? If you were in Reznik's position, would you accept the offer? Be sure to incorporate ethical reasoning into your responses.

2. Notwithstanding the existence of the Whistleblower Act, assume that Reznik is a certified public accountant (CPA) working in the accounting office at the Department of Transportation, and the fraud she identifies concerns financial statement items. Would you advise Reznik to blow the whistle on the financial wrongdoing? What if she were a CMA (Certified Management Accountant) or CIA (Certified Internal Auditor)? What ethical and professional considerations are relevant in making such a decision, and what action would you advise?

Source: Steven M. Mintz, *Cases in Accounting Ethics and Professionalism*, 3rd ed., New York: McGraw-Hill, 2005.

discussion
EXERCISE 7.2

JAMES ALDERSON

James Alderson became the chief financial officer of the North Valley Hospital in Whitefish, Montana, after a 17-year career at the hospital. Shortly afterwards, the management of the hospital was taken over by Quorum Health Group, a division of the Hospital Corporation of America (HCA), based in Nashville, Tennessee. As part of Alderson's introduction to Quorum's accounting methods, he was told that Quorum kept two sets of books: one for operational management and a second for reporting higher-than-actual expenses to the government for reimbursement. Alderson refused to use the new accounting method on the grounds that it was illegal and unethical. He was fired five days later.

After tracking down copies of the false claims being filed, and learning that other Quorum hospitals were using the same accounting methods, Alderson eventually filed a whistle-blower lawsuit under the federal False Claims Act against Quorum and HCA, expecting the case to be "a sprint to the finish line." In the end, the case became "an exhausting marathon" as Alderson and his family moved to five different towns in 10 years, gathering additional evidence and working to cover their bills.

In 1998, Alderson's undercover work was abruptly made public when the U.S. government became involved in his lawsuit and the CBS 60 Minutes program profiled him.

With mounting evidence against them, the CEO and several top executives of the now merged Columbia/HCA were relieved of their positions. HCA eventually reimbursed the U.S. government a total of $840 million in 2001—$745 million in civil damages and $95 million in criminal penalties. In June 2003, the U.S. District Court of Columbia approved a further payment of $881 million to settle all remaining fraud charges against the company.

The federal False Claims Act (1986) allows whistle-blowers to receive between 15 and 25 percent of any settlement proceeds. Alderson says, "I won't deny that money provided an incentive, but it was only part of the motivation. What Quorum and HCA were doing was wrong, and it took me 13 years and my career to prove it. Fortunately, I received enough money from the settlement to retire." Alderson's wife, Connie, doesn't feel quite so vindicated: "Knowing what I know now and knowing how long it's been, I'm not sure I would have agreed to pursuing the case. I don't think any amount of money is going to take care of what we've been through." Alderson and his colleague, John Schilling, ended up splitting an award of $100 million.

Discussion Questions

1. Do you think Alderson and his family would have made as many sacrifices if the federal False Claims Act did *not* allow whistle-blowers to receive the 15–25 percent compensation on any settlement?

2. If you were faced with the same situation, would the money make a difference to you? Explain your answer.

3. Do you think the compensation provides an unethical incentive for prospective whistle-blowers to "go public" with proprietary information?

4. The prospect of a long, drawn-out legal battle is probably a major obstacle to many prospective whistle-blowers. If legislation existed to expedite such cases, do you think insiders would reveal more corporate scandals? Why or why not?

5. In many cases, whistle-blowers face the loss of their careers as a result of their actions. What could be done to prevent this?

6. Could you go back to work for the same company after you had revealed unethical corporate behavior? What about a similar job with a different company?

Source: Grover L. Porter, "Whistle-Blowers: A Rare Breed," *Strategic Finance*, August 2003; Leslie Griffin, "Watch Out for Whistle-blowers," *Journal of Law, Medicine & Ethics* 33, no. 1 (Spring 2005), p. 160.

THE OLIVIERI CASE

In April 1993, Dr. Nancy Olivieri, head of the hemoglobinopathy program at the Hospital for Sick Children (HSC), the teaching hospital for the University of Toronto in Canada, signed an agreement with the Canadian drug company Apotex to undertake clinical trials on a drug called deferiprone (referred to as L1 during the study). The drug was designed to help children with thalassemia, an inherited blood disorder that can cause the fatal build-up of iron in the blood. The agreement that Olivieri signed with Apotex included a clause (later referred to as a "gag clause") that specifically prevented the unauthorized release of any findings in the trial for a period of three years:

"As you now [sic], paragraph 7 of the LA-02 Contract provides that all information whether written or not, obtained or generated by you during the term of the LA-02 Contract and for a period of three years thereafter, shall be and remain secret and confidential and shall not be disclosed in any manner to any third party except with the prior written consent of Apotex. Please be aware that Apotex will take all possible steps to ensure that these obligations of confidentiality are met and will vigorously pursue all legal remedies in the event that there is any breach of these obligations."

The existence of this clause was to prove significant to the relationship between Olivieri and Apotex. After reporting some initial positive findings in the trial in April 1995, Olivieri reported in December 1996 that long-term use of the drug appeared to result in the toxic build-up of iron in the liver of a large number of her pediatric patients—a condition known as hepatic fibrosis. When she reported the findings to Apotex, the company determined that her interpretation of the data was incorrect. Olivieri then contacted the hospital's Research Ethics Board (REB), which instructed her to change the consent form for participation in the trial to ensure that patients were made aware of the risks of long-term use of the drug.

After copying Apotex on the revised form, the company notified Olivieri that the Toronto trials were being terminated effective immediately, and that she was being removed as chair of the steering committee of the global trial that included patients in Philadelphia and Italy. When Olivieri notified Apotex that she and her research partners, including Dr. Gary Brittenham of Case Western Reserve University in Cleveland, were planning to publish their findings in the August 1998 issue of the New England Journal of Medicine, Apotex Vice President Michael Spino threatened legal action for breaching the confidentiality clause in her agreement with the company.

Olivieri then asked the HSC administration for legal support in her forthcoming battle with Apotex. The administrators declined. She then approached the University of Toronto, where the Dean of the Faculty of Medicine declined to get involved on the grounds that her contract with Apotex had been signed without university oversight and that the university would never have agreed to the confidentiality clause in the first place.

"Olivieri forged ahead with the publication despite this (lack of support) and instantly became celebrated as a courageous whistleblower in the face of corporate greed."

The situation was further clouded by reports that the University of Toronto and HSC were, at the time, in the process of negotiating a $20 million donation from Bernard Sherman, the CEO and founder of Apotex.

The bitter relationship with her employers was to continue for several years, during which time she was referred to the Canadian College of Physicians and Surgeons for research misconduct and dismissed from her post at HSC, only to be reinstated following the aggressive support of several of her academic colleagues, including Dr. Brenda Gallie of the division of immunology and cancer at HSC, who led a petition drive that succeeded in garnering 140 signatures in support of a formal enquiry into Dr. Olivieri's case.

That enquiry was undertaken by both the College of Physicians and Surgeons, which found her conduct to be "exemplary," and by the Canadian Association of University Teachers, whose 540-page report concluded that Dr. Olivieri's academic freedom had been violated when Apotex stopped the trials and threatened legal action against her.

«« «« The two-and-a-half-year battle ended in January 1999 when an agreement was brokered between the University, HSC, and Olivieri thanks to the efforts of two world-renowned experts in blood disorders–Dr. David Nathan of Harvard and Dr. David Weatherall of Oxford who intervened on the basis of the international importance of Dr. Olivieri's research. Working with the President of the University of Toronto, Robert Pritchard, and lawyers for both parties, a compromise settlement was reached that reinstated Olivieri as head of the hemoglobinopathy program at HSC, covered her legal expenses up to $150,000, and withdrew all letters and written complaints about her from her employment file.

As part of the agreement, a joint working group appointed by the University of Toronto and the University's Faculty Association was chartered with the task of making "recommendations on changes to university policies on the dissemination of research publications and conflict of interest and the relationship of these issues to academic freedom."

Discussion Questions

1. Was it ethical for Apotex to include a three-year gag clause in the agreement with Dr. Olivieri?

2. Even though Dr. Olivieri later admitted that she should never have signed the agreement with Apotex that included a confidentiality clause, does the fact that she *did* sign it have any bearing on her actions here? Why or why not?

3. Was Olivieri's decision to publish her findings about the trial an example of *universalism* or *utilitarianism*? Explain your answer.

4. If we identify the key players in this case as Dr. Olivieri, Apotex, the Hospital for Sick Children, and the University of Toronto, what are the conflicts of interest between them all?

5. What do you think would have happened if Dr. Olivieri's fellow academics had not supported her in her fight?

6. How could this situation have been handled differently to avoid such a lengthy and bitter battle?

Source: Robert A. Phillips and John Hoey, "Constraints of Interest: Lessons at the Hospital for Sick Children," *Canadian Medical Association Journal* 159 (October 20, 1998), p. 8.
John Hoey and Anne Marie Todkill, "The Olivieri Story, Take Three," *Canadian Medical Association Journal* 173 (October 11, 2005), p. 8.
David Hodges, "Dr. Olivieri, Sick Kids, U of T Resolve Disputes," *Medical Post*, 38, no. 43 (November 26, 2002), p. 4.

chapter 8

Ethics and Technology

" *Big Brother Is Watching You.*

—George Orwell, 1984, Part 1, Chapter 1 "

LEARNING OBJECTIVES

After studying this chapter, you should be able to:

1. Evaluate the ethical ramifications of recent technological advances.

2. Explain the employer view of privacy at work.

3. Explain the employee view of privacy at work.

4. Distinguish between thin and thick consent.

5. Evaluate the concept of vicarious liability.

6. Analyze an organization's employee-surveillance capabilities.

7. Discuss the future of corporate surveillance for employees.

Problems at ComputerWorld

Steve has just been hired as a computer repair technician (CRT) for ComputerWorld, a large retail computer store. As a recent graduate from the local technical college, Steve is eager to put his new diploma to good use and make a name for himself at ComputerWorld. "Who knows," he thinks to himself, "in a couple of years I could be running the whole department!" Steve is working with Larry, who's been a CRT at this location for five years. Larry seems nice enough and has promised to "show him the ropes."

Their first customer of the day is Mr. Johnson, who admits to not being "very PC-savvy." Larry hooks up the laptop and announces that the hard drive has crashed and needs to be replaced. "The good news," he tells Mr. Johnson, "is that your repair is under warranty so we can switch that hard drive out for you, no problem—leave it with us and it'll be ready tomorrow morning." Steve is suitably impressed with Larry's quick diagnosis and his firm commitment to Mr. Johnson that his laptop will be ready in the morning. Mr. Johnson, however, doesn't seem so pleased. "What about the old hard drive?" he asks. "There's a lot of personal information on there—can I have it back when you put in the new one?

"Sorry, no can do," says Larry. "We have to return warranty-replaced parts to the manufacturer—company policy—but don't worry, their technicians will erase all the data on it before they recycle it—we're very careful about that."

Mr. Johnson thinks for a few moments and then decides that he can live with that and leaves the store. Larry quickly replaces the hard drive and throws the old one into a box that Steve notices is labeled "Flea Market" under Larry's workstation.

"What are you doing?" asks Steve. "I thought we had to send that back to the manufacturer for a warranty repair?" "Are you crazy?" laughs Larry. "We just tell the customers that—all the manufacturer needs is a serial number and the paperwork. That's a perfectly good hard drive—all he had was a file conflict. I've already fixed it—but since it's under warranty, he gets a nice new hard drive for free, we get a nice warranty contract, and I get a slightly used hard drive that I can sell at the flea market this weekend."

"But what about all his personal information on the hard drive?" asks Steve. "Aren't you going to erase it?"
"If I have time," laughs Larry.

1. The Computer Ethics Institute developed "Ten Commandments of Computer Ethics," listed on page 196 in this chapter. How many of those commandments are being broken here?

2. Larry seems pretty happy with the prospect of selling those slightly used hard drives at the flea market, but what happens if the information on them doesn't get erased? Would ComputerWorld be liable here? Read the section "Vicarious Liability" on page 194 to find out more.

3. What should Steve do now?

Ethics and Technology

Technological advances often deliver new and improved functional capabilities before we have had the chance to fully consider the implications of those improvements. Consider the dramatic changes in workplace technology over the last two decades—specifically desktop computing, the Internet, and the growth of email and instant messaging (IM). These technological advances arrived with the promise of "ease of access," "ease of use," and the ever-popular "increased worker productivity."

There is some truth to this assessment of the advantages of technology in the workplace. Consider the following:

- Companies are now able to make vast amounts of information available to employees and customers on their Internet, **intranet,** and **extranet** sites. Information previously distributed in hard-copy format—handbooks, guidebooks, catalogs, policy manuals—can now be posted to a site and made available to employees and/or customers anywhere in the world in a matter of minutes, and updating that material can be accomplished in hours rather than weeks.

- JetBlue Airlines was able to achieve significant cost savings by avoiding the expensive overhead of developing call centers for its reservations department. Using available call-routing technology with a desktop computer and dedicated phone line, JetBlue was able to hire 700 part-time workers in the Salt Lake City area to become its reservations department, working from the comfort of their dens, dining rooms, or spare bedrooms with no costly buildings to staff and maintain, and a much more flexible and satisfied workforce that can log on at a time that's convenient for them with no commute or office dress code.

> **Intranet** A company's internal Web site, containing information for employee access only.
>
> **Extranet** A private piece of a company's Internet network that is made available to customers and/or vendor partners on the basis of secured access by unique password.

However, now that these tools have become part of our everyday work environment, many of those wonderful promises have been overshadowed by concerns over loss of privacy in two key areas:

1. Customers must be aware that companies now have the technical capability to send their personal data to any part of the world to take advantage of lower labor costs.

2. Employees must be aware that employers now have the capability of monitoring every email you send and Web site you visit in order to make sure that you really are delivering on the promise of increased worker productivity.

Do You Know Where Your Personal Information Is?

With the availability of a network of fiber-optic cable that spans the globe and an increasingly educated global workforce that is fluent in English, the potential cost savings for American corporations in shipping work overseas to countries with lower labor costs is becoming increasingly attractive. Technically, anything that can be digitized can be sent over a fiber-optic cable.

The first wave of this technological advance came with the establishment of call centers in other parts of the world (predominantly India) to answer, for example, your customer service calls to your credit card company or for tech support on your computer. Very polite young people with suitably American names but with a definite accent can now answer your call as if you were calling an office park in the Midwest. This is just the beginning, as Thomas L. Friedman points out in *The World Is Flat*[1]:

A few weeks after I spoke with [Jaithirth "Jerry"] Rao, the following e-mail arrived from Bill Brody, the president of Johns Hopkins University, whom I had just interviewed for this book:

Dear Tom, I am speaking at a Hopkins continuing education medical meeting for radiologists (I used to be a radiologist). . . . I came upon a very fascinating situation that I thought might interest you. I have just learned that in many small and some medium-size hospitals in the US, radiologists are outsourcing reading of CAT scans to doctors in India and Australia!!! Most of this evidently occurs at night (and maybe weekends) when the radiologists do not have sufficient staffing to provide in-hospital coverage. While some radiology groups will use teleradiology to ship images from the hospital to their home (or to Vail or Cape Cod, I suppose) so that they can interpret images and provide a diagnosis 24/7, apparently the smaller hospitals are shipping CAT images to radiologists abroad. The advantage is that it is daytime in Australia or India when it is nighttime here—so after-hours coverage becomes more readily done by shipping the images across the globe. Since CAT (and MRI) images are already in digital format and available on a network with a standardized protocol, it is no problem to view the images anywhere in the world. . . . I assume that the radiologists on the other end . . . must have trained in [the] US and acquired the appropriate licenses and credentials. . . . The groups abroad that provide these after-hours readings are called "Nighthawks" by the American radiologists that employ them.

The ethical obligations of this new technical capability are just being realized. Should the customer be notified where the call center is based? Should the customer be notified that the person answering the call who introduces himself as "Ray" is really Rajesh from Mumbai? If you are referred to a radiologist for treatment, are you entitled to know that your CAT scan is being beamed across the globe for another radiologist on the opposite side of the world to read? Advocates argue that assigning patient ID numbers rather than full names or personal information can guarantee patient confidentiality, but once the information is in digital format on a network, what guarantees are there that someone else isn't tapping into that network?

1. How would you feel if you found out that someone halfway around the world from your doctor's office was reading your CAT scan?

2. Would your opinion change if you knew the cost savings from outsourcing were putting American radiologists out of a job? What if they were being read this way because there was a shortage of qualified medical personnel here? Would that change your opinion?

3. Should your doctor be obligated to tell you where your tests are being read? Why or why not?

4. Storing private information in digital format simplifies the storage and transfer of that information and offers cost savings to companies that are (hopefully) passed on to their customers. Does using ID numbers instead of names meet their obligation to maintain your privacy in this new digital world?

The Promise of Increased Worker Productivity

Desktop computers, email, instant messaging, and the Worldwide Web have changed our work environments beyond recognition over the last two decades, but with those changes have come a new world of ethical dilemmas. With a simple click, you can check the news on CNN, email a joke to a friend, check the weather forecast for your trip next weekend, check in with that friend you've been meaning to call, and spread some juicy "dirt" that you just overheard in the break room—but the question is, should you? We can identify two distinct viewpoints on this issue: the employer view and the employee view.

The Employer Position

As an employee of the organization, your productivity during your time at work represents the performance portion of the pay-for-performance contract you entered into with the company when you were hired. Therefore, your actions during that time—your allotted shift or normal work period—are at the discretion of the company. Other than lunch and any scheduled breaks, all your activity should be work-related, and any monitoring of that activity should not be regarded as an infringement of your privacy. If you want to do something in private, don't do it at work.

The organization has an obligation to its stakeholders to operate as efficiently as possible, and to do so it must ensure that company resources are not being misused or stolen and that company data and proprietary information are being closely guarded.

The Employee Position

As an employee of the company, I recognize that my time at work represents the productivity for which I receive an agreed amount of compensation—either an hourly rate or an annual salary. However, that agreement should not intrude upon my civil rights as an individual—I am an employee, not a servant. As such, I should be notified of any electronic surveillance and the purpose of that surveillance. The actions of a small number of employees in breaking company rules should not be used as a justification to take away everyone's civil rights. Just because the guy in the cube next to me surfs the Web all day doesn't mean that we all do. Electronic monitoring implies that we can't be trusted to do our jobs—and if you can't trust us, why are you employing us in the first place?

Arriving at a satisfactory resolution of these opposing arguments has proven to be difficult for two reasons. First, the availability of ongoing technological advancements has made it increasingly difficult to determine precisely where work ends and personal life begins. Second, the willingness to negotiate or compromise has risen and fallen in direct relation to the prevailing job market.

ETHICAL dilemma

CASE 8.1 A Failure to Disclose

My name is Sally Jones and I am the office manager for Chuck Wilson, CPA, a small accounting firm in the Midwest. Life is good—it's a healthy business with a good mix of small business and individual returns, and Chuck has been a great guy to work for. He's well respected in our community as an active member of the local Chamber of Commerce; he does pro bono work for several local nonprofit organizations; and he's built up a loyal customer base over the years. The problem is Chuck Junior. It's always been Chuck's plan that Junior would take over the business, and with Junior having just passed his CPA exams, that time would seem to be now. The number of boating and fishing magazines that have suddenly appeared on Chuck's desk make me believe that he is thinking more seriously about retirement than ever before.

I don't begrudge Chuck his retirement—he's earned it. My job here is secure. I have done good work for Chuck and his customers like me. However, Chuck Junior is already looking to put his mark on the business. I wouldn't be surprised if he's having some "Under New Management" signs prepared for the day when he does take over the practice. Junior likes to think of himself as "on the cutting edge of new technology" and "ready to take it to the streets" to take on the local H&R Block and Jackson Hewitt offices that take such a large portion of the individual tax returns every year. He's all excited about an article he read in one of his business magazines that he thinks will give us an advantage over the big guys—and he's already been in contact with the company that was featured in the article.

His plan is to send all our individual tax returns to a company in India that will guarantee the return will be prepared in less than 48 hours by accountants in its offices who are U.S.-licensed CPAs. The term for this is *outsourcing*. This, says Junior, will allow us to go after the more labor-intensive but profitable corporate returns at tax time instead of having all our time taken up with the individual returns. It will also save us from hiring any additional staff for the season. He's even figured out that, with the cost of each return this company will charge us, we can undercut the big guys and take away some of their business. He's already planning a big advertising campaign in the local papers and radio stations.

I'm happy to give him the benefit of the doubt on this idea, but here's my concern—he's not planning to tell anyone how we're going to do this. He's not going to mention that someone else (whom he's never met) will be preparing the tax return or that the customers' personal information will be emailed to India to complete the return. He says that the customers won't care as long as the return is quick, accurate, and cheaper than the other guys. With all those ads for "immediate refunds," I can see his point, but his failure to disclose just doesn't sit right with me.

> **Telecommuting** The ability to work outside of your office (from your home or anywhere else) and log in to your company network (usually via a secure gateway such as a VPN, virtual private network).

1. Is Sally right to be concerned about Chuck's plan? Explain why or why not.

2. Chuck Junior is obviously focusing on the money to be saved (and made) with this plan. What are the issues he is not considering?

3. Do you think Chuck Senior has signed off on this plan? If not, should Sally tell him? Explain why or why not.

4. Would the plan still succeed if Chuck Junior disclosed all the details?

Source: Adapted from "The Ethical Dilemmas of Outsourcing," Steven Mintz, *The CPA Journal* 74 (March 2004), p. 3.

When Are You "at Work"?

The argument over privacy at work has traditionally centered on the amount of time that employees were on-site—in the office or at the factory or store or hospital or call center, and so on. With the advances in computer technology and the new capability of **telecommuting,** which allows you to work from home (or anywhere) and log in to your company's network remotely, the concept of "at work" has become blurred.

With the availability of technology has come the expectation that you can check emails at home or finish a presentation the night before the big meeting. The arrival of the Blackberry (affectionately known as the "crackberry" by many users and their partners) has made many employees available to their boss at all times of the day and night—24/7 unless they turn off the message notification function!

In this new environment, the concept of being at work has become far more flexible. Availability has now become defined by accessibility. If I can reach you by phone or email, I can ask you a question or assign you a task. The time of day or the day of the week is of secondary importance—it's a competitive world out there and only the truly committed team players get ahead.

Employees, in return, have begun to expect the same flexibility in taking care of personal needs during working hours. If I stay up late working on a presentation for an important meeting the next day, shouldn't I then be allowed to call my dentist and make an appointment during my workday? What

Telecommuting is a growing trend in business. What are some obstacles to being a good employee from a remote location?

happens if I forget to send my mother some flowers for Mother's Day? If I order them online during my workday, am I still technically goofing off and therefore failing to meet my boss's expectations as a dedicated and productive employee?

If employee rights were recognized in this argument, then for those rights to have any validity, it would follow that employees should give their consent to be monitored by all this technology. However, as Adam Moore points out, the state of the job market will inevitably create a distinction between two types of consent: **thin** and **thick**.[2]

Thin Consent When an employee receives formal notification that the company will be monitoring all email and Web activity—either at the time of hire or during employment—and it is made clear in that notification that his or her continued employment with the company will be dependent on the employee's agreement to abide by that monitoring

Thick Consent When jobs are plentiful and the employee would have no difficulty in finding another position, then the employee has a realistic alternative if he or she finds a monitoring policy unacceptable, and consent can be classified as thick.

Thin Consent If an employee receives formal notification that the company will be monitoring all e-mail and Web activity—either at the time of hire or during employment—and it is made clear in that notification that his or her continued employment with the company will be dependent on the employee's agreement to abide by that monitoring, then the employee may be said to have given thin consent. In other words, there are two options: agree to the monitoring or pursue other employment opportunities. You could argue that the employee has at least been notified of the policy, but the notification is based on the assumption that jobs are hard to come by and the employee is not in a position to quit on principle and risk temporary unemployment while seeking a position with another company.[2]

Thick Consent If employment conditions are at the other end of the scale—that is, jobs are plentiful and the employee would have no difficulty in finding another position—then consent to the monitoring policy could be classified as thick since the employee has a realistic alternative if he or she finds the policy to be unacceptable.

✓ PROGRESS CHECK QUESTIONS

5. Define the term *telecommuting*.

6. Summarize the employer position on privacy at work.

7. Summarize the employee position on privacy at work.

8. Explain the difference between thin and thick consent.

Abstract notions of notification and consent are idealistic at best. Consider the following account of life in a call center in the United Kingdom documented by "Jamie"[3]:

> Back in October 1999, I started work at a call centre for a very large UK company. There were about 1,000 staff there, split into teams which would compete with each other on sales volumes. Winning teams might get a case of wine to share, or something like that. There was also a personal bonus scheme driven by sales.
>
> I was an "outbound telesales agent." This means we phoned customers at home with the aim of selling the company's services. I knew that most customers don't like to be phoned while at home, and if any customer clearly didn't want the call, I would end it, and flag their account for "no future correspondence," though we were specifically told only to do this in extreme cases.
>
> The bonus scheme encouraged some of my colleagues (mostly students) to sell aggressively—selling products that customers didn't want—for the bonus.

These staff would usually have left the company by the time there were any repercussions.

A lot of customers imagine telesales agents as being spotty idiots trawling phonebooks ringing people as they go through the book. But the company's call system is quite complex. A database of all customers is kept (obviously!) and the computers dial these customers (depending on flags set on their accounts). As soon as someone picks the phone up, the computer transfers it to the next available agent. The agent has no physical control over the call, the headphones beep, and there's a customer on the other end saying "Hello?" and that's it. The agent then performs the schpiel.

There would probably be about 30 seconds between coming off a call, and the next one coming in (when I started, I was told there was about 90 seconds) and this continues throughout the shift.

The call centre is a pretty stressful place, with most of the agents getting as stressed or more stressed than the customers.

Increasingly higher sales targets started coming in, and more products were being introduced. Unfortunately, the training to go with these products was pretty poor, being in the form of glossy—but shallow—PowerPoint presentations. We knew the basics of the products, but we could not answer all questions, and this didn't go down well with some of the more knowledgeable customers. If it was something we might have an idea on, then I'm afraid we would sometimes bullsh*t.

I think telesales calls were targeted not to exceed about six minutes.

One day, they decided to open an inbound sales channel. The idea was to try to sell products to customers who were calling in to us. I signed up, thinking maybe things would be a bit easier. What a surprise to come onto the sales floor and take incessant customer complaint calls, having completed three weeks of training for inbound sales!

We were expected to take all manner of calls. We had to use different systems for logging orders and calls, and those systems were very difficult to use—with DOS-like command-line interfaces.

There would be a command to look up a customer's address/general details. Another command would look up an order on a customer's account. Instead of having a mouse and clicking things, we had to use commands and order codes to issue products on customers' accounts. We would then have to use a different command if we wanted to enter the customer's delivery address details. Another command later, and we would then be able to confirm the dates for the order. And after another command, the order would be confirmed.

So, the customer would be waiting impatiently on the phone, thinking the agent was a slow typist. The agent may then get stressed, because they cannot find a particular order code for a certain product, or cannot remember a certain command, or might make a typing error—that sort of thing.

This all had to be done within nine minutes.

After dealing with the complaint, we then had to try to sell them extra products using our inbound sales training. And this is far from easy—nothing like ringing up a company to complain and having one of their agents try to flog you more products!

I started to question my manager as to whether there was any point in this, but got nowhere. Managers, in general, seemed uninterested in what we were doing, beyond telling us of the new products we were to try to sell, or relaying irrelevant upper-management news. The general level of management skill seemed low to me.

Eventually, I resigned and was escorted off the premises by security.

✓ PROGRESS CHECK QUESTIONS

9. How would you describe the atmosphere in this call center?

10. Jamie's calls were monitored at all times by a call center supervisor. Is that ethical? Why or why not?

11. What would you say is the worst part of working in this call center?

12. When Jamie resigned, he was escorted from the building by security. Is that ethical? Why or why not?

LIFEskills

The mixed blessing of technology

Take a moment and think about how many benefits we are able to derive from the Internet, personal computers, and cellphones. Without them, you could still call someone on a landline, but for a long-distance friend you would probably write a letter and send it by snail-mail. To do research for a homework assignment you would go to the library to use an encyclopedia rather than Google or Wikipedia, and then type your paper on a typewriter!

The world of instant access—emails, IM, texting on your Sidekick, Blackberry, or iPhone—has certainly made communication faster and easier, but have you ever stopped to consider the downside of that instantaneous access? You may pride yourself on your ability to multitask and do homework, emails, texts, shop online, and check out some YouTube videos, all at the same time, but how often do you turn everything off and really focus on the subject you are working on?

In the work environment, instant access goes both ways. To your boss, you are just an email, phone call, or text message away—so what if you are at home eating dinner? She needs that information now or needs that report on her desk by 9 a.m., so why shouldn't she call you?

Recent technological advances have blurred the lines between work and home life, and while being a team player can help your long-term career prospects, you're no good to your company if you are a burned-out shell who never finds downtime to rest and recharge your batteries. So, find the time to switch off, unplug and, as the saying goes, just chill!

The Dangers of Leaving a Paper Trail

We may resent the availability of technology that allows employers to monitor every keystroke on our computers, but it is often the documents written on the machines that do the most harm. Consider the following recent events:

- In 1997, British insurance giant Norwich Union was forced into an out-of-court settlement for alleged defamation by email against a competitor, Western Provident Association (WPA). Norwich Union staff sent emails falsely claiming that WPA was insolvent. By the time a writ had been issued, the email messages had been deleted at Norwich Union. Western Provident obtained a court order forcing Norwich Union to search their backup systems to retrieve the data. Norwich Union made an apology required by the High Court and paid £450,000 in damages and costs to settle the case.[4]

- In November 1998, the Chevron Corporation settled a sexual harassment lawsuit for $2.2 million that was brought in response to "offensive" email postings within the company's network, such as "25 reasons why beer is better than women."[5]

- In October 1999, the Xerox Corporation fired 40 of its employees for viewing pornographic Web sites at work.[6]

- On September 11, 2001, scarcely one hour after the Twin Towers attacks in New York, Jo Moore, a special advisor to the Labour Secretary of State for Transportation in the United Kingdom, sent an email suggesting that "today would be a good day to bury bad news." Her email was leaked to the media, which attacked her already-unpopular role as a "spin doctor" for the Labour Party. In February 2002, Moore made the same suggestion over the release of negative safety figures for the United Kingdom's rail system—she sent another email suggesting that the figures be released on the same day as the funeral of the Queen's sister, Princess Margaret. This email was also leaked to the media, and Moore resigned on February 15, 2002.[7]

- In October 2003, Microsoft contractor Michael Hanscom was fired after posting a picture on his personal weblog (blog). The picture showed some new Apple Macintosh G5 computers being delivered to Microsoft's Redmond, Washington, headquarters—presumably for a detailed "inspection."[8]

- In March 2005, Boeing CEO Harry Stonecipher was dismissed after emails "of a romantic nature" were brought to the attention of the board of directors, revealing Stonecipher's affair with a Boeing vice president of operations.[9]

With the immediate nature of Internet communication and the potential damage that evidence gathered from the electronic trail of emails can do, it's easy to see why organizations have become so concerned about the activities of their employees. If the negative effect on your corporate brand and reputation weren't enough of a reason to be concerned, then the legal concept of **vicarious liability** should grab any employer's attention.

Vicarious Liability

Vicarious liability is a legal concept that means a party may be held responsible for injury or damage even when he or she was not actively involved in an incident. Parties that may be charged with vicarious liability are generally in a supervisory role over the person or parties personally responsible for the injury or damage. The implications of vicarious liability are that the party charged is responsible for the actions of his or her subordinates.

There are a variety of situations in which a party may be charged with vicarious liability. Contractors may face charged [sic] of vicarious liability if their subcontractors fail to complete a job, perform the job incorrectly, or are found guilty of other contract violations. Parents have been charged with vicarious liability when the actions of their children cause harm or damage. Employers can face a number of situations involving vicarious liability issues, including sexual harassment of one employee by another, discriminatory behavior by an employee against fellow employees or customers, or any other action in which one of their employees personally causes harm, even if that employee acts against the policies of the employer.[10]

So as an employer, you could be held liable for the actions of your employees through Internet communications to the same degree as if they had written those communications on company letterhead. The new term for this is **cyberliability,** which applies the existing legal concept of liability to a new world—computers. The extent of this new liability can be seen in the top categories of litigation recorded by Elron Software[11]:

- Discrimination
- Harassment
  - Obscenity and pornography
  - Defamation and libel
  - Information leaks
  - Spam

> **Vicarious Liability** A legal concept that means a party may be held responsible for injury or damage even when he or she was not actively involved in an incident.
>
> **Cyberliability** Employers can be held liable for the actions of their employees in their Internet communications to the same degree as if those employers had written those communications on company letterhead.

ETHICAL dilemma

CASE 8.2 Top 20 Blonde Jokes

Bill Davis was really torn about the complaint that had just landed on his desk from a female employee in the accounting department. As HR director for Midland Pharmaceuticals, it was his job to address any complaints about employee behavior. Over the years, the company had invested a lot of money in training employees on the biggest employee behavior issues—sexual harassment and discrimination—probably, Bill suspected, because of the real danger of lawsuits that could cost the company tens if not hundreds of thousands of dollars to settle. However, this complaint had Bill stumped.

Midland was a midsize regional company of about 180 employees. Their rural location provided a good quality of life for their employees—no commuting headaches, good schools, and salaries that were competitive with their more metropolitan competitors. Turnover was not an issue—in fact, the last employee newsletter had featured eight members of the same family working for Midland, and the next edition would feature one family with three generations working for the company. This was a good company to work for and Bill enjoyed his job as HR director.

Jane Williams was a new employee in accounting. She had moved here as part of her husband's relocation to the area with another company about three months ago. Bill's conversation with her manager had revealed that she was a model employee—punctual, reliable, and very productive. Then Steve Collins in the warehouse had decided to brighten everyone's Friday by forwarding an email that one of his buddies had sent to him. The title of the email was "Top 20 Blonde Jokes." Collins had used the corporate email directory to send the email to everyone with a simple "Happy Friday!" message, so Bill had opened it and, he confessed to himself, laughed at a couple of the jokes. He had then moved on to the quarterly report he was working on and thought nothing more of it.

Jane, who was blonde ("a natural blonde," as she had pointed out in her email), did not find the email funny at all—in fact, she took such offense to it that she filed a formal grievance against Collins, claiming that the email created "a hostile working environment" for her (one of the key phrases the lawyers had emphasized in the harassment training). Bill had also been told that Jane was trying to get some of the other women in the department on her side by complaining that since the blonde jokes were always about females, they were discriminatory to women.

Bill had interviewed Jane personally when she was hired, and she didn't strike him as the type of employee who would try to hold the company for ransom over such a thing, so he suspected that the "hostile work environment" comment was meant more as an indication of her emotional response to the email than a serious threat of legal action. However, her complaint was a formal one and he needed to act on it. Unfortunately, Midland's policies on email communication had always been fairly informal. It had never been raised as an issue before now. People were always sending jokes and silly stories and Midland had relied upon the common sense of their employees not to send anything offensive or derogatory.

The IT folks took all the necessary precautions for network and data security, but as a family-owned company, the thought of monitoring employee emails never been considered. Now, Bill feared, the issue would have to be addressed.

1. Was Steve Collins wrong to send the email? Why?

2. Is Jane Williams overreacting in filing her formal complaint? Explain why or why not.

3. What impact do you think any change in the employee privacy policies would have at Midland?

4. What are Bill Davis's options here?

If we acknowledge the liabilities employers face that are a direct result of the actions of their employees, does that justify employee monitoring to control (and hopefully prevent) any action that might place the company at risk? Or are employees entitled to some degree of privacy at work?

The Right to Privacy—Big Brother Is in the House

Listen for this generic statement the next time you call a company and navigate through the voicemail menu—this is usually the last thing you hear before you are (hopefully) connected to a live person.

[*"Calls may be monitored for quality control and training purposes."*

"It was terribly dangerous to let your thoughts wander when you were in any public place or within range of a telescreen. The smallest thing could give you away. A nervous tic, an unconscious look of anxiety, a habit of muttering to yourself— anything that carried with it the suggestion of abnormality, of having something to hide. In any case, to wear an improper expression on your face . . . was itself a punishable offense. There was even a word for it in Newspeak: facecrime . . ."

—George Orwell, 1984, Book 1, Chapter 5

In his novel *1984,* George Orwell created a dark and bleak world where Big Brother monitored everything you did and controlled every piece of information to which you were given access. Many supporters of employee privacy rights argue that we have reached that state now that employers have the technology to monitor every keystroke on your computer, track every Web site you visit, and record every call you make. The vicarious liability argument is presented to justify these actions as being in the best interests of shareholders, but what is in the best interests of the employees?

The liability argument and the recent availability of capable technology may be driving this move towards an Orwellian work environment, but what are the long-term effects likely to be? Employee turnover costs organizations thousands of dollars in recruitment costs, training, and lost productivity. Creating a "locked-down" place to work may protect your liability, but it may also drive away those employees who really aren't comfortable being treated like lab rats.

1. Thou Shalt Not Use A Computer To Harm Other People.

2. Thou Shalt Not Interfere With Other People's Computer Work.

3. Thou Shalt Not Snoop Around In Other People's Computer Files.

4. Thou Shalt Not Use A Computer To Steal.

5. Thou Shalt Not Use A Computer To Bear False Witness.

6. Thou Shalt Not Copy Or Use Proprietary Software For Which You Have Not Paid.

7. Thou Shalt Not Use Other People's Computer Resources Without Authorization Or Proper Compensation.

8. Thou Shalt Not Appropriate Other People's Intellectual Output.

9. Thou Shalt Think About The Social Consequences Of The Program You Are Writing Or The System You Are Designing.

10. Thou Shalt Always Use A Computer In Ways That Ensure Consideration And Respect For Your Fellow Humans.

Ten Commandments of Computer Ethics[12]

(Created by the Computer Ethics Institute.)

✓ PROGRESS CHECK QUESTIONS

13. Which of the "Ten Commandments of Computer Ethics" carry the strongest ethical message? Why?

14. Define the term *vicarious liability.*

15. List four of the top categories of litigation related to Internet communications.

16. Define the term *cyberliability.*

Big Brother Is Here to Stay

The Computer Ethics Institute offers some simple guidelines on the appropriate use of technology, but the debate over whether all this technology demands a new techno-friendly school of ethics is likely to continue. However, addressing the issue in real time requires us to consider how many of the issues have really changed from the variables we have been discussing in the previous seven chapters of this book. We are still talking about the same stakeholders, conducting the same business transactions in the same fiercely competitive markets. What have changed are the platforms on which those transactions can now take place and, more importantly, the speed with which they occur.

Should the same rules that apply to recording telephone calls apply to emails in the same way, or should there be a different set of rules? The reality is that our working lives have changed dramatically since the arrival of all this technology. We all spend a lot more time at work, and the availability of instant access to our work means that the line between work life and private life is now much less clearly defined. This change should mean that the employer's ability to intrude on our personal lives with an urgent request would be balanced by an equal flexibility in our time at work—but does that really happen where you work? If you think this debate is being overhyped in the media, consider the following summary of employee surveillance capabilities.[13]

> Remarkably invasive tools exist to monitor employees at the workplace. These include:
>
> - Packet-sniffing software can intercept, analyze, and archive all communications on a network, including employee email, chat sessions, file sharing, and Internet browsing. Employees who use the workplace network to access personal email accounts not provided by the company are not protected. Their private accounts, as long as they are accessed on workplace network or phone lines, can be monitored.
>
> - Keystroke loggers can be employed to capture every key pressed on a computer keyboard. These systems will even record information that is typed and then deleted.
>
> - Phone monitoring is pervasive in the American workplace. Some companies employ systems that automatically monitor call content and breaks between receiving calls.
>
> - Video surveillance is widely deployed in the American workplace. In a number of cases, video surveillance has been used in employee bathrooms, rest areas, and changing areas. Video surveillance, under federal law, is acceptable where the camera focuses on publicly accessible areas. However, installment in areas where employees or customers have a legitimate expectation of privacy, such as inside bathroom stalls, can give the employee a cause of action under tort law.
>
> - "Smart" ID cards can track an employee's location while he or she moves through the workplace. By using location tracking, an employer can monitor whether employees spend enough time in front of the bathroom sink to wash their hands. New employee ID cards can even determine the direction the worker is facing at any given time.

Problems at Computerworld—
Steve Makes a Decision

Steve thought long and hard about what he should do now. As a new employee, he really didn't want to get a reputation as a troublemaker, and he liked working with Larry most of the time. Anyway, there was no harm done. Mr. Johnson got a new hard drive under his warranty, ComputerWorld got the replacement contract (keeping Larry and him employed!), and Larry got his perk of a slightly used hard drive to sell at the flea market next weekend. As far as ComputerWorld was concerned, the drives were destroyed—their employee manual instructed them to drill holes through the drives and throw them away. What else was the manufacturer going to do with them? Break them up and recycle them for scrap? That seemed like a waste of a perfectly good hard drive.

"Larry's a reliable guy," thought Steve. "I'm sure he'll remember to erase those drives before he sells them.

Before he knew it, Steve was "one of the guys." Larry taught him all the "tricks of the trade" and between them they built a lucrative side business of used computer parts repaired under warranty, listed as "destroyed," and then sold at the flea market on the weekends.

Unfortunately, two months later, Mr. Johnson received a telephone call from someone who had bought a used hard drive at the flea market. The seller had told him that the drive had been erased, but when he installed it, he found all Mr. Johnson's personal information still on the hard drive.

1. What could Steve have done differently here?

2. What do you think will happen now?

3. What will be the consequences for Steve, Larry, Mr. Johnson, and ComputerWorld?

[KEY TERMS]

Cyberliability *p. 194*

Extranet *p. 185*

Intranet *p. 185*

Telecommuting *p. 189*

Thick Consent *p. 190*

Thin Consent *p. 190*

Vicarious Liability *p. 194*

[REVIEW QUESTIONS]

1. Should you be allowed to surf the Web at work? Why or why not?

2. Are your telephone calls monitored where you work? If they are, how does that make you feel? If they aren't monitored, how would you feel if that policy were introduced?

3. What would you do if someone sent you an email at work that you found offensive? Would you just delete it or say something to that person?

4. If you had the chance to work from home and telecommute, would you take it? If the opportunity meant that you had to allow your company to monitor every call on your phone and every keystroke on your computer, would you still take it? Explain why or why not.

[REVIEW EXERCISE]

Removing temptation. I'm the customer service director for Matrix Technologies, a manufacturer of design software. We've recently upgraded our customer service extranet service to allow our clients to download software updates (including any patches or "bug fixes") directly from our extranet site. The initial response from the majority of our customers has been very positive—the new process is convenient, quick, and reliable—they love it. Everyone, that is, except for our large local government client. The new service doesn't help them at all—and the reason for that really has me stumped. Earlier this year, this client made the decision to remove access to the Internet from all their desktop computers, so no access to the Internet means no access to our customer service site to download our upgrades. When I asked the IT director if he was pulling my leg, he got mad at me. Apparently they installed some monitoring software on their system and found that employees were spending almost 40 percent of their time surfing the Web—mostly to news and entertainment sites, but sometimes to places that would make you blush! Their response was swift and effective. The employees came in one morning and found that they no longer had access to the Web from their desktops. Now we have to come up with a plan to mail upgrade CDs to 24 regional offices.

1. How well did Matrix's client handle this situation?

2. What kind of message does this send to the employees of Matrix's client?

3. What other options were available here?

4. On the assumption that their downloadable software patches can greatly improve updates for their client, does Matrix have an ethical obligation to get involved here? Explain your answer.

INTERNET EXERCISE

Visit the Web site for the LRN Corporation at www.lrn.com.

1. What does the LRN Corporation do?
2. What are the five core values of the LRN culture?
3. What is the stated purpose of the LRN-RAND Center for Corporate Ethics, Law and Governance?

TEAM EXERCISES

1. **When are you "at work"?** Divide into two teams. One team must defend the *employer* position on employee monitoring. The other team must defend the *employee* position. Draw on the policies and experiences you have gathered from your own jobs.

2. **A new billing system.** A new system that bills corporate clients is under development, and there is a discussion over how much to invest in error checking and control. One option has been put forward so far, and initial estimates suggest it would add about 40 percent to the overall cost of the project but would vastly improve the quality of the data in the database and the accuracy of client billing. Not spending the money would increase the risk of overcharging some midsize clients. Divide into two groups and prepare arguments *for* and *against* spending the extra money on error checking and control. Remember to include in your argument how stakeholders would be impacted and how you would deal with any unhappy customers.

3. **Email privacy.** Divide into two groups and prepare arguments *for* and *against* the following behavior: Your company has a clearly stated employee surveillance policy that stipulates that anything an employee does on a company-owned computer is subject to monitoring. You manage a regional office of 24 brokers for a company that offers lump-sum payments to people receiving installment payments—from lottery winnings or personal injury settlements—who would rather have a large amount of money now than small monthly checks for the next 5, 10, or 20 years.

   You have just terminated one of your brokers for failing to meet his monthly targets for three consecutive months. He was extremely angry about the news and when he went back to his cube, he was observed typing feverishly on his computer in the 10 minutes before building security arrived to escort him from the premises.

   When your IT specialist arrives to shut down the broker's computer, he notices that it is still open and logged-in to his Gmail account and that there is evidence that several emails with large attachments had been sent from his company email address to his Gmail address shortly after the time he was notified that he was being fired. The emails had been deleted from the folder of sent items in his company account. The IT specialist suggests that you take a look at the emails and specifically the information attached to those emails. Should you?

4. **Software piracy.** Divide into two groups and prepare arguments *for* and *against* the following behavior: You run your own graphic design company as a one-person show, doing primarily small-business projects and subcontracting work for larger graphic design agencies. You have just been hired as an adjunct instructor at the local community college to teach a graphic design course. You decide that it's easier to use your own laptop rather than worry about having the right software loaded on the classroom machines, and so the college IT department loads the most current version of your graphic design software on your machine. Business has been a little slow for you and you haven't spent the money to update your own software. The version that the IT department loads is three editions ahead of your version with lots of new functionality.

   You enjoy teaching the class, although the position doesn't pay very well. One added bonus, however, is that you can be far more productive on your company projects using the most current version of the software on your laptop, and since you use some of that work as examples in your class, you're not really doing anything unethical, right?

STUMBLING OVER GMAIL

In spring 2004, with business booming and Google basking in the glow of its ever-growing popularity, Larry [Page] and Sergey [Brin] prepared to dazzle Internet users with a different kind of email. Building on the strong Google brand name, they called the new service "Gmail." . . . Larry and Sergey wanted to make a big splash with Gmail. There was no reason to provide the service unless it was radically better than email services already offered by Microsoft, Yahoo, AOL, and others. They built Gmail to be smarter, easier, cheaper, and superior. Otherwise Google users wouldn't be impressed, and its creators wouldn't be living up to their own high standards . . . [Larry and Sergey] had identified email problems that Google, with its immense computing power, could address. For example, it was difficult, if not impossible, to find and retrieve old emails when users needed them. America Online automatically deleted emails after 30 days to hold down systems costs. There was no easy way to store the mountain of emails that an accumulative Internet user amassed without slowing personal computers or paying Microsoft, Yahoo, or another firm to provide additional storage.

To blow the competition away and add a Google "wow" factor, Larry and Sergey, and the Gmail team inside the Googleplex addressed all these issues and then some. To make the new service an instant hit, they planned to give away one free gigabyte of storage (1,000 megabytes) on Google's own computer network with each Gmail account. That was 500 times greater than the free storage offered by Microsoft and 250 times the free storage offered by Yahoo. . . . One gigabyte was such an amazing amount of storage that Google told Gmail users they would never need to delete another email.

Finally, to inject Gmail with that Googley sense of magic, computer users would be able to find emails instantly, without ever having to think about sorting or storing them. A Gmail search would be fast, accurate, and as easy to perform as a Google search, making the service an instant hit among trusted employees who sampled it inside the Googleplex.

Unlike most of its new products, Gmail was designed to make money even during the test phase. With demand for advertising increasing, the company needed to increase the available space it could sell. It made sense to Larry and Sergey to profit from Gmail by putting the same type of small ads on the right-hand side of Gmails that Google put on the right-hand side of search results. The ads would be "contextually relevant," triggered by words contained in the emails. It was a proven business model that served advertisers and users well as part of Google's search results. By giving advertisers more space on the Google network, Gmail would provide a healthy new stream of profits for the company that would grow over time as the communications technology caught on.

Looking at the world through Google-colored lenses, this seemed like a superb idea in every respect. It didn't occur to Larry, Sergey, or any of the other engineers in senior roles at Google that serious people they respected would strenuously object to the privacy implications of having Google's computers reading emails and then placing ads in them based on the content of those messages . . .

As word spread of Google's plans to put ads in emails, politicians and privacy groups attacked the company and its plans, kicking off a media firestorm. In Massachusetts, anti-Gmail legislation was introduced. Shocked privacy advocates urged the company to pull the product immediately and began circulating anti-Google petitions. One California lawmaker threatened the company, saying that if Google didn't dump Gmail, she would press for legislation banning it. Her bill passed the Senate's Judiciary Committee with only one opposing vote. She decried the ad-driven profiteering in emails as a gross, unwarranted invasion of privacy. For the first time, Google was being viewed with suspicion in a major way. People considered their emails private, and the notion of Google's putting ads in them based on their content seemed to cross the line . . .

Because from their perspective this was much ado about nothing, Larry and Sergey saw no need to be defensive or respond to crazed critics. In fact, all the publicity would certainly heighten awareness of the Google search engine and its Gmail progeny. Soon enough, friendly columnists who tested Gmail and fell in love with it would begin writing about why the outcry was unjustified. Tradition-bound companies might have seriously considered pulling Gmail, at least temporarily, to quell the uprising. But this was Google, and it had clout, and confident leadership, to ride this out without flinching. The founders began to respond on-message.

"It sounded alarming, but it isn't," Sergey said. "The ads correlate to the message you're reading at the time. We're not keeping your mail and mining it or anything like that. And no information whatsoever goes out. We need to be protective of the mail and the people's privacy. Any Web service will scan your mail. It scans it in order to show it to you; it scans it for spam. All we're doing is showing ads. It's automated. No one is looking, so I don't think it's a privacy issue. I've used Gmail for a while, and I like having the ads. Our ads aren't distracting. They're helpful."

When Google tested Gmail, people bought lots of things by clicking on the ads. To Larry, this was proof that computer users, advertisers, and Google's coffers were all well served by the small ads on the right-hand side of a Gmail. "Even if it seems a little spooky at first, it's useful," he said.

Discussion Questions

1. Google sent out a press release about the Gmail service without mentioning the intention to put ads in the emails or how those ads would be selected. Was that ethical? Explain why or why not.

2. Sergey Brin offered the argument that all email providers scan your e-mails for content to ensure that it is yours and that it isn't a spam email. Does that argument justify their decision to scan emails for content in order to place "contextually relevant" ads? Explain why or why not.

3. Does the fact that the scanning process is done by computer, with no people reading the emails, make the act any less of an invasion of your privacy?

4. Does the availability of 1 gigabyte of free storage, which was 500 times greater than the storage offered by Microsoft at the time, make the placement of ads in your emails a fair trade? Explain your answer.

5. Give four examples of ads that could be shown in emails that you would send or receive.

6. Could Google have launched Gmail in a way that would have avoided the media firestorm over privacy? Explain your answer.

Source: David A. Vise, "The Google Story," New York: Delacorte Press, Random House, 2005, pp. 152–156.

CANADIAN IMPERIAL BANK OF COMMERCE: DIGITAL EMPLOYEE PRIVACY

Introduction

"We could have a lively situation on our hands if some of these email privacy scenarios come true," remarked Bob Jones, compliance manager at Canadian Imperial Bank of Commerce (CIBC). It was May 16, 2000, and Jones was aware that Toronto-based CIBC had implemented word-recognition software in its U.S. brokerage to comb email messages sent by employees for specified business words. What if these routine searches flagged an email message that also contained personal information about an employee? In the wake of an email "worm" that crippled corporate networks in the first week of May 2000, use of email at work was a hot topic of discussion in management circles.

Canadian Imperial Bank of Commerce

As of May 2000, Canadian Imperial Bank of Commerce had 45,000 employees worldwide serving six million individual customers, 350,000 small businesses, and 7,000 corporate and investment banking customers. The bank had total assets of $250 billion, and a net income of $1.029 billion in 1999.

Richard Ivey School of Business
The University of Western Ontario

Employee Privacy in the Banking Industry

Employee privacy was somewhat different than customer privacy. By design, in most banks, customers were provided with the best level of privacy protection available. However, there were legitimate reasons why banks might want to monitor what employees were doing on company time and with company equipment.

For banks like CIBC, providing employees with access to company email had become a strategic necessity. However, with email access came the possibility of unwittingly receiving or transmitting an email worm or virus, much like the ones which swept across the world in early 2000. Computer Economics Inc., a research firm based in Carlsbad, California, reported that the ILOVEYOU virus alone had infected three million computers around the world, causing US$2 billion in direct economic losses and a further US$6.7 billion in lost productivity. Insurer Lloyd's of London announced on May 8, 2000, that computer viruses would prove to be the biggest insurance risk in upcoming years, prompting business analysts to call for a widespread change in company email policies.

In addition to protecting company systems from viruses, employers like CIBC had obligations to ensure that employees were not acting illegally, (for example in perpetrating frauds) or immorally. Without appropriate security, employees could use email to make inappropriate or defamatory comments or to transmit sensitive corporate information.

CIBC's Electronic Communication Policy

Email and voice mail were both included in Section 4.6 of CIBC's *Principles of Business Conduct*. CIBC recognized that occasional personal use could not be avoided:

> E-mail and voice mail are essential ways to communicate with employees, customers, suppliers, and other parties. Although all e-mail and voice mail facilities supplied by CIBC are its property, CIBC recognizes that incidental or occasional personal use of both is unavoidable.

CIBC reserved the right to access and monitor both internal and external email and voice mail, including stored messages, and to restrict the use of both, without prior notice. The company also reserved the right to produce all office communications in legal proceedings.

Assentor Software

To ensure that its brokerage employees were not acting inappropriately in their dealings with customers through email communications, CIBC relied on software to screen and archive email messages in a central database. The software had the ability to screen not only key words, but also combinations of words and sentences (so-called natural language technology). The software allowed CIBC to flag and hold potentially inappropriate email communications, such as high-pressure sales tactics and insider information, as well as other potentially litigious issues, such as sexual harassment. These flagged emails were then held for human analysis and review before being sent.

The market for email screening software was worth $17 million in 1999, and was growing at a rate of 45 percent per year. According to a report by the Tower Group (www.towergroup.com), natural language technology was a significant improvement in screening technology allowing for more flexible and accurate monitoring than keyword or phrase search alone.

An excerpt from a news release from SRA International Inc. (which markets Assentor email screening software), dated February 22, 1999, read:

> (Tower Group) predicts that natural language functionality will become the technology of choice for e-mail compliance tools. . . . Securities firms of all sizes are using Assentor to apply technology to the compliance review process and take advantage of the many benefits of e-mail technology for communicating with their clients. Assentor uses a sophisticated, linguistics-based natural language pattern matching engine and highly refined compliance patterns developed closely with securities industry associations, compliance experts, and major broker/dealers to ensure that the technology is effective for all types of compliance requirements.

Companies in the financial services industry that used Assentor included CIBC, A. G. Edwards, BancBoston, Southwest Securities, and the National Association of Securities Dealers. Many others used other email screening methods, most of which were less powerful.

Call centers typically tape conversations for quality control, and most organizations announce to the customer at the beginning of the call that the conversation will be taped. Employees working at call centers knew when they arrived at work that their conversations would be taped due to the possibility of disputes—for example, replaying a taped call would confirm if the customer requested a buy order of 500 shares instead of a sell order for 5,000 shares of the same stock. It was much easier, on the other hand, to forget that email use could be monitored.

CIBC had recently developed an electronic mail policy, which went into more detail than the previous entry in its *Principles of Business Conduct* document. This policy outlined appropriate and inappropriate use of this company resource. A short summary of the policy read:

> Electronic mail (e-mail) systems, provided by the CIBC Group of Companies (CIBC Group) are its property. Employees are to use these systems for company business primarily within the boundaries of this policy and its standards. Business information and the ability to freely communicate it are valuable assets that play a significant role in CIBC's success. The protection and appropriate use of these assets is everyone's responsibility.
>
> All messages sent or received by electronic mail are CIBC records and must be handled in a manner consistent with CIBC record management policies and practices. Caution and discretion should be used in the nature and content of all messages sent, stored or distributed.
>
> CIBC recognizes that incidental or occasional use of e-mail for personal communications is unavoidable. However, all users with access to CIBC e-mail systems should be aware that the CIBC reserves the right to access, to monitor and to archive all e-mail messages, transmitted, received or stored on its systems, without further prior notice.

"Email use is often similar to casual conversations rather than formal written communications," Jones recognized, "because employees forget that it is recorded and can be monitored." He went on to stress that email is a business resource covered by a separate email policy. He concluded by asking, "how should employees be discouraged from inappropriate language, content, and usage?"

Jones knew that these were not easy questions to answer. Recent articles in newspapers and trade journals on email privacy, such as the following excerpt from the *Wall Street Journal* article "Prying Times: Those Bawdy E-Mails Were Good for a Laugh—Until the Ax Fell" (February 4, 2000), had brought the issue to CIBC's attention once more.

> In the course of their inquiry, workers say, managers found a number of potentially offensive e-mails, some of which had been sent by or forwarded to other employees in the office. That led to a wider investigation, and ended Nov. 30, 1999 when the *Times* fired

22 people in Norfolk, plus one in New York. Roughly 20 more workers, who the company determined had received offensive messages but didn't forward them to others, got warning letters. Most of the fired employees were otherwise in good standing; one had just received a promotion, and another had recently been commended as "employee of the quarter."

Some corporations, like CIBC, used email screening to catch email misuse, but since these filters tended to slow down network traffic, the practice was not universal. A second option, according to Jordan Worth, an Internet Analyst with International Data Corporation, an Internet research firm, was to put in place policies that banned certain types of attachments. A third approach was to archive email, but only access it in the event of a complaint.

What Should CIBC Do?

Jones found that making the decision to implement the Assentor software was a lot easier than deciding what to do in the event that the software found something improper.

"What if an employee sends a personal message using a business word flagged by Assentor and his or her direct manager finds out about a private situation?" wondered Jones. "What are the legal ramifications if the employee is reassigned or fired and subsequently claims bias on the part of the manager? What about the question of company ethics? Should we be reading personal email from employees?"

Jones wondered how to best reinforce the email policy at CIBC.

Discussion Questions

1. Is the risk of an email virus enough justification to monitor all email traffic at CIBC?

2. A second option is to ban the types of attachments that typically include email viruses. Is this a more ethical alternative? Explain why or why not.

3. A third option is to simply archive the email without reading it and only access it in the event of a complaint. Is this a more ethical alternative? Explain why or why not.

4. Which stakeholders are impacted by the decisions made in this case?

5. Do you think CIBC's email policy is an example of thin or thick consent? Explain your answer.

6. What would you recommend in this situation?

Source: M. Wade, and K. Mark, "Canadian Imperial Bank of Commerce: Digital Employee Privacy," Richard Ivey School of Business, University of Western Ontario, 2001.

Ken Mark prepared this case under the supervision of Mike Wade solely to provide material for class discussion. The authors do not intend to illustrate either effective or ineffective handling of a managerial situation. The authors may have disguised certain names and other identifying information to protect confidentiality.

THE HIPAA PRIVACY RULE

On August 21, 1996, Congress enacted the Health Insurance Portability and Accountability Act (HIPAA), a piece of legislation designed to clarify exactly what rights patients have over their own medical information and to specify what procedures needed to be in place to enforce appropriate sharing of that information within the healthcare community. "This law required Congress to pass legislation within 3 years to govern privacy and confidentiality related to (a patient's) medical record. If that action did not occur, then the Department of Health and Human Services (DHHS) was to identify and publish the appropriate legislation. Because Congress did not pass required legislation, the DHHS developed and publicized a set of rules on medical record privacy and confidentiality" that required compliance from most healthcare providers by April 14, 2003.

Since then, the HIPAA legislation has often been referred to as a privacy rule, but in reality it is disclosure legislation that "offers a floor, rather than a ceiling, for health privacy." As such, the true purpose behind the commitment to patient privacy is to control how patient information is collected and by whom, how and where it will be stored safely for future retrieval, and how healthcare providers and other healthcare organizations will use it, ideally on a need-to-know basis only.

As Bill Trippe explains the law in an *Econtent* article, "The key. . .is to provide authorized (healthcare professionals) with precisely the information they need, when they need it—but only the precise information they need so that (patient) privacy is not compromised."

However, while advances in information technology—specifically database technology—appear to offer the promise of functionality to do precisely that, the sheer number of combinations of users and needs in the provision of healthcare would seem to exceed even those grand promises. Compare, for example, the patient records needs of a doctor prescribing a specific medication, as opposed to those of a doctor giving a full physical examination. The former might need lab results and any relevant research about the medication; the latter would prefer to have the patient's full medical history. It may be possible to retrieve that information from one comprehensive database, but if everyone has different information needs, how do you set up that database to restrict access where appropriate under the banner of need to know or to summarize information where needed to maximize patient privacy?

The logistical challenges of this scenario are further complicated when you consider that the legislation covers not only patient care but also the administrative aspects of the healthcare system. For example, according to Richard Sobel of the *Hastings Center Report,* HIPAA gave "six hundred thousand 'covered entities'—such as health care plans, clearing houses, and health maintenance organizations—'regulatory permission to use or disclose protected health information for treatment, payment, and health care operations' (known as TPO) without patient consent. Some of these 'routine purposes' for which disclosures are permitted are far removed from treatment. . . 'health care operations' (HCO) include most administrative and profit-generating activities, such as auditing, data analyses for plan sponsors, training of non-healthcare professionals, general administrative activities, business planning and development, cost management, payment methods improvement, premium rating, underwriting, and asset sales—all unrelated to patient care."

HIPAA was enacted to address privacy concerns in the face of increasingly sophisticated database technology that can send your most private information to the other side of the globe in a split second. Ironically, however, many violations of the privacy rule have little connection, if any, with direct patient care and treatment. Consider the following two examples:

1. "Patient MW, a victim of domestic abuse, informs (her nurse) that her status as a patient in the hospital must be kept confidential. (The nurse) assures MW that she's safe and that the staff won't share information with anyone who inquires about her. (The nurse) informs the unit clerk not to release any information

on MW, but fails to remove MW's name and room number from the assignment board (at the nurse's station). Later in the shift, MW's husband enters the nurse's station and asks the unit clerk for his wife's number. The unit clerk, following the nurse's instructions, states that she has no information on the person named. The spouse, upon looking around the nurse's station, sees his wife's name and room number. He rushes to the room and physically abuses her. The unit clerk calls hospital security, which promptly arrives and escorts the spouse off the unit. He's subsequently jailed for spousal abuse."

2. "A member of the electronic medical record (EMR) staff was conducting a training session for resident physicians and medical students at an outpatient facility. . . . The trainer used fictional patient records specifically created for EMR training purposes for the demonstrations and exercises. During the Q&A session one of the residents stated that just that morning he had had problems prescribing a specific medication in the medication module of the EMR, which had created an inaccurate entry in the patient's electronic chart. The resident

asked how he could correct the mistake. Since the trainer knew that many new EMR users had had similar problems with this feature of the EMR, she thought this would be a good 'teachable moment.' She asked the resident the name of the patient. She then looked up the patient's chart and projected the patient's medication list on the screen for all the class to see. The trainer proceeded to correct the error in the EMR."

While the first example represents a clear violation of the HIPAA legislation, since the patient's room information was publicly accessible simply by visiting the nurse's station, the situation is not so straightforward in the second example. The residents and medical students being trained were employees of a covered entity, and since training falls under the heading of approved healthcare operations, no violation occurred. Of course, it is debatable as to whether it was appropriate to display the patient's records to the entire group rather than helping the one student after the class, since that choice calls into question the issue of using the minimum information on a need-to-know basis. What is clear, however, is that while the purpose of HIPAA may be clearly stated, the interpretation of the legislation lacks the same degree of clarity.

Discussion Questions

1. What is the stated purpose of the HIPAA legislation?

2. Is the term *privacy rule* accurate in describing the HIPAA legislation? Why or why not?

3. What are the key objectives in providing patient information?

4. Is it ethical for covered entities to be excused from getting patient permission to use their private information for routine purposes? Why or why not?

5. Based on the limited information in this article, do you think the HIPAA legislation achieves its objective of securing patient privacy?

6. How could this issue of patient privacy have been handled in a more ethical manner?

Source: Judith A. Erlen, "HIPAA-Clinical and Ethical Considerations for Nurses," *Orthopaedic Nursing* 23, no. 6 (November/December 2004). J. Mack, "Beyond HIPAA-Ethics in the e-Health Arena," *Healthcare Executive*, September/October 2004, pp. 32–33.
Bill Trippe, "First Do No Harm: Can Privacy and Advanced Information Technology Coexist?" *Econtent* 26, no. 3 (March 2003).
Richard Sobel, "The HIPAA Paradox: The Privacy Rule That's Not," *The Hastings Center Report* 37, no. 4 (July/August 2007).
Patricia D. Blair, "Make Room for Patient Privacy," *Nursing Management*, June 2003, pp. 28–29.
Bob Brown, "Did They Break the Rules?" *Journal of Health Care Compliance* 10, no. 2 (March/April 2008).

THE FUTURE OF BUSINESS
ETHICS

» » Having examined the challenges involved in developing an ethical culture within an organization, we can now consider what lies ahead for companies as they grow on an international and global scale. Crossing national boundaries to conduct business often involves crossing cultural boundaries at the same time. How do organizations address those cultural differences while staying true to their own ethical principles?

Chapter 9 examines the challenges organizations face in the pursuit of global ethics. While they may prefer to adopt their own policies as a universal standard of ethics, the reality is that the organizations and customers from other countries with whom they conduct business will bring their own moral standards and ethical principles into the relationship. What happens when there is a conflict in those standards?

Chapter 10 examines the big-picture issue of maintaining an ethical culture in the face of all these challenges. This far into the text, we have examined all the issues and the resources available to help organizations and their employees with those issues, but the challenge of maintaining and enforcing a code of ethics must be faced on a daily basis. » »

chapter 9

Ethics and Globalization

" The World has become small and completely interdependent. "
—Wendell L. Wilkie, Republican presidential nominee
defeated by Franklin D. Roosevelt in 1940

LEARNING OBJECTIVES

After studying this chapter, you should be able to:

1. Understand the ethical issues arising in global business.

2. Explain the issue of ethical relativism in a global environment.

3. Compare the ethical challenges in doing business in developing and developed economies.

4. Explain the challenges in developing a global code of ethics.

5. Analyze the ramifications of the UN Global Compact.

6. Explain the OECD Guidelines for Multinational Enterprises.

A Matter of Definition

Kevin is a copywriter with a regional ad agency that has a very lucrative contract with the Smith's national retail chain. He likes working for a smaller agency even though he could probably make more money with a larger national organization. At least here everyone knows each other and works together as a team, and he likes the culture here—they do good work for good clients and they have been known to turn down contracts for campaigns that conflicted with their corporate values. In fact, their decision to turn down a campaign for a local bourbon distillery made the trade press.

Kevin has friends at a couple of the national agencies and they describe the culture as a totally cutthroat one where it's everyone for himself and any business is good business as long as the check clears.

Landing the Smith's account was a big deal for their regional agency and they all worked hard to make it happen (and celebrated with a party that will probably go down in company history as one of the best ever!). Now they had to deliver on everything they promised in their bid for the work. Their first big project is the new campaign for the July 4th sales event coming up. The theme of the event is "Made in America," which the company thinks will tap into a sense of patriotism. Smith's has lined up several very low-priced "loss leaders" to get customers into the store, and they are promoting them heavily as being "made in America."

Kevin has been assigned to write the copy for a series of ads featuring BBQ utensil sets featuring the American flag and red, white, and blue color combinations. As part of his prep kit, Kevin receives the product specifications on the items along with the photographs that his copy will support.

As he is reading through the material, Kevin notices that his contacts at Smith's included a copy of the original billing paperwork for the shipment by mistake—paperwork that shows that the items were actually made in Indonesia by a company named Jakarta Enterprises.

The name seems very familiar to Kevin and he looks the company up on Google. To his dismay, he finds several articles criticizing the business practices of Jakarta Enterprises—specifically in the area of employing young children in sweatshop working conditions.

1. Ten guidelines for organizations doing business with developing nations are listed on page 217. Do you think Smith's is following any of these?

2. Review the UN Global Compact on page 220. How many violations has Smith's incurred by doing business with Jakarta Enterprises?

3. What are Kevin's options here?

Ethics and Globalization

Up to now we have focused primarily on a domestic approach to business ethics—how we as North American organizations get our own house in order and ensure that we have a clearly defined code of ethics which all our stakeholders can relate to and understand.

Once we step outside the domestic environment and conduct business on an international or even a global scale, the concept of business ethics changes dramatically. Business transactions in different countries in different languages and different cultures inevitably force North American companies to revisit the ethical principles to which they are committed and to recognize which principles and policies they are willing to negotiate in favor of the client country with which they are looking to do business.

Ethics in Less-Developed Nations

Any discussion of business ethics in this arena must distinguish between the developed and **less-developed nations** of the world. If we follow the traditional stereotypes, companies in the **developed nations** know how the game is played. Business is typically conducted in English and all international business travelers have read and reread their copy of *Kiss, Bow, or Shake Hands: How to Do Business in Sixty Countries.*[1]

These nations are busy playing the game of globalization—everyone is pursuing the same goal of maximum profits with minimum costs, and if individual cultures present some challenges, those can be overcome with translations and cultural adaptations. That, of course, is easier said than done. The assumption that "what works here works there" has managed to get a lot of companies into hot water over the years[2]:

Less-Developed Nation Country that lacks the economic, social, and technological infrastructure of a developed nation.

Developed Nation Country that enjoys a high standard of living as measured by economic, social, and technological criteria.

- The name Coca-Cola in China was first rendered as Ke-kou-ke-la. Unfortunately, the Coke company did not discover until after thousands of signs had been printed that the phrase means, "bite the wax tadpole" or "female horse stuffed with wax," depending on the dialect. Coke then researched 40,000 Chinese characters and found a close phonetic equivalent, "ko-kou-ko-le," which can be loosely translated as "happiness in the mouth" (though a marketing "classic," this story has been denounced as an urban legend).

- In Taiwan, the translation of the Pepsi slogan "Come alive with the Pepsi Generation" came out as "Pepsi will bring your ancestors back from the dead."

- When Parker Pen marketed a ballpoint pen in Mexico, its ads were supposed to say, "It won't leak in your pocket and embarrass you." However, the company mistakenly thought the Spanish word *embarazar* meant "embarrass"; instead, the ads said, "It won't leak in your pocket and make you pregnant."

- An American T-shirt manufacturer in Miami printed shirts for the Spanish market that promoted the Pope's visit. But instead of the desired "I Saw the Pope" in Spanish, the shirts proclaimed "I Saw the Potato."

- In Italy, a campaign for Schweppes Tonic Water translated the name into Schweppes *Toilet* Water.

- Bacardi concocted a fruity drink with the name "Pavian" to suggest French chic, but "Pavian" means "baboon" in German.

- Clairol introduced the "Mist Stick," a curling iron, into Germany, only to find out that *mist* is slang for manure.

- When Gerber first started selling baby food in Africa, they used the same packaging as in the United States—jars with pictures of the cute little baby on the label. Only later did they learn that in Africa, companies routinely put pictures on the label that describe what's inside, since most people can't read.

- And, as America's favorite chicken magnate, Frank Perdue, was fond of saying, "It takes a tough man to make a tender chicken." In Spanish, however, his words took on a whole new meaning: "It takes a sexually stimulated man to make a chicken affectionate."

These are all amusing anecdotes, but the economic reality underlying them is far more serious. International markets represent growth and with profitable growth come happy shareholders and rising stock prices. In addition, international markets represent new customers as well as sources of cheaper materials and cheap labor.

From a business ethics perspective, this constant hunger for growth at any cost presents some challenges. As we recall from our discussion of **utilitarianism** in Chapter 1, any questionable behavior in overseas markets can be explained away by serving the greatest good for the greatest number of people. However, as we discussed in Chapter 1, when you focus on doing the greatest good for the greatest number of people, there is no accountability for individual actions.

So what happens if you simply transplant your "take no prisoners" aggressive business style from the United States to whatever market you happen to be in? Do the same rules apply? Or do you focus on not breaking any local laws and fall back on the old adage, "if it's legal, it must be ethical"? Are American companies bound by their domestic ethical policies when they conduct business overseas, or are they free to adopt (or completely overlook) local ethics? Is this a uniquely American phenomenon or do French, German, Russian, or Chinese companies adopt similarly flexible attitudes to business ethics when they step outside their national boundaries?

Before we examine these questions in detail, we should clarify some terminology. The term **globalization** has applications in commercial, economic, social, and political environments. For our purposes, we are concerned with globalization as the expansion of international trade to a point where regional trade blocs (Latin America, Europe, Africa) have overtaken national markets, leading eventually to a global marketplace. As these national markets become interdependent, questions arise over the ethical behavior of economically advanced nations toward developing ones.

Operating in this increasingly globalized business world are **multinational corporations (MNCs)**—also referred to as transnational corporations—that pursue revenue (and hopefully profit) on the basis of operating strategies that ignore national boundaries as merely bureaucratic obstacles. Economists disagree over the correct definition of an MNC: Some argue that to be truly multinational, an organization must have owners from more than one country (such as Shell's Anglo-Dutch structure); others argue that an organization is multinational when it

Utilitarianism Ethical choices that offer the greatest good for the greatest number of people.

Globalization The expansion of international trade to a point where national markets have been overtaken by regional trade blocs (Latin America, Europe, Africa), leading eventually to a global marketplace.

Multinational Corporation A company that provides and sells products and services across multiple national borders.

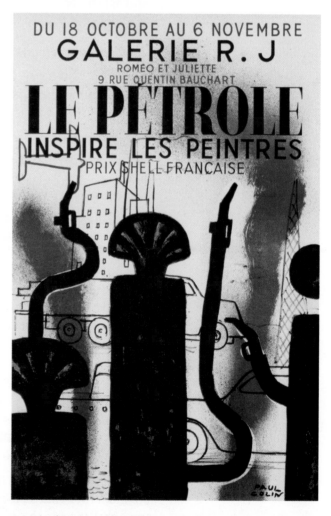

As a multinational corporation Shell must reach different markets with different needs. How might this impact local employees at a Shell Service Station?

generates products and/or services in multiple countries and when it implements operational policies (marketing, staffing, production) that go beyond national boundaries.

It is here that the global ethics dilemma becomes apparent: What happens when you go beyond national boundaries? If ethical standards are based on cultural and social norms and customs, what happens when you are operating in an environment that is representative of multiple cultures and societies?

Critics have argued that most MNCs have chosen to ignore all ethical standards in the pursuit of the almighty dollar on the basis of the following two arguments:

- If they didn't pursue the business, somebody else would.
- They are operating in full compliance with local laws and regulations, which conveniently happen to be far less restrictive than those they would face in their own country.

✓ PROGRESS CHECK QUESTIONS

1. Explain the term *globalization.*

2. What is an MNC?

3. When is "operating in full compliance with local laws and regulations" unethical?

4. Explain the term *utilitarianism.*

For the less-developed nations, the concept of globalization has a different meaning.

Economist Lester Thurow explains[3]:

> Among countries, the big losers are in Africa, south of the Sahara. They are not losing, however, because they are being crushed by globalization. . . . [T]hey are losing because they are being ignored by globalization. They are not in the global economy. No one in the business community wants anything to do with countries where illiteracy is high, where modern infrastructure (telecommunications, reliable electrical power) does not exist, and where social chaos reigns. Such countries are neither potential markets nor potential production bases.

E T H I C A L dilemma

CASE 9.1 Questionable Payments

Gulf Oil is in talks to sell one of its refineries to Transworld Oil at a substantial premium over Gulf's cost of construction for the refinery. However, there are some challenges to the deal:

1. The refinery is operating at a processing capacity of 5.8 million tons of crude per year.

2. The refinery operating permit is for 3.9 million tons per year.

3. Any public application for an increase in capacity is likely to be met with extreme opposition from the press, local communities, and various citizens and environmental groups that have plagued the construction of the refinery from the beginning.

4. The permit authorizing the utilization of full capacity of the refinery would have to be issued jointly by seven different agencies representing the national ministries of Industry, Commerce, Finance, Petroleum Affairs, and several local agencies.

Gulf Oil assessed the likelihood of getting all the agencies to sign off on the permit and decided to enlist the help of a local public relations and financial consulting firm, run by Thomas "Butch" Calhoun, who claimed to have several long-standing relationships with key members of all the agencies needed to sign the permit.

Gulf Oil contracted Calhoun's services for the lump sum of $2 million to provide "public relations consulting at a national, regional and local level to facilitate the procurement of a permit for increased production capacity to the level of 5.8 million tons per annum." The funds were paid in advance.

The permit was granted eight months later and the plant continued to operate under full capacity under the new ownership of Transworld Oil. However, Gulf's external auditor had flagged the $2 million payment for "public relations consulting" as outside the control parameters in place for all financial transactions exceeding $1 million and requested a formal board review of the transaction.

Suspecting kickbacks to Gulf Oil employees in the creation of the contract, the board initially requested an itemized account of the services provided for the $2 million. What they received was a statement from Calhoun documenting the following:

> As requested, we are happy to confirm that no amount from the original fee of $2 million was returned to employees, dependents, or agents of Gulf Oil. The funds were budgeted as follows: 50–55% to newspapers and other media specializing in the petroleum sector, about 35% to consultants and other experts, and the remaining balance to my company to address overhead expenses.

Calhoun did not furnish the board with copies of any documents representing the work performed on the project. However, the board did not feel it was in any position to demand any further documentation since the lump-sum payment had been paid in advance without any contractual specification to account for the expenditure of the funds.

1. Was this an ethical transaction? Explain why or why not.

2. Mr. Calhoun delivered the permit as requested. Did he do anything unethical?

3. Does the investigation by the board represent sufficient effort to resolve this situation?

4. What kind of policies should Gulf Oil put in place to make sure this doesn't happen again?

Source: Adapted from Christopher A. Bartlett, "Questionable Payments Abroad: Gulf in Italy," Cambridge, MA: Harvard Business School (PRIMIS: 9-382-080).

In such environments, the ideal "black and white" world of ethics must give way to a gray area of **ethical relativism.** Policies and procedures can be hard to follow when your customers don't have comparable policies in their own organizations. In addition, policies that have been outlawed here in an

Ethical Relativism Where your ethical principles are defined by the traditions of your society, your personal opinions, and the circumstances of the present moment.

attempt to legally enforce ethical corporate behavior may be standard operating procedure in less-developed nations. Social and political chaos can generate a bureaucracy that bears no relation to a logical reality, leaving companies with the tough decision whether to stand by their Western principles of ethical conduct or submit to the practical reality of the local market and "grease the appropriate palms" to get things done.

The Pursuit of Global Ethics

Globalization can be seen to have both an upside and a downside. Supporters of the upside argue that globalization is bringing unprecedented improvements in the wealth and standards of living of citizens in developing nations as they leverage their natural resources or low costs of living to attract foreign investment. For the more economically advanced nations, access to those resources enables lower production costs that equate to lower prices and higher income standards for their customers.

Advocates for the downside of globalization argue that it is merely promoting the dark side of capitalism onto the global stage—developing countries are ravaged for their raw materials with no concern for the longer-term economic viability of their national economies; workers are exploited; and corporations are free to take full advantage of less-restrictive legal environments.

So, how do you take advantage of the upside of globalization while maintaining your ethical standards and avoiding the downside?

As we have seen in previous chapters, any organization that commits itself to establishing and sticking with a clearly defined code of ethics will face considerable challenges, and their commitment will be tested when the quarterly numbers fall a little short of the forecast. However, moving that ethical commitment to a global stage requires a great deal more planning than simply increasing the scale of the policies and procedures. Just because it was developed here does not mean it can be applied in the same manner elsewhere in the world, and it's likely that the ethical policy will require a lot more refinement than simply translating it into the local language.

Critics have argued that the moral temptations of global expansion have simply been too strong for MNCs to ignore. Faced with constant pressure to increase revenue, cut costs, maximize profitability, and grow market share—ideally all in the next 90 days—companies find themselves tempted to take

Are there differences in the ethical issues employees face at a multinational company versus a locally owned company? Which environment do you think would be preferable?

maximum advantage of the less stringent laws and regulations of local markets and (in what critics consider to be the worst transgression), if there are no clear local ethical standards, to operate in the absence of any standards rather than reverting to their own domestic ethical policies.

So what is the answer here? Is the development of a **global code of conduct** a realistic solution to this issue?

Even though we are now seeing the development of larger trading blocs as neighboring countries (such as the European Economic Community) work together to leverage their size and geographic advantage to take a bigger role on the global economic stage, the individual countries within those trading blocs are not disappearing. For this reason, the customs and norms of those individual societies are likely to prevail.

For advocates of global ethics, this means that a *flexible* solution has to be found—one that provides standards of practice to guide managers as they conduct business across national boundaries in the name of global commerce, while at the same time respecting the individual customs of the countries in which they are operating.

Richard DeGeorge offers the following guidelines for organizations doing business in these situations[4]:

> **Global Code of Conduct** A general standard of business practice that can be applied equally to all countries over and above their local customs and social norms.

1. Do no intentional harm.
2. Produce more good than harm for the host country.
3. Contribute to the host country's development.
4. Respect the human rights of their employees.
5. Respect the local culture; work with it, not against it.
6. Pay their fair share of taxes.
7. Cooperate with the local government to develop and enforce just background institutions.
8. Majority control of a firm includes the ethical responsibility of attending to the actions and failures of the firm.
9. Multinationals that build hazardous plants are obliged to ensure that the plants are safe and operated safely.
10. Multinationals are responsible for redesigning the transfer of hazardous technologies so that such technologies can be safely administered in host countries.

✓ PROGRESS CHECK QUESTIONS

5. Why would a global code of conduct be unrealistic?

6. Select your top five from DeGeorge's guidelines for organizations doing business in less-developed countries and defend your selections.

7. Can you think of any reasons why international organizations wouldn't follow these guidelines? Provide three examples.

8. Do you think DeGeorge's guidelines represent a sufficiently "flexible" solution? Why or why not?

DeGeorge's guidelines present something of an ethical ideal that can at best provide a conceptual foundation, but at worst they overlook some of the most severe transgressions that have brought such negative attention to the ethical behavior of MNCs. In the pursuit of profit and continued expansion, MNCs have been found guilty of bribery, pollution, false advertising, questionable product quality, and, most prominently, the abuse of human rights in the utilization of "sweatshop" production facilities that fail to meet even the minimum health and safety standards of their home countries and that utilize child labor, often at wage levels that are incomprehensible to Western consumers.

The situation becomes even more complicated when we acknowledge that many global companies have reached such a size that they have a dramatic impact on trade levels just with their own internal transactions. As economist William Greider observed in *One World, Ready or Not*[5]:

> The growth of transnational corporate investments, the steady dispersal of production elements across many nations, has nearly obliterated the traditional understanding of trade. Though many of them know better, economists and politicians continue to portray the global trading system in terms that the public can understand—that is, as a collection of nations buying and selling things to each other. However, as the volume of world trade has grown, the traditional role of national markets is increasingly eclipsed by an alternative system: trade generated within the multinational companies themselves as they export and import among their own foreign-based subsidiaries.

ETHICAL dilemma

CASE 9.2 What Is a Global Business?

On December 7, 2004, IBM announced that it was selling its whole Personal Computing Division to the Chinese computer company Lenovo to create a new worldwide PC company—the globe's third largest—with approximately $12 billion in annual revenue. Simultaneously, though, IBM said that it would be taking an 18.9 percent equity stake in Lenovo, creating a strategic alliance between IBM and Lenovo in PC sales, financing, and service worldwide. The new combined company's worldwide headquarters, it was announced, would be in New York, but its principal manufacturing operations would be in Beijing and Raleigh, North Carolina; research centers would be in China, the United States, and Japan; and sales offices would be around the world. The new Lenovo will be the preferred supplier of PCs to IBM, and IBM will also be the new Lenovo's preferred supplier of services and financing.

Are you still with me? About 10,000 people will move from IBM to Lenovo, which was created in 1984 and was the first company to introduce the home computer concept in China. Since 1997, Lenovo has been the leading PC brand in China. My favorite part of the press release is the following, which identifies the new company's senior executives.

> Yang Yuanqing—Chairman of the Board. [He's currently CEO of Lenovo.] Steve Ward—Chief Executive Officer. [He's currently IBM's senior vice president and general manager of IBM's Personal Systems Group.] Fran O'Sullivan—Chief Operating Officer. [She's currently general manager of IBM's PC division.] Mary Ma—Chief Financial Officer. [She's currently CFO of Lenovo.]

Talk about horizontal value creation: This Chinese-owned computer company headquartered in New York with factories in Raleigh and Beijing will have a Chinese chairman, an American CEO, an American COO, and a Chinese CFO, and it will be listed on the Hong Kong stock exchange. Would you call this an American company? A Chinese company? To which country will Lenovo feel most attached? Or will it just see itself sort of floating above a flat earth?

This question was anticipated in the press release announcing the new company anticipated this question: "Where will Lenovo be headquartered?" it asked.

Answer: "As a global business, the new Lenovo will be geographically dispersed, with people and physical assets located worldwide." Sort that out.

1. "The new Lenovo will be geographically dispersed, with people and physical assets located worldwide." Which culture will provide the greatest influence in establishing a code of ethics? Explain your answer.

2. Do you think Lenovo will have one code of ethics for the whole company or separate codes to reflect its different cultures? Explain your answer.

3. What would be the challenges in establishing one code of ethics for a global company of this size?

4. Do you think the issue of managing business ethics on a global scale was considered in this transaction?

Source: Excerpts from Thomas L. Friedman, "The World Is Flat: A Brief History of the Twenty-First Century." Copyright © 2005 by Thomas L. Friedman. Reprinted by permission of Farrar, Straus, and Giroux, LLC.

With such a negative track record to begin with, how do you enforce ethical behavior in an organization that is trading with itself? Do the ethical norms of the parent company dominate the corporation's business practices in complete disregard of local customs and traditions? Or is it simply more expedient to "go with the flow" and take advantage of whatever the local market has to offer? Unfortunately, in this new environment, simply categorizing the "parent company" can prove to be a challenge.

Enforcing Global Ethics

While companies may be held accountable for ethical performance within their home countries (America's Foreign Corrupt Practices Act, for example), enforcing ethical behavior once they cross national boundaries becomes extremely difficult. What happens if the behavior is illegal in the company's home country, but not in the local country in which the alleged transgression took place? Would the enforcement of penalties in their home country automatically prevent any future transgressions? What if the profit margins are high enough to simply pay the fines as a cost of doing business?

Enforcing a global ethical standard would require all parties involved to agree on acceptable standards of behavior and appropriate consequences for failing to abide by those standards. Given the fact that many of the hundreds of nations in the world still experience difficulty governing their own internal politics, it would seem that we are many years away from achieving a truly global standard.

In the meantime, organizations such as the United Nations (UN) and the Organization for Economic Cooperation and Development (OECD) have approached the issue of standardizing global ethical conduct by promoting behavior guidelines that MNCs can publicly support and endorse as a strong message to their stakeholders that they are committed to ethical corporate conduct wherever they do business in the world.

The UN Global Compact

Launched in a speech to the World Economic Forum on January 31, 1999, by UN Secretary-General Kofi Annan, the **UN Global Compact** became operational in July 2000. It represents a commitment on the part of its members to promote good corporate citizenship with a focus on four key areas of concern: the environment, anticorruption, the welfare of workers around the world, and global human rights.

UN Global Compact A voluntary corporate citizenship initiative endorsing 10 key principles that focus on four key areas of concern: the environment, anticorruption, the welfare of workers around the world, and global human rights.

The Global Compact is not a regulatory instrument—it does not "police," enforce, or measure the behavior or actions of companies. Rather, the Global Compact relies on public accountability, transparency, and the enlightened self-interest of companies, labor and civil society to initiate and share substantive action in pursuing the principles upon which the Global Compact is based.

With over 2,000 companies in more than 80 countries making a voluntary commitment to this corporate citizenship initiative, the Global Compact is widely recognized as the world's largest initiative of its kind. By endorsing and actively promoting the message of the Global Compact, companies make public commitments to a set of core values that are captured in 10 key principles that address the four areas of concern[6]:

Human Rights

1. Businesses should support and respect the protection of internationally proclaimed human rights.
2. Businesses should make sure they are not complicit in human rights abuses.

Labor Standards

3. Businesses should uphold the freedom of association and the effective recognition of the right to collective bargaining.
4. Businesses should uphold the elimination of all forms of forced and compulsory labor.
5. Businesses should uphold the effective abolition of child labor.
6. Businesses should uphold the elimination of discrimination in employment and occupation.

Environment

7. Businesses should support a precautionary approach to environmental challenges.

8. Businesses should undertake initiatives to promote greater environmental responsibility.

9. Businesses should encourage the development and diffusion of environmentally friendly technologies.

Anticorruption

10. Businesses should work against all forms of corruption, including extortion and bribery.

✓ PROGRESS CHECK QUESTIONS

9. What is the UN Global Compact?

10. When and why was it created?

11. Explain the 10 key principles of the Global Compact.

12. What would a multinational corporation gain from signing the Global Compact?

LIFEskills

A subtle influence

In Chapter 1 we examined the work of Lawrence Kohlberg and his argument that we develop a reasoning process (and our individual ethical standards) over time, moving through six distinct stages as we are exposed to major influences in our lives.

When we consider ethics from a global perspective and begin to recognize the impact of cultural influences on our personal value system, we come to the realization that our individual ethical standards can often be sheltered from a broader global awareness by those cultural influences.

What do you consider to be your primary cultural influences? As the child of immigrant parents, for example, your value system would be directly impacted by influences from both the American culture you live in, and your parents' native culture—and if your parents happen to be from two different cultures, then things can really get interesting!

Do you think those cultural influences impact your daily behavior? Much of what you learn about the world in terms of education and daily information is subject to the perspective of the country in which you live. Are you open to that or would you describe yourself as being open to other viewpoints from other countries?

The development of a reasoning process over time allows these influences to work gradually so that you may not be fully aware of their impact until someone criticizes your viewpoint as being blinkered or, even worse, discriminatory. So, if you find yourself in a situation where you are making a decision that involves different cultures or employees from different countries, consider your starting point first.

The OECD Guidelines for Multinational Enterprises

Originally adopted as part of the larger Declaration on International Investments and Multinational Enterprises in 1976, the **Organization for Economic Cooperation and Development (OECD) Guidelines for Multinational Enterprises** represents a more governmental approach to the same issues featured in the UN's nongovernmental Global Compact.

OECD Guidelines for Multinational Enterprises A governmental initiative endorsed by 30 members of Organization for Economic Cooperation and Development and 9 nonmembers (Argentina, Brazil, Chile, Estonia, Israel, Latvia, Lithuania, Romania, and Slovenia), the OECD guidelines promote principles and standards of behavior in the following areas: human rights, information disclosure, anticorruption, taxation, labor relations, environment, competition, and consumer protection.

Supporters argue that the government backing adds credibility to the issues being promoted, but the guidelines carry no criminal or civil enforcement and are not regarded as legally binding. What they do offer are principles and standards of behavior that draw on the same core values as the UN Global Compact across a broader series of issues captured in 10 "chapters"[7]:

I. **Concepts and Principles:** sets out the principles which underlie the Guidelines, such as their voluntary character, their application worldwide, and the fact that they reflect good practice for all enterprises.

II. **General Policies:** contains the first specific recommendations, including provisions on human rights, sustainable development, supply chain responsibility, and local capacity building; and, more generally, calls on enterprises to take full account of established policies in the countries in which they operate.

III. **Disclosure:** recommends disclosure on all material matters regarding the enterprise such as its performance and ownership, and encourages communication in areas where reporting standards are still emerging such as social, environmental, and risk reporting.

IV. **Employment and Industrial Relations:** addresses major aspects of corporate behavior in this area including child and forced labor, nondiscrimination and the right to bona fide employee representation, and constructive negotiations.

V. **Environment:** encourages enterprises to raise their performance in protecting the environment, including performance with respect to health and safety impacts. Features of this chapter include recommendations concerning environmental management systems and the desirability of precautions where there are threats of serious damage to the environment.

VI. **Combating Bribery:** covers both public and private bribery and addresses passive and active corruption.

VII. **Consumer Interests:** recommends that enterprises, when dealing with consumers, act in accordance with fair business, marketing, and advertising practices; respect consumer privacy; and take all reasonable steps to ensure the safety and quality of goods or services provided.

VIII. **Science and Technology:** aims to promote the diffusion by multinational enterprises' of the fruits of research and development activities among the countries where they operate, thereby contributing to the innovative capacities of host countries.

IX. Competition: emphasizes the importance of an open and competitive business climate.

X. Taxation: calls on enterprises to respect both the letter and spirit of tax laws and to cooperate with tax authorities.

✓ PROGRESS CHECK QUESTIONS

13. What are the OECD Guidelines for Multinational Enterprises?

14. How do they differ from the UN Global Compact?

15. How are they similar to the UN Global Compact?

16. Can you think of a situation in which a multinational corporation would endorse one or the other? Or should they both be endorsed? Explain your answer.

If an organization is committed to ethical business conduct, that commitment should remain constant wherever that business is conducted in the world. Unfortunately, the more evidence of ethical misconduct at home, the greater the likelihood that organizations will fall victim to the temptations offered in the less-regulated developing nations.

Carrying a reputation as a good corporate citizen may bring some positive media coverage and win the business of critical consumers who pay close attention to where the products they buy are sourced and manufactured. However, the real test comes when the quarterly numbers aren't looking as good as Wall Street would like and the need to trim costs will mean the difference between a rising stock price and a falling one.

As the Wendell Wilkie quote at the beginning of this chapter indicates, the world is now completely interdependent, and that interdependence extends to both *operations* and *information*. You may be able to save money by contracting with vendors who manufacture goods in sweatshop conditions, and you may be able to let contractors handle your hazardous waste without worrying too much about where they put it, but these will be short-lived savings and conveniences. Once those actions are made public through investigative media agencies or consumer advocacy groups, your status as a "good corporate citizen" may never be regained.

The concept of global ethics remains frustratingly complex. Advocates of a global code of conduct may rally against sweatshops and the employment of children at unspeakably low wages. However, their proposed solutions for the prohibition of these working conditions often fail to address the replacement of family income when the children are no longer allowed to work, which, in turn, can cause financial devastation to the families involved.

It can be argued that true global citizens should remain ethically involved in all their markets, rather than (as the critics maintain) taking advantage of the weak for the betterment of the strong. Supporters of Milton Friedman's *instrumental* contract may argue that corporations carry no moral obligation to the countries in which they operate beyond abiding by their laws, but when we consider the public backlash against Nike's sweatshops and Kathie Lee Gifford's child labor scandal, it would seem that there is a strong enough financial incentive to address these issues whether you accept a moral obligation or not.

A Matter of Definition—
Kevin Makes a Decision

Kevin considered his options very carefully. If the media found out about these sweatshops, would that negative publicity make it back to their agency? After all, they just wrote the ad copy and negotiated the placement of the ads. They didn't order the items, and if Kevin hadn't received the billing paperwork by mistake, his agency wouldn't know where the items were made.

"Even so," thought Kevin, "manufacturing any goods in sweatshop conditions is wrong and our agency doesn't do business with customers that subscribe to the abuse of human rights."

Kevin lost no time in bringing this new information about the Smith's campaign to his boss, Charles Cooper, the founder and president of their agency:

"Mr. Cooper, this Smith's campaign could be a big problem for us. Their leading sales items weren't 'made in America' at all. This paperwork shows that the items came from a sweatshop in Indonesia. I did some research on the company that manufactures these items and they've already been fined on several occasions for human rights violations."

Then Kevin took a deep breath. "I know this is a big contract for us, Mr. Cooper, but is this the type of work we are going to do now? I didn't think our agency worked on these kinds of campaigns. Little kids working in sweatshops just so we can have cookouts on the fourth of July doesn't seem right, sir."

Charles Cooper thought for several minutes before responding: "Are you sure this information is accurate, Kevin?"

"Yes Sir. This billing paperwork came with the original prep kit directly from Smith's."

"Then let's get our friends at Smith's on the phone. I'm afraid they are going to be looking for a new agency."

1. What do you think Charles Cooper will say to his counterpart at Smith's?

2. What do you think Smith's reaction will be?

3. Is there a chance that Kevin's company could save its relationship with Smith's?

Developed Nation *p. 212*

Ethical Relativism *p. 215*

Global Code of Conduct *p. 217*

Globalization *p. 213*

Less-Developed Nation *p. 212*

Multinational Corporation *p. 213*

OECD Guidelines for Multinational Enterprises *p. 222*

UN Global Compact *p. 220*

Utilitarianism *p. 213*

[REVIEW QUESTIONS]

1. Do you think global businesses would be willing to subscribe to a global code of conduct? Explain your answer.
2. Would it be easier to just follow the business practices and customs of the country in which you're doing business? Why or why not?
3. Are there more stakeholders for an international/global company than a domestic one? Explain your answer.
4. What is the most ethical way to do business internationally?

[REVIEW EXERCISE]

Universal Training Solutions. Kathy James was Universal Training Solutions' top trainer. She had delivered client presentations, one-day open workshops on sales calls, and had led national rollouts for large training implementations. The opportunity to lead the training for Universal's new South African client, National Bank of SA, was simply too good to miss. She had met with Universal's account manager for National Bank and felt that she had a strong grasp of what the client was looking for.

National Bank of SA had recently invested $10 million (about 60 million rand) in upgrading its call center equipment, and its managers were looking for customer service training to ensure that the call center representatives (CCRs) could provide the highest level of service in their market. Market research had shown that South Africans weren't accustomed to good service from their banks, so this initiative was seen as a good way to gain some market share.

Universal's customer service training program—First Class Service (FCS)—had a phenomenal reputation with dozens of *Fortune* 500 companies and several global implementations to its credit. It was designed to be delivered in three days with average class sizes of 10 to 12 employees. It was a logical choice for National, which was eager to get the program rolling.

Kathy asked to lead the cultural adaptation team, working with a translator in Johannesburg to translate FCS into Afrikaans (although she had been told by the account manager that most of National's employees spoke very good English). She anticipated that most of the group activities within the program would remain the same—that was what National's buyers had seen at the demonstration. She set up the first of what she thought would be several conference calls with the translator and looked forward to another successful project.

However, the first call brought things to a dramatic halt. As Kathy and the translator got to know each other, the translator asked how much Kathy knew about the South African culture. Kathy had been doing some extensive research on the Web after she had been assigned to the project and she did her best to dazzle the translator with her knowledge. Then the translator asked a question that stumped Kathy: "Why are you only translating this into Afrikaans? Did you know there are 11 national languages in South Africa and that not recognizing those languages is considered to be a social blunder?"

The translator went on to describe how in many formal presentations (such as the training events Universal was planning to roll out in all National's regional offices over the next six months), it was considered rude not to recognize all the nationalities present in the room—particularly in group activities.

Kathy started to panic. How was she supposed to turn an American three-day program into a South African three-day program that allows time to recognize 11 different languages and nationalities in the group exercises?

1. What is the right thing to do here?
2. Why shouldn't National just deliver the American version of CFS? If it works here, it should work there.
3. Which stakeholders will be impacted by Kathy's decision?
4. What are her options here?

INTERNET EXERCISE

Visit the International Ethics and Integrity page for Seagate Technology at www.seagate.com/newsinfo/citizenship/work_environment/international_ethics.html.

1. How does Seagate define *international ethics?*
2. What is Seagate's position on international ethics?
3. What are the consequences of violating Seagate's ethics policies?

TEAM EXERCISES

1. **Global or local?** Divide into two teams. One team must prepare a presentation advocating for the development of a standardized global code of conduct. The other team must prepare a presentation arguing for the development of a more flexible local code of conduct that takes into account the cultural norms of individual nations.

2. **Restoring a reputation.** Divide into groups of three or four. Each group must map out its proposal for restoring the ethical reputation of a multinational corporation that has been fined for one of the following transgressions: bribery, pollution, operating sweatshops, employing child labor. Prepare a presentation outlining your plan for restoring the reputation of the company with its stakeholders.

3. **Tamiflu:** Divide into two groups and prepare arguments *for* and *against* the following behavior:

Your American company operates manufacturing plants throughout Asia, with a combined staff of 20,000 employees. In 2003, after Asia was hit with the severe acute respiratory syndrome (SARS) epidemic, your company introduced a policy to stockpile drugs in locations where employees don't have access to high quality healthcare. In 2005, SARS was replaced by avian influenza–bird flu–as the primary risk for the next pandemic. Your company responded by stockpiling quantities of the drug Tamiflu, the antiviral drug that is regarded as the best treatment for bird flu in humans.

There has been a reported outbreak of bird flu in a remote region of Vietnam, about 100 miles from where you have a manufacturing plant. The government clinic has a small supply of Tamiflu but, aware of your company's stockpile, they have approached your local plant manager to share some of your supply. The plant manager contacted you for help in responding to their request. Your company policy on this is to make sure employees are taken care of first, and so you decline the request of for assistance, claiming that you have insufficient quantities of Tamiflu to meet your immediate needs.

4. **Looking the other way:** Divide into two groups and prepare arguments *for* and *against* the following behavior:

"You have been sent to investigate a fraud claim made against your company by the Customs [department] in one of the countries where you do business. On arrival, an officer explains that your company is being fined for underdeclaring the number of safety boots imported into the country. You notice he is wearing a pair of the 'missing' boots."

In preparation for your trip you verified that all the shipment and customs paperwork was in order and you are certain that the number of safety boots has not been underdeclared. Since your company's strategic plan features high growth expectations from this region, you are tempted to simply pay the fine and get the officer's name and address so you can send him some other samples of your company's products. However, your company's senior management team recently returned from a strategic planning retreat in which they made a clear commitment to enforce the organization's code of ethics in all business transactions, here and abroad, even at the risk of losing short-term business. Your CEO was quoted in the company newsletter as saying: "We should use our higher moral standards as an opportunity to win customers who want to do business with a reputable organization."

So, you reach into your briefcase for your copies of the customs paperwork and begin to challenge the officer's accusation of underdeclaring.[8]

CONSCIENCE OR THE COMPETITIVE EDGE?

The plane touched down at Mumbai airport precisely on time. Olivia Jones made her way through the usual immigration bureaucracy without incident and was finally ushered into a waiting limousine, complete with uniformed chauffeur and soft black leather seats. Her already considerable excitement at being in India for the first time was mounting. As she cruised the dark city streets, she asked her chauffeur why so few cars had their headlights on at night. The driver responded that most drivers believed that headlights use too much petrol! Finally, she arrived at her hotel, a black marble monolith, grandiose and decadent in its splendor, towering above the bay.

The goal of her four-day trip was to sample and select swatches of woven cotton from the mills in and around Mumbai, to be used in the following season's youthwear collection of shirts, trousers, and underwear. Her hosts, who were invariably Indian factory owners or British agents for Indian mills, therefore treated her with the utmost deference. For three days she was ferried from one air-conditioned office to another, sipping iced tea or chilled lemonade, poring over leather-bound swatch catalogs, which featured every type of stripe and design possible. On the fourth day, Jones made a request which she knew would cause some anxiety in the camp. "I want to see a factory," she declared.

After much consultation and several attempts at dissuasion, she was once again ushered into a limousine and driven through a part of the city she had not previously seen. Gradually, the hotel and the western shops dissolved into the background and Jones entered downtown Mumbai. All around was a sprawling shantytown, constructed from sheets of corrugated iron and panels of cardboard boxes. Dust flew in spirals everywhere along the dirt roads and open drains. The car crawled along the unsealed roads behind carts hauled by man and beast alike, laden to overflowing with straw or city refuse—the treasure of the ghetto. More than once the limousine had to halt and wait while a lumbering white bull crossed the road.

Finally, in the very heart of the ghetto, the car came to a stop. "Are you sure you want to do this?" asked her host. Determined not to be fainthearted, Jones got out of the car.

White-skinned, blue-eyed, and blond, clad in a city suit and stiletto-heeled shoes, and carrying a briefcase, Jones was indeed conspicuous. It was hardly surprising that the inhabitants of the area found her an interesting and amusing subject, as she teetered along the dusty street and stepped gingerly over the open sewers.

Her host led her down an alley, between the shacks and open doors and inky black interiors. Some shelters, Jones was told, were restaurants, where at lunchtime people would gather on the rush mat floors and eat rice together. In the doorway of one shack there was a table that served as a counter, laden with ancient cans of baked beans, sardines, and rusted tins of a fluorescent green substance that might have been peas. The eyes of the young man behind the counter were smiling and proud as he beckoned her forward to view his wares.

As Jones turned another corner, she saw an old man in the middle of the street, clad in a waist cloth, sitting in a large tin bucket. He had a tin can in his hand with which he poured water from the bucket over his head and shoulders. Beside him two little girls played in brilliant white nylon dresses, bedecked with ribbons and lace. They posed for her with smiling faces, delighted at having their photograph taken in their best frocks. The men and women moved around her with great dignity and grace, Jones thought.

Finally, her host led her up a precarious wooden ladder to a floor above the street. At the top Jones was warned not to stand straight as the ceiling was just five feet high. There, in a room not 20 feet by 40 feet, 20 men were sitting at treadle sewing machines, bent over yards of white cloth. Between them on the floor were rush mats, some occupied by sleeping workers awaiting their next shift. Jones learned that these men were on a 24-hour rotation, 12 hours on and 12 hours off, every day for six months of the year. For the remaining six months they returned to their families in the countryside to work the land, planting and building with the money they had earned in the city. The shirts they were working on were for an order she had placed four weeks earlier in London, an order of which she had been particularly proud because of the low price she had succeeded in negotiating. Jones reflected that this sight was the most humbling experience of her life. When she questioned her host about these conditions, she was told that they were typical for her industry—and for most of the Third World, as well.

Eventually, she left the heat, dust, and din of the little shirt factory and returned to the protected, air-conditioned world of the limousine.

"What I've experienced today and the role I've played in creating that living hell will stay with me forever," she thought. Later in the day, she asked herself whether what she had seen was an inevitable consequence of pricing policies that enabled the British customer to purchase shirts at £12.99 instead of £13.99 and at the same time allowed the company to make its mandatory 56 percent profit margin? Were her negotiating skills—the result of many years of training—an indirect cause of the terrible conditions she had seen?

Once Jones returned to the United Kingdom, she considered her position and the options open to her as a buyer for a large, publicly traded retail chain operating in a highly competitive environment. Her dilemma was twofold: Can an ambitious employee afford to exercise a social conscience in his or her career? And can career-minded individuals truly make a difference without jeopardizing their future?

Discussion Questions

1. From an ethical perspective, what was wrong with the working conditions Olivia witnessed in the shirt factory?

2. Her company mandates a minimum 56 percent profit margin. Is that unethical?

3. Which stakeholders would be impacted by any changes Olivia tried to implement back in London?

4. The conditions Olivia observed were described as "typical for the industry—and for most of the Third World as well." Does that make it an ethical situation?

5. Are there other ways to reduce the price a customer pays for a shirt?

6. Olivia's visit to the shirt factory affected her deeply and prompted her to reconsider her pursuit of corporate success. What do you think she will do when she returns to London? Explain your answer.

Source: Kate Button and Christopher K. Bart, "Conscience or the Competitive Edge," North American Case Research Association, 1994, www.nacra.net.

discussion
EXERCISE 9.2

SOCCER BALLS MADE FOR CHILDREN BY CHILDREN: CHILD LABOR IN PAKISTAN

Child Labor in History and Today

Although child labor is, by all accounts, common in the developing world, estimates vary widely, if for no other reason than because the definition of "child labor" is in itself a matter of debate. A child employed in a factory or mine is undoubtedly working. So is a child begging in the streets with his parents. But what about a boy herding cattle on his parents' farm in the morning before school? What about a girl helping with household chores while her mother is working outside the home? The answer depends on what is included in the definition of "child labor."

Child labor is a perennially divisive issue. Some argue that it is inherently exploitative while others see putting children to work in factories as being no better or worse than sending them away to be apprenticed in a trade skill—a common practice prior to the Industrial Revolution. Social engineers and activists see child labor as a violation of fundamental human rights in the same manner as slavery and prison labor. Children, they argue, deserve time for play and personal development, for a childhood.

Many activists in Pakistan and many outside observers seem to share this view. According to Zahid Siddiqi, a founder of the nongovernmental organization Sudhaar, child labor in Pakistan creates a kind of underground market for parents willing to exploit their families:

> The more children they put to work, the more money they can get. Lots of their fathers even stop working themselves. Why should they work when they can get five or six of their own children working for them? This has to stop.

New International Activism

In the mid-1990s, a number of television news magazines visited Bangladesh and Pakistan to report on alleged cases of bonded child labor, a kind of modern slavery through the debt obligations of their parents.

While consumers remained unwilling to pay higher prices for goods produced by socially responsible methods—they preferred known brands, price, and quality—their perceptions of "exploitive" multinationals were beginning to change for the worse. Fearing that these perceptions would affect their bottom line, many marketers of craft products from the third world began to refuse imports of goods produced by children and other victims of human rights abuses.

In 1996, a sweatshop-related discovery helped to catapult the issue of child labor into the international spotlight: a line of clothing sponsored by U.S. television personality Kathie Lee Gifford, reporters found, relied on children who were paid only US$0.30 per hour in Honduran sweatshops. Entering an arena that had long been the concern of a few politicians and professionals in international organizations, scores of activists suddenly became concerned about working children. Armies of reporters, some of them celebrities in their own right, joined the cause, scouring the Third World for examples of abuse and exploitation of children; their harrowing tales of brushes with mysterious thugs, some clad like local policemen, lent them credibility and élan. In addition to stories of slave labor and cruel punishments—one famous reporter claimed to have found children "branded, beaten, blinded as punishment for wanting to go home"—alarming estimates began to surface. A movement to end child labor coalesced around soccer ball manufacturers in the "Foul Ball" campaign.

Zaka-ud-Din and M. Yunas Ratra (managing director of a sporting goods company that bore his name) remembered vividly when the spotlight fell on them as soccer ball manufacturers in Sialkot, located in the Punjab province near the disputed border of Kashmir. "An American friend, who was a business associate and customer, called me at home," Zaka-ud-Din recalled. "He told me he was watching the news on television, and asked me whether it was true that I used children to stitch soccer balls. I was surprised by his question because I had never looked into it. . . . All we did was subcontract out kits that were taken to villages and stitched. We didn't know who stitched them."

These campaigns could backfire. As a result of a high-profile public opinion campaign in the United States and in fear of trade sanctions, garment factory owners in Bangladesh had turned out approximately 50,000 working children into the street virtually overnight. Unfortunately, rather than return to school, instead many of the children lost status within their families, becoming an insupportable burden—in a country where 65 percent of the children were malnourished, their earnings had been desperately needed. As a result, the number of homeless children increased, while many others were forced into more hazardous occupations, such as brick baking, street scavenging, and even prostitution.

Multinational Corporations: Seeking the Lowest Possible Costs

Having been thrust into the international spotlight by accusations of exploitation and hypocrisy regarding child labor, a number of sporting goods multinationals imposed their own policies on Sialkot. Reebok, one of America's premier designers and marketers of sporting goods, took the vanguard, lobbying its sports industry association to abolish child labor and undertaking its own extensive investigations at approximately 40 Reebok subcontractor factories in the Third World. According to Douglas Cahn, Reebok's vice president for human rights, "[B]ecause we wanted to move quickly, we proceeded on our own . . . in a tripartite approach: (1) bring stitching out of the home and into larger factories; (2) set up a vigorous monitoring system; (3) start remediation programs in education." The fourth element consisted of labeling Reebok's finished soccer balls, to be purchased from a local contractor who had built a new child-free factory, as "child labor free."

In February 1997 at the annual sports trade fair in the United States, an agreement (dubbed "The Atlanta Agreement" after the location of the trade fair) was unveiled in a media blitz of high drama and expectation. Brand manufacturers in the Sporting Goods Manufacturers Association of the United States pledged to "eliminate child labor"—workers under 14 years of age—from the stitching and production of soccer balls, as did the members of the SCCI (Sialkot Chamber of Commerce & Industry), within two years.

In a major departure from its role as a local observer and funder of small-scale initiatives, the International Labor Organization stepped forward to monitor the agreement, acting as a kind of guarantor of the integrity of the process.

The agreement, which was formulated to avoid the problems experienced by child laborers in Bangladesh, juggled a number of provisions and requirements:

- Stitching centers were to be established, which would bring the work out of the household and into official manufacturing facilities.
- Workers were to be systematically registered in corporate records for the first time, an additional mechanism for verification of worker age.
- In order to create alternative activities and employment for displaced workers, programs would be created for purposes of both education for children and wider economic development.
- A system of rewards, warnings, and penalties was set up to encourage company compliance.
- Members of the World Federation of the Sporting Goods Industry would favor vendors who did not use child labor. For its part, SCCI undertook a commitment to expand the elimination of child labor to additional industries.

Financial support for the agreement came from a wide variety of sources. The U.S. Department of Labor promised to supply US$500,000 for the first two years of the program. SCCI members would provide US$360,000 to finance independent monitors. UNICEF would provide US$200,000. Finally, the Soccer Industry Council of America (the industry association of brand sporting goods manufacturers) would add US$100,000. The bulk of foreign contributions was targeted for education and prevention programs for the children and other affected workers. Financed largely by SCCI monitoring funds, the ILO had hired 15 staff monitors to work in teams of two, traveling on motorbikes for random, unannounced visits to the stitching centers. According to Antero Vahapassi, the ILO official in charge of the initiative, "This is the first program in which the ILO is getting its hands dirty in the details of implementation. We cannot afford to fail. It is a very bold step for us."

SCCI members fulfilled their promises on schedule: as of November 1998, 50 percent of their manufacturing took place in the approximately 500 new stitching centers they had set up; 36 manufacturers—about half of the manufacturers in Sialkot—participated under SCCI auspices, which represented 65–70 percent of total annual production of export-quality soccer balls. But all this did not come for free. According to Naeem Javed, managing director of the Sublime Group of Companies, in the new centers, "each ball costs about 15 rupees more to produce; we used to be able to do it for 30–35 rupees, but now it costs us 50–55 rupees." Because Sublime enjoyed a solid relationship with Adidas for the high-quality ball market, it did not lose its business, but it did need to produce more to keep the same profit. Sialkot employers, of course, deeply resented this requirement. "We talk about ethics and fair trade," said M. Yunas Ratra "But when I ask my buyers to share the cost, they refuse." By and large, SCCI member profits were down by a significant margin. While the exact figures were confidential, one executive of a major firm confided that his cumulative gross profit had fallen from 18 percent of revenues to about 10 percent since the program began. The drop in profits, which differed from company to company, was due primarily to the costs of opening and running larger stitching centers, that is, providing the infrastructure that home-based cottage industries had long allowed them to avoid.

Local contractors footed the entire bill for these stitching centers. As a result, soccer ball manufacturers were struggling to improve their efficiency—reducing rejection rates by a factor of almost 90 percent, investing in whatever labor-saving technologies they could find, and training their labor forces. In addition, to maintain profits with the higher overhead costs of their stitching centers, the larger firms increased the scale of production. For less efficient small- and medium-sized producers, the bottom line was squeezed to a new low. "It is becoming a matter of survival," Ratra said. "For now we [the larger firms] are keeping our heads above water." But many others were likely to be pushed out of business by an industrywide consolidation in the next few years.

The initiative also had an unforeseen impact on Punjabi women. By taking labor out of the home environment to outside stitching centers, the new manufacturing arrangement would effectively prevent them from working for a variety of reasons. First, were the prohibitions of religion, which in Pakistan coexisted with caste: According to increasingly influential Islamic law and custom, women were not allowed to mingle with men who were not in their immediate families, which included working alongside men; caste restrictions added to the complexity of women's work opportunities, effectively limiting many "higher" caste women from traveling outside their villages. Second, despite the relative wealth of Punjab province, the state of the local infrastructure often hindered women from traveling. Bus services for women effectively ended at 4 p.m., which meant that they could not be at home to "take care" of their husbands when they returned from work, as dictated by regional custom. Preventing women from working would compound the income-loss problem created by the elimination of child labor, as the male household head would then become the sole wage earner.

Was the Atlanta Agreement a success? Have the Sialkot children gained? In the words of Fawad Usman Khan, a founder of Sudhaar,

> [I]f it were up to me, I would take all child laborers out of the more hazardous professions and put them into the soccer ball industry—there are no chemicals, they are well paid, and the hours are flexible. The children can work at home in their spare time, mixing it with housework or after school. I am very worried that the children taken out will end up in more dangerous occupations. This is an easy sector when compared to carpets or leather tanneries.

Have Pakistani women, whose position is most vulnerable, gained in the new arrangement? If the Atlanta Agreement was indeed a success, does it provide a model that can be emulated elsewhere, say in the carpet industry? Is it likely to have ripple effects in other industries?

Discussion Questions

1. Is it wrong to put children to work?

2. The soccer ball industry was seen as less hazardous because there were no chemicals involved, good pay, and flexible hours. Does that make it more ethical? Explain your answer.

3. The global market for soccer balls carries a high profile because of all the international associations involved. Do you think that all these changes would have occurred in a lower-profile industry?

4. Which stakeholders have been impacted by these changes?

5. Do you think that the industry has improved as a result of all these changes? Is it a more ethical industry now?

6. These changes have led to negative consequences for the children, their mothers, and the families as a whole. How could this situation have been handled differently?

Source: Adapted from K. E. Goodpaster, L. L. Nash, and H-C de Bettignies, "Soccer Balls Made for Children by Children: Child Labor in Pakistan," Business Ethics: Policies and Persons, 4th Ed., New York: McGraw-Hill, 2006, pp. 559–570.

THE ETHICS OF OFFSHORING CLINICAL TRIALS

The process of offshoring (outsourcing an organizational function overseas) is being applied to clinical drug trials with the same speed and enthusiasm as major U.S. corporations transplanting their customer service call centers to countries such as Ireland, India, and increasingly further eastern locations.

For United States–based pharmaceutical companies, the rush is driven by both attractive options and practical realities:

- Pursuing the same cost advantages as other U.S. corporations, drug companies are now discovering that trials in countries in such regions as Eastern Europe, Asia, Latin America, and Africa can produce the same quality of data at a lower cost and often in a shorter time frame.

- After safety concerns over drugs like the anti-inflammatory Vioxx, which was withdrawn from sale in 2004, regulators such as the Food and Drug Administration (FDA) are now requiring even more data as a prerequisite for the approval of a new drug. That equates to more trials enrolling more people for longer periods of time—sometimes many thousands of patients over 12 months or longer.

- Patients in North America are increasingly unwilling to participate in Phase 1 experimental trials, preferring instead to participate in Phase 2 or 3 trials where the effectiveness of the drug has already been established and the trials are focused on identifying appropriate dosage levels or potential side effects.

- In contrast, these new overseas trial sites offer "large pools of patients who are "treatment naïve" because the relatively low standard of healthcare compared with Western countries means they have not had access to the latest and most expensive medicines."

- In North American trials, each doctor may only be able to offer a handful of patients who are willing and able to participate, whereas in populous nations such as India and China, a single doctor may see dozens of patients a day who would be willing trial participants, allowing faster recruitment from a smaller number of sites.

However, pharmaceutical companies don't have everything their own way. Developing countries or not, restrictions are in place to either directly prevent trials or, at the very least, to ensure the professional and ethical management of those trials:

- Many developing countries have laws against "first in man" trials to prevent the treatment of their citizens as guinea pigs in highly experimental drug trials.

- Russia and China have both limited the export of blood and patient tissue samples in recent years, partly out of concern over illegal trafficking in human organs.

- The FDA recently set up an office in China to increase inspections of the rapidly growing number of clinical trials.

- The World Medical Association's 2004 Helsinki declaration called for stringent ethical practices in drug trials, but these remain voluntary practices.

In addition, the rush to take advantage of these cost savings and practical benefits has produced some problems ranging from questionable data to patient deaths:

- In 2003, several patients with AIDS died after an experimental drug trial in Ditan Hospital in Beijing. Viral Genetics, a California biotechnology company, was criticized for failing to explain adequately to participants that they were taking part in a drug trial rather than receiving a proven medicine.

- Further criticism was levied at Viral Genetics for an issue that has become a greater concern for clinical drug trials in general—specifically the use of a sugar pill or placebo as a comparative measure of the efficacy of the drug. In the Ditan trial questions were raised as to why an antiretroviral treatment—the most effective treatment for AIDS in the west—wasn't used as a comparative treatment.

- The lack of education and lower standards of care in these developing countries also raise questions about patient eligibility for participation in these trials. While they may qualify by diagnosis, do they really understand the concept of informed consent and, more importantly still, do they realize that once the

trial has ended it may be months or years before they have access to the drug for a prolonged treatment regimen for their condition?

In the end, it is likely that basic economics will win out. Increasingly stringent standards in North America, driven, some would argue, by the litigious nature of our society, will only serve to increase the attractiveness of overseas trials. Without a suitable regulatory framework to oversee these trials and ensure that patients are treated in an ethical manner, the feared picture of uneducated citizens from developing countries being used as guinea pigs in experimental trials that citizens from developed nations are unwilling to participate in will become a reality.

Discussion Questions

1. Is it ethical to offshore clinical drug trials? Explain your answer.

2. Identify three factors that are driving pharmaceutical companies to host clinical drug trials overseas.

3. What regulations are in place to oversee the professional and ethical management of these trials?

4. If patients lack the language skills or education to understand the significance of informed consent or the use of a placebo, is it ethical to allow them to participate in the drug trial? Why or why not?

5. Is it right to offer patients treatment in a drug trial only to deprive them of access to that drug on a treatment plan for months or years after the completion of the trial? Explain your answer.

6. What proposals would you offer to make the offshoring of clinical drug trials a more ethical process for all the stakeholders involved?

Source: Andrew Jack, "New Lease on Life? The Ethics of Offshoring Clinical Trials," *Financial Times*, London (UK), January 29, 2008, p. 9.

chapter 10

Making It Stick: Doing What's Right in a Competitive Market

> "As long as fallible human beings are in charge, we can expect more businesses to get into big trouble. Generally they're going to fail through bad luck or bad business judgment, but sometimes they're going to fail through negligence or active malfeasance or even active criminal behavior. The challenge our society faces is to study these events and to take lessons from them about ethical conduct personally and ethical conduct as representatives of our companies, and about public policy responses. I ask myself, what should I do differently in my job. . . . What should my company do differently?"
>
> —James A. Baker III, White House Chief of Staff for President Ronald Reagan and Secretary of State for President George H. W. Bush[1]

LEARNING OBJECTIVES

After studying this chapter, you should be able to:

1. Develop the key components of an ethics policy.

2. Understand the key components of a job description for an ethics officer.

3. Reward ethical behavior within your department/organization.

4. Promote your organization's ethics policy to your stakeholders.

5. Monitor ethical behavior in your department/organization.

6. Understand the difference between *reactive* and *proactive* ethical policies.

You Scratch My Back

Adam is a sales rep for a leading pharmaceutical company. His company is in a fierce battle with its largest competitor over the highly lucrative blood pressure medication market. Blood pressure medication is a multibillion-dollar market in the United States, the largest selling medication after drugs for cholesterol and diabetes. Adam's company has the number one drug and its competitor the number two drug in the market, but like Coke and Pepsi, they are locked in a fierce battle for market share with aggressive marketing campaigns and sales promotions. The company has produced every possible giveaway item with the name of the drug on it, and the trunk and back seat of Adam's company car (not to mention his garage) are crammed with boxes of those items to give away to any doctor who shows an interest in prescribing the medicine.

Today, Adam is visiting a new doctor. The office is actually one he has worked with for a long time, but the partners he knew recently sold their practice and retired, so Adam has a meeting with the new owner of the practice, Dr. Green.

As Adam pulls into the parking lot, he has a problem finding a parking space. "This place is busier than ever," he thinks. "I hope old Doc Stevens and his partners got a good price for this practice—it's got to be a gold mine."

In the waiting room, Adam sees all the old familiar faces behind the counter but notices that no one is smiling—all are very serious and focused on paperwork. Jennifer, the office manager, takes him back to Dr. Green's office and leaves him with a word of advice: "Watch yourself, Adam; it's not like the old days."

After 15 minutes, Dr. Green walks in. Adam stands up and introduces himself and politely thanks Dr. Green for making time for him in his busy schedule.

Dr. Green doesn't smile or make small talk. He gets straight to the point: "Adam, is it? Well, Adam, let me explain my philosophy in working with pharmaceutical reps. The way I see it, you make as much money on your pills as you can until the patent runs out, and I'd like to see some of that money being spent for the benefit of this practice—lots of free samples for my patients and lots of evidence that your company appreciates my support of their medicines—do you follow me?"

Adam wasn't sure what "lots of evidence" meant, but he was pretty sure that Dr. Green was about to explain it to him, so he nodded and smiled.

"This practice represents a long-term investment for me and I paid top dollar for it. Old Man Stevens built a good base of patients, but I think we can do better—this place just needs a firm hand and it will double in size within the year. Unfortunately, with growth comes additional expense. Did I mention I paid top dollar for this place?" Dr. Green suddenly stopped and smiled—one of the most artificial smiles Adam had ever seen.

"Here's what I'm thinking, Adam. Rather than wasting money on notepads and pens that the other reps give me by the case, I'd like some support—we can call it marketing funds if you'd like—in decorating my office. Some high-end furniture worthy of a doctor with a growing practice—what do you think?"

Adam coughed, trying desperately to come up with an answer: "Well, sir, that's a very unusual request, um, and while we greatly appreciate your support of our medicines, um, I don't think I could get that approved by my regional manager."

Dr. Green's fake smile disappeared as quickly as it had arrived. "Here's the deal, Adam. I had a very productive meeting with a delightful young man named Zachary this morning. He works for your competition, I believe."

continued

Adam winced at the mention of Zach's name.

"Zachary didn't seem to think there would be a problem with such an unusual request. In fact, he has a friend who is an interior designer and he was confident that her services could be included in those "marketing funds." So what are we going to do here?"

1. The four key points of a code of ethics are outlined on page 239. If we assume that Adam's company has such a code, what guidance could Adam find in those four key points?

2. Do you think Zachary is willing to provide those "marketing funds" in order to win the business away from Adam, or is Dr. Green just bluffing?

3. What should Adam do now?

Making It Stick—Key Components of an Ethics Policy

Ask any CEO to describe the market she is working in and she will probably describe the same set of characteristics:

- *Demanding customers* who want new and better products and services at lower prices.
- *Impatient stockholders* who want the stock price to rise each and every quarter.
- *Aggressive vendors* who want to sell you more of everything.
- *Demanding federal, state, and local officials* who want to burden you with more rules and regulations while encouraging you to hire more people and pay more taxes.
- *Demanding creditors* who want their loan payments on time.
- *Aggressive competitors* who want to steal your customers from you.

When you are operating a business in such a tough environment, holding on to your promise to run an ethical business and to do "the right thing" for all your stakeholders can be very challenging. It's easy to see why so many executives, after the unethical behavior of their companies has been exposed, point to the ruthless competition of the business world as their excuse for not doing the right thing.

So how do you make it stick? How do you make sure your company holds on to its ethical principles even if everyone else in your marketplace doesn't? For an ethical culture to be **sustainable,** it has to persist within the operational policies of the organization long after the latest public scandal or the latest management buzzword.

Sustainable Ethics An ethical culture that persists long after the latest public scandal or the latest management buzzword.

We have seen in the last nine chapters how a company's commitment to ethical behavior impacts every managerial level and every department of the organization. So making ethical behavior *sustainable* requires the involvement of every member of the organization in committing to a formal structure to support an ongoing process of monitoring and enforcement. This can be summarized in the following six stages:

1. Establish a code of ethics.
2. Support the code of ethics with extensive training for every member of the organization.
3. Hire an ethics officer.
4. Celebrate and reward the ethical behavior demonstrated by your employees.
5. Promote your organization's commitment to ethical behavior.
6. Continue to monitor the behavior as you grow.

Establish a Code of Ethics

In order for everyone to begin from the same starting point, the organization's commitment to ethical behavior must be documented in a code of ethics. A well-written code of ethics can do several things:

- It can capture what the organization understands ethical behavior to mean—your values statement.
- It can establish a detailed guide to acceptable behavior.
- It can state policies for behavior in specific situations.
- It can document punishments for violations of those policies.

The audience for the code of ethics would be every stakeholder of the organization. Investors, customers, and suppliers would see how serious you are about ethical performance, and employees would understand clearly what standard of behavior is expected from them and what the consequences would be for failing to meet that standard.

Review the following appendixes for examples of codes of ethics from the following organizations:

- Society of Professional Journalists (SPJ)—Appendix 7.
- Association for Computing Machinery (ACM)—Appendix 8.
- The Institute of Internal Auditors (IIA)—Appendix 9.
- American Society of Civil Engineers (ASCE)—Appendix 10.

As you can see from those four examples and others that have been featured throughout this book, there is no perfect model for a code of ethics: Some are very specific in their commitments to their profession (consider the "Canons" of the ASCE code) and others are operational in their focus, giving very clear guidance as to the consequences if employees transgress the code.

If you are involved in creating a code of ethics from scratch, consider the following advice from the Institute of Business Ethics[2]:

1. *Find a champion.* Unless a senior person—hopefully the CEO—is prepared to drive the introduction of a business ethics policy, the chances of it being a useful tool are not high.
2. *Get endorsement from the chairman and the board.* Corporate values and ethics are matters of governance. The board must be enthusiastic not only about having such a policy but also about receiving regular reports on its operation.
3. *Find out what bothers people.* Merely endorsing a standard code or copying that of another will not suffice. It is important to find out on what topics employees require guidance.

4. *Pick a well-tested model.* Use a framework that addresses issues as they affect different constituents or shareholders of the company. The usual ones are: shareholders employees, customers, suppliers, and local/national community. Some might even include competitors.

5. *Produce a company code of conduct.* This should be distributed in booklet form or via a company intranet. Existing policies, for example on giving and receiving gifts or the private use of company software, can be incorporated. Guidance on how the code works should also be included.

6. *Try it out first.* The code needs piloting—perhaps with a sample of employees drawn from all levels and different locations. An external party such as the Institute of Business Ethics will comment on drafts.

7. *Issue the code and make it known.* Publish and send the code to all employees, suppliers, and others. State publicly that the company has a code and implementation program that covers the whole company. Put it on your Web site and send it to joint venture and other partners.

8. *Make it work.* Practical examples of the code in action should be introduced into all company internal (and external) training programs as well as induction courses. Managers should sign off on the code regularly and a review mechanism should be established. A code "master" needs to be appointed.

Support the Code of Ethics with Extensive Training for Every Member of the Organization

Writing the code of ethics is the easy part. Getting your commitment to ethical performance down on paper and specifying the standards of behavior you will accept and the punishments you will enforce is a good starting point. However, the code can only be a guide—it cannot cover every possible event. The real test of any company's ethics policy comes when one of your employees is presented with a potentially unethical situation.

Moreover, even though your code of ethics is written for employees to follow, your stakeholders aren't required to follow it.

For example, what do you do when a supplier offers one of your employees a bribe or kickback for signing an order or a customer asks for a kickback from you for giving you their business? Is that example going to be in your code? If not, what guidance are you going to offer your employees?

This is where an extensive training program to support the published code of ethics becomes so important. Since the code can't capture every possible example, each department of the organization should take the code and apply it to examples that could arise in their area. In these department or team meetings, employees can work on

- Recognizing the ethical issue.

- Discussing options for an appropriate response.

- Selecting the best option for the organization.

Employees in all job functions need to be familiar with their company's code of ethics. How might a code of ethics apply to these factory workers?

1. List six characteristics of a tough market.

2. List four key items in a code of ethics.

3. Provide three examples of unethical behavior by a customer.

4. Provide three examples of unethical behavior by a supplier.

Smaller organizations can strengthen this employee training with additional training for supervisors and managers in ethical conflict resolution. If an individual employee or team of employees is unable to resolve an ethical issue, they can then turn to their supervisor or manager for guidance and support. In larger organizations, that role is made more significant by the creation of the position of ethics officer.

Hire an Ethics Officer

The hiring of an **ethics officer** represents a formal commitment to the management and leadership of an organization's ethics program. The role is usually developed as a separate department with the responsibility of enforcing the code of ethics and providing support to any employees who witness unethical behavior. It sends a clear message to your stakeholders and provides an appropriate person for employees and their managers to turn to when they need additional guidance and support. This person can be promoted from within the organization (selecting a familiar face who can be trusted) or hired from outside (selecting an independent face who is new to company history and office politics).

Ethics Officer A senior executive responsible for monitoring the ethical performance of the organization both internally and externally.

The Ethics and Compliance Officers Association (a professional group of ethics and compliance officers with over 1,000 members) documented the chief responsibilities of their members in a survey, which may be summarized as follows:

89% Oversight of hotline/guideline/internal reporting.

89% Preparation and delivery of internal presentations.

88% Organizationwide communications.

85% Senior management and/or board briefings/communications.

84% Training design.

83% Assessing/reviewing vulnerabilities.

83% Assessing/reviewing success/failure of initiatives.

79% Overseeing investigations of wrongdoing.

79% Management of program documentation.

77% Direct handling of hotline/guideline/internal reporting.

72% Preparation and delivery of external presentations.

68% Establishing company policy and procedures.

64% International program development.

61% Training delivery.

56% International program implementation.

52% Conducting investigations of wrongdoing.

ETHICAL dilemma

CASE 10.1 What Would Julie Do?

CEO Michael Capellas's Introduction to MCI's Code of Ethics and Business Conduct

At MCI, ethical conduct forms the foundation for our business success. Our commitment to high standards in no way diminishes our determination to aggressively pursue success in the marketplace as a superior provider of the industry's most innovative products and services. Indeed, over the long term, being—and being recognized as—a highly ethical company will provide us with a sustainable competitive advantage. History has proven that while some may achieve short-term success by cutting corners, at the end of the day, only the true ethics leaders in industry will remain standing. We shall stand tall among them.

What would Julie do? That's the question MCI's 55,000 employees have been trained to ask themselves and each other every day as the telecommunications giant seeks to remake its image in the wake of the more than $9 billion accounting scandal (back when it was called WorldCom) that led it into the largest bankruptcy in history.

As part of its settlement with the bankruptcy court and the SEC (Securities and Exchange Commission), MCI was required to put about 1,200 executive and financial employees through mandatory ethics training. Chairman and CEO Michael Capellas decided instead that since the issue of ethics was so critical to the future survival of MCI, every employee in the organization should go through the training.

The training course consists of an online program that takes 30 to 60 minutes to complete and presents the employee with a series of ethical situations. Developed over a nine-month period with the New York University School of Continuing and Professional Studies' Corporate Learning Services, the program requires you to think through a set of theoretical ethical dilemmas facing Julie, a fictitious MCI employee.

The dilemmas range from the abstract—"are you justified if you kill an attacker in order to defend your family"—to the more industry specific—should Julie ignore the error she discovers in a colleague's financial report as a co-worker suggests, or should she confront the colleague, who is a friend, and get the mistake fixed?

The company put 20,000 employees through the program in one week, and another 20,000 the next week—placing a considerable strain on the University's Web servers in the process. "People at MCI are really very embarrassed about what happened at their company," says Nancy Higgins, who joined the carrier in October 2004 as its first chief ethics officer. "Employees are really happy to see the company spending time [on ethics training]."

While it's too soon to say whether the program will bring about cultural change at MCI or wind up as an elaborate public relations exercise, the carrier appears to be taking its second chance seriously. At MCI headquarters, where about 5,000 employees work, the company's focus on ethics is hard to miss, from the "What would Julie do?" T-shirts to banners and posters down hallways and in conference rooms that remind employees "Our code is the standard, you make the difference" and "Do the right thing, because it's the right thing to do."

From the MCI Code of Ethics and Business Conduct: MCI's 10 Guiding Principles

- Build Trust and Credibility. Do what you say and say what you do.
- Respect for the Individual. Treat each other with dignity and integrity.
- Create a Culture of Open and Honest Communications. Everyone should feel comfortable to speak his or her mind.
- Set the Tone at the Top. Management leads by example.
- Uphold the Law. Put the law of the land on a pedestal.
- Avoid Conflicts of Interest. Carefully and consciously manage various stakeholder interests.
- Set Metrics and Report Results Accurately. Balance between the short and long term.
- Promote Substance over Form. Focus on what is important and not what is convenient.
- Be Loyal. To your families, your company, yourselves.
- Do the Right Thing. Because it's the right thing to do.

Several key questions can help to identify situations that may be unethical, inappropriate, or illegal. Ask yourself

- Does what I am doing comply with the letter and the spirit of MCI's Guiding Principles and company policies?
- Have I been asked to misrepresent information or deviate from normal procedure?
- Would I feel comfortable describing my decision at a staff meeting?
- How would it look if it made the headlines?
- Am I being loyal to my family, my company, and myself?
- What would I tell my child to do?
- Is it the right thing to do?

Communicating the company's message of integrity and educating employees on how to avoid misconduct is an ongoing effort for Higgins, who previously oversaw ethics at Lockheed Martin and Boeing. "We can't deal with any of the problems we don't know about. We want to create an environment where people will feel comfortable reporting [questionable ethics]," she says.

Higgins says there are certain actions over which MCI doesn't have control. For instance, if the reported misconduct results in legal prosecution, MCI couldn't prevent certain information from being revealed if the company were subpoenaed. One way MCI addresses such concerns is through an anonymous toll-free number where employees can seek additional clarity on any topic covered in the training or report suspected unethical practices. MCI says it logged more than 400 calls into this system in November 2004, a tenfold jump from July, before the training program went into effect.

While browsing through the company's 16-page code of ethics and business conduct, cynics might see a more pragmatic motivation behind MCI's new-found commitment to an ethical culture. The federal government's General Services Administration (GSA) had banned MCI from bidding on new government contracts because of questions it had regarding the company's ethics and corporate governance programs. The restriction was later removed. In addition, the comforting and reassuring commitment to people as the key to ethical operations has been diluted with the departure of over 24,000 employees as MCI struggled to emerge from bankruptcy.

1. List the 10 guiding principles that form the foundation of MCI's Code of Ethics and Business Conduct.

2. List six of the questions that MCI employees are encouraged to ask themselves in identifying inappropriate, unethical, or illegal situations.

3. If MCI had not been facing a ban from bidding for GSA contracts, do you think the company would have been as eager to introduce such a far-reaching ethics initiative? Explain why or why not.

4. What else could MCI have done to restore investor and customer confidence in the wake of the accounting scandal?

Source: Adapted from Denise Pappalardo, "Doing the Right Thing, MCI Style," *Network World* 21, no. 7 (February 16, 2004), http://global.mci.com/about/governance/values/coc.pdf.

Celebrate and Reward the Ethical Behavior Demonstrated by Your Employees

With standards of behavior specified in the code of ethics, along with the punishment served for failing to follow those standards, your ethics program can become harsh. This goes against your goal of increasing employee loyalty and customer satisfaction. So the threats of punishment must be balanced with promised rewards for successful behavior:

- Celebrate examples of good ethical behavior in your company newsletter.

- Award prizes for ethical behavior—and let the employee choose the reward.

- Award prizes for new and creative ideas—and let the employee choose the reward.

- Recognize employees who represent the standard of behavior to which you are committing.

- Declare an Ethics Day and allow every department to share their successes.

5. When hiring an ethics officer, is it better to promote someone from within the company or hire someone from outside? Explain your answer.

6. List six key responsibilities of an ethics officer.

7. Give three examples of celebrating ethical behavior.

8. If you publicly celebrate ethical behavior, should you also publish punishment for unethical behavior? Why or why not?

Promote Your Organization's Commitment to Ethical Behavior

An ethics policy commits you to doing the right thing for all your stakeholders, so that message must be shared with *all* your stakeholders—both inside and outside the company. Make clear and firm promises to them and then deliver on those promises. Offer concrete examples that your organization is committed to winning the trust (and the business) of your customers by building a reputation they can count on. For example:

- Offer a no-questions-asked refund policy like Lands' End.
- Offer a 110-percent price-match guarantee like Home Depot.
- If you overcharge clients by mistake, give them a refund *plus* interest *before* their accounting department figures out the error and asks for the money.
- Get your clients involved in the development of your ethics policies. Ask them to tell you what forms of behavior or guarantees will make them feel reassured that they are dealing with an ethical company.
- Let your employees visit client sites to talk about your code of ethics in person.
- Share your success stories with all of your stakeholders, not just your employees.
- Invite your stakeholders to your Ethics Day celebration.

ETHICAL dilemma

CASE 10.2 Just a Small Favor

My Tuesday morning wasn't looking good. I had a few minutes to try to catch up on my e-mails, and then a meeting with Doug Slater, the head of one of our smaller business units. Slater wasn't one of my favorite people. It's not that I'd ever had problems with him in his work performance; it was just a nagging feeling that he couldn't be trusted. He was bright enough, and he certainly knew how to work a room, but he was just too slick for my taste. He was always ready to agree at a moment's notice with anyone above him on the organizational chart, while belittling those who couldn't touch him because he was the head of a business unit. He seemed to be focused on nothing more than getting ahead, and I got the impression he would manipulate anyone and anything to get there.

Slater walked casually into my office on the stroke of 10:00 a.m., punctual as always. He was "all smiles," spending just the right amount of time on small talk and last night's triple overtime football game, before he dropped his "small favor." All he wanted, he said, was a slight delay in paying his unit's bills this month.

Our company is highly automated, and the companies we do business with operate in much the same manner. When we receive their bills and approve them for payment, they go to accounts payable, where they're matched electronically against the contracts or purchase orders for payment terms. As with all good cash flow management programs, if the terms are net 10 days, we automatically pay in 10 days. If they're 30 days, then we pay in 30. Messing with this system requires multiple signatures, in triplicate, and it's usually only possible if one of our vendors offers us a deal for early payment that's too good to pass up.

This was precisely Slater's "small favor," and I knew why he wanted it. Our monthly business-unit profitability reports are calculated on a cash basis—actual receipts against actual expenses. So if Slater could keep the expense figure artificially low by delaying payment on some bills, his margin figures would look that much better. Obviously, the figures would catch up with him in the end, but he was gambling that a few good quarters would catch the attention of the right people in the right places and he'd be promoted to another position, leaving his poor unsuspecting replacement to deal with it.

I didn't answer immediately—I needed a minute to get my temper under control. Did he really think I was so dumb that I wouldn't know what he was trying to do, or had he assumed that I didn't care enough about our code of ethics to mind? Either way, it was a poor reflection on me. The only bright side was that I figured he was in my office because no one in my IT team had been willing to help him with his "small favor." Even if he had found someone to help him, if it were to come to light, the internal auditors would be notified because it would indicate a violation of our controls. If we manually change the terms on a contract (to modify payment terms, for example), an exception report is printed that goes straight to the chief financial officer. He obviously either didn't realize how tightly we monitor such things or he thought he would be long gone by the time it was discovered and he could blame someone else.

I told Slater that I wouldn't override the software nor would I authorize one of my team to do it. I also warned him that if anyone on the IT team did it for him, that person would be clearing out his desk by the end of the day. He replied, "It's not such a big deal! Anyway, you can't blame a guy for trying," and walked out.

1. Why is Slater's "small favor" unethical?
2. Are there any federal or legal safeguards in place to prevent this type of behavior?
3. Should Slater's request be reported to anyone? Who and why?
4. If Slater had requested his "small favor" from members of the IT team, they had obviously refused to do it. Why?

Source: Adapted from Herbert W. Lovelace, "But It's a Business Favor, Herb, Not Ethics," *Information Week*, Aug 12, 2002, p. 62.

Continue to Monitor the Behavior as You Grow

Any organization's commitment to ethical performance must be watched constantly. It is easy for other business issues to take priority and for the code of ethics to become taken for granted. Also, the continued growth of technology will present new situations for ethical dilemmas such as policies on e-mail monitoring and Web surfing, so your code may need to be rewritten on a regular basis. A large organization can make that one of the responsibilities of its designated ethics officer. Smaller companies need to include their code of ethics as part of any strategic planning exercise to make sure it is as up-to-date as possible.

Reactive Ethical Policies Policies that result when organizations are driven by events and/or a fear of future events.

Proactive Ethical Policies Policies that result when the company develops a clear sense of what they stand for as an ethical organization.

Transparent Organization An organization that maintains open and honest communications with all stakeholders.

✓ PROGRESS CHECK QUESTIONS

9. List six examples of commitments that companies can make to win the trust of their stakeholders.

10. Provide four of your own examples.

11. Why would a code of ethics need to be updated?

12. Find out when your company's code of ethics was last updated.

Becoming a Transparent Organization

Many organizations have been prompted to introduce or modify their codes of ethics by the sight of CEOs pleading the Fifth Amendment in front of congressional committees. Others have been inspired by the large number of zeroes that can now be tacked on to financial penalties for corporate misconduct. Unfortunately, neither motivation is enough. These are examples of **reactive policies,** which result when organizations are driven by events and/or a fear of future events. True ethical policies are **proactive,** which occur when the company develops a clear sense of what it stands for as an ethical organization—not only what ethics means to them and their stakeholders, but also the extent of the actions they will take (and the necessary punishments they will enforce) to get there.

One characteristic that is common to such organizations is **transparency,** which means the company is open and honest in all its communications with all its stakeholders. However, the financial markets that govern stock prices (and the profits to be made as corporate executives cash in their stock options) have proven to be remarkably indifferent to "open and honest communications." Consider the two situations in Case 10.3.

No matter how big or small your business, transparency is important. What are some ways an employee can promote transparency?

ETHICAL dilemma

CASE 10.3 To Be or Not to Be

Situation A: "What You Don't Know Won't Hurt You"

"Chainsaw Al" Dunlap at Scott Paper Co.

[When Al Dunlap became CEO of Scott Paper in April 1994] he told employees that his goal was to reinvest in the business and fashion a clear vision for the future. But many survivors said it soon became clear he was only interested in selling out . . . within two months of his arrival [he had announced] there would be major changes in management, a restructuring that would eliminate 35 percent of the employees, outright sales of units unrelated to Scott's core tissue business, and a new strategy for the future. . . . [He] slashed the company's research and development budget in half and eliminated 60 percent of the staffers in R&D. He put off all major plant and equipment maintenance for the 1995 year. . . . "What he did was borrow a year, maybe two from the future," said Jerry Ballas, Scott's head of manufacturing and technology worldwide. "At some point, you have to pay it back. If you wait too long, you'll pay it back double because the plants will operate inefficiently and the machines will begin to break down. We strung it out as far as we could without getting into unsafe conditions."

Dunlap ran Scott's factories and drove people as if the company were going out of business. As Ballas, who had spent 33 years working for Scott, put it: "You don't allow factory shutdowns. You do no training whatsoever. You don't hire anybody. You buy nothing unless you need it today. And you try to sell everything you make. We were down to the bare bones. People were working unbelievable hours doing unbelievable stuff. We could not have continued to run the business the way we were for the future."

To push more product into the marketplace, the company's consumer sales force gave huge discounts to customers that were earned only when the product sold through at retail. The result was that Scott's financial staff could book the sale and profit at standard rates and only had to provide the discount in the future when retailers applied for the credit. That way, the paper company could show dramatic increases in sales without an immediate erosion in profit margins. Typically, such trade promotion discounts ran at 10 percent to 20 percent of revenue. To drive volume at Scott, especially in the final months before the company was sold, the discounts were doubled.

When Kimberly-Clark agreed to buy Scott Paper for $9.4 billion, Scott shareholders saw their investment in the company rise by 225 percent. Under Dunlap's leadership, the company's market capitalization went up by an extraordinary $6.3 billion. Going into the merger, however, Scott's budget projected income of $100 million in the fourth quarter of 1995. Instead, Kimberly-Clark lost $60 million on Scott's business, according to company insiders, a profit swing of $160 million that did not include a massive $1.4 billion restructuring charge the company declared to cover its "integration plan for Scott." Among the acquisition's hidden costs was a hit of $30 million on the promotion credits for the discounted sales Scott gave retailers to build inventory. In the first three months after the takeover, Kimberly-Clark spent nearly $30 million more on plant and equipment maintenance that had been postponed under Dunlap. "We had to get the condition of our equipment back to where it should have been," explained Ballas, who spent 15 months with Kimberly-Clark to assist with the transition. . . . Among other things, Ballas found himself undoing "80 percent of what we did the year before."

Kimberly-Clark was forced to take a second restructuring charge in early 1998 to close plants and slash 5,000 workers, bringing total job cuts since the Scott merger to 11,000. . . . Dunlap's brief stint at Scott earned him $100 million.

Situation B: "Here We Are, Warts And All"

Ricardo Semler, CEO of Brazil-Based Semco for the Last Two Decades

It often takes a customer time to get used to Semco's way of doing business. Many of them are wary of our reputation for democracy, dissent, and flexibility. Those freedoms just mean chaos to people who don't appreciate them. While customers are not expected to adopt our philosophies when they hire us, we make our practices clear, and that has caused some unexpected culture clashes.

My own people have often been flabbergasted at my admission of guilt for product deficiencies during customer presentations. Dismayed, they would see our case going down the drain. More often than not, however, the customer would be taken aback by my frankness, and believe in the rest of what we had to say.

In one famous incident, we'd been battling with Anglo-American Mines over who was at fault in a mishap with gold mixing equipment. I went to see them and confessed that we had found drawings that definitely proved that the fault was ours. Though the drawings had been found sometime before, I had only just learned about them.

Our people were shaken. The $450,000 cost of redoing the equipment was a lot to us at the time, but Anglo-American reacted as I had hoped. They thanked us for our honesty, and ordered two more mixing machines. We used the money to fund the replacement of the older machines. They're our avid customers to this day.

So, in the world of business ethics, the corporate philosophies that Ricardo Semler adopted at Semco earned him the title of "maverick" and the curiosity of academics and business analysts alike, who couldn't understand why a company that continued to "break" so many rules had managed to stay in business. Meanwhile, Al Dunlap, who went on to additional (albeit brief) financial success at Sunbeam Corporation, rode the Wall Street rollercoaster of fame as "Rambo in Pinstripes," a nickname earned for his "take no prisoners" approach to "slashing and burning" as he turned around companies and appeared to resurrect their stock prices in record time. He was eventually fired by Sunbeam and sued for fraud.

1. "Dunlap ran Scott's factories and drove people as if the company were going out of business." Give four examples of this behavior.
2. Explain why Ricardo Semler's decision to tell the truth in the Anglo-American Mines incident was "the right thing to do."
3. Who would you rather work for, Dunlap or Semler? Explain your answer.
4. Why is Semler called a maverick?

Source: John A. Byrne, "*Chainsaw: The Notorious Career of Al Dunlap in the Era of Profit at Any Price*," New York: HarperBusiness, New York, 1999, pp. 26–33. Ricardo Semler, *The Seven-Day Weekend*, New York: Portfolio, 2003, pp. 128–9.

✓ PROGRESS CHECK QUESTIONS

13. What is a *reactive* ethical policy?
14. What is a *proactive* ethical policy?
15. Why would a company want to be transparent?
16. Would you say the company you work for is transparent? Explain your answer.

Conclusion

The intense media coverage of the many corporate scandals that have been uncovered over the last few years has brought the subject of business ethics to

the attention of a large portion of this country's population. That increased attention has proven to be something of a mixed blessing.

On the one hand, the average investor can be forgiven for thinking that the business world is full of crooks whose only purpose is to make as much money as possible. Problems with product quality, poor customer service, made-up financial reports, and out-of-court settlements with no admission of guilt paint a very negative picture.

The response to this negative picture has been new rules (Sarbanes-Oxley and others) and tighter controls that now represent a greater risk for organizations that fail to comply with the expected standard of behavior. Large financial penalties and expensive lawsuits can now place a substantial dollar figure on the cost of unethical behavior.

On the other hand, ethics has also become an issue that positively impacts the business world. Stockholders want to invest in companies with solid reputations and strong ethical programs. Employees prefer to work for companies they can trust where they feel valued. That sense of value results in increased commitment and reduced turnover, which means greater profits for the company. Customers prefer to buy from companies with proven track records of integrity in their business

You Scratch My Back— Adam Makes A Decision

Dr. Green continued to stare at Adam. He was obviously looking for an answer now, and Adam knew that if he tried to stall by asking to check with his regional manager, Green would show him the door.

One small part of Adam wanted to laugh out loud at this ridiculous situation. Doctors had asked him for extra free samples before, and the industry had always been willing to underwrite lunches and tickets to sports events or shows as appropriate marketing expenses, but no one had ever asked him outright for money to decorate his office—and this guy was dead serious!

For a moment Adam wondered if he was bluffing about Zach. He knew Zach was a tough competitor and they fought a tough battle in this region, usually managing to win clients away from each other on a couple of occasions. "Come to think of it," thought Adam, "Zach probably would go along with this deal. Winning this practice would be a real catch for his territory."

Then Adam looked at Dr. Green again. Something was bothering him about this guy. He got the feeling that this wasn't a one-time special request. If Adam gave in on this, he knew there would be other requests for "marketing funds" in the future, always with the threat of switching to the competition.

Suddenly Adam, almost as a surprise to himself, knew what he had to do: "I'm sorry Dr. Green. We value our relationships with our doctors very highly—that's how we were able to work so closely with Dr. Stevens for as long as we did. Unfortunately, that type of relationship doesn't include 'marketing funds.' I hope Zach's interior designer friend does a good job for you."

With that, Adam got up and turned to leave.

Six weeks later, the local paper featured a very unflattering picture of Dr. Green and Zach on the front page. Dr. Green had developed a very close relationship with Zach and his company—so close, in fact, that Dr. Green had been willing to massage some of his patient data to help Zach's company in a new drug trial.

1. What do you think the reaction of Adam's regional manager was to the initial news of the loss of Dr. Green's business?

2. Do you think Zach's company supported his willingness to provide Dr. Green's "marketing funds"?

3. What do you think will happen to Zach and Dr. Green now?

---

dealings—even if that choice costs them a little more. So if the threat of negative publicity, ruined reputations, and million-dollar legal settlements won't lead a company into developing an ethics policy, perhaps the promise of increased profits, happy stockholders, happy employees, and happy customers will!

Recognizing the concept of *business ethics* allows us to categorize behavior as unethical, but when you are looking to manage the reputation and policies of an organization, the commitment to doing the right thing becomes more about **organizational integrity** than any sense of a written ethics policy. Understanding that your company does not operate independently from its community, its customers, its employees, its stockholders, and its suppliers is vital to the long-term survival of the organization. Winning the trust and confidence of all your stakeholders would be a great achievement in today's business world, but *keeping* that trust and confidence over the long term would be an even greater one.

> **Organizational Integrity** A characteristic of publicly committing to the highest professional standards and sticking to that commitment.

[KEY TERMS]

REVIEW QUESTIONS

1. You have been asked to join a team as the representative of your department. The team has been tasked with the development of an ethics training program to support the company's new code of ethics. What would your recommendations be?

2. Your company wrote its code of ethics in 1986. You have been assigned to a team that has been tasked with updating the code to make it more representative of current business ethics issues like the Internet and modern business technology. What are your recommendations?

3. Do you think you could be an ethics officer? Why or why not?

4. When you go shopping, do you pay attention to how *transparent* the company is in its business practices? Why or why not?

TEAM EXERCISES

1. **A different Scott Paper.** Divide into two teams. One team must defend the actions of Al Dunlap at Scott Paper. The other team must criticize them and come up with a proposal to make Scott Paper more transparent in its business practices.

2. **An ethics charter.** Divide into groups of three or four. Each group develops a charter that documents its company's commitment to ethical behavior. What industry is your company in? What does ethical behavior look like in that industry? What will your company's commitment consist of? A code of ethics? Performance guarantees? Corporate governance policies?

ROMP

Do your shoes have a name? Not a brand name, Lobb or Blahnik, but a real name such as Snuffles or Piggly Wiggly? UK leather goods brand Romp wants you to get to know your shoes a bit better, right down to the animal they used to be, scratching around in the hay.

Now in its seventh year, Romp is a Soil Association–accredited organic leather manufacturer, with a range of products that includes coats, shoes, and corsets. Selling across eight markets, including Russia, the company provides ethically sourced designer clothing, and its holding company will turn over an estimated $35 million (£19 million) this year. To ensure its practices are ethical and transparent, Romp claims customers can trace its products back through 48 stages of its supply chain, right to the animal on the farm. All the chemicals used are listed by code and everyone who has touched the product is named, with contact details. The company's policy is defined in this statement:

The "I-Button"

Every time you buy a product you are supporting and encouraging all the systems that went into the production and sale of that item. So how do you know that you do actually support such systems, and would you still buy the item if you knew that you didn't? Our solution is an "I-button."

As with most legislation, labeling requirements are both complex and virtually unworkable as a deterrent to bad or unfair practice. Clever people will always seek ways to gain advantage by positioning their response to legislation as close to breaching the requirements, without actually doing so, as they can. If you don't believe me, try to find the no longer legally required, Country of Origin label on many high street garments. If you can't see it immediately, check the bottom of the inside pocket. You'll be surprised how frequently the label that is concealed or is not there at all does not mention a democratic country.

Labeling is there, in spirit, to protect the consumer and to level the playing field for the retailer. So what does it say about the retailer's or brand's opinion of their customers if they don't even bother to conform to that spirit?

The [UK] Trade Descriptions Act 1968 makes it an offence to apply a false description to any goods. It means that people selling goods should not make false claims about the product, and neither should any packaging, labeling or advertising. However if nothing is said you must be very careful of drawing your own conclusions about the goods.

The important examples to Romp of information which is not currently required are: The Country of Origin, the legislative standards of animal husbandry, pollution, and labor law for a product.

These are all important, as currently, these are the areas that virtually dictate the cost of production.

For Romp, the customer deserves all the information that we can give him or her about what they are buying. It is the only way to offer free choice.

There are different types of product in our range (Stages 1, 2, 3) with different origins and impacts and so a simple label inside each garment was never going to be enough.

Every product that we sell has a photograph in the boutique section and under the photograph is an "I" button. Before you buy always read this 21st Century Label. Where any customer is unhappy with this level of information we will always seek to provide more. Each individual product sold will be provided with all the required labels but also will have a unique identification number of its own. Your product will, in most cases be made to order, so the trace information provided on the site is for the coat shown. When you receive your item simply check the unique number and type it into any one of the Get History Boxes. The information with it will be genuine, accurate and verifiable.

Romp believes that you have the right to care or not to care about what your money is supporting but we do not believe that we or any other vendor has the right to take that choice away.

In other words ignorance is not bliss, for the people, animals and planet involved.

Romp founder and chief executive, Greg Sturmer, agrees that most consumers won't want to be on first-name terms with the pig whose skin they are now wearing, but he believes it sets the benchmark for how business needs to behave. "If you are prepared to work with the full glare of traceability, you come up with a naturally better product."

Tim Kitchen, partner in the relationship management consultancy The Glasshouse Partnership, outlines what this philosophy means for brands. "The Romp revolution is its traceability and transparency," he explains. "The challenge for brands is to take this process and make it user specific."

Sturmer doesn't believe that this degree of product traceability has only niche appeal. "Seventy-seven percent of households—4.5 million—buy organic, and 23 percent of those are heavy users," he reveals. "All of them are prepared to pay more to get a better quality product. These people are also the sort to buy designer clothing, so I think we have a large customer pool."

Both Kitchen and Sturmer agree that they may be ahead of the consumer curve in revealing quite so much about the supply chain, but Sturmer claims it's only a matter of time. "We're saying 'look, this coat is pretty and if you want more detail, we'll give you more.' Once people know what's possible, they'll think your brand is shabby if you're not providing it. Soon you won't be able to market a quality product without its traceability."

Scott Bedbury, chief executive of brand consultancy Brandstream, agrees customer-driven transparency is the movement of the future. "The more transparent we are as a company, the world will be a better place. We're all going to be buck naked."

Discussion Questions

1. If you purchased a pair of Romp shoes, would you want to know the name of the animal they came from? Why or why not?

2. Most consumers looking to do business with an ethical company want reassurance that the company operates in a fair and decent manner with all its stakeholders. Does the notion of traceability provide that?

3. Could the practice of traceability be applied to all industries? Provide three examples of industries where it would be difficult (or impossible) to introduce this practice.

4. There are differences between providing traceability information to all customers and simply making it available to those customers who want it. How would you approach each option?

5. Explain the term *transparency* when used in reference to corporate operations.

6. Can you assume that a transparent company is an ethical company? Explain why or why not.

Source: "Romp," *Brand Strategy*, London: Nov 2, 2005, pg. 28. www.romp.co.uk.

THE TRANSFORMATION OF SHELL

In the late 1990s, Shell International underwent a remarkable transformation. Variously termed by observers a "sea change," a "midlife crisis," and a "dramatic overhaul," the company undertook a deep and systematic effort to remake itself. In the process, Shell radically changed its organizational structure, its culture, its relationship with stakeholders (including its most vocal critics), its reporting practices, and, indeed, even its very business principles. In the end, it set out to become an organization in which financial, social, and environmental performance were equally valued and fully integrated.

A cover story in *Fortune* in 1997 was pointedly titled "Why Is the World's Most Profitable Company Turning Itself Inside Out?" To some, this transformation represented wrongheaded New Age tampering with a proven management formula. To some, it was nothing more than a sophisticated public relations offensive to repair a reputation badly tarnished by human rights abuses in Nigeria, the controversy over the disposal of the oil rig Brent Spar, and struggles with shareholder activists over corporate governance. To others, though, it represented more. To them, Shell's multilevel struggle to transform itself was the most ambitious effort ever by a major multinational corporation to define a new relationship between business and society in a world of rapidly changing public expectations.

The Campaigns Against Shell

The early to mid-1990s were a period when international environmentalist, human rights, and shareholder campaigns directed against Shell gathered intensity. Three separate but related campaigns—opposing at-sea disposal of old offshore oil facilities, alleging human rights abuses in Nigeria, and backing shareholder resolutions for reforms in corporate governance—focused a spotlight of often negative publicity on the world's most profitable multinational corporation.

The Brent Spar Incident

A watershed event in Shell's transformation was what came to be known at the Brent Spar incident. The Brent Spar was an oil storage and loading buoy in the North Sea, about 100 miles off the coast of Scotland. Although a unique structure, it was one of several hundred North Sea installations, many nearing the end of their useful lives.

In 1991, Shell took the Brent Spar out of service and began looking at options for disposing of it. According to international and British law, operators were required to determine the best practical environmental option for disposal. This could involve either sinking the platform in the deep sea or removing and dismantling it on land. Government approval was required. In April 1995, after extensive consultations with outside experts about possible options, Shell announced its intention to dispose of the Brent Spar at sea, and British authorities agreed.

The plan quickly ran into resistance from Greenpeace, however. At the time, Greenpeace was the largest environmental organization in the world, with a full-time staff of 120, a budget of about $50 million, and a penchant for confrontational tactics. Greenpeace believed that toxic residue in the Brent Spar's tanks would harm the marine environment and that its disposal at sea would set a precedent for other, soon-to-be-decommissioned oil installations.

On April 30, 1995, Greenpeace activists boarded and occupied the abandoned buoy. After a three-week standoff, Shell personnel, aided by local law officers, evicted the protesters nonviolently. The company defended its decision to sink the Brent Spar in full-page newspaper advertisements and began towing the rig toward the open sea. However, the Greenpeace occupation and resulting media coverage had galvanized public opinion, especially on the Continent. By mid-June, government officials in Belgium, Denmark, Sweden, the Netherlands, and Germany had asked Shell to postpone sinking the Brent Spar. Meanwhile, a consumer boycott had gathered steam. In Germany, Shell franchise owners reported a 50 percent decline in sales over a two-week period. Several Shell gas stations, also in Germany, were anonymously firebombed. The British prime minister continued to support Shell, however, and the boycott was less successful in Britain.

On June 20, Shell abruptly changed course, announcing that it had decided to abandon its plan to dispose of the Brent Spar at sea and to seek a permit for onshore disposal. In a statement, the company said, "The European Companies of the Royal Dutch/Shell Group find themselves in an untenable position and feel that it is not possible to continue without wider support." The company moved the buoy to a Norwegian fjord while it considered further actions. Greenpeace later acknowledged that it had seriously erred in its estimate of the amount of toxic residue in the Brent Spar's tanks and apologized.

Human Rights in Nigeria

Just a few months later, the execution of Ken Saro-Wiwa and his colleagues in Nigeria on November 10, 1995 . . .led to what *Fortune* referred to as a "global uproar." Much of it was directed at the government of Nigeria, which was summarily suspended from the Commonwealth of Nations at the urging of President Nelson Mandela of South Africa. Other countries called for an arms embargo, sports boycott, and freezing the foreign bank accounts of the pariah nation's military leaders.

But much outrage was also directed at Shell, which was perceived by many as not acting forcefully to prevent Saro-Wiwa's execution. Environmentalist organizations, particularly, spoke out. The chairman of Greenpeace UK told the press, "There is blood on Shell's hands. Ken Saro-Wiwa was hanged for speaking out against Shell. He was trying to secure the most basic of human rights—the right to clean air, land, and water." The Sierra Club promoted a boycott of the company under the slogan "(S)hell no, corporate accountability yes," and urged its supporters to cut up their Shell credit cards, boycott Shell products, and participate in protest demonstrations.

One of the organizations most involved in the protests against Shell was The Body Shop International (BSI), the beauty products retailer chaired by social activist Anita Roddick. BSI initiated a major protest campaign against Shell, which included the perhaps unprecedented event of one corporation publicly accusing another of murder. Greenpeace, The Body Shop International, and Friends of the Earth ran a full-page advertisement with a photograph of a gas flare under the heading, "Dear Shell, This is the Truth. And it Stinks." Protest demonstrations featured hooded dummies dangling from nooses.

Initiating Organizational Change

In early 1994, more than a year before the Brent Spar, Nigeria, and shareholder campaigns erupted, Shell management had initiated a process of internal organizational change, aimed at improving the Group's financial performance relative to its competitors.

Since the 1950s, Royal Dutch/Shell had used a matrix form of organization. Under this structure, the chief executive of the national operating companies reported simultaneously to two superiors: a regional manager and a product manager. For example, the managing director of Shell Nigeria would report both to a regional coordinator for Africa and to the coordinator for exploration and production. In addition, staff at Shell's headquarters in London and The Hague provided functional expertise in finance, legal matters, human resources management, and external affairs. (Shell U.S., the largest of the Group companies, maintained its own staff of functional specialists and operated for most purposes independently.) At the time, it was believed that this matrix organization benefited Shell by devolving power and balancing interests.

In March 1995, Shell concluded the first phase of its internal review by announcing a plan to reorganize into five worldwide business units. These were exploration and production, oil products, chemicals, gas and coal, and central staff functions. The five units would be overseen by committees of senior executives, who would report to the committee of managing directors (CMD). Under this plan, managers of the operating companies would report only to their business unit superiors, in a single line of command, thus eliminating the matrix, which was perceived as unnecessarily complicated. Excess staff at the center was also cut. The restructuring was intended to enable the company to focus more efficiently on the needs of its business and retail customers.

Social and Environmental Reporting

Shell considered that an important element in its corporate responsibility initiative was to be publicly accountable not only to its shareholders but also to its other stakeholders and society at large. Accordingly, it began publishing a series of reports that went well beyond traditional annual financial reports.

In April 1998, the company published its first annual Shell Report, subtitled "Profits and Principles—Does There Have to Be a Choice?" This unusual document reported on Shell's commitment to human rights, environmental protection, and corporate citizenship. It also invited others to join with the company in a global debate on the responsibilities of multinational corporations. In its introduction, the report stated:

> This Report is about values. It describes how we, the people, companies, and businesses that make up the Royal Dutch/Shell Group, are striving to live up to our responsibilities—financial, social, and environmental. It is also an invitation to you to tell us what you think of our performance.

The report described the revised SGBP in detail, gave examples of each principle, and explained the company's efforts to make sure they were honored by the operating companies and Shell's joint venture partners and contractors. It presented a series of challenging ethical questions and invited readers to share their reactions. Many of these questions had already been the subjects of extensive public debate, in connection with Nigeria and Brent Spar. For example, one question asked, "Under what circumstances, if any, should a major company use its economic power to deliver, or at least influence, political change—especially in nations with undemocratic governments and poor human rights records?" The report presented Shell's approach to a number of difficult issues, such as climate change.

The report also included an essay by John Elkington, chairman of SustainAbility, a consultancy specializing in advising corporations on sustainable development. In this essay, Elkington presented his concept of the triple bottom line, arguing that companies had a duty to provide audited reports not only of their financial performance but of their social and environmental performance as well. The report concluded with a road map for the future. Shell followed up "Profits and Principles" with its "Health, Safety, and Environment Report" and "Shell's Investment in Society," reporting specifically on its environmental and social performance. All three reports were intended to be annual publications.

Although Shell had opposed PIRC's 1997 shareholder resolution calling for external auditing of its environmental performance, it now undertook to provide independent verification of its social and environmental reports. This goal presented unique challenges. The scope of practices to be audited was worldwide and complex. Moreover, unlike financial reporting, where auditing practices were well established, meaningful measures of social and environmental performance were not generally accepted. The

company set out to work with its auditors, KPMG and Price Waterhouse, and others to develop social and environmental accounting and assurance standards. In "Profits and Principles," the company set out a timetable leading to integrated, externally verified reporting for its financial, social, and environmental performance by 2002.

The company's July 1998 "Health, Safety, and Environment Report" was the first independently verified audited environmental report ever published by a multinational oil company. The auditors, KPMG and Price Waterhouse, acknowledged that the job had "proved to be a considerable challenge" because of the "absence of established generally accepted international standards for the verification of HSE data." The initial cost to audit Shell's health, safety, and environmental data in 30 entities worldwide in 1998 was around $2 million.

To bring the message of these reports to a wider public, Shell in 1999 initiated a $25 million "profits and principles" advertising campaign. Its purpose, in the words of Mark Moody-Stuart, was "to keep all of our stakeholders informed, both about the issues themselves and the work we at Shell are doing to address those issues."

Dialogue With Stakeholder Organizations

During this period, Shell also maintained an ongoing dialogue with stakeholders, including some of its most vocal critics. It called this process *engagement*. In part, this was accomplished through tear-off "Tell Shell" cards in various reports, such as Profits and Principles, which readers were invited to fill out and mail back to the company. In part, it was accomplished through an interactive feature on Shell's Web site, which permitted anyone to submit comments for all to see. Scores of people did, including many who were morally outraged at Shell's behavior. Their comments were posted, without censorship, creating the unusual spectacle of a corporate Web site peppered with negative remarks, which activists could use to find each other and create a community of anti-Shell interest.

In addition to opening itself up for freewheeling public comment, Shell also engaged in written and face-to-face dialogue with stakeholders, including community activists and human rights, environmentalist, and corporate governance organizations. The engagement process was coordinated by Shell's Department of External Affairs, but it involved managers at many levels throughout the Group.

The Human Rights Dialogue

One such dialogue occurred with two human rights organizations, Amnesty International and Pax Christi. In December 1995, in the wake of Ken Saro-Wiwa's execution, Pax Christi—a Catholic lay organization devoted to promoting world peace, human rights, and economic justice—wrote Shell asking the company to speak out on the issue of human rights in Nigeria. Herkströter replied, responding to specific points in the letter and inviting Pax Christi to engage in further discussions.

Pax Christi asked Amnesty International, with which it shared many concerns, to join it in this process. At that time, Amnesty International was probably the best-known human rights organization in the world, with more than a million members worldwide. Over the following three years, these two organizations engaged in an ongoing dialogue with Shell, involving an exchange of position papers, public forums, and face-to-face meetings.

In these discussions, Pax Christi and Amnesty International focused on several issues. They argued that it was imperative that the company incorporate explicit support for the Universal Declaration of Human Rights in its Statement of General Business Principles. The two human rights organizations urged Shell to appoint a director for human rights and to institute better training in human rights for its staff, particularly its security personnel. They recommended independent auditing of the company's human rights practices. Other portions of the discussion focused specifically on the situation in Nigeria and on Shell's role during the Saro-Wiwa trial and its relationship to the Nigerian military authorities.

In some cases, the company made specific changes in response to the NGOs' recommendations. For example, the NGOs raised questions about the adequacy of the guidance provided to police assigned to protect Shell's property and for failing to require accountability for possible police misconduct. In response, Shell reviewed its policies and made specific changes to bring them into compliance with United Nations standards. The company also updated the plastic wallet-sized cards distributed to police assigned to Shell facilities, summarizing the company's revised human rights policies. In other situations, by contrast, Shell declined the NGOs' recommendations. For example, the company declined to appoint a director of human rights, saying that its current corporate governance procedures were sufficient.

The Brent Spar Dialogue

After reversing its initial decision to seek deep-sea disposal of the Brent Spar, Shell initiated a two-year-long dialogue with its environmental critics, including Greenpeace. In October 1995, the company announced an international competition to solicit innovative solutions to the problem of what to do with the decommissioned rig. It also sponsored open meetings in the United Kingdom, Germany, Denmark, and the Netherlands to discuss various options. These gatherings were facilitated by an independent organization, the Environmental Council, which worked with groups to find common ground in environmental disputes. After winnowing the list of possible options, in 1997 Shell held yet another round of public meetings in all four countries, accompanied by a CD-ROM describing the short-listed options.

Finally, in January 1998 Shell announced its selection of a solution: to recycle the Brent Spar as a ferry quay near Stavanger, Norway. So-called Ro/Ro (roll-on, roll-off) ferries, which carried both cars and people, were widely used in Norway, with its mountainous terrain and miles of coastline. Under the plan, the Spar would be disassembled, and its flotation tanks and other parts reused to construct a Ro-Ro dock. The ferry quay solution appealed to environmentalists, who liked the idea of putting the old rig to good use. The British government quickly approved the plan, and construction began in late 1998.

Shell later commented that the Brent Spar experience "taught us the value of dialogue with our critics and other interested parties. . .. This unique consultation exercise has helped promote a different approach to decision making in the Group, and has shown new ways in which Shell companies can be more open and accountable." In a speech, a Shell executive later described this new approach as a switch from DAD—decide, announce, and defend, to DDD—dialogue, decide, and deliver.

In addition to its dialogues with human rights organizations and environmentalists, Shell also continued to meet with shareholder activists, religious leaders, and other stakeholders during this period.

Continuing Challenges of Corporate Responsibility

Over a four-year period, Shell had undergone a major transformation. It had undertaken a revision of its business principles, an internal structural reorganization, a survey of its global reputation, and externally audited reports on its social and environmental performance.

It had conducted hundreds of meetings with stakeholders, and changed its corporate policies in many areas.

What did the "new" Shell's proclaimed environmental and social commitments mean in practice? What changes did managers and employees on the ground in the Group's scores of operating companies do differently, if anything, as a result of the transformation of Shell? In its far-flung worldwide operations, the company continued to face daily challenges to act in a manner consistent with its support for human rights, sustainable development, and social responsibility. To some, the company was making marked progress toward meeting society's changing expectations. To others, it continued to fall short, focusing more on changing the public's perception than on changing its actual practice.

In an interview in July 1999, chairman Mark Moody-Stuart reflected on Shell's transformation process:

I think that the main goals [of the transformation] were to make sure that we were internally effective, that we made best use of our resources, our assets, our people. . . . But, also, that we had this connection to society and to the customers. . . . [It] is the society that commercial organizations have to serve, no matter what you do. Even if you are a baker making bread, you had better know what the trends are on bread in the society. If people are going to give up eating bread, you had better know about it. If they like chocolate bread, you had better know about that. . . . You can't divorce the two. People sometimes try to do that. They say, all this societal stuff is woolly, we should stick to commerce. The two are absolutely linked. . . . These soft issues are really business issues because we are part of society, and members of society are our customers. So, our impact on society really matters commercially.

Discussion Questions

1. In the late 1990s, Shell underwent a transformation. What were the key changes that Shell made in the areas of organizational structure and culture, relationships with stakeholders, reporting practices, and business principles? What additional changes, if any, do you believe Shell should have made?

2. In your opinion, what was the most important cause of Shell's transformation? Do you believe the company was motivated more by external pressures or by internal pressures? Why do you think so?

3. Some people believe that Shell was sincere in the changes it made, and others believe that the company's transformation was mainly an effort to manipulate public opinion. What is your opinion? How could you best determine the answer to this question?

Source: Anne T. Lawrence. Copyright © 2000 by the Council on Ethics in Economics. Slightly abridged and used by permission of the Council on Ethics in Economics. All rights reserved. In A. T. Lawrence, J. Weber, and J. E. Post, *Business and Society: Stakeholders, Ethics, Public Policy,* 11th ed., New York: McGraw-Hill, 2005, pp. 492–501.

discussion

ERIN BROCKOVICH AND PG&E

The story of Erin Brockovich, a legal assistant with the law firm of Masry & Vittitoe in Los Angeles, California, drew global attention with the launch of the Julia Roberts movie that bore her name in 2000. In the movie, Ms. Brockovich was portrayed as a heroic single mother fighting for the legal rights of the citizens of Hinkley, California, against the Pacific Gas & Electric Company (PG&E). The lawsuit accused PG&E of allowing a rust inhibitor referred to as Chromium-6 to leach into the water table, thus contaminating the groundwater for the residents of the Southern California desert town. It was alleged that this contamination over a 30-year period in the 1960s, 70s, and 80s caused illnesses including breast cancer, chronic nosebleeds, Hodgkin's disease (lymphoma), lung cancer, brain stem cancer, stress, chronic fatigue, miscarriages, chronic rashes, gastrointestinal cancer, Crohn's disease, spinal deterioration, kidney tumors, and many other medical maladies.

PG&E, a $28 billion corporation, eventually reached a $333 million settlement with 600 residents of Hinkley as compensation for their pain and suffering—the largest settlement ever paid in a direct-action lawsuit in U.S. history at the time. As the plaintiffs' attorneys, the law firm of Masry & Vittitoe received more than $133.6 million in fees (40 percent of the total) and Ms. Brockovich received a postsettlement bonus of $2 million.

The case won global attention for Masry & Vittitoe and Ms. Brockovich, and the firm went on to fight other large-profile cases (including additional lawsuits against PG&E) with the now-famous Erin Brockovich as their lead investigator. Universal Studios produced a blockbuster movie with *Erin Brockovich* and Julia Roberts took home an Oscar for her portrayal. Add all that to the large financial settlement granted to the residents of Hinkley, and the story appears to have a Hollywood happy ending.

However, shortly after the release of the movie, author and columnist Michael Fumento started to make accusations against some of the facts associated with the case:

- "Chromium-6, derived from ubiquitous chromite ore, is considered by the U.S. Environmental Protection Agency and other regulators as a human carcinogen within certain limits. Its connection is only to two types of cancer, that of the lungs and of the septum (the piece that separates your nostrils). Further, as one might guess from these two cancers, it's only a carcinogen when inhaled."

- Joe Schwarz, director of McGill University's Office for Chemistry and Society, explains why. The difference, he says, "is that ingested chromium-6 encounters hydrochloric acid in the stomach's gastric juices, and is converted to chromium-3 which is innocuous." Anyway, he points out, "No single toxin causes the wide array of conditions that afflict Hinkley residents."

- "Cancer aside, exhaustive, repeated studies of communities living adjacent to landfills with huge concentrations of chromium-6, including that detectable in residents' urine, have found no ill health effects. A report out of Glasgow, Scotland, in January [2000] indicated exposed residents showed 'no increased risk of congenital abnormalities (birth defects), lung cancer, or a range of other diseases.'"

- "Coincidentally, a study by [Dr. William J.] Blot [head of the International Epidemiology Institute] and others just published in *The Journal of Occupational and Environmental Medicine* evaluated almost 25,000 workers who worked at three PG&E plants over a quarter of a century. One was the Hinkley plant, and another is near Kettleman, California, where Miss Brockovich's firm is also rounding up plaintiffs. The researchers found that not only was there no excess of cancer when compared to the general California population, but the overall PG&E worker death rate was significantly much lower than those of other Californians."

- "Unfortunately, much of the medical evidence came in after PG&E settled. Further, Miss Brockovich's small firm had brought in an Iowa-class battleship in the form of Thomas V. Girardi, a specialist in toxic pollution suits, who makes everybody's short list of the most powerful attorneys in the United States."

Erin Brockovich was given the opportunity to respond to these accusations in a "Letter to the Editor" published in *The Wall Street Journal*. She cited PG&E's own documentation confirming that chromium-6 was toxic and dismissed the research of William Blot as a "paid expert for PG&E, who has earned as much as $400 an hour testifying on behalf of the utility." She also pointed out that Blot's study was funded by PG&E.

"There is no doubt that PG&E irresponsibly dumped chromium-6, and that the substance is a carcinogen." However, the behavior of many "interested parties" around this case has demonstrated questionable ethical judgment.

Discussion Questions

1. Have any ethical principles been violated in this situation?

2. Why do you think PG&E chose to settle with so much information available to refute the claims that Chromium-6 was responsible?

3. Do you think that Ms. Brockovich and the team at Masry & Vittitoe acted unethically in bringing this lawsuit against PG&E on behalf of the residents of Hinkley?

4. Do you think Michael Fumento acted unethically in his critical campaign against Erin Brockovich?

5. Do you think the residents of Hinkley were suitably compensated by the settlement (60 percent of the $333 million shared between 600 claimants according to the severity of their conditions).

6. Is it ethical for attorneys to take 40 percent (or more) of the settlements they win for their clients?

Source: Michael Fumento, "The Dark Side of Erin Brockovich," *The National Post*, March 29, 2000. Leon Jaroff, "Erin Brockovich's Junk Science," *Time*, July 11, 2003. Michael Fumento, Michael, "Erin Brockovich Exposed," *The Wall Street Journal*, editorial, March 28, 2000. Erin Brockovich, "Letters to the Editor," *The Wall Street Journal*, April 6, 2000.

discussion

MAZDA'S DILEMMA

Mark Fields, the dapper new president of Mazda Motors, is behind the wheel of a company with two noisy back-seat drivers: impatient shareholders and nervous unions. While investors in the company, which is one-third owned by Ford Motor Company, seek a turbocharged shortcut to higher profits by moving more production overseas, the car maker's Hiroshima-based rank and file want to ride the brakes and plod along the local scenic route, ensuring everyone comes along for the ride. "It's a real balancing act," says Fields, 39. "That's the toughest part of the job."

Mazda's dilemma is simple: More than 80 percent of the cars it sells are made in Japan and the strong yen is eroding the value of its profits in key overseas markets. But long-time company hands are resisting pressure to shift production away from domestic plants like the flagship Hiroshima factory, located next to Mazda headquarters.

It's easy to see why. A glance at a map of Hiroshima shows Mazda's overwhelming presence in the community. Stretching across seven kilometers of reclaimed land on the southern border of the city, Mazda's massive complex dominates the shoreline of the Inland Sea. The company employs about 24,000 people in the Hiroshima area and [it is estimated that another] 20,000 people are said to owe their jobs to Mazda indirectly. For years, the town prospered as a steady stream of shiny new Mazda models rolled off the production line and into showrooms worldwide.

At its peak in 1990, the Hiroshima plant produced 1.2 million vehicles a year. But over the past decade the plant's annual output has been more than halved to just 507,000 vehicles, and the founding family from Hiroshima has been replaced by controlling shareholder Ford. Next year, when rivals introduce a plethora of additions to their product lineups, Mazda won't debut a single model. Even more troubling, the company's promising earnings turnaround appears to have stalled.

That's bad news for Hiroshima, the economic anchor of southwestern Japan, nicknamed the country's "rust belt" because of the many factories there that operate below capacity. "When Mazda sneezes,

Hiroshima catches a cold," says Hiroshi Yamamoto, chief plant manager and a second-generation Mazda employee. Recently, the company has begun to show some flu-like symptoms.

Fields says the company will get a boost from a "new generation" of Mazda vehicles to be introduced in 2002 that will share "platforms"—chassis, engine and other major components—with cars produced by parent company Ford. The idea is to cut production costs through joint parts procurement and streamlined manufacturing. As benefits are realized from synergies with Ford and streamlining of distribution, says Fields, "you're going to see a lot of that fall to the bottom line."

But critics complain that Mazda hasn't done nearly enough to resolve its fundamental problem—it exports too many vehicles from its high-cost manufacturing bases in Japan. That's critical because the Japanese car market is stuck in neutral and unable to absorb Mazda's domestic production capacity. Fields responds by saying Mazda is considering moving manufacturing of some cars to Ford plants in Europe, most likely models with shared platforms such as the new version of its subcompact Demio. Japan's leading business newspaper reported earlier this year that Mazda may slash domestic output by 20 percent and cut 4,000 jobs at its Hiroshima plant. Fields insists a decision isn't due before year-end.

Analysts say the obvious answer is to move much more production offshore and increase procurement of imported parts. That would allow Mazda to rationalize manufacturing facilities in Japan, resulting in significant cost savings . . .Mazda has gingerly taken some steps in that direction, following in the footsteps of other major Japanese car makers that moved many facilities offshore in the 1980s. Imported parts now account for roughly 15 percent of components procured by Mazda, more than double the level a few years ago. The company also opened a pick-up truck production plant in Rayong, Thailand, two years ago and began making a four-door compact sedan there in January 2000. Export volumes at the Thai plant in the first half of 2000 rose 17 percent over the same period a year earlier to 20,530 trucks. All new Tribute sports utility vehicles built for sale outside Japan are being made at a Ford plant near Kansas City, Missouri.

But impatient analysts and investors wonder why, more than six months into the job, Fields says he still needs time before moving forward more aggressively. The reason for the procrastination has everything to do with building a consensus in Hiroshima, where Mazda's "social responsibility" looms large over the local community.

For Takeshi Morikawa, president of Mazda's chief labor union, that means stopping jobs being transferred overseas. "Of course we're against moving production abroad," says the gruff labor leader. "That would cause an unacceptable hollowing out of the manufacturing base in Hiroshima."

The union is unhappy with talk of boosting output outside Japan, especially at a time when Ford, which owns 33.3 percent of Mazda, has just won preferred bidding rights to buy South Korea's Daewoo Motors for $7 billion. "Why can't they invest a little bit of that money in Mazda?" Morikawa grumbles. Company executives seem keenly aware of the challenge they face in trying to placate both shareholders such as Ford and stakeholders like the unions and hometown loyalists in management.

Discussion Questions

1. What is Mazda's social responsibility to the Hiroshima region?

2. What evidence is there that they are acknowledging this responsibility?

3. Is there a mutually beneficial outcome for all the stakeholders in this situation? Explain your answer.

4. Which stakeholder will take priority here?

5. Do you think the outcome would be different if the founding family of Mazda still had an active interest in running the company? Explain why or why not.

6. How do you think this situation will be resolved?

Source: Chester Dawson, "Mazda's Dilemma," *Far Eastern Economic Review* 163, no. 30 (July 27, 2000), p. 42.

APPENDICES

1. Enron Code of Ethics

How to Use This Booklet

Enron has long had a set of written policies dealing with rules of conduct to be used in conducting the business affairs of Enron Corp., its subsidiaries, and its affiliated companies (collectively the "Company"). It is very important that you understand the scope of those policies and learn the details of every one that relates to your job.

In order to do this, please take the following steps:

1. Carefully read the summaries of each of the Enron policies in this booklet;

2. If you have a concern or question, talk it over with your supervisor, manager, or Enron legal counsel; and/or

3. Report your concerns or possible violations to the Enron Corp. Compliance Officer as described in the section on Responsibility for Reporting at page 60 of this booklet.

Enclosed with this booklet is a Certificate of Compliance to be signed by you as a statement of your personal agreement to comply with the policies stated herein during the term of your employment with the Company. Please carefully review this booklet, then sign and return the Certificate of Compliance to Elaine V. Overturf, Deputy Corporate Secretary and Director of Stockholder Relations, Enron Corp.

These policies are not an employment contract. The Company does not create any contractual rights by issuing these policies.

The Company reserves the right to amend, alter, and terminate policies at any time.

Principles of Human Rights

As a partner in the communities in which we operate, Enron believes it has a responsibility to conduct itself according to certain basic tenets of human behavior that transcend industries, cultures, economics, and local, regional and national boundaries.

And because we take this responsibility as an international employer and global corporate citizen seriously, we have developed the following principles on human rights.

Enron's Vision and Values are the platform upon which our human rights principles are built.

Vision

Enron's vision is to become the world's leading energy company—creating innovative and efficient energy solutions for growing economies and a better environment worldwide.

Values

Respect

We treat others as we would like to be treated ourselves. We do not tolerate abusive or disrespectful treatment. Ruthlessness, callousness and arrogance don't belong here.

Integrity We work with customers and prospects openly, honestly and sincerely. When we say we will do something, we will do it; when we say we cannot or will not do something, then we won't do it.

Communication We have an obligation to communicate. Here, we take the time to talk with one another . . . and to listen. We believe that information is meant to move and that information moves people.

Excellence We are satisfied with nothing less than the very best in everything we do. We will continue to raise the bar for everyone. The great fun here will be for all of us to discover just how good we can really be.

Principles of Human Rights

- Enron stands on the foundation of its Vision and Values. Every employee is educated about the Company's Vision and Values and is expected to conduct business with other employees, partners, contractors, suppliers, vendors and customers keeping in mind respect, integrity, communication and excellence. Everything we do evolves from Enron's Vision and Values statements.

- At Enron, we treat others as we expect to be treated ourselves. We believe in respect for the rights of all individuals and are committed to promoting an environment characterized by dignity and mutual respect for employees, customers, contractors, suppliers, partners, community members and representatives of all levels of Government.

- We do not and will not tolerate human rights abuses of any kind by our employees or contractors.

- We believe in treating all employees fairly, regardless of gender, race, color, language, religion, age, ethnic background, political or other opinion, national origin, or physical limitation.

- We are dedicated to conducting business according to all applicable local and international laws and regulations, including, but not limited to, the U.S. Foreign Corrupt Practices Act, and with the highest professional and ethical standards.

- We are committed to operating safely and conducting business worldwide in compliance with all applicable environmental, health, and safety laws and regulations and strive to improve the lives of the people in the regions in which we operate. These laws, regulations, and standards are designed to safeguard the environment, human health, wildlife, and natural resources. Our commitment to observe them faithfully is an integral part of our business and of our values.

- We believe that playing an active role in every community in which we operate fosters a long-term partnership with the people with whom we come into daily contact. Strengthening the communities where our employees live and work is a priority. We focus community relations activities on several areas, with particular emphasis on education, the environment, and promoting healthy families.

- We believe in offering our employees fair compensation through wages and other benefits.
- We believe that our employees and the employees of our contractors working in our facilities should have safe and healthy working conditions.

Education/Communication

Because we take these principles seriously, we should act decisively to ensure that all those with whom we do business understand our policies and standards.

Providing clearly written guidelines reinforces our principles and business ethics. Enron employees at all levels are expected to be active proponents of our principles and to report without retribution anything they observe or discover that indicates our standards are not being met.

Compliance with the law and ethical standards are conditions of employment, and violations will result in disciplinary action, which may include termination. New employees are asked to sign a statement, and employees are periodically asked to reaffirm their commitment to these principles.

Furthermore, Enron's contractors, suppliers and vendors should be expected to uphold the same respect for human rights that we require of ourselves, and we should seek to include appropriate provisions in every new contract entered with these parties. When we are joint venture partners with other companies, we will work to gain board approval for similar measures in joint venture contracts with contractors, suppliers and vendors.

Securities Trades by Company Personnel

No director, officer, or employee of Enron Corp. or its subsidiaries or its affiliated companies (collectively referred to herein as "Company") shall, directly or indirectly, trade in the securities of Enron Corp., Northern Border Partners, L.P., EOTT Energy Partners, L.P., or any other Enron Corp. subsidiary or affiliated company with publicly-traded securities, or any other publicly-held company while in the possession of material non-public information relating to or affecting any such company, disclose such information to others who may trade, or recommend the purchase or sale of securities of a company to which such information relates. Advice should be sought in respect of equivalent requirements under other applicable jurisdictions.

The Need for a Policy Statement

The Securities and Exchange Commission ("SEC") and the Justice Department actively pursue violations of insider trading laws. Historically, their efforts were concentrated on individuals directly involved in trading abuses. In 1988, to further deter insider trading violations, Congress expanded the authority of the SEC and the Justice Department, adopting the Insider Trading and Securities Fraud Enforcement Act (the "Act"). In addition to increasing the penalties for insider trading, the Act puts the onus on companies and possibly other "controlling persons" for violations by company personnel.

Although the Act is aimed primarily at the securities industry, application of the laws may be made to companies in other industries. Many experts have concluded that if companies like Enron Corp. do not take active steps to adopt preventive policies and procedures covering securities trades by Company personnel, the consequences could be severe.

In addition to responding to the Act, we are adopting this Policy Statement to avoid even the appearance of improper conduct on the part of anyone employed by or associated with the Company (not just so-called insiders). We have all worked hard over the years to establish our reputation for integrity and ethical conduct. We cannot afford to have it damaged.

The Consequences

This policy applies to all employees of the Company. It is intended to provide guidance to employees with respect to existing legal restrictions. It is not intended to result in the imposition of liability on employees that would not exist in the absence of such policy. Any breach of this policy, however, may subject employees to criminal penalties.

The consequences of insider trading violations can be staggering:
For individuals who trade on inside information (or tip information to others):

- A civil penalty of up to three times the profit gained or loss avoided;
- A criminal fine (no matter how small the profit) of up to $1 million; and
- A jail term of up to ten years.

For a company (as well as possibly any supervisory person) that fails to take appropriate steps to prevent illegal trading:

- A civil penalty of the greater of $1 million or three times the profit gained or loss avoided as a result of the employee's violation; and
- A criminal penalty of up to $2.5 million.

Moreover, if an employee violates the Company's insider trading policy, the Company may impose sanctions against such individual, including dismissing him or her for cause.

Our Policy

If a director, officer, or any employee of the Company (as defined herein) has material non-public information relating to Enron Corp., Northern Border Partners, L.P., EOTT Energy Partners, L.P., or any other Enron Corp. subsidiary or affiliated company with publicly-traded securities, it is the Company's policy that neither that person nor any related person may buy or sell securities of Enron Corp., Northern Border Partners, L.P., EOTT Energy Partners, L.P., or other Enron Corp. subsidiary or affiliated company with publicly traded securities, or engage in any other action to take advantage of, or pass on to others, that information. This policy also applies to material non-public information relating to any other company, including our customers or suppliers, obtained in the course of employment.

A transaction that may be necessary or justifiable for independent reasons (such as the need to raise money for an emergency expenditure) does not constitute an exception. Even the appearance of an improper transaction must be avoided to preserve the Company's reputation for adhering to the highest standards of conduct.

> *Material Information.* Material information is any information that a reasonable investor would consider important in a decision to buy, hold, or sell stock: in short, *any information which could reasonably be expected to affect the price of the stock.* If you are considering buying or selling a security

because of information you possess, you should assume such information is material.

Examples. Common examples of information that will frequently be regarded as material are: projections of future earnings or losses; news of a pending or proposed merger, acquisition, or tender offer; news of a significant sale of assets or the disposition of a subsidiary; changes in dividend policies or the declaration of a stock split or the offering of additional securities; changes in management; significant new products or discoveries; impending bankruptcy or financial liquidity problems; and the gain or loss of a substantial customer or supplier. Either positive or negative information may be material. The foregoing list is by no means exclusive.

Twenty-Twenty Hindsight. If your securities transactions become the subject of scrutiny, they will be viewed after-the-fact with the benefit of hindsight. As a result, before engaging in any transaction you should carefully consider how regulators and others might view your transaction in hindsight.

Transactions by Family Members. The very same restrictions apply to your family members and others living in your household. Employees are expected to be responsible for the compliance of their immediate family and personal household.

Tipping Information to Others. Whether the information is proprietary information about the Company or information that could have an impact on our stock prices, employees must not pass material nonpublic information on to others; this is called tipping. The above penalties may apply, whether or not you derive any direct benefit from another's actions.

When Information Is Public. Information is "non-public" until it has been disseminated in a manner making it available to investors generally. This is typically satisfied by distribution of such information by means of a press release. However, even after such information is released to the press, you should wait a period of time (at least one business day and often two or three business days) before trading or disclosing such information to others. Again, it is a good idea to exercise caution and wait a longer period of time following the release of material information than you might first consider warranted.

Company Assistance

No set of specific rules will be adequate in every circumstance. Any person who has any questions about specific transactions may obtain additional guidance from Elaine Overturf, Deputy Corporate Secretary and Director of Stockholder Relations, at (713) 853-6062, who will consult with Company counsel as appropriate. Remember, however, that the ultimate responsibility for adhering to the Policy Statement and avoiding improper transactions rests with you. In this regard, it is imperative that you act in good faith and use your best judgment.

Business Ethics

Employees of Enron Corp., its subsidiaries, and its affiliated companies (collectively the "Company") are charged with conducting their business affairs in accordance with the highest ethical standards. An employee shall not conduct himself or herself in a manner which directly or indirectly would be detrimental to the best interests of the Company or in a manner which would bring to the employee financial gain separately derived as a direct consequence of his or her employment with the Company. Moral as well as legal obligations will be fulfilled openly, promptly, and in a manner which will reflect pride on the Company's name.

Products and services of the Company will be of the highest quality and as represented. Advertising and promotion will be truthful, not exaggerated or misleading.

Agreements, whether contractual or verbal, will be honored. No bribes, bonuses, kickbacks, lavish entertainment, or gifts will be given or received in exchange for special position, price, or privilege.

Employees will maintain the confidentiality of the Company's sensitive or proprietary information and will not use such information for their personal benefit.

Employees shall refrain, both during and after their employment, from publishing any oral or written statements about the Company or any of its officers, employees, agents, or representatives that are slanderous, libelous, or defamatory; or that disclose private or confidential information about their business affairs; or that constitute an intrusion into their seclusion or private lives; or that give rise to unreasonable publicity about their private lives; or that place them in a false light before the public; or that constitute a misappropriation of their name or likeness.

Relations with the Company's many publics—customers, stockholders, governments, employees, suppliers, press, and bankers—will be conducted in honesty, candor, and fairness.

It is Enron's policy that each "contract" must be reviewed by one of our attorneys prior to its being submitted to the other parties to such "contract" and that it must be initialed by one of our attorneys prior to being signed. By "contract" we mean each contract, agreement, bid, term sheet, letter of intent, memorandum of understanding, amendment, modification, supplement, fax, telex, and other document or arrangement that could reasonably be expected to impose an obligation on any Enron entity. (Certain Enron entities utilize standard forms that have been preapproved by the legal department to conduct routine activities; so long as no material changes are made to these preapproved forms, it is not necessary to seek legal review or initialing prior to their being signed.) Please bear in mind that your conduct and/or your conversations may have, under certain circumstances, the unintended effect of creating an enforceable obligation; consult with the legal department with respect to any questions you may have in this regard.

Additionally, it is Enron's policy that the selection and retention of outside legal counsel be conducted exclusively by the legal department. (Within the legal department, the selection and retention of counsel is coordinated and approved by James V. Derrick Jr., Enron's Executive Vice President and General Counsel.) In the absence of this policy, it would not be possible for our legal department to discharge its obligation to manage properly our relationships with outside counsel.

Employees will comply with the executive stock ownership requirements set forth by the Board of Directors of Enron Corp., if applicable.

Laws and regulations affecting the Company will be obeyed. Even though the laws and business practices of foreign nations may differ from those in effect in the United States, the applicability of both foreign and U.S. laws to the Company's operations will be strictly observed. Illegal behavior on the part of any employee in the performance of Company duties will neither be condoned nor tolerated.

Ownership of Information

All information, ideas, concepts, improvements, discoveries, and employee inventions, whether patentable or not, which are conceived, made, developed, or acquired by an employee, individually or in conjunction with others, during the employee's employment by Enron Corp., its subsidiaries, and its affiliated companies (collectively the "Company") (whether during business hours or otherwise and whether on the Company's premises or otherwise) which relate to the Company's business, products, or services shall be disclosed to the Company and are and shall be the sole and exclusive property of the Company.

For this purpose, the Company's business, products, or services, include, without limitation, all such information relating to corporate opportunities, research, financial and sales data, pricing and trading terms, evaluations, opinions, interpretations, acquisition prospects, the identity of customers or their requirements, the identity of key contacts within the customer's organization (or within the organization of acquisition prospects), marketing and merchandising techniques, and prospective names and marks.

Moreover, all documents, drawings, memoranda, notes, records, files, correspondence, manuals, models, specifications, computer programs, e-mail, voice mail, electronic databases, maps, and all other writings or materials of any type embodying any of such information, ideas, concepts, improvements, discoveries, and inventions are and shall be the sole and exclusive property of the Company.

If, during an employee's employment by the Company, the employee creates any original work of authorship fixed in any tangible medium of expression which is the subject matter of copyright (such as videotapes, written presentations on acquisitions, computer programs, e-mail, voice mail, electronic databases, drawings, maps, architectural renditions, models, manuals, brochures, or the like) relating to the Company's business, products, or services, whether such work is created solely by the employee or jointly with others (whether during business hours or otherwise and whether on Company's premises or otherwise), the employee shall disclose such work to the Company.

The Company shall be deemed to be the author of such work if the work is prepared by the employee in the scope of his or her employment; or, if the work is not prepared by the employee within the scope of his or her employment but is specially ordered by the Company as a contribution to a collective work, as a part of a motion picture or other audiovisual work, as a translation, as a supplementary work, as a compilation, or as an instructional text, then the work shall be considered to be work made for hire and the Company shall be deemed to be the author of the work. If such work is neither prepared by the employee within the scope of his or her employment nor a work specially ordered and is deemed to be a work made for hire, then the employee hereby agrees to assign, and by these presents does assign, to the Company all of the employee's worldwide right, title and interest in and to such work and all rights of copyright therein.

Confidential Information and Trade Secrets

You may have access to or become aware of confidential and/or proprietary information of the Company—that is, information relating to the Company's business which is not generally or publicly known. This information includes but is not limited to:

Internal telephone lists and directories; bid, trading, and financial data; planned new projects and ventures; advertising and marketing programs; lists of potential or actual customers and suppliers; wage and salary or other personnel data; capital investment plans; changes in management or policies of the Company; suppliers' prices; and other trade secrets.

The Company's confidential or proprietary information could be very helpful to suppliers and the Company's competitors, to the detriment of the Company. To help protect the Company's interests, business units have established and implemented computer and electronic security measures to ensure that employees have the means to communicate domestically and internationally in a secure fashion. Employees should use these means and, in disclosing or using Company confidential or proprietary information, should follow these guidelines.

- Do not use, either for your own personal benefit or for the benefit of others, Company information that is not publicly known;
- Do not disclose Company proprietary or confidential information to other employees or outsiders, except as required in the conduct of the Company's business;
- Dispose of documents containing the Company's confidential or proprietary information with care so as to avoid inadvertent disclosure; and
- Guard against inadvertently disclosing such information in public discussions where you may be overheard and in discussions with family members.

As a result of the employee's employment by the Company, the employee may also from time to time have access to, or knowledge of, confidential business information or trade secrets of third parties, such as customers, suppliers, partners, joint venturers, and the like, of the Company. Each employee agrees to preserve and protect the confidentiality of such third party confidential information and trade secrets to the same extent, and on the same basis, as the Company's confidential business information and trade secrets.

These obligations of confidence apply even if the information has not been reduced to a tangible medium of expression (e.g., is only maintained in the minds of the Company's employees) and, if it has been reduced to a tangible medium, irrespective of the form or medium in which the information is embodied (e.g., documents, drawings, memoranda, notes, records, files, correspondence, manuals, models, specifications, computer programs, e-mail, voice mail, electronic databases, maps, and all other writings or materials of any type.)

Information Acquisition

Acquiring and having access to accurate and current market information is of significant interest to the Company. The Company therefore encourages employees to share within the Company potentially useful information they receive. This includes information properly obtained from outside sources. On the other hand, using improper means to obtain trade secret information of others, or using such trade secret information, could expose the Company, or individual employees, to potentially significant civil fines or liabilities, or even criminal penalties. The use of improper means to obtain trade secret information and the use of others' trade secrets is therefore prohibited. This policy explains the types of information that employees are encouraged to obtain and the types of activities they can pursue in obtaining information, as well as the types of improper activities to obtain trade secret information that they are prohibited from engaging in.

Publicly Available Information A vast amount of information is freely available to the public and the acquisition and use of this type of information is encouraged. Publicly available information includes information:

- found in books and magazines;
- available on the Internet;
- made public by federal, state, or local government agencies;
- revealed in legal filings and pleadings;
- disclosed or discussed in public places, at conferences or trade shows, or in specialized trade or technical publications;
- contained in patent applications or issued patents; and
- obtainable from simple observation from the street or another legally permissible location.

While all of this information is publicly available, it is not necessarily widely known. To the degree that this information could have particular relevance to the Company, employees are encouraged to find this information and share it within the Company.

"Trade Secret" Information Generally, information is considered a "trade secret" only if:

- the information is in fact secret, i.e., not generally known to and not readily ascertainable by the public;
- the owner has taken reasonable measures to keep the information secret; and
- the information has independent economic value because it is not widely known.

In 1996, the U.S. Congress passed the Economic Espionage Act which makes it a crime to steal trade secrets. More specifically, the Economic Espionage Act prohibits you from acquiring trade secrets of others through improper means, such as deceit or misrepresentation, and prohibits the receipt or use of information illegally acquired by a third party, or from present or former employees who are not authorized to disclose it. The Economic Espionage Act provides for criminal fines for the Company of up to $10 million and criminal fines for an employee of up to $500,000 and up to 15 years imprisonment. Accordingly, an employee should not knowingly:

1. take, carry away, or obtain a third party trade secret without authorization or obtain a third party trade secret by fraud or deception;
2. copy, download, mail, deliver, send, transmit, or communicate a third party trade secret without authorization; or
3. receive, buy, or possess a third party trade secret knowing it has been stolen or obtained without authorization.

Non-Public, Non-"Trade Secret" Information Certain information is not "public" in the sense that it is not published or widely available to the public, but neither is it a "trade secret." This would include, for example, information about a company that the Company itself made no effort to keep secret. Nothing would bar an employee from obtaining such information in a casual conversation and subsequently reporting or using that information. Accordingly, Company employees are encouraged to obtain, share, and use such non-public, non-trade secret information, *provided* that no improper means are used. If improper means are necessary to obtain information, a good chance exists that the party who would divulge the information knows that he or she should keep the information secret, thus raising the likelihood that the information could be considered a trade secret. "Improper Means" would include:

- lying, engaging in deception, or creating a false impression in order to induce the disclosure of trade secrets;
- paying someone to reveal trade secrets;
- blackmailing or threatening someone to reveal trade secrets;
- paying someone who had already improperly obtained trade secrets to reveal those secrets to you; and
- engaging in any activity that is itself illegal (such as theft or computer "hacking") in order to obtain secrets.

The preceding list is not exhaustive. Other types of activity engaged in to obtain trade secrets could be considered "improper." Therefore, if you have any doubts about activities you are thinking of pursuing to obtain information, *do not engage in those activities* until you have first discussed them with the Company's General Counsel. Only if you have first obtained the advice and clearance of the Company's General Counsel may you engage in any activity of a questionable nature to obtain information from others.

Copyright and Trademark

The federal Copyright Act provides for criminal fines for an employee of up to $250,000 and up to 5 years imprisonment for the first offense. The federal Trademark Counterfeiting Act provides for criminal fines for the Company of up to $1 million and criminal fines for an employee of up to $250,000 and up to 5 years imprisonment for the first offense.

An employee will not willfully infringe for purposes of commercial advantage or private financial gain a third party's copyright in a work by copying the work, distributing copies of the work, using the work to prepare derivative works, or in the case of some works, by publicly displaying or performing the work. Similarly, an employee will not intentionally traffic in goods or services using a counterfeit or spurious trademark.

Conclusion and Summary

Each employee agrees to act with honesty, candor, and fairness with respect to competitors and third parties and to comply in all respects with applicable laws prohibiting the misappropriation of trade secrets, copyright infringement, or use of counterfeit or spurious trademarks. Under no circumstances will any activity be authorized or undertaken by an employee which violates the federal Economic Espionage Act, the federal Copyright Act, the federal Trademark Counterfeiting Act, or any other applicable domestic or foreign laws.

If an employee has any questions concerning the meaning of the laws summarized in this Policy, the employee should contact the Company's General Counsel.

Upon signing the Certificate of Compliance, an employee acknowledges and agrees that:

1. the business of the Company is highly competitive, and its strategies, methods, books, records, and documents, its technical information

concerning its products, equipment, services, and processes, procurement procedures and pricing techniques, and the names of and other information (such as credit and financial data) concerning its customers and its business affiliates all comprise confidential business information and trade secrets which are valuable, special, and unique assets which the Company uses in its business to obtain a competitive advantage over its competitors;

2. the protection of such confidential business information and trade secrets against unauthorized disclosure and use is of critical importance to the Company in maintaining its competitive position;

3. he or she will not, at any time during or after his or her employment by the Company, make any unauthorized disclosure of any confidential business information or trade secrets of the Company, or make any use thereof, except in the carrying out of his or her employment responsibilities hereunder;

4. the Company shall be a third party beneficiary of the employee's obligations under this policy; and

5. he or she agrees to act with honesty, candor, and fairness with respect to competitors and third parties and to comply in all respects with applicable laws prohibiting the misappropriation of trade secrets, copyright infringement, or the use of counterfeit or spurious trademarks.

All documents, drawings, memoranda, notes, records, files, correspondence, manuals, models, specifications, computer programs, e-mail, voice mail, electronic databases, maps, and all other writings or materials of any type made by, or coming into possession of, employee during the period of employee's employment by the Company which contain or disclose confidential business information or trade secrets of the Company shall be and remain the property of the Company. Upon termination of employee's employment by the Company, for any reason, employee promptly shall deliver the same, and all copies thereof, to the Company.

Safety

Employees of the Company have a responsibility to comply with all applicable laws and regulations regarding the safe design, construction, maintenance, and operation of Company facilities. It is the responsibility of every employee to perform his or her work and to conduct the Company's operations in a safe manner. Employees should be aware that health and safety laws may provide for significant civil and criminal penalties against individuals and/or the Company for failure to comply with applicable requirements. Accordingly, each employee must comply with all applicable safety and health laws, rules, and regulations, including occupational safety and health standards.

Policy on Use of Communication Services and Equipment

The term "Communication Services and Equipment" as used in this Policy and the accompanying Procedures shall mean any and all communications systems or equipment owned or possessed by Enron Corp., its divisions, its subsidiaries, and its affiliated and related companies (the "Company"), or used in connection with the Company's business, including but not limited to, telephones, facsimile machines, computers, computer modems, special long-distance services, cellular phones, voice mail, pagers, electronic mail, mail and delivery services, storage means of all types for the physical or electronic storage of the

Company's information or data, transaction services, or any other services of any nature whatsoever in connection with any communication systems necessary or desirable to promote the conduct of the Company's business.

General Application of This Policy and the Accompanying Procedures

This Policy and the accompanying Procedures apply to all employees, third party contractors, guests, licensees, or invitees of the Company who utilize, possess, or have access to the Company's Communication Services and Equipment (cumulatively referred to herein as the "Users" of the Company's Communication Services and Equipment).

General Policy of the Company with Respect to Its Communication Services and Equipment

It is the general policy of Company:

- To provide or contract for effective Communication Services and Equipment for use by the Company in connection with its business;
- To preserve and protect the confidentiality of the information and data of the Company and its customers and contractors;
- To preserve and protect the legal privileges provided by the law with respect to attorney/client communications, work product, and investigations of the Company and its customers and contractors; and
- To operate and maintain the Company's Communication Services and Equipment in a manner that is in full compliance with the law.

Limits on Expectations of Privacy

All Users of the Company's Communication Services and Equipment are advised and placed on notice that:

1. The United States government, and the various state and local governments, may monitor contemporaneous communications of all types (including communication by telephone, facsimile machine, computer modems, special long-distance services, cellular phones, voice mail, pagers, electronic mail, mail, and other delivery services) or access stored communications, data, or information of all types, subject to the protections of the Fourth Amendment of the United States Constitution, which generally requires the issuance of a court order or warrant. Moreover, the United States government, and the various state and local governments, may monitor contemporaneous oral, wire, or electronic communications of all types subject to federal statutes such as the First Amendment Privacy Protection Act and the Omnibus Crime Control and Safe Streets Act, as amended by the Electronic Communications Privacy Act of 1986.

2. The Federal Rules of Civil Procedure and the rules of civil procedure for almost all states permit requests for production of documents that are likely to lead to the discovery of relevant evidence. Both the Federal Rules of Civil Procedure and the Texas Rules of Civil Procedure specifically allow the discovery of electronically maintained data. For example, Rule 34 of the Federal Rules of Civil Procedure and Rule 166b(2)(b) of the Texas Rules of Civil Procedure permit the discovery of data compilations from which information can be obtained and, if necessary,

translated by the respondent through detective devices into reasonably readable form.

3. There should be no expectations of privacy with respect to communications sent to or received from public electronic bulletin boards or public electronic communications systems such as the Internet.

4. Under the regulations of the United States Postal Service, any mail addressed to a non-governmental organization, including but not limited to corporations, firms, sole proprietorships, partnerships, joint ventures, and associations, or to an individual, such as an official, employee, contractor, client, agent, etc. by name or title at the address of the organization, shall be delivered to the organization. This is also true with respect to mail addressed in this manner to former officials, employees, contractors, agents, clients, etc. Moreover, mail addressed in this manner but bearing the term "personal" is no different from other mail and will be delivered by the United States Postal Service to the Company. For example, the United States Postal Service will deliver each of the following to the offices of the Company:

Sam Smith	Sam Smith	Sam Smith
Enron Corp.	1400 Smith	Personal and Confidential
1400 Smith Street	Houston,	P.O. Box 1188
P.O. Box 1188	Texas 77251	Houston, Texas 77251
Houston, Texas 77251		

All such mail belongs to the Company until such time as the Company determines that the information contained in the mail does not pertain to the business of the Company. The Company has the right to open the mail if there is some question as to its deliverability and/or to forward the mail to a superior or Company-designated recipient if the person to whom the mail is addressed is no longer with the Company or is ill or on extended leave. Moreover, all incoming or outgoing mail containing information owned by the Company is the property of the Company, and the Company has the right to open any Company mail to protect its business interests or to prevent illegal conduct.

5. The Company reserves the right to monitor on a continuous basis the contemporaneous communications of certain of its functions, such as communications conducted on the telephones used in connection with certain training functions and communications conducted on the telephones on the floors in which certain of its traders operate. There should be no expectation of privacy by anyone with respect to communications conducted on those telephones.

6. The Company reserves the right to monitor on a contemporaneous basis communications transmitted by or stored within its Communication Services and Equipment in the ordinary course of the Company's business to ensure that no improper, illegal, or criminal activities are being conducted. Such monitoring shall be effected in accordance with the provisions of the Omnibus Crime Control and Safe Streets Act, as amended by the Electronic Communications Privacy Act of 1986 and shall be effected only if authorized by an officer of the Company.

7. The Company reserves the right to delete or destroy any and all communications, including e-mail and voice mail messages, stored in the Company's Communication Services and Equipment. As a general rule,

the Company's Communication Services and Equipment is not backed-up and should, therefore, be thought of as a very temporary storage media. If a machine failure in the Company's Communication Services and Equipment occurs, all messages and data could be lost. Therefore, Users must not consider e-mail and voice mail messages to be permanently stored by the Company. On the other hand, the Company also reserves the right in its discretion to maintain any and all communications, including e-mail and voice mail messages, transmitted by or stored within the Company's Communication Services and Equipment. Users therefore also should take care that the messages they transmit or store comply with all of the Company's policies and with the law.

8. The Company reserves the right to access e-mail messages, voice mail messages, data, or information stored on the Company's computers or other electronic devices or media owned or controlled by the Company or comprising the Company's Communication Services and Equipment. Therefore, there should be no expectation of privacy with respect to such stored e-mail messages, voice mail messages, data, or information.

9. Because all of the Company's Communication Services and Equipment are the property of the Company, the Company reserves the right to monitor its Communication Services and Equipment to ensure that its property is being properly and legally used.

10. Users do not have a personal privacy right in any data or information created, received, or sent on the Company's Communication Services and Equipment. Any data or information transmitted or stored on the Company's Communication Services and Equipment, whether or not they relate or pertain to the Company's business, goods, or services, may be accessed by the Company. Any employee or contractor who elects to utilize the Company's Communication Services and Equipment to transmit or store data or information recognizes that the Company may access and monitor such data or information and has no obligation to continue to store such data and information.

Ownership and Confidentiality of Information

1. All of the Company's Communication Services and Equipment are the property of the Company. Any and all communication, data, or information created, received, or sent on the Company's Communication Services and Equipment are the property of the Company. Users have no right, title, or interest in such Communication Services and Equipment or in any communications, data, or information created, received, or sent on the Company's Communication Services and Equipment. All means of identifying communications, such as the use of domain names on the Internet or other networks or systems, that embody or use the Company's image, names, or marks (such as an Internet domain name incorporating Enron.Com) shall belong to the Company.

2. This Policy and the accompanying Procedures do not modify in any way the Company's policy that the Company is and remains the owner of all information created by the Company's employees during their employment by the Company that relates to the business, goods, or services of the Company, irrespective of where such information is stored or maintained, e.g., in electronic form on the hard drives of the Company's computers, in electronic form in servers maintained by the Company as part

of its network, or in diskettes or computers purchased by the Company that are possessed by the employees.

3. This Policy and the accompanying Procedures do not modify in any way the Company's policy that users remain obligated to protect the confidentiality of the Company's information irrespective of where such information is stored or maintained, e.g., in electronic form on the hard drives of the Company's computers, in electronic form in servers maintained by the Company as part of its network, or in diskettes or computers purchased by the Company that are possessed by the employees.

The right to use the Company's Communication Services and Equipment is at the will of the Company and is conditioned on continued compliance with the Company's rules and policies.

1. Users are allowed to utilize the Company's Communication Services and Equipment only at the will and discretion of the Company. The Company has the right to prohibit users from utilizing the Company's Communication Services and Equipment at any time for any reason.

2. Moreover, the users' right to use the Company's Communication Services and Equipment is conditioned on acceptance of the terms of this *Policy* and the accompanying *Procedures* as well as continued compliance with this and all of the Company's other rules and policies.

Acceptance, Disciplinary Action, Interpretation, and Modification

Employment by the Company, agreement by a contractor to do business with the Company, or use of the Company's Communication Services and Equipment by a user each constitutes acceptance of and consent to the terms of this *Policy* and the accompanying *Procedures*.

Improper use of the Company's Communication Services and Equipment may result in discipline, up to and including termination.

Questions about interpretation of this *Policy* and the accompanying *Procedures* should be referred to the Company's Legal Department.

Purpose

To set forth the procedures for the use of the Company's Communication Services and Equipment in accordance with the Policy.

General Application of the Policy and These Procedures

The *Policy* and these *Procedures* apply to all Users of the Company's Communication Services and Equipment.

Requirements for the Use of the Company's Communication Services and Equipment

1. The Company's Communication Services and Equipment should be used for Company purposes only. Employees should limit use of the Company's Communication Services and Equipment for personal purposes to those circumstances where such personal use enhances such employee's efficiency during office hours or otherwise does not detract from such employee's activities on behalf of the Company. When personal usage is unavoidable, employees must properly log any user charges and reimburse the Company for them. However, whenever possible, personal

communications that incur user charges should be placed on a collect basis or charged directly to the employee's personal credit card or account. Users may not use the Company's Communication Services and Equipment for non-Company businesses, such as "moonlighting" jobs.

2. Users should not utilize the Company's Communication Services and Equipment to send or receive private, personal messages they do not wish monitored or accessed by the government, third parties, or the Company.

3. Users shall refrain absolutely from any activity that may cause harm or damage to the Company's Communication Services and Equipment or any communications, data, or information transmitted by or stored within such Communication Services and Equipment.

4. Users may not use the Company's Communication Services and Equipment for or in connection with any illegal or criminal activity. Users may not use the Company's Communication Services and Equipment for any activity which violates any Company policy. For example, Users may not use the Company's Communication Services and Equipment to copy, duplicate, or use software that is not properly licensed or the use of which infringes the copyright of a third party. Users may not use the Company's Communication Services and Equipment to infringe third party intellectual property rights. Accordingly, users should download information and software from the Internet and other public or third party systems into communications systems and equipment only when such downloads do not infringe on third party copyrights or intellectual property rights.

5. No confidential or proprietary information of the Company and no privileged communications (e.g., attorney/client communications) may be transmitted via public electronic communication systems unless the transmissions are properly encrypted and no third party copyright or intellectual property rights are violated.

6. Users may not use the Company's Communication Services and Equipment to forward messages without a legitimate business purpose under circumstances likely to lead to embarrassment of the sender or to violate a clearly expressed desire of the sender to restrict additional dissemination.

7. Users may not connect incompatible equipment to the Company's Communication Services and Equipment. Users may not use in the Company's Communication Services and Equipment any software that is infected with a virus. If any such software is found to be infected with a virus, users will immediately alert those who have received a copy and will work with their systems management to remove the virus.

8. Employees and contractors must understand that whatever they reduce to a tangible form and maintain in their physical or electronic files may possibly, under the appropriate circumstances, be discovered by third parties in litigation. Employees and contractors are cautioned that all such documents must comply with the Company's policies with respect to the protection of confidential information, the Company's policies with respect to the protection of privileged communications, and the Company's document retention policies.

9. Users may not use the Company's Communication Services and Equipment to transmit "chain" letters.

10. Users should keep the number of messages and data stored in the Company's Communication Services and Equipment under control and should purge old Communication Services and Equipment messages and data regularly.

11. Employees should exercise care so that no personal correspondence appears to be an official communication of the Company. Personalized Company stationery and business cards may only be issued by the Company and may only be used in connection with Company business. Employees may not use the Company's address for receiving personal mail or use Company stationery or postage for personal matters.

Passwords

Users must change their passwords every 60 days. Passwords must be no shorter than six characters and must be a mixture of alpha, special, and numeric symbols so that the password code is difficult for others to determine using "password cracking" software.

Passwords should not contain any codes, names, words, or phrases that someone familiar with the owner might associate with that person and thereby have an advantage in cracking the code and using it illegally.

Passwords are not to be shared by two or more people. Each user should have a unique code that only he or she knows.

Files containing user account names, log-on codes, and passwords (i.e., security files) in Company Communication Services and Equipment should be examined at least weekly for persons who no longer work for the Company, and their access authority should be removed immediately.

Users who have not used their access identification code and password for longer than 90 consecutive calendar days should have their need for continued access reviewed at least monthly.

All Company Communication Services and Equipment that allow persons to connect to the service or equipment from a remote location (dial-up access) should require all users to authenticate themselves through the use of passwords or other types of technology, such as voice recognition systems, that ensure the person is who he or she claims to be.

Whenever possible, all remote access Company Communication Services and Equipment should have a preset maximum number of attempts to authenticate the remote user, e.g., 3 attempts. Failure to successfully remotely authenticate within the preset maximum number of attempts should result in that access session being terminated or forwarded to a Company security officer for verification of the requesting party.

Monitoring Communication Services and Equipment Access

All Company Communication Services and Equipment should be designed/equipped to accurately and quickly determine and log all attempted or successful intrusions of the system or network by someone not authorized to use that system or network. Any such "hacker" attempts should be immediately investigated and measures should be taken quickly to prevent that type of unauthorized access in the future.

Internet Security Policy: Scope of Use of Electronic Media and Services

Introduction—General Application of This Policy This Internet Security Policy defines roles, responsibilities, and policies for the Company's employees, agents, and contractors using the Company's communications facilities to access third party electronic media and services such as the Internet.

As an advanced technology company, we increasingly use and exploit electronic forms of communication and information exchange. Company employees, agents, and contractors may have access to one or more forms of electronic media and services, computers, e-mail, telephones, voicemail, fax machines, external electronic bulletin boards, wire services, on-line services, and the Internet. The Company encourages the use of these media and associated services because information technology is part of our business, because they make communication more efficient and effective, and because they are valuable sources of information about vendors, customers, new products, and services. However, Company-provided access to electronic media and services (e.g., an Internet account) are the Company's property, and their purpose is to facilitate Company business.

Because of the rapidly changing nature of electronic media, and because the "neti-quette" is developing among users of external on-line services and the Internet, this Internet Policy cannot lay down rules to cover every situation. Instead, this Internet Policy expresses the Company's philosophy and sets forth general principles to be applied to the use of electronic media and services. This Internet Policy applies to all Company employees, agents, and contractors using electronic media and services which are: accessed on or from Company premises; accessed using Company computer equipment or via Company-paid access methods; and/or used in a manner which identifies the individual with the Company. Collectively, and individually, such individuals will be referred to in this Policy as "Internet Users."

Use of Company-provided access to the Internet is intended to be primarily for the Company's business-related purposes. Internet access is monitored, and actual Web-site connections are recorded. Excessive use of Company-provided access to the Internet for non-business-related purposes will result in loss of access privileges.

Procedures, Guidelines, and Restrictions

Accounts and Account Passwords

a. Internet users are responsible for the security of their account password(s) and will be held responsible for all use or misuse of their account. Internet users must maintain secure passwords to their account. Internet users accessing the Internet over a Company network may be required to use an ID and password at the firewall (in addition to their usual LAN sign on). Passwords are machine generated and will be changed every thirty days. Internet users must follow all directions of the Company's system administrators with respect to security of passwords and take reasonable precautions against unauthorized access.

b. Remote login to the Company network is prohibited unless permission to do so is granted. Do not remotely log into (or otherwise use) any workstation or computer not designated explicitly for public logins over the Company network—even if the configuration of the computer permits remote access—unless you have explicit permission from the owner and the current user of that computer to log into that machine.

c. Access to selected Internet hosts or networks which the Company designates as inappropriate may be denied. You may not use any account set up for another Internet User and you may not attempt to find out the password of a service for which you have not been authorized, including accounts set up for other Internet users.

(i) File Transfer Protocol ("FTP") may be used to initiate transfer of data from/to specified Company hosts and from/to selected Internet hosts. Initiation of FTP sessions to Company hosts from the Internet is prohibited.

(ii) Access to "network news" is allowed with restrictions. The Company will apply filters as appropriate to block certain news groups.

(iii) Access to the "World Wide Web" is permitted. Inappropriate sites may be blocked from the Company network.

(iv) All services not explicitly allowed are prohibited. Use of games or other non-work related objects over the Internet is prohibited.

d. Network services and World Wide Web sites can and do monitor access and usage and can identify at least which company—and often which specific individual—is accessing their services. Thus, accessing a particular bulletin board or Website leaves Company-identifiable electronic "tracks" even if the Internet user merely reviews or downloads the material and does not post any message. As a general rule, all Internet use should be conducted with this in mind so as to always portray the Company as a reputable company and to maintain its reputation and goodwill.

Intended Uses

Electronic media and services are primarily for Company business use. All Company systems and related equipment are intended for the communication, transmission, processing, and storage of Company-authorized information. Limited, occasional, or incidental use of electronic media (sending or receiving) for personal, non-business purposes is understandable and acceptable—as is the case with personal phone calls. However, Internet users need to demonstrate a sense of responsibility and may not abuse the privilege.

Assuring Ethical and Legal Uses

a. Electronic media may not be used for knowingly transmitting, retrieving, or storing any communication which is (i) discriminatory, harassing, or threatening, (ii) derogatory to any individual, (iii) obscene, (iv) defamatory, (v) a "chain letter" or junk mail, (vi) untrue or fraudulent, (vi) illegal or against Company policy or contrary to the Company's interest, or (vii) for personal profit.

b. In downloading any material from the World Wide Web or by FTP transfer, or in distributing any material by e-mail or FTP transfer, you must bear in mind any proprietary or intellectual property rights of third parties in the material. You must not and may not copy material where such copying would infringe the proprietary or intellectual property rights of third parties. Such infringement is an offense which may render you liable for civil claims and, where appropriate, may also be a criminal offense.

c. You may not download or store any indecent or obscene material from the World Wide Web, or any such material received by e-mail or by FTP transfer, and you may not distribute any such material by FTP transfer or by e-mail.

d. No e-mail or other electronic communications may be sent which attempt to hide the identity of the sender or represent the sender as someone else or as someone from another company. Whenever Internet users send e-mail, Internet user name, Internet user ID, and the Company's name are included in each e-mail message. Internet users are solely responsible for all electronic mail originating from their Internet user ID. When using the Company's e-mail facilities, the following are prohibited: (i) forgery or attempted forgery of e-mail messages; and (ii) reading, deleting, copying, or modifying the e-mail of others.

e. Employees must respect the confidentiality of other people's electronic communications and may not attempt to (i) "hack" into third party systems, (ii) read other people's logins or "crack" passwords, (iii) breach computer or network security measures, or (iv) intercept or monitor electronic files or communications of other employees or third parties, except by explicit direction of Company management.

f. Many software programs and computer data, and related materials such as documentation, are owned by individual users or other companies and are protected by copyright and other laws, together with licenses and other contractual arrangements. Anyone obtaining electronic access to another company's or individual's materials must respect all rights (including copyrights) therein, and may not copy, retrieve, modify, disclose, examine, rename, or forward such materials except as permitted by the person owning the data, software programs, and/or other materials. Such restrictions include:

  (i) copying programs or data;
  (ii) reselling programs or data;
  (iii) using programs or data for non-Company business purposes;
  (iv) using programs or data for personal financial gain;
  (v) using programs or data without being one of the licensed individuals or groups; and
  (vi) publicly disclosing information about software programs without the owner's permission.

FAILURE TO ABIDE BY THESE RESTRICTIONS MAY SUBJECT EMPLOYEES TO CIVIL AND/OR CRIMINAL PROSECUTION.

Consent to Monitoring

Electronic information created and/or communicated by an Internet user using e-mail, word processing, utility programs, spreadsheets, voicemail, telephones, Internet/Bulletin Board System (BBS) access, etc. may be monitored by the Company, and the Company reserves the right to engage in monitoring activities:

a. The Company routinely monitors usage patterns for both voice and data communications (e.g., number called or site accessed; call length; times of day when calls were initiated). Reasons include cost analysis/allocation and the management of our gateway to the Internet.

b. The Company also reserves the right, in its discretion, and the employee upon signing the Certificate of Compliance consents to such action from the Company, to review and disclose any electronic files and messages (including e-mail) and usage to the extent necessary to ensure that electronic media and services are being used in compliance with the law and with this and other Company policies. The Company may also find it necessary to monitor the system for signs of illegal or unauthorized entry. Accordingly, the Company reserves the right, in its discretion, and the undersigned hereby consents to such action by the Company, to intercept and disclose any electronic files and messages (including e-mail) at any time with or without prior notification to the users or owners of such files or resources. The undersigned hereby waives any right to privacy in such electronic files.

c. Employees should therefore understand that electronic communications are not totally private and confidential. Sensitive or confidential information should be transmitted by more secure means.

Assuring Proper Use of the Company's System Resources

Electronic media and services should be used in an efficient and economical manner and not in a way that is likely to cause network congestion or significantly hamper the ability of other people to access and use the Company's computer systems. Any software that is designed to destroy data, provide unauthorized access to the Company's computer systems, or disrupt computing processes is prohibited.

Confidentiality and Encryption In accordance with the Policy on Use of Communication Services and Equipment, Internet users will maintain the confidentiality of the Company's confidential and/or proprietary information and will not use such information for their personal benefit. Any messages or information sent by an Internet user to one or more individuals via an electronic network (e.g., bulletin board, on-line service, or Internet) are statements identifiable and attributable to the Company. While some users include personal "disclaimers" in electronic messages, it should be noted that there would still be a connection with the Company, and the statement might still be legally imputed to the Company. All communications sent by employees via a network must comply with this and other Company policies and may not disclose any confidential and/or proprietary Company information.

Protecting information that is material to Enron's business decision making is a vital part of maintaining our competitive edge. To that end, Enron will take steps to protect proprietary information while ensuring that the necessary transparency for an information-driven business is maintained.

In keeping with the Policy on Use of Communication Services and Equipment, Enron employees, contractors, and consultants are prohibited from posting or otherwise contributing Enron-related information to Internet message/bulletin boards. Additionally, access to certain Internet sites through Enron IT Systems may be monitored or restricted.

To ensure the Company's continuous access to information on the Company's computer systems, no Internet user shall use personal hardware or software to encrypt any e-mail, voicemail, or any other data stored in or communicated by the Company's computer systems, except in accordance with express prior written permission from the Company's management. Should an Internet user have a need to use security measures to encrypt any e-mail, voicemail, or any other data stored in or communicated by the Company's computer systems, such Internet user should contact the appropriate information systems personnel to assist in and facilitate such encryption. The Company will retain the encryption keys for all encrypted data stored in or communicated by the Company's computer systems, except in accordance with express prior written permission from the Company's management. Because there may be a need for the Company to access an Internet user's system or files when he/she is away from the office, Company management, at their discretion, may request that authorized systems personnel reset the password of an Internet user who uses any security measures on any Company-supplied PC, Macintosh, UNIX workstation, or any other Company-supplied workstation for Company use if required.

To meet the Company's public disclosure responsibilities as required by the Securities and Exchange Commission and to ensure that we are communicating a consistent message, public disclosure restrictions apply to interactions over the Internet as well as any other methods of communications. Any employees found to be abusing the privilege of Company-facilitated access to electronic media or services will be subject to corrective action up to and including termination and will risk losing Internet user privileges for himself/herself and possibly for other employees.

Any unauthorized attempts to penetrate or subvert Company computer systems will be thoroughly and promptly investigated and resolved on a case-by-case basis. If circumstances warrant, such attempts will be vigorously pursued and prosecuted to the full extent of the law.

Governmental Affairs and Political Contributions

The Company's official policy concerning all governmental, political, and public matters in which the Company has an interest shall be determined and announced by the Executive Committee of Enron Corp.'s Board of Directors. No alteration of or deviation from such official policy will be made without the approval of the Chairman of the Board and Chief Executive Officer of Enron Corp.

The Company employs governmental relations and public policy personnel who are assigned the responsibility of fulfilling its corporate public affairs responsibility, communicating with public bodies and officials pertaining to the Company's position on public policy questions, and maintaining the good will and understanding of public officials.

Communications of the Company's position to public officials or bodies by personnel of the Company and its subsidiaries must be coordinated with the governmental relations and public policy personnel at corporate headquarters.

The Company may also provide factual information to employees and stockholders concerning the impact on the Company of specific issues, legislation, and other governmental, political, and public matters. Such communications must be approved by the Chairman of the Board and Chief Executive Officer of Enron Corp. or the President and Chief Operating Officer of Enron Corp.

To establish restrictions with regard to corporate participation in the political system as imposed by law, the following guidelines will be followed:

1. No funds, assets, or services of the Company will be used for political contributions, directly or indirectly, unless allowed by applicable foreign and U.S. law and approved in advance by the Chairman of the Board or President of Enron Corp.

2. If eligible under applicable foreign and U.S. law, Company contributions to support or oppose public referenda or similar ballot issues are permitted, but only with advance approval of the Chairman of the Board or President of Enron Corp.

3. Employees, if eligible under applicable foreign and U.S. law, may make political contributions through legally established Company-sponsored and -approved political support funds. Any such personal contribution is not a deductible expense for federal or other applicable income tax purposes and is not eligible for reimbursement by the Company as a business expense. Political action committees are permitted under U.S. law.

Under no circumstances will any activity be authorized or undertaken by an employee which violates the provisions of the Foreign Corrupt Practices Act, federal and state election laws, bribery, or other applicable domestic or foreign laws.

The Company encourages its employees, management, and stockholders to exercise their voting rights and take an active interest and participate in public affairs at local, state, and national levels.

Employees, regardless of their Company position, are free to express their views on public affairs matters through political or non-political measures of their choice and engage in partisan political activities. Employees should conduct themselves in contacts with others so as to make clear that the views expressed are their own and not those of the Company.

Consulting Fees, Commissions, and Other Payments

Agreements with consultants, agents, or representatives must be in writing and must state the services to be performed, the fee basis, amounts to be paid, and other material terms and conditions, and the form and content must be approved by the Company's legal counsel and with respect to foreign consultants, agents, or representatives by Mr. Jack Urquhart, Senior Advisor to the Chairman of the Board of Enron Corp. Payments must bear a reasonable relationship to the value of the services rendered, must be completely documented and recorded, and must not violate the provisions of the Foreign Corrupt Practices Act or any other applicable law, including, without limitation, those relating to bribery. Payments will be made by check or wire transfer in accordance with the following procedure:

1. In any lawful currency in the country where the services are performed; and

2. To the person directly or to the person's bank account in the country where the services are performed; provided, however, that payment may be made other than in the place of performance with the approval of Company legal counsel.

When payments are requested to be made in any manner, currency, or place other than in accordance with the above procedure, the person who has made such request shall be advised that such payments shall not be made except upon notification to the governments of both the country of residence and the country where the services are performed, unless Company legal counsel determines that such notice is not required by law and is not otherwise advisable under the circumstances. Such notification shall be made to both governments even though the requested manner of payment does not apparently violate applicable domestic or foreign law. Notification with respect to the requested manner of payment should normally be made to the tax, finance, or other governmental authorities, as shall be appropriate under the circumstances.

The Company policy discourages but does not prohibit customary expediting payments to low-level employees of foreign governments, properly recorded in the Company's books, which are not excessive in amount and which meet the following criteria:

1. The making of such payments is an established and well-recognized practice in the area.

2. Such payments are to expedite or assure performance of a routine governmental action (such as obtaining customs clearances, visas, and work

permits) to which the Company or the Company's employee is clearly entitled.

3. The payment does not violate any provisions of the Foreign Corrupt Practices Act or any applicable law, including, without limitation, those relating to bribery.

Compliance with the Foreign Corrupt Practices Act

The United States Foreign Corrupt Practices Act (the "Act") applies to the Company in its worldwide operations as well as individually to all Company employees with respect to their worldwide activities. The Act prohibits the corrupt offer, payment or gift of money or anything of value to a foreign governmental official or employee or to any foreign political candidate or party for the purpose of influencing any act or decision of a governmental body in order to obtain or retain business, to direct business to any person, or to secure any improper advantage. The Act also prohibits the offer, payment, or gift of money or anything of value to any third party with knowledge that all or a portion of such money or thing of value will be transferred to a governmental official or employee or political candidate for a prohibited purpose. The Act contains certain narrow affirmative defenses to its prohibitions.

The Act provides for stiff criminal and civil penalties. Criminal fines of up to $2,500,000 or twice the gain per offense can be imposed on the Company. Individuals may be imprisoned for up to 10 years per violation and may have to pay criminal fines ranging from $1,000,000 to twice the gain from the violation. In addition, a civil penalty of $10,000 per violation may be imposed on both the Company and any individual. The Company will not reimburse any fine paid by any individual. Accordingly, Company policy requires strict compliance with the Act.

Due to the broad nature of the Act's prohibitions, it may be implicated by a wide range of activities in addition to direct bribery of a foreign official. For instance, arrangements with foreign joint venture partners, foreign agency or sponsorship arrangements, and any direct dealings with, including lavish entertainment of, foreign governmental officials or employees may raise issues under the Act.

Any questions with respect to the application of the Act to any proposed activity by the Company should be referred immediately to Company legal counsel.

Compliance with Antitrust Laws

All employees of the Company are expected to comply fully with all applicable federal, state, and foreign antitrust laws. Whenever any doubt exists as to the legality of any action or arrangement, such transaction must be submitted to Company legal counsel for prior approval and continuing review. Both the spirit and the letter of antitrust laws are to be followed, so as to avoid creating any unlawful restraints on competition or the appearance of any unlawful restraints.

In the United States, certain types of agreements with third parties, including competitors, suppliers, or customers, are unlawful per se under federal antitrust law. That is, such agreements are automatically in violation of such laws, regardless of the agreement's commercial reasonableness, its purpose, or its actual effect on competition. Other agreements with competitors or customers, although not unlawful per se, may be unlawful under the antitrust "rule of reason."

Formal or informal arrangements with actual or potential competitors (a broadly defined group) which limit or restrict competition may constitute per se violations. Such unlawful agreements include those which: fix, stabilize, or control prices (also a broadly defined term which includes not only price but any element of price such as credit terms, discounts, freight rates, etc.) or terms or conditions of sale; allocate products, markets, customers, or territories; boycott customers or suppliers; or limit or prohibit a party from carrying on a particular commercial enterprise. To assure compliance with antitrust laws, Company employees are not to enter into any discussion or arrangement with an actual or potential competitor which could result in any such per se violation. Further, since the existence of an unlawful agreement may be inferred from the mere exchange of competitively sensitive information between competitors, absent prior review and approval by Company counsel that such actions are lawful no employee shall give to or accept from a competitor any information concerning prices, terms, and conditions of sale, or any other competitive information.

Certain types of restrictive understandings between a customer and supplier are also deemed to be anticompetitive and may be per se antitrust violations. Some such agreements are clearly per se illegal, such as an agreement between a supplier and a distributor setting the distributor's minimum resale prices. Others may be per se illegal if the party imposing the agreement has market power, such as an agreement imposing a requirement of reciprocal dealing, (for example, an agreement that one party buys goods from another only or the understanding that the second party will buy goods from the first), or tying a customer's right to buy one product or service to the obligation to buy another. These possible per se illegal arrangements must not be agreed to or discussed with a customer, absent prior review and approval by Company counsel that the arrangement is lawful.

Agreements that do not unambiguously injure competition (i.e., that are not per se illegal) are analyzed under the antitrust rule of reason. Under the antitrust "rule of reason" test, a court determines whether a particular agreement acts as an "unreasonable" restraint on trade and thus is anticompetitive and unlawful. Such a determination is based on a particular set of facts and circumstances, including the terms of the agreement, the purposes, the relationship of the parties, and the probable effects on competition. Since the circumstances surrounding any arrangement change from time to time, it is essential that agreements which could potentially cause an unreasonable restraint on trade be subject to continuing review by Company legal counsel.

Unilateral action by the Company (in other words, conduct not involving an agreement) may also violate the antitrust laws. Any transaction or practice that would appear to result in the Company gaining a monopoly in a particular line of business in a particular market or geographic area, or which indicates an intent to drive a competitor out of business or to prevent a competitor from entering a market, should therefore be avoided and discussed with Company legal counsel.

Also, discriminating pricing can violate a complicated antitrust statute known as the Robinson-Patman Act.

The sanctions resulting from violations of the antitrust laws can be severe, both as to corporations and as to individuals; they include both criminal penalties and civil treble damages. Whenever any question arises as to the significance or application of antitrust laws, Company legal counsel must be consulted, and any agreements with possible antitrust implications shall be made only with prior approval of Company legal counsel.

International operations may be subject to antitrust laws of either the United States or foreign countries, so employees should be aware of the implication of any such laws to Company transactions.

Advice should be sought in respect of equivalent requirements under other applicable jurisdictions, including the European Commission.

Compliance with Environmental Laws

Employees of Enron Corp., its subsidiaries, and its affiliated companies (collectively the "Company") must conduct Company operations in compliance with all applicable environmental laws and regulations including those of other countries which have jurisdiction over Company activities. These laws are designed to protect the environment in which we live and work, human health, wildlife, and natural resources. Environmental laws either prohibit or severely restrict the release of pollutants to the air, land, surface water, and groundwater. They contain numerous waste management requirements. They impose on owners and operators of most types of facilities the duty to protect the environment by requiring them to obtain permits for certain emissions, to report releases and spills of materials which may cause pollution, and to create and maintain certain records. The Company is committed to environmental protection, and it expects employees to abide by the letter and the spirit of these laws. Employees who do not follow environmental rules and regulations shall be subject to appropriate disciplinary action.

Those responsible for the construction and the operation of Company facilities must ensure that the Company has the necessary environmental permits and clearances for these activities and that the Company complies with the terms and conditions of its permits. These individuals are charged with the responsibility of ensuring that the Company makes all required environmental reports and maintains, at the appropriate location, all required environmental records. Employees must consider the environmental consequences of all aspects of Company operations and proposed changes to our operations.

One of the major environmental laws of the United States may have significant legal and economic consequences for companies which fail to consider the environmental aspects of proposed transactions. The Comprehensive Environmental Response, Compensation and Liability Act (CERCLA, commonly known as "Superfund") was passed to provide a means for cleaning up abandoned waste disposal sites and for responding to environmental emergencies. CERCLA imposes sweeping liability (i) on those who sent hazardous substances to sites that may be cleaned up under CERCLA, (ii) on those who owned or operated these sites when hazardous substances were sent there, (iii) on those who transported hazardous substances to these sites, and (iv) on those who now own or operate these sites. These four classes of persons are potentially responsible for the entire cost of cleaning up the site. Employees must attempt to avoid actions which would increase the Company's Superfund liability. Those who are responsible for disposing waste offsite should ensure that the disposal facility is well managed by a reputable firm. Those who engage in real estate transactions of any nature, particularly acquiring property rights, should make all appropriate inquiry about environmental conditions at the property before completing the real estate transaction.

Environmental regulations change constantly both in the United States and abroad. Those who are responsible for environmental compliance should make every effort to stay abreast of changes to regulations which affect the Company and to plan accordingly for the implementation of regulations which have been proposed.

Environmental audits may be used to verify compliance with environmental regulations. The U.S. Environmental Protection Agency and the Department of Justice encourage the performance of periodic, internal environmental audits to ensure compliance with regulatory requirements. The Company likewise encourages those in charge of operations to conduct periodic environmental audits of Company facilities.

The Company encourages the efforts of employees to minimize the quantity of waste generated by Company operations and to recycle waste which is produced. Innovative waste minimization not only protects the environment by reducing the volume of waste generated, it may also result in reduced operating costs for the Company.

All employees should be aware that the violation of environmental laws may result in the imposition of significant civil and criminal penalties for the Company as well as for individual employees. Many of the laws that apply to the Company's operations in the U.S. provide for civil penalties in the amount of $25,000 per violation, and they make each day of violation a separate offense. Criminal penalties for environmental violations may be as much as fifteen (15) years imprisonment per violation. Severe criminal and civil penalties for environmental violations may also be imposed in other countries in which the Company conducts its business.

Advice should be sought with respect to requirements and powers of enforcement agencies in jurisdictions outside of the United States.

Conflicts of Interests, Investments, and Outside Business Interests of Officers and Employees

Employees of the Company have inquired from time to time as to the propriety of their association with, or the investment of their personal funds in, business enterprises similar in character to certain activities of the Company. In response, the Company has established certain principles for the guidance of officers and employees with respect to personal business and investment interests.

The primary consideration of each full-time (regular as well as temporary) officer and employee should be the fact that the employer is entitled to expect of such person complete loyalty to the best interests of the Company and the maximum application of skill, talent, education, etc., to the discharge of his or her job responsibilities, without any reservations. Therefore, it follows that no full-time officer or employee should:

a. Engage in any outside activity or enterprise which could interfere in any way with job performance;

b. Make investments or perform services for his or her own or related interest in any enterprise under any circumstances where, by reason of the nature of the business conducted by such enterprise, there is, or could be, a disparity or conflict of interest between the officer or employee and the Company; or

c. Own an interest in or participate, directly or indirectly, in the profits of any other entity which does business with or is a competitor of the Company, unless such ownership or participation has been previously disclosed in writing to the Chairman of the Board and Chief Executive Officer of Enron Corp. and such officer has determined that such interest or participation does not adversely affect the best interests of the Company.

Notwithstanding any provision to the contrary in this Policy on Investments, securities of publicly-owned corporations which are regularly traded on the open market may be owned without disclosure if they are not purchased as a result of confidential knowledge about the Company's operations, relations, business, or negotiations with such corporations.

If an investment of personal funds by an officer or employee in a venture or enterprise will not entail personal services or managerial attention, and if there appears to be no conflict or disparity of interest involved, the following procedure nevertheless shall be followed if all or any part of the business of the venture or enterprise is identical with, or similar or directly related to, that conducted by the Company, or if such business consists of the furnishing of goods or services of a type utilized to a material extent by the Company:

a. The officer or employee desiring to make such investment shall submit in writing to the Chairman of the Board and Chief Executive Officer of Enron Corp. a brief summary of relevant facts; and

b. The Chairman of the Board and Chief Executive Officer of Enron Corp. shall consider carefully the summary of relevant facts, and if he concludes that there appears to be no probability of any conflict of interest arising out of the proposed investment, the officer or employee shall be so notified and may then make the proposed investment in full reliance upon the findings of the Chairman of the Board and Chief Executive Officer of Enron Corp.

In the event the Chairman of the Board and Chief Executive Officer of Enron Corp. should desire to make such an investment, he may do so only upon approval of the majority of a quorum of the Executive Committee of the Board of Directors of Enron Corp., other than himself, at any regular or special meeting of such Committee.

Every officer and employee shall be under a continuing duty to report, in the manner set forth above, any situation where by reason of economic or other interest in an enterprise there is then present the possibility of a conflict or disparity of interest between the officer or employee and the Company. This obligation includes but is not limited to (1) any existing personal investment at the date of promulgation of this policy, (2) any existing personal investment at the time of employment of any officer or employee by the Company, and (3) any existing personal investment, whether or not previously approved, which may become in conflict with the provisions of this policy because of changes in the business of the Company or changes in the business of the outside enterprise in which investment has been made.

In the event of a finding by the Chairman of the Board and Chief Executive Officer of Enron Corp. (or by the Executive Committee of the Board of Directors of Enron Corp., if applicable) that a material conflict or disparity of interest does exist with respect to any existing personal investment of an officer or employee, then, upon being so notified, the officer or employee involved shall immediately divest himself or herself of such interest and shall notify the Chairman and Chief Executive Officer of Enron Corp. (or the Executive Committee, if applicable) in writing that he or she has done so.

Responsibility for Reporting

The Company has established a reporting system that allows officers, employees, and other agents of the Company to report violations of any of the policies set forth in this booklet, or other Company policies, as well as any suspected criminal conduct by any officer, employee, or agent of the Company relating to the performance of his or her duties.

Upon observing or learning of any such violation or criminal conduct, employees should report the same by writing a letter describing the suspected violation or criminal conduct with as much detail as possible and sending the letter to:

Enron Compliance Officer

CONFIDENTIAL—Conduct of Business Affairs

P.O. Box 1188

Houston, Texas 77251-1188.

Employees may also report the same by telephoning the Office of the Chairman of the Company at (713) 853-7294 or sending e-mail addressed to the Office of the Chairman. If an employee places the call from his or her extension, or an outside line, the message will be completely anonymous. Similarly, e-mail addressed to the Office of the Chairman will also be completely anonymous.

The employee may (but is not required to) sign the letter or e-mail. Anonymous letters and anonymous e-mail will be investigated and acted upon in the same manner as letters and e-mail which contain a signature. All letters and e-mail should contain as much specific detail as possible to allow the Company to conduct an investigation of the reported matter.

All letters, e-mail, and telephone calls submitted shall be kept in confidence and acted upon only by designated objective Company personnel unless disclosure is required or deemed advisable in connection with any governmental investigation or report, in the interest of the Company, or in the Company's legal handling of the matter. The Company will not condone any form of retribution upon any employee who uses the reporting system in good faith to report suspected wrongdoers, unless the individual reporting is one of the violators. The Company will not tolerate any harassment or intimidation of any employee using the reporting system.

Compliance; Administration

It is a condition of employment that each employee accept the responsibility of complying with the foregoing policies. The Company will require each employee of the Company to complete and submit a statement in a form designated by the Company pertaining to such employee's compliance with the policies set forth in this booklet. The Company reserves the right to request any employee to complete and submit such statement at any time or as frequently as the Company may deem advisable.

The Chairman of the Board and Chief Executive Officer of Enron Corp. may from time to time at the Chairman's discretion delegate any of the responsibilities to be fulfilled by the Chairman as hereinabove set forth. Such delegation may be made to any executive officer of the Company.

An employee who violates any of these policies is subject to disciplinary action including but not limited to suspension or termination of employment, and such other action, including legal action, as the Company believes to be appropriate under the circumstances.

2. American Marketing Association (AMA) Code of Ethics

Ethical Norms and Values for Marketers

The American Marketing Association commits itself to promoting the highest standard of professional ethical norms and values for its members. Norms are established standards of conduct that are expected and maintained by society and/or professional organizations. Values represent the collective conception of what people find desirable, important and morally proper. Values serve as the criteria for evaluating the actions of others. Marketing practitioners must recognize that they not only serve their enterprises but also act as stewards of society in creating, facilitating and executing the efficient and effective transactions that are part of the greater economy. In this role, marketers should embrace the highest ethical norms of practicing professionals and the ethical values implied by their responsibility toward stakeholders (e.g., customers, employees, investors, channel members, regulators and the host community).

General Norms

1. Marketers must do no harm. This means doing work for which they are appropriately trained or experienced so that they can actively add value to their organizations and customers. It also means adhering to all applicable laws and regulations and embodying high ethical standards in the choices they make.

2. Marketers must foster trust in the marketing system. This means that products are appropriate for their intended and promoted uses. It requires that marketing communications about goods and services are not intentionally deceptive or misleading. It suggests building relationships that provide for the equitable adjustment and/or redress of customer grievances. It implies striving for good faith and fair dealing so as to contribute toward the efficacy of the exchange process.

3. Marketers must embrace, communicate and practice the fundamental ethical values that will improve consumer confidence in the integrity of the marketing exchange system. These basic values are intentionally aspirational and include honesty, responsibility, fairness, respect, openness and citizenship.

Ethical Values

Honesty—to be truthful and forthright in our dealings with customers and stakeholders.

- We will tell the truth in all situations and at all times.
- We will offer products of value that do what we claim in our communications.
- We will stand behind our products if they fail to deliver their claimed benefits.
- We will honor our explicit and implicit commitments and promises.

Responsibility—to accept the consequences of our marketing decisions and strategies.

- We will make strenuous efforts to serve the needs of our customers.
- We will avoid using coercion with all stakeholders.
- We will acknowledge the social obligations to stakeholders that come with increased marketing and economic power.
- We will recognize our special commitments to economically vulnerable segments of the market such as children, the elderly and others who may be substantially disadvantaged.

Fairness—to try to balance justly the needs of the buyer with the interests of the seller.

- We will represent our products in a clear way in selling, advertising and other forms of communication; this includes the avoidance of false, misleading and deceptive promotion.
- We will reject manipulations and sales tactics that harm customer trust.
- We will not engage in price fixing, predatory pricing, price gouging or "bait-and-switch" tactics.
- We will not knowingly participate in material conflicts of interest.

Respect—to acknowledge the basic human dignity of all stakeholders.

- We will value individual differences even as we avoid stereotyping customers or depicting demographic groups (e.g., gender, race, sexual orientation) in a negative or dehumanizing way in our promotions.
- We will listen to the needs of our customers and make all reasonable efforts to monitor and improve their satisfaction on an ongoing basis.
- We will make a special effort to understand suppliers, intermediaries and distributors from other cultures.
- We will appropriately acknowledge the contributions of others, such as consultants, employees and co-workers, to our marketing endeavors.

Openness—to create transparency in our marketing operations.

- We will strive to communicate clearly with all our constituencies.
- We will accept constructive criticism from our customers and other stakeholders.
- We will explain significant product or service risks, component substitutions or other foreseeable eventualities that could affect customers or their perception of the purchase decision.
- We will fully disclose list prices and terms of financing as well as available price deals and adjustments.

Citizenship—to fulfill the economic, legal, philanthropic and societal responsibilities that serve stakeholders in a strategic manner.

- We will strive to protect the natural environment in the execution of marketing campaigns.
- We will give back to the community through volunteerism and charitable donations.
- We will work to contribute to the overall betterment of marketing and its reputation.
- We will encourage supply chain members to ensure that trade is fair for all participants, including producers in developing countries.

Implementation

Finally, we recognize that every industry sector and marketing subdiscipline (e.g., marketing research, e-commerce, direct selling, direct marketing, advertising) has its own specific ethical issues that require policies and commentary. An array of such codes can be accessed through links on the AMA Web site. We encourage all such groups to develop and/or refine their industry and discipline-specific codes of ethics to supplement these general norms and values.

Source: The American Marketing Association, www.marketingpower.com.

3. American Institute of Certified Public Accountants (AICPA) Code of Ethics

Section 50: Principles of Professional Conduct:

Membership in the American Institute of Certified Public Accountants is voluntary. By accepting membership, a certified public accountant assumes an obligation of self-discipline above and beyond the requirements of laws and regulations.

These Principles of the Code of Professional Conduct of the American Institute of Certified Public Accountants express the profession's recognition of its responsibilities to the public, to clients, and to colleagues. They guide members in the performance of their professional responsibilities and express the basic tenets of ethical and professional conduct. The Principles call for an unswerving commitment to honorable behavior, even at the sacrifice of personal advantage.

Article I—Responsibilities

In carrying out their responsibilities as professionals, members should exercise sensitive professional and moral judgments in all their activities.

As professionals, certified public accountants perform an essential role in society. Consistent with that role, members of the American Institute of Certified Public Accountants have responsibilities to all those who use their professional services. Members also have a continuing responsibility to cooperate with each other to improve the art of accounting, maintain the public's confidence, and carry out the profession's special responsibilities for self-governance. The collective efforts of all members are required to maintain and enhance the traditions of the profession.

Article II—The Public Interest

Members should accept the obligation to act in a way that will serve the public interest, honor the public trust, and demonstrate commitment to professionalism.

A distinguishing mark of a profession is acceptance of its responsibility to the public. The accounting profession's public consists of clients, credit grantors, governments, employers, investors, the business and financial community, and others who rely on the objectivity and integrity of certified public accountants to maintain the orderly functioning of commerce. This reliance imposes a public interest responsibility on certified public accountants. The public interest is defined as the collective well-being of the community of people and institutions the profession serves.

In discharging their professional responsibilities, members may encounter conflicting pressures from among each of those groups. In resolving those conflicts, members should act with integrity, guided by the precept that when members fulfill their responsibility to the public, clients' and employers' interests are best served.

Those who rely on certified public accountants expect them to discharge their responsibilities with integrity, objectivity, due professional care, and a genuine interest in serving the public. They are expected to provide quality services, enter into fee arrangements, and offer a range of services—all in a manner that demonstrates a level of professionalism consistent with these Principles of the Code of Professional Conduct.

All who accept membership in the American Institute of Certified Public Accountants commit themselves to honor the public trust. In return for the faith that the public reposes in them, members should seek continually to demonstrate their dedication to professional excellence.

Article III—Integrity

To maintain and broaden public confidence, members should perform all professional responsibilities with the highest sense of integrity.

Integrity is an element of character fundamental to professional recognition. It is the quality from which the public trust derives and the benchmark against which a member must ultimately test all decisions.

Integrity requires a member to be, among other things, honest and candid within the constraints of client confidentiality. Service and the public trust should not be subordinated to personal gain and advantage. Integrity can accommodate the inadvertent error and the honest difference of opinion; it cannot accommodate deceit or subordination of principle.

Integrity is measured in terms of what is right and just. In the absence of specific rules, standards, or guidance, or in the face of conflicting opinions, a member should test decisions and deeds by asking: "Am I doing what a person of integrity would do? Have I retained my integrity?" Integrity requires a member to observe both the form and the spirit of technical and ethical standards; circumvention of those standards constitutes subordination of judgment.

Integrity also requires a member to observe the principles of objectivity and independence and of due care.

Article IV—Objectivity and Independence

A member should maintain objectivity and be free of conflicts of interest in discharging professional responsibilities. A member in public practice should be independent in fact and appearance when providing auditing and other attestation services.

Objectivity is a state of mind, a quality that lends value to a member's services. It is a distinguishing feature of the profession. The principle of objectivity imposes the obligation to be impartial, intellectually honest, and free of conflicts of interest. Independence precludes relationships that may appear to impair a member's objectivity in rendering attestation services.

Members often serve multiple interests in many different capacities and must demonstrate their objectivity in varying circumstances. Members in public practice render attest, tax, and management advisory services. Other members prepare financial statements in the employment of others, perform internal auditing services, and serve in financial and management capacities in industry, education, and government. They also educate and train those who aspire to admission into the profession. Regardless of service or capacity, members should protect the integrity of their work, maintain objectivity, and avoid any subordination of their judgment.

For a member in public practice, the maintenance of objectivity and independence requires a continuing assessment of client relationships and public responsibility. Such a member who provides auditing and other attestation services should be independent in fact and appearance. In providing all other services, a member should maintain objectivity and avoid conflicts of interest.

Although members not in public practice cannot maintain the appearance of independence, they nevertheless have the responsibility to maintain objectivity in rendering professional services. Members employed by others to prepare financial statements or to perform auditing, tax, or consulting services are charged with the same responsibility for objectivity as members in public practice and must be scrupulous in their application of generally accepted accounting principles and candid in all their dealings with members in public practice.

Article V—Due Care

A member should observe the profession's technical and ethical standards, strive continually to improve competence and the quality of services, and discharge professional responsibility to the best of the member's ability.

The quest for excellence is the essence of due care. Due care requires a member to discharge professional responsibilities with competence and diligence. It imposes the obligation to perform professional services to the best of a member's ability with concern for the best interest of those for whom the services are performed and consistent with the profession's responsibility to the public.

Competence is derived from a synthesis of education and experience. It begins with a mastery of the common body of knowledge required for designation as a certified public accountant. The maintenance of competence requires a commitment to learning and professional improvement that must continue throughout a member's professional life. It is a member's individual responsibility. In all engagements and in all responsibilities, each member should undertake to achieve a level of competence that will assure that the quality of the member's services meets the high level of professionalism required by these Principles.

Competence represents the attainment and maintenance of a level of understanding and knowledge that enables a member to render services with facility and acumen. It also establishes the limitations of a member's capabilities by dictating that consultation or referral may be required when a professional engagement exceeds the personal competence of a member or a member's firm. Each member is responsible for assessing his or her own competence—of evaluating whether education, experience, and judgment are adequate for the responsibility to be assumed.

Members should be diligent in discharging responsibilities to clients, employers, and the public. Diligence imposes the responsibility to render services promptly and carefully, to be thorough, and to observe applicable technical and ethical standards.

Due care requires a member to plan and supervise adequately any professional activity for which he or she is responsible.

Article VI—Scope and Nature of Services

A member in public practice should observe the Principles of the Code of Professional Conduct in determining the scope and nature of services to be provided.

The public interest aspect of certified public accountants' services requires that such services be consistent with acceptable professional behavior for certified public accountants. Integrity requires that service and the public trust not be subordinated to personal gain and advantage. Objectivity and independence require that members be free from conflicts of interest in discharging professional responsibilities. Due care requires that services be provided with competence and diligence.

Each of these Principles should be considered by members in determining whether or not to provide specific services in individual circumstances. In some instances, they may represent an overall constraint on the nonaudit services that might be offered to a specific client. No hard-and-fast rules can be developed to help members reach these judgments, but they must be satisfied that they are meeting the spirit of the Principles in this regard.

In order to accomplish this, members should

1. Practice in firms that have in place internal quality-control procedures to ensure that services are competently delivered and adequately supervised.

2. Determine, in their individual judgments, whether the scope and nature of other services provided to an audit client would create a conflict of interest in the performance of the audit function for that client.

3. Assess, in their individual judgments, whether an activity is consistent with their role as professionals.

Source: The American Institute of Certified Public Accountants, revised May 15, 2000, www.aicpa.org.

4. The Social Responsibility of Business Is to Increase Its Profits

by Milton Friedman

When I hear businessmen speak eloquently about the "social responsibilities of business in a free-enterprise system," I am reminded of the wonderful line about the Frenchman who discovered at the age of 70 that he had been speaking prose all his life. The businessmen believe that they are defending free enterprise when they declaim that business is not concerned "merely" with profit but also with promoting desirable "social" ends; that business has a "social conscience" and takes seriously its responsibilities for providing employment, eliminating discrimination, avoiding pollution and whatever else may be the catchwords of the contemporary crop of reformers. In fact they are—or would be if they or anyone else took them seriously—preaching pure and unadulterated socialism. Businessmen who talk this way are unwitting puppets of the intellectual forces that have been undermining the basis of a free society these past decades.

The discussions of the "social responsibilities of business" are notable for their analytical looseness and lack of rigor. What does it mean to say that "business" has responsibilities? Only people have responsibilities. A corporation is an artificial person and in this sense may have artificial responsibilities, but "business" as a whole cannot be said to have responsibilities, even in this vague sense. The first step toward clarity in examining the doctrine of the social responsibility of business is to ask precisely what it implies for whom.

Presumably, the individuals who are to be responsible are businessmen, which means individual proprietors or corporate executives. Most of the discussion of social responsibility is directed at corporations, so in what follows I shall mostly neglect the individual proprietors and speak of corporate executives.

In a free-enterprise, private-property system, a corporate executive is an employee of the owners of the business. He has direct responsibility to his employers. That responsibility is to conduct the business in accordance with their desires, which generally will be to make as much money as possible while conforming to their basic rules of the society, both those embodied in law and those embodied in ethical custom. Of course, in some cases his employers may have a different objective. A group of persons might establish a corporation for an eleemosynary purpose—for example, a hospital or a school. The manager of such a corporation will not have money profit as his objective but the rendering of certain services.

In either case, the key point is that, in his capacity as a corporate executive, the manager is the agent of the individuals who own the corporation or establish the eleemosynary institution, and his primary responsibility is to them.

Needless to say, this does not mean that it is easy to judge how well he is performing his task. But at least the criterion of performance is straightforward, and the persons among whom a voluntary contractual arrangement exists are clearly defined.

Of course, the corporate executive is also a person in his own right. As a person, he may have many other responsibilities that he recognizes or assumes voluntarily—to his family, his conscience, his feelings of charity, his church, his clubs, his city, his country. He may feel impelled by these responsibilities to devote part of his income to causes he regards as worthy, to refuse to work for particular corporations, even to leave his job, for example, to join his country's armed forces. If we wish, we may refer to some of these responsibilities as "social responsibilities." But in these respects he is acting as a principal, not an agent; he is spending his own money or time or energy, not the money of his employers or the time or energy he has contracted to devote to their purposes. If these are "social responsibilities," they are the social responsibilities of individuals, not business.

What does it mean to say that the corporate executive has a "social responsibility" in his capacity as businessman? If this statement is not pure rhetoric, it must mean that he is to act in some way that is not in the interest of his employers. For example, that he is to refrain from increasing the price of the product in order to contribute to the social objective of preventing inflation, even though a price increase would be in the best interests of the corporation. Or that he is to make expenditures on reducing pollution beyond the amount that is in the best interests of the corporation or that is required by law in order to contribute to the social objective of improving the environment. Or that, at the expense of corporate profits, he is to hire "hardcore" unemployed instead of better qualified available workmen to contribute to the social objective of reducing poverty.

In each of these cases, the corporate executive would be spending someone else's money for a general social interest. Insofar as his actions in accord with his "social responsibility" reduce returns to stockholders, he is spending their money. Insofar as his actions raise the price to customers, he is spending the customers' money. Insofar as his actions lower the wages of some employees, he is spending their money.

The stockholders or the customers or the employees could separately spend their own money on the particular action if they wished to do so. The executive is exercising a distinct "social responsibility," rather than serving as an agent of the stockholders or the customers or the employees, only if he spends the money in a different way than they would have spent it.

But if he does this, he is in effect imposing taxes, on the one hand, and deciding how the tax proceeds shall be spent, on the other.

This process raises political questions on two levels: principle and consequences. On the level of political principle, the imposition of taxes and the expenditure of tax proceeds are governmental functions. We have established elaborate constitutional, parliamentary and judicial provisions to control these functions, to assure that taxes are imposed so far as possible in accordance with the preferences and desires of the public—after all, "taxation without representation" was one of the battle cries of the American Revolution. We have a system of checks and balances to separate the legislative function of imposing taxes and enacting expenditures from the executive function of collecting taxes and administering expenditure programs and from the judicial function of mediating disputes and interpreting the law.

Here the businessman—self-selected or appointed directly or indirectly by stockholders—is to be simultaneously legislator, executive and jurist. He is to decide whom to tax by how much and for what purpose, and he is to spend the proceeds—all this guided only by general exhortations from on high to restrain inflation, improve the environment, fight poverty and so on and on.

The whole justification for permitting the corporate executive to be selected by the stockholders is that the executive is an agent serving the interests of his principal. This justification disappears when the corporate executive imposes taxes and spends the proceeds for "social" purposes. He becomes in effect a public employee, a civil servant, even though he remains in name an employee of a private enterprise. On grounds of political principle, it is intolerable that such civil servants—insofar as their actions in the name of social responsibility are real and not just window-dressing—should be selected as they are now. If they are to be civil servants, then they must be elected through a political process. If they are to impose taxes and make expenditures to foster "social" objectives, then political machinery must be set up to make the assessment of taxes and to determine through a political process the objectives to be served.

This is the basic reason why the doctrine of "social responsibility" involves the acceptance of the socialist view that political mechanisms, not market mechanisms, are the appropriate way to determine the allocation of scarce resources to alternative uses.

On the grounds of consequences, can the corporate executive in fact discharge his alleged "social responsibilities"? On the one hand, suppose he could get away with spending the stockholders' or customers' or employees' money. How is he to know how to spend it? He is told that he must contribute to fighting inflation. How is he to know what action of his will contribute to that end? He is presumably an expert in running his company—in producing a product or selling it or financing it. But nothing about his selection makes him an expert on inflation. Will his holding down the price of his product reduce inflationary pressure? Or, by leaving more spending power in the hands of his customers, simply divert it elsewhere? Or, by forcing him to produce less because of the lower price, will it simply contribute to shortages? Even if he could answer these questions, how much cost is he justified in imposing on his stockholders, customers and employees for this social purpose? What is his appropriate share and what is the appropriate share of others?

And, whether he wants to or not, can he get away with spending his stockholders', customers' or employees' money? Will not the stockholders fire him? (Either the present ones or those who take over when his actions in the name of social responsibility have reduced the corporation's profits and the price of its stock.) His customers and his employees can desert him for other producers and employers less scrupulous in exercising their social responsibilities.

This facet of "social responsibility" doctrine is brought into sharp relief when the doctrine is used to justify wage restraint by trade unions. The conflict of interest is naked and clear when union officials are asked to subordinate the interest of their members to some more general purpose. If the union officials try to enforce wage restraint, the consequence is likely to be wildcat strikes, rank-and-file revolts and the emergence of strong competitors for their jobs. We thus have the ironic phenomenon that union leaders—at least in the U.S.—have objected to Government interference with the market far more consistently and courageously than have business leaders.

The difficulty of exercising "social responsibility" illustrates, of course, the great virtue of private competitive enterprise—it forces people to be responsible for their own actions and makes it difficult for them to "exploit" other people for either selfish or unselfish purposes. They can do good—but only at their own expense.

Many a reader who has followed the argument this far may be tempted to remonstrate that it is all well and good to speak of Government's having the responsibility to impose taxes and determine expenditures for such "social" purposes as controlling pollution or training the hard-core unemployed, but that the problems are too urgent to wait on the slow course of political processes, that the exercise of social responsibility by businessmen is a quicker and surer way to solve pressing current problems.

Aside from the question of fact—I share Adam Smith's skepticism about the benefits that can be expected from "those who affected to trade for the public good"—this argument must be rejected on the grounds of principle. What this amounts to is an assertion that those who favor the taxes and expenditures in question have failed to persuade a majority of their fellow citizens to be of like mind and that they are seeking to attain by undemocratic procedures what they cannot attain by democratic procedures. In a free society, it is hard for "evil" people to do "evil," especially since one man's good is another's evil.

I have, for simplicity, concentrated on the special case of the corporate executive, except only for the brief digression on trade unions. But precisely the same argument applies to the newer phenomenon of calling upon stockholders to require corporations to exercise social responsibility (the recent G.M. crusade, for example). In most of these cases, what is in effect involved is some stockholders trying to get other stockholders (or customers or employees) to contribute against their will to "social" causes favored by activists. Insofar as they succeed, they are again imposing taxes and spending the proceeds.

The situation of the individual proprietor is somewhat different. If he acts to reduce the returns of his enterprise in order to exercise his "social responsibility," he is spending his own money, not someone else's. If he wishes to spend his money on such purposes, that is his right and I cannot see that there is any objection to his doing so. In the process, he, too, may impose costs on employees and customers. However, because he is far less likely than a large corporation or union to have monopolistic power, any such side effects will tend to be minor.

Of course, in practice the doctrine of social responsibility is frequently a cloak for actions that are justified on other grounds rather than a reason for those actions.

To illustrate, it may well be in the long-run interest of a corporation that is a major employer in a small community to devote resources to providing amenities to that community or to improving its government. That may make it easier to attract desirable employees, it may reduce the wage bill or lessen losses from pilferage and sabotage or have other worthwhile effects. Or it may be that, given the laws about the deductibility of corporate charitable contributions, the stockholders can contribute more to charities they favor by having the corporation make the gift than by doing it themselves, since they can in that way contribute an amount that would otherwise have been paid as corporate taxes.

In each of these—and many similar—cases, there is a strong temptation to rationalize these actions as an exercise of "social responsibility." In the present climate of opinion, with its widespread aversion to "capitalism," "profits," the "soulless corporation" and so on, this is one way for a corporation to generate goodwill as a by-product of expenditures that are entirely justified in its own self-interest.

It would be inconsistent of me to call on corporate executives to refrain from this hypocritical window-dressing because it harms the foundation of a free society. That would be to call on them to exercise a "social responsibility"! If our institutions, and the attitudes of the public make it in their self-interest to cloak their actions in this way, I cannot summon much indignation to denounce them. At the same time, I can express admiration for those individual proprietors or owners of closely held corporations or stockholders of more broadly held corporations who disdain such tactics as approaching fraud.

Whether blameworthy or not, the use of the cloak of social responsibility, and the nonsense spoken in its name by influential and prestigious businessmen, does clearly harm the foundations of a free society. I have been impressed time and again by the schizophrenic character of many businessmen. They are capable of being extremely far-sighted and clear-headed in matters that are internal to their businesses. They are incredibly short-sighted and muddle-headed in matters that are outside their businesses but affect the possible survival of business in general. This short-sightedness is strikingly exemplified in the calls from many businessmen for wage and price guidelines or controls or income policies. There is nothing that could do more in a brief period to destroy a market system and replace it by a centrally controlled system than effective governmental control of prices and wages.

The short-sightedness is also exemplified in speeches by businessmen on social responsibility. This may gain them kudos in the short run. But it helps to strengthen the already too prevalent view that the pursuit of profits is wicked and immoral and must be curbed and controlled by external forces. Once this view is adopted, the external forces that curb the market will not be the social consciences, however highly developed, of the pontificating executives; it will be the iron fist of Government bureaucrats. Here, as with price and wage controls, businessmen seem to me to reveal a suicidal impulse.

The political principle that underlies the market mechanism is unanimity. In an ideal free market resting on private property, no individual can coerce any other, all cooperation is voluntary, all parties to such cooperation benefit or they need not participate. There are not values, no "social" responsibilities in any sense other than the shared values and responsibilities of individuals. Society is a collection of individuals and of the various groups they voluntarily form.

The political principle that underlies the political mechanism is conformity. The individual must serve a more general social interest—whether that be determined by a church or a dictator or a majority. The individual may have a vote and say in what is to be done, but if he is overruled, he must conform. It is appropriate for some to require others to contribute to a general social purpose whether they wish to or not.

Unfortunately, unanimity is not always feasible. There are some respects in which conformity appears unavoidable, so I do not see how one can avoid the use of the political mechanism altogether.

But the doctrine of "social responsibility" taken seriously would extend the scope of the political mechanism to every human activity. It does not differ in philosophy from the most explicitly collective doctrine. It differs only by professing to believe that collectivist ends can be attained without collectivist means. That is why, in my book *Capitalism and Freedom,* I have called it a "fundamentally subversive doctrine" in a free society, and have said that in such a society, "there is one and only one social responsibility of business—to use its resources and engage in activities designed to increase its profits so long as it stays within the rules of the game, which is to say, engages in open and free competition without deception or fraud."

Source: Milton Friedman, "The Social Responsibility of Business Is to Increase Its Profits," *New York Times Magazine,* September 13, 1970.

5. Getting to the Bottom of "Triple Bottom Line"

By Wayne Norman and Chris MacDonald*

Abstract

In this paper, we examine critically the notion of "Triple Bottom Line" accounting. We begin by asking just what it is that supporters of the Triple Bottom line idea advocate, and attempt to distil specific, assessable claims from the vague, diverse, and sometimes contradictory uses of the Triple Bottom Line rhetoric. We then use these claims as a basis upon which to argue (a) that what is sound about the idea of a Triple Bottom Line is not novel, and (b) that what is novel about the idea is not sound. We argue on both conceptual and practical grounds that the Triple Bottom Line is an unhelpful addition to current discussions of corporate social responsibility. Finally, we argue that the Triple Bottom Line paradigm cannot be rescued simply by attenuating its claims: the rhetoric is badly misleading, and may in fact provide a smokescreen behind which firms can avoid truly effective social and environmental reporting and performance.

Introduction

The notion of "Triple Bottom Line" (3BL) accounting has become increasingly fashionable in management, consulting, investing, and NGO circles over the last few years. The idea behind the 3BL paradigm is that a corporation's ultimate success or health can and should be measured not just by the traditional financial bottom line, but also by its social/ethical and environmental performance. Of course, it has long been accepted by most people in and out of the corporate world that firms have a variety of obligations to stakeholders to behave responsibly. It is also almost a truism that firms cannot be successful in the long run if they consistently disregard the interests of key stakeholders. The apparent novelty of 3BL lies in its supporters' contention that the overall fulfillment of obligations to communities, employees, customers, and suppliers (to name but four stakeholders) should be measured, calculated, audited and reported—just as the financial performance of public companies has been for more than a century. This is an exciting promise. One of the more enduring clichés of modern management is that "if you can't measure it, you can't manage it." If we believe that ethical business practices and social responsibility are important functions of corporate governance and management, then we should welcome attempts to develop tools that make more transparent to managers, shareholders and other stakeholders just how well a firm is doing in this regard.

In this article we will assume without argument both the desirability of many socially responsible business practices, on the one hand, and the potential

*Much of the preliminary research for this paper was carried out while Wayne Norman was a Visiting Scholar at the Center for Social Innovation at the Graduate School of Business, Stanford University, and we thank the Center for its generous support. We are also grateful for numerous challenges and suggestions from audiences at the Conference on Developing Philosophy of Management, St. Anne's College, Oxford, and the Université de Montréal. Special thanks go out to Christopher Cowton, Jim Gaa, Marya Hill-Popper, and Bryn Williams-Jones, as well as to the referees of this Journal.

usefulness of tools that allow us to measure and report on performance along these dimensions, on the other. These are not terribly controversial assumptions these days.[1] Almost all major corporations at least pay lip service to social responsibility—even Enron had an exhaustive code of ethics and principles—and a substantial percentage of the major corporations are now issuing annual reports on social and/or environmental performance.[2] We find controversy not in these assumptions, but in the promises suggested by the 3BL rhetoric.

The term "Triple Bottom Line" dates back to the mid 1990s, when management thinktank AccountAbility coined and began using the term in its work.[3] The term found public currency with the 1997 publication of the British edition of John Elkington's *Cannibals With Forks: The Triple Bottom Line of 21st Century Business*.[4] There are in fact very few references to the term before this date, and many (including the man himself) claim that Elkington coined it. In the last three or four years the term has spread like wildfire. The Internet search engine, Google, returns roughly 25,200 Web pages that mention the term.[5] The phrase "triple bottom line" also occurs in 67 articles in the *Financial Times* in the year preceding June 2002. Organisations such as the Global Reporting Initiative and AccountAbility have embraced and promoted the 3BL concept for use in the corporate world. And corporations are listening. Companies as significant as AT&T, Dow Chemicals, Shell, and British Telecom have used 3BL terminology in their press releases, annual reports and other documents. So have scores of smaller firms. Not surprisingly, most of the big accounting firms are now using the concept approvingly and offering services to help firms that want to measure, report or audit their two additional "bottom lines." Similarly, there is now a sizable portion of the investment industry devoted to screening companies on the basis of their social and environmental performance, and many of these explicitly use the language of 3BL.[6] Governments, government departments and political parties (especially Green parties) are also well represented in the growing documentation of those advocating or accepting 3BL "principles." For many NGOs and activist organisations 3BL seems to be pretty much an article of faith. Given the rapid uptake by corporations, governments, and activist groups, the paucity of academic analysis is both surprising

---

[1] According to a comprehensive poll conducted for *BusinessWeek* magazine's issue of September 11, 2000, fully 95% of respondents agreed with the following claim: "U.S. corporations should have more than one purpose. They also owe something to their workers and the communities in which they operate, and they should sometimes sacrifice some profit for the sake of making things better for their workers and communities." By contrast, only 4% agreed with the position most closely associated with Milton Friedman in his oft-reprinted article, namely that: "U.S. corporations should have only one purpose—to make the most profit for their shareholders—and their pursuit of that goal will be best for America in the long run." The poll was conducted by Harris, with a sample of over 2,000 respondents and a margin of error of plus-or-minus 3%.

[2] Enron's code of ethics (July, 2000) runs to over 60 pages. According to Helle Bank Jørgensen of PriceWaterhouse Coopers, 70% of the British FTSE 350 report on their environmental and social performance. According to KPMG's *International Survey of Corporate Sustainability Reporting 2002,* 45% of the *Fortune* global top 250 companies (GFT250) are now issuing environmental, social or sustainability reports in addition to their financial reports. The number of companies participating in the Global Reporting Initiative now numbers "in the thousands." (*Trust Us: The Global Reporters 2002 Survey of Corporate Sustainability Reporting,* 2002).

[3] *Trust Us,* 4.

[4] John Elkington, *Cannibals With Forks: The Triple Bottom Line of 21st Century Business,* Stony Creek, CT: New Society Publishers, 1998.

[5] Informal search conducted March, 2003.

[6] There is now a huge annual "Triple Bottom Line Investing" conference (www.tbli.org). The Washington, D.C.–based Social Investment Forum (www.socialinvest.org) claims that in 2001 there was more than $2 trillion in professionally managed investment portfolios using social and environmental screening.

and worrisome. Our recent search of the principal academic databases turned up only about a dozen articles, mostly concentrated in journals catering to the intersection of management and environmentalism. One book beyond Elkington's has been published, but this was written by a former IBM executive, not an academic.[7] (The generally languid pace of the academic publishing industry may be partly to blame here, given the relative novelty of the concept.)

In this paper, we propose to begin the task of filling this academic lacuna. We do this by seeking answers to a number of difficult questions. Is the intent of the 3BL movement really to bring accounting paradigms to bear in the social and environmental domains? Is doing so a practical possibility? Will doing so achieve the goals intended by promoters of the 3BL? Or is the idea of a "bottom line" in these other domains a mere metaphor? And if it is a metaphor, is it a useful one? Is this a form of jargon we should embrace and encourage?

Our conclusions are largely critical of this "paradigm" and its rhetoric. Again, we are supportive of some of the aspirations behind the 3BL movement, but we argue on both conceptual and practical grounds that the language of 3BL promises more than it can ever deliver. That will be our bottom line on Triple Bottom Line.

What Do Supporters of 3BL Believe?

There are two quick answers to the question in the above section heading: first, different supporters of 3BL seem to conceive of the 3BL in a variety of ways; and second, it is rarely clear exactly what most people mean when they use this language or what claims they are making on behalf of "taking the 3BL seriously." Despite the fact that most of the documents by advocates of 3BL are explicitly written to introduce readers to the concept and to sell them on it, it is difficult to find anything that looks like a careful definition of the concept, let alone a methodology or formula (analogous to the calculations on a corporate income statement) for calculating one of the new bottom lines. In the places where one is expecting a definition the most that one usually finds are vague claims about the aims of the 3BL approach. We are told, for example, that in the near future "the world's financial markets will insist that business delivers against" all three bottom lines.[8] If "we aren't good corporate citizens"—as reflected in "a Triple Bottom Line that takes into account social and environmental responsibilities along with financial ones"—"eventually our stock price, our profits and our entire business could suffer."[9] 3BL reporting "defines a company's ultimate worth in financial, social, and environmental terms." Such reporting "responds to *all* stakeholder demands that companies take part in, be accountable for, and substantiate their membership in society." Further, 3BL is "a valuable management tool—that is, an early warning tool that allows you to react faster to changes in stakeholders' behaviour, and incorporate the changes into the strategy before they hit the [real?] bottom line."[10] Many claims on 3BL's behalf are very tepid indeed, suggesting little more than that the concept is "an important milestone in our journey toward sustainability," or an approach that "places emphasis"[11]

---

[7] Bob Willard, *The Sustainability Advantage: Seven Business Case Benefits of a Triple Bottom Line*. Gabriola Island, BC: New Society Publishers, 2002.

[8] Elkington, p. 20.

[9] From AT&T, at www.att.com/ehs/annual_reports/ehs_report/triple_bottom_line.html.

[10] Quotes in these last three sentences from Helle Bank Jorgensen of PriceWaterhouse Coopers from an article published in 2000 on www.pwcglobal.com (grammar corrected).

[11] Luciano Respini, (President, Dow Europe). "The Corporation and the Triple Bottom Line," www.dowchemical.at/dow_news/speeches/10-18-00.htm.

on social and environmental aspects of the firm, along with economic aspects, and that "should move to the top of executives' agendas."[12]

From these many vague claims made about 3BL it is possible to distil two sets of more concrete propositions about the meaning of the additional bottom lines and why it is supposed to be important for firms to measure and report on them. (For the sake of brevity and economy of illustration, from this point on we will look primarily at the case of the so-called social/ethical bottom line.[13] But most of the conceptual issues we will explore with this "bottom line" would apply equally to its environmental sibling.)

A. What Does It Mean to Say There Are Additional Bottom Lines?

- (*Measurement Claim*) The components of "social performance" or "social impact" can be measured in relatively objective ways on the basis of standard indicators. (See Appendix 1 for examples of indicators used in actual social performance reports.) These data can then be audited and reported.

- (*Aggregation Claim*) A social "bottom line"—that is, something analogous to a net social "profit/loss"—can be calculated using data from these indicators and a relatively uncontroversial formula that could be used for any firm.

B. Why Should Firms Measure, Calculate and (Possibly) Report Their Additional (and in Particular Their Social) Bottom Lines?

- (*Convergence Claim*) Measuring social performance helps improve social performance, and firms with better social performance tend to be more profitable in the long run.

- (*Strong Social-Obligation Claim*) Firms have an obligation to maximise (or weaker: to improve) their social bottom line—their net positive social impact—and accurate measurement is necessary to judge how well they have fulfilled this obligation.

- (*Transparency Claim*) The firm has obligations to stakeholders to disclose information about how well it performs with respect to all stakeholders.

In short, 3BL advocates believe that social (and environmental) performance can be measured in fairly objective ways, and that firms should use these results in order to improve their social (and environmental) performance. Moreover, they should report these results as a matter of principle, and in using and reporting on these additional "bottom lines" firms can expect to do better by their financial bottom line in the long run.

We will not examine each of these claims in isolation now. Rather we will focus on some deeper criticisms of the 3BL movement by making reference to these five central claims about the project and its aims. The most striking general observation about the two sets of claims is how vaguely one has to formulate

---

[12] Patricia Panchack, "Editor's Page: Time for a Triple Bottom Line," *Industry Week,* 1 June 2002.

[13] The collapsing of the categories of "ethical," "socially responsible," "social performance," etc., in many discussions of CSR raises serious conceptual issues. In particular, judging the extent to which one is ethical or responsible can rarely be reduced to a calculation of net impact. We will address some of these problems toward the end of this article.

most of them in order for them to be plausible. That is, the truth of many of these claims is salvaged at the expense of their power. Consider, for example, the Transparency Claim. Of course everyone accepts that there are obligations (or at the very least, good reasons) to report *some* information to various stakeholders. The question is, what information do stakeholders actually have a right to, and how would one justify such rights claims? When is it perfectly legitimate to keep secrets from outsiders, including competitors? We have not found any guidance on these issues in the burgeoning literature on the 3BL.

In a moment we will turn to the most distinctive and novel aspect of the 3BL idea—the Aggregation Claim. We will argue that this claim, which is essential to the very concept of a bottom line, is untenable. We can sum up our critique with the slogan, "what's sound about the 3BL project is not novel, and what is novel is not sound."

What Is Sound about 3BL Is Not Novel

Again, it goes without saying that all 3BL advocates believe that corporations have social responsibilities that go beyond maximizing shareholder value. Indeed, many uses of "Triple Bottom Line" are simply synonymous with "corporate social responsibility" (CSR)—for example, when the CEO of VanCity (Canada's largest credit union) defines "the 'triple bottom line' approach to business" as "taking environmental, social and financial results into consideration in the development and implementation of a corporate business strategy."[14] Nowhere does one find advocates of measuring, calculating and reporting on the "social bottom line" who nevertheless maintain that the financial bottom line, or shareholder value, is the only thing that really counts. But again, the belief in CSR was alive and well long before the 3BL movement. The same is true of faith in the general belief that attention to social responsibility and ethics should help a firm sustain profits in the long run (the Convergence Claim, above). This belief has increasingly been part of mainstream management theory at least since the publication of Edward Freeman's 1984 classic, *Strategic Management: A Stakeholder Approach.*[15]

Now it might be argued that what is new about the 3BL movement is the emphasis on measurement and reporting. But this is not true either. Those who use the language of 3BL are part of a much larger movement sometimes

---

[14] Dave Mowat, "The VanCity Difference: A Case for the Triple Bottom Line Approach to Business," Corporate Environmental Strategy: the International Journal of Corporate Sustainability v. 9, no.1 (2002), p. 24. In an article in the on-line magazine, *Salon.com,* 13 August 2002, Arianna Huffington writes that the "key idea" of 3BL is "that corporations need to pay attention to both their stockholders and their stakeholders—those who may not have invested money in the company but clearly have a de facto investment in the air they breath, the food they eat and the communities they live in." In other words, put this way, it is nothing more than the idea that corporations have obligations beyond maximizing shareholder value. One of the problems with this overly loose way of framing the idea of 3BL is that it is completely at odds with the ubiquitous claim that 3BL is a new concept and a new movement. Huffington echoes this spirit in the same article when she reports that "More than a hundred companies in America are seeking to redefine the bottom line—moving away from conventional corporate accounting, where the only consideration is profit, to one that also includes the social and environmental impact the company is having. It's called the Triple Bottom Line."

[15] R. Edward Freeman, *Strategic Management: A Stakeholder Approach,* Boston: Pitman, 1984. A recent survey article (Thomas M. Jones, Andrew C. Wicks and R. Edward Freeman, "Stakeholder Theory: The State of the Art," in N. Bowie (ed), *The Blackwell Guide to Business Ethics,* Oxford: Blackwell, 2002, pp. 21–22), traces the insights of the stakeholder approach in mainstream management theory back as far as the 1930s. PriceWaterhouse Cooper's *Global CEO Survey,* released in January 2002, shows 68% of responding CEOs agreeing that corporate social responsibility is vital to the profitability of any company.

identified by the acronym SEAAR: social and ethical accounting, auditing and reporting. This movement (to use that term loosely) has grown in leaps and bounds over the past decade, and has produced a variety of competing standards and standard-setting bodies, including the Global Reporting Initiative (GRI), the SA 8000 from Social Accountability International, the AA 1000 from AccountAbility, as well as parts of various ISO standards.[16] The most important function of these standards is to identify indicators of social performance as well as methodologies for measuring and auditing performance along these indicators (again, see Appendix 1 for some examples of social-performance indicators). In general it would be safe to say that anyone supporting the SEAAR movement would endorse at least four of the five 3BL claims listed above—and certainly the Measurement and Transparency Claims—if only because of the relative weakness or generality of these claims. But only the Aggregation Claim is truly distinctive of a "bottom line" approach to social performance, and this claim is definitely not endorsed by any of the major social performance standards to date.[17] In the following sections we will try to show why this rejection of the Aggregation Claim is justified and why this should lead us to avoid the rhetoric of 3BL even if one endorses the general aims of the SEAAR movement.

One often has the impression that 3BL advocates are working with a caricature that has traditional "pre-3BL" or "single-bottom-line" firms and managers focussing exclusively on financial data, like *le businessman* mindlessly and forever counting "his" stars in Saint-Exupéry's *Le Petit Prince*. But obviously, even a pure profit-maximiser knows that successful businesses cannot be run like this. Indeed, most of the data to be reported on the so-called social-bottom-line is already gathered by the standard departments in any large organisation. For example, Human Resource departments will typically keep records on employee turnover, employee-demographic information by gender and/or ethnicity, and various measures of employee satisfaction; good Marketing and Sales departments will try to track various measures of customer satisfaction; Procurement departments will monitor relationships with suppliers; Public Relations will be testing perceptions of the firm within various external communities, including governments; the Legal department will be aware of lawsuits from employees, customers or other stakeholders; and so on. Of

---

[16] For a critical evaluation of the "movement's" progress, see Rob Gray, "Thirty Years of Social Accounting, Reporting and Auditing: What (if Anything) Have We Learnt?" *Business Ethics, A European Review,* January 2001, vol. 10, no.1, pp. 9–15; and David Owen and Tracey Swift, "Introduction: Social Accounting, Reporting and Auditing: Beyond the Rhetoric?" *Business Ethics, A European Review,* January 2001, vol. 10, no. 1, pp. 4–8. For something of a how-to guide, see Simon Zadek, Peter Pruzan and Richard Evans, *Building Corporate Accountability: Emerging Practices in Social and Ethical Accounting, Auditing and Reporting,* London: Earthscan Publications, 1997.

[17] The GRI provides an instructive contrast to 3BL. With the agreement of hundreds of corporations and other organisations, this standard identifies a large array of minimal standards that corporations should meet without any attempt to aggregate or to rank or score companies on how far they exceed some of these minimal standards. A similar approach is defended in George Enderle and Lee A. Tavis, "A Balanced Concept of the Firm and the Measurement of Its Longterm Planning and Performance," *Journal of Business Ethics* 17:1129–1144, 1998; see especially pp. 1135–36. By focusing on standards that are both agreed-upon and minimal, this rival approach makes it easier for outsiders to identify "rear-guard" firms that fail to meet some of the minimal standards. But it does this at the cost of not being able to identify or to guide the strategic deliberations of "vanguard" firms, since most "mainstream" firms can expect to meet the minimal standards. All of the rhetoric of 3BL advocates suggests that they could never be satisfied with the less ambitious approach taken by the GRI. At any rate, this rival approach is completely at odds with the metaphor of bottom lines and the inherent idea of continual, measurable improvement.

course, what is distinctive of the recent trend in corporate social responsibility is that many of these various figures are now being externally verified and reported, not to mention gathered in one document rather than being scattered among many departments oriented toward different stakeholders. But the only point we wish to make here is that much of the information that goes into any report or calculation of a 3BL already figures in the deliberations of strategic planners and line managers even in the most "single-bottom-line"–oriented corporations.

In short, if there is something distinctive about the 3BL approach, it cannot be merely or primarily that it calls on firms and senior managers to focus on things besides the traditional bottom line: it has never been possible to do well by the bottom line without paying attention elsewhere, especially to key stakeholder groups like employees, customers, suppliers and governments. To give but one clear example, a firm that has consistently done as well as any of the "profit-maximising" rivals in its sector is Johnson & Johnson. Some six decades ago J&J published its Credo announcing that its primary stakeholders were its customers, employees and the communities it operated in—in that order, and explicitly ahead of its stockholders. The Credo, which is the first thing to greet visitors to J&J's homepage (www.jnj.com) ends by affirming that "Our final responsibility is to our stockholders. . . . When we operate according to these principles [i.e., those outlining obligations to other stakeholders], the stockholders should realize a fair return." These words were written in the 1940s and are hardly revolutionary today.

Now we are certainly not claiming that most major corporations are already functioning the way 3BL advocates would like them to. The point is merely that once we formulate 3BL principles in a way that makes them plausible, they become vague enough that many mainstream executives would not find them terribly controversial (nor, perhaps, terribly useful). 3BL advocates would certainly have corporations *report* more of the data they collect on stakeholder relations than they typically do at present. But even here, as we shall explain in a moment, there is nothing distinctive to the 3BL approach to the call to audit and report social and environment performance. If there are good justifications for firms to report such data, these will be independent of the distinctive feature of the 3BL: namely the Aggregation Claim, the idea that it is possible in some sense to quantify a firm's social performance in a way that arrives at some kind of "bottom line" result.

What Is Novel about 3BL Is Not Sound

The keenest supporters of the 3BL movement tend to insist, if only in passing, that firms have social and environmental bottom lines *in just the same way* that they have "financial" or "economic" bottom lines. We submit that the only way to make sense of such a claim is by formulating it (roughly) in the way we have with the Aggregation Claim, above. That is, we cannot see how it could make sense to talk about a bottom line analogous to the bottom line of the income statement unless there is an agreed-upon methodology that allows us, at least in principle, to add and subtract various data until we arrive at a net sum.

Probably the most curious fact about the 3BL movement—certainly the one that surprised us most as we researched it—is that none of the advocates of so-called 3BL accounting ever actually proposes, presents or even sketches a methodology of the sort implied by the Aggregation Claim. In other words, for all the talk of the novelty of the 3BL idea, and for the importance of taking all three "bottom lines" seriously, nobody (as far as we know) has actually proposed a way to use the data on social performance to calculate some kind of a net social bottom line.[18] The charitable interpretation of this stunning omission is that advocates of the concept see these as early days for the idea of real social and environmental bottom lines, and hope that progress on a methodology will come once the general desirability of the idea has gained acceptance.[19] In this section we will suggest that this is probably a vain hope. We will first try to give some indication of how disanalogous the evaluations of financial and social performance are. Then we will argue that in fact there is good reason to think that it would be *impossible* to formulate a sound and relatively uncontroversial methodology to calculate a social bottom line.

If it makes sense to say that there is a bottom line for performance in some domain, x, that is directly analogous to the financial bottom line, then it makes sense to ask what a given firm's x-bottom line is. And there should be a relatively straightforward answer to this question, even if we do not yet know what that answer is. So we might reasonably ask of firms like The Body Shop, or British Telecom, or Dow Chemical—all companies that have claimed to believe in the 3BL—what their social bottom line actually was last year. But just posing this question conjures up visions of Douglas Adams's comic tour de force, *The Hitchhiker's Guide to the Galaxy,* in which the greatest of all computers is asked to come up with an answer to "the great question of Life, the Universe and Everything." That answer, which takes seven-and-a-half million years to calculate, is "42."

At least part of the charm in this *Hitchhiker* shtick is that "42" seems wrong not because it arrives at the wrong number, but because it is ridiculous to think that the answer to such a question could be expressed numerically or even just with one word (especially a dangling adjective—42 *what?*). We do not know exactly what the answer should look like—indeed we may not really know what that question means—but we are pretty sure such a "great question" cannot be solved that succinctly.

Perhaps this is how you would feel if you asked what the social or environmental "bottom line" of a firm was, and someone told you it was 42, or 42-thousand, or 42-million. We may not be sure what the right answer should look like, but this kind of answer, even (or especially?) if it were expressed in monetary units, just does not seem right. So it is worth reflecting for a moment about what *would* look like a plausible answer to the question of what some particular firm's social bottom line is. We can have good grounds for thinking that one firm's social performance (say, BP's) is better than another's (say, Enron's); or that a given firm's social/ethical performance improved (Shell) or declined (Andersen) over a five-year period. And indeed, our judgments in these cases would be at least partly based on, or reflected in, the kind of indicators that various proposed social standards highlight—including,

---

[18] We limit our claim here to the current generation of writers, consultants and activists who are explicitly endorsing a 3BL paradigm. There are surely some very valuable lessons for this generation in the generally unsuccessful attempts of a previous generation—largely from within the accounting profession—to develop a calculus of social accounting that could attach values to social benefits and losses. In addition to the articles cited in the preceding note, see Rob Gray, Dave Owen, Carol Adams, *Accounting and Accountability: Changes and Challenges in Corporate Social and Environmental Accounting,* Prentice Hall, 1996. We are grateful to Christopher Cowton and Jim Gaa for drawing our attention to these earlier debates.

[19] Elkington (p. 72) writes that "the metrics are still evolving." AccountAbility describes social and environmental accounting as "embryonic." See AccountAbility's "Triple Bottom Line in Action," www.sustainability.com/people/clients/tbl-in-action4.asp.

for example, charitable donations, various measures of employee satisfaction and loyalty, perceptions in the community, and so on. But this is still a long way from saying that we have any kind of systematic way of totting up the social pros and cons, or of arriving at some global figure for a firm's social performance.

The problem with alleged analogy between the "traditional" bottom line and social or environmental bottom lines runs deeper still. The traditional bottom line, of course, is the last line of the income statement indicating net income (positive or negative). Net income is arrived at by subtracting the expenses incurred by the organisation from the income earned by it within a given period.[20] We have just suggested that we are not sure what the social version of this "line" should look like, or in what sort of units it should be expressed. But we are also puzzled when we look for conceptual analogies *above* the bottom line, so to speak. What are the ethical/social equivalents or analogues of, say, revenue, expenses, gains, losses, assets, liabilities, equity, and so on? The kinds of raw data that 3BL and other SEAAR advocates propose to collect as indications of social performance do not seem to fit into general categories, analogous to these, that will allow for a straightforward subtraction of "bads" from "goods" in order to get some kind of net social sum.

With reference to typical SEAAR criteria we could imagine a firm reporting that:

a. 20% of its directors were women,

b. 7% of its senior management were members of "visible" minorities,

c. it donated 1.2% of its profits to charity,

d. the annual turnover rate among its hourly workers was 4%, and

e. it had been fined twice this year for toxic emissions.

Now, out of context—e.g., without knowing how large the firm is, where it is operating, and what the averages are in its industrial sector—it is difficult to say how good or bad these figures are. Of course, in the case of each indicator we often have a sense of whether a higher or lower number would generally be better, from the perspective of social/ethical performance. The conceptual point, however, is that these are quite simply not the sort of data that can be fed into an income-statement-like calculation to produce a final net sum. For one thing, most of these figures are given in percentages, and one obviously cannot add or subtract percentages attached to different figures—for example, (a) and (b), above, do not add up to 27% of *anything*. But even when there are cardinal numbers involved (e.g., ". . . 8 employees of Shell companies . . . lost their lives in 1997. . . .,"[21] it is not at all clear where on a given sliding scale we treat a figure as a "good" mark to raise the "social bottom line" and where we treat it as a "bad" mark that takes away from the bottom line. (Is eight a high number or a low number for fatalities from the worldwide operations of a firm like Shell? Something to be proud of or ashamed of?) Again, we are not disputing that these are relevant considerations in the evaluation of a firm's level of social responsibility; but it does not seem at all helpful to think of this evaluation as

---

[20] It really should be noted that the income statement, with its famous "bottom line," is but one of the principal financial statements used to evaluate the health of a firm. The others include the balance sheet, the statement of cash flows and the statement of owners' equity. For the sake of charity, we are assuming that when 3BL advocates speak of traditional management preoccupations with "the bottom line" they are using this as shorthand for the use of all of the major financial statements—including the details revealed in the footnotes to these statements.

[21] Reported in *The Shell Report 1999: People, Planet and Profits*, p. 18.

in any way analogous to the methodology of adding and subtracting used in financial accounting.[22]

An Impossibility Argument

Ultimately, we argue, there are fundamental philosophical grounds for thinking that it is impossible to develop a sound methodology for arriving at a meaningful social bottom line for a firm. There is a strong and a weak version of the argument: the strong version says that it is in principle impossible to find a common scale to weigh all of the social "goods" and "bads" caused by the firm; and the weak version says, from a practical point of view, that we will never be able to get broad agreement (analogous, say, to the level of agreement about accounting standards) for any such proposed common scale.[23] We would not pretend to be able to demonstrate the strong version here, since it would require a significant detour into the realm of moral epistemology. But we do think we can give a glimpse at why the weaker version of our critique is plausible, and that should be enough to cast doubt on the prospects of Triple Bottom Line accounting.

We can begin by expressing this "impossibility" argument in the decidedly less metaphysical terminology of accountancy. One of the three basic assumptions underlying the methodologies of the standard financial statements, including the income statement, is the so-called "unit of measure" assumption—that all measures for revenue, expenses, assets, and so on, are reducible to a common unit of currency.[24] What is lacking in the ethical/social realm is an obvious, and obviously measurable, common "currency" (whether in a monetary or non-monetary sense) for expressing the magnitude of all good and bad produced by the firm's operations and affecting individuals in different stakeholder groups.

Part of the problem is that it is difficult to make *quantitative* assessments of how good or bad some action or event is; and partly it is that we seem to be dealing with *qualitative* as well as quantitative distinctions when we evaluate

---

[22]Another kind of methodology for evaluating performance would be a *rating scheme* that assigned scores to various levels of performance on certain key indicators. For example, a rating organisation might score firms out of 100 with, say, 10 of those points derived from data about charitable contributions as a percentage of the firm's profits. Perhaps a firm would get 2 points for each half-percent of its profits donated to charity up to a maximum of 10 points. Similar scores could be assigned on the basis of the percentage of women and minorities in senior positions, and so on. Schemes like these are sometimes used by firms that screen investment funds on ethical grounds, and one is described in detail and employed in a book produced by the ethics consultancy EthicScan, *Shopping with a Conscience,* Toronto: John Wiley & Sons, 1996. Now any such scheme will be loaded with inherently controversial value judgments about how morally worthy these various factors are; and for this reason, such schemes are unlikely ever to receive the kind of widespread support and legitimacy that is enjoyed, say, by most of the basic accounting standards. Our point here, however, is simply that ratings schemes like this constitute a very different paradigm for evaluation than the one used in financial accounting; and not simply because they are more controversial. Not surprisingly, none of the major organisations that has tried to develop international, cross-sector standards for reporting and auditing social performance has gone this route of trying to develop an overall rating scheme. Nor have the major ("Final Four") accounting firms who are lining up to sell 3BL auditing services.

[23] We do not wish to imply that setting "ordinary" accounting standards is an uncontroversial process; but simply that inherently moralistic social accounting will be significantly more controversial.

[24] Two of the other basic assumptions are the "separate entity" assumption (the assumption that the economic events measured can be identified as happening to the entity in question, an entity separable from other individuals or organizations for accounting purposes), and the "time period" assumption (the assumption that the economic events measured occur within a well-defined period of time). For these assumptions, see Thomas Beechy and Joan Conrod, *Intermediate Accounting, Volume 1,* Toronto: McGraw-Hill/Ryerson, 1998, among other sources. These three assumptions sometimes go by different names, and are often accompanied by other assumptions not named here.

the social impact of corporate activities. Again, let us start with the "objective" indicators of social performance that are now being used in corporate social reports and in the leading social-auditing standards. Let us consider the comparatively simple task of merely trying to determine whether some particular "good" score outweighs another particular "bad" score. Imagine a firm with any one of the following pairs of scores in its record:

- Pair 1: a generous family-friendly policy that includes extended maternity-leave as well as part-time and job-sharing provisions for women returning to the firm after maternity leave, but also three sexual-harassment suits against it in the past year.

- Pair 2: an "ethical sourcing" policy for its overseas contractors that is audited by an international human-rights NGO, but also a spotty record of industrial relations at home, including a bitter three-month strike by members of one union.

- Pair 3: a charitable donation equal to 2% of gross profits, but also a conviction for price-fixing in one of its markets.

Other things equal, is there any obvious way to judge whether any one of these pairs of data would result in a net gain or loss on the firm's social bottom line? We could also consider the challenge of comparing good to good and bad to bad. For example, would a firm do more social good by donating one million dollars to send underprivileged local youths to college, or by donating the same amount to the local opera company? How should we evaluate the charitable donation by a firm to a not-for-profit abortion clinic, or to a small fundamentalist Christian church? Examples like these make it clear that although there are many relevant and objective facts that can be reported and audited, any attempt to "weigh" them, or tot them up, will necessarily involve subjective value judgments, about which reasonable people can and will legitimately disagree. (And of course this task can only get more difficult when there are hundreds of data points, rather than just two, to tot up.)

The power of this illustration does not rest on acceptance of any deep philosophical view about whether all value judgments are ultimately subjective or objective; it rests only on a realistic assessment of the open-ended nature of any attempt to make a global assessment of a firm's social impact given the kind of data that would go into such an evaluation. In the language of moral philosophers, the various values involved in evaluations of corporate behaviour are "incommensurable"; and reasonable and informed people, even reasonable and informed moral philosophers, will weigh them and trade them off in different ways. To say they are incommensurable is to say that there is no overarching formula that can be appealed to in order to justify all of these trade-offs (e.g., to decide definitively what the net social impact is for any of the pairs listed in the preceding paragraph).[25] In short, whatever is going on in this sort of normative evaluation, it would seem to be about as

---

[25] Utilitarians might object in principle to these claims that there is (a) no common "currency" for evaluating the impact of corporate activities, and (b) no overarching formula to justify trade-offs involving different values affecting different individuals. In its most straightforward, classical formulations, utilitarians believe that "utility" is this currency, and that anything of value can ultimately be judged in terms of its impact on the amount of utility. We will ignore the fact that utilitarianism is no longer especially popular among academic moral philosophers. Even if it were in some sense the best moral theory, it would hardly rescue the 3BL model of social accounting. The theory itself does not provide any objective formula for extrapolating "utility impact" from the kinds of data that are typically reported in social reports (again, see Appendix 1 for examples of typical social indicators). Any two reasonable and well informed utilitarians would be just as likely to disagree about the net social impact of a firm's many operations as would two non-utilitarians.

far as you could get from the paradigm of the accountant performing calculations on the basis of verifiable figures and widely accepted accounting principles.

One suspects that numerous problems with the aggregative assumptions underlying 3BL have gone unnoticed in part because they are also implicit in many discussions of CSR. It is common for advocates of 3BL and CSR to talk of the "social performance" or "social impact" of a firm, as if this captured everything that was relevant for an ethical evaluation of the firm. (Indeed, in articulating these theories throughout this paper we have had to use these expressions.) On this view, what is morally relevant is how the firm improves its positive impact on individuals or communities (or reduces its negative impact). Presumably "social impact" here must be closely related to "impact on well-being" (including the well-being of non-human organisms). In the language of moral philosophy, this is to locate all of business ethics and social responsibility within the *theory of the good*: asking, roughly, how does the firm add value to the world? Obviously, this is a very relevant question when evaluating a corporation. But much of what is ethically relevant about corporate activities concerns issues in what moral philosophers call the *theory of right*: e.g., concerning whether rights are respected and obligations are fulfilled. Now clearly there are important links between our views about rights and obligations, on the one hand, and the question of what actions make the world better or worse, on the other. But unless we are the most simple-minded act-utilitarians, we recognize that the link is never direct: that is, we do not simply have one obligation, namely, to maximize well-being.[26] Sometimes fulfilling a particular obligation or respecting a particular person's rights (e.g., by honouring a binding contract that ends up hurting the firm or others) might not have a net positive "social impact"—but it should be done anyway. More importantly, for our purposes here, obligation-fulfillment and rights respecting are not what we might call "aggregative" concepts. They are not things that a good individual or firm should necessarily be trying to increase or *maximize*. If you have an obligation, then you should try to fulfill it. But there is no special value in obligation fulfillment per se. If you promised to pay someone back in the future then you must do your best to pay them back. And if you do, that is something that improves our ethical evaluation of you, so to speak. But you do not become more ethical by maximising the number of promises you can make in order to maximise your social performance as promise fulfiller. Put another way, for a firm and its managers to keep their promises is a good thing, an ethical thing, a socially responsible thing. But other things equal, you are not more ethical or responsible by making and keeping ten promises than you are by making and keeping one promise. To conceive of ethics and social responsibility as necessarily aggregative is to confuse very different ethical categories; and yet that is what happens in the logic of 3BL (and much of CSR) when we treat all ethically relevant aspects of a firm as if they can be measured in terms of social impact.[27]

---

[26] In a longer critique of 3BL and CSR it would be worth trying to identify just how much of the basic logic of these views is a reiteration of act utilitarianism. For a good summary of some of the stock criticisms of utilitarianism—particularly in the context of measuring social development—see Amartya Sen, *Development as Freedom*, Oxford University Press, 1999, pp. 54–61.

[27] It must be said that the brute notion of "social performance" or "social impact" also seems to flatten out the concept of *responsibility*. In effect, for advocates of CSR, the most socially responsible corporation is the one that has the greatest net social impact. But this erases many important "deontic" categories that are relevant for determining the nature of specific obligations. We are not always obliged to maximise "social impact." There are good and noble actions that we are not obliged to do (sometimes called supererogatory duties); other things that we are permitted to do but not obliged to do; other things that we are obliged to do even if they do not improve welfare; and so on. For a much richer notion of responsibility than the one implied in most writings on 3BL and CSR, see Enderle and Tavis, op. cit., pp. 1131–37.

Conclusion: What Use Bottom Lines without a Bottom Line?

We cannot help but conclude that there is no meaningful sense in which 3BL advocates can claim there is a social bottom line. (Again, we believe that analogous arguments would undermine the idea of an environmental bottom line; but that argument deserves more space than we could devote to it here.) This piece of jargon is, in short, *inherently misleading:* the very term itself promises or implies something it cannot deliver. This raises two issues worth reflecting upon. First, why has the idea spread so quickly, not just among Green and CSR activists, but also among the top tier of multinational corporations? And secondly, should we be concerned about the use, and propagation of the use, of jargon that is inherently misleading?

There is no simple answer to the first question, and certainly no general explanation for why so many different kinds of individuals and groups have found the language of 3BL so attractive. There are no doubt many conflicting motivations at play here, and by and large we can do no more than speculate about the mental states of different key actors. For many grassroots activists it is likely that the metaphor of bottom lines captured perfectly their long-held sense that social responsibility and environmental sustainability are at least as important as profitability when evaluating the performance and reputations of firms. After all, in ordinary discourse, when one announces that one's "bottom line" on a given subject is *P,* it rarely means more than that the speaker wants to convey that *P* is something worth noting, perhaps as a way of summing up.[28] For some of the initiators and early adopters of the concept within activist circles (including Elkington himself), it is likely that there were also perceived rhetorical advantages to borrowing from the "hard-headed" language and legitimacy of accountancy.[29] Perhaps senior executives would find it easier to take seriously the fuzzy notions of CSR and sustainability if they could be fit into more familiar paradigms with objective measures and standards. Many of these early movers (including Elkington himself [30]) were also offering large corporations consulting and auditing services that were built, at least in part, around the 3BL paradigm; and they would soon be joined, as we noted at the outset, by some of the most powerful "mainstream" accounting and consulting firms. Paid consultants have, of course, mixed motives for promoting and legitimising something like the 3BL paradigm: on the one hand, they can be committed to the utility for the clients of collecting, auditing, and reporting social and environmental data (for reasons given in list B, above); but on the other, they cannot be blind to the fact that this opens up a market niche that might not otherwise have existed. Corporations are almost certainly paying more for SEAAR-related services now than they were previously paying for ethics and CSR consultants.

More fanciful leaps of speculation are necessary for explaining the motivations of some of the early adopters of 3BL rhetoric and principles among multinational corporations. As we have noted already, there are a number of corporations that have long prided themselves on their traditions of social responsibility and good corporate citizenship. Having succeeded despite putting principles ahead of short-term profits is part of the lore in the cultures of

---

[28] For example, a hockey broadcaster summed up a game in which team A defeated team B with the remark, "the bottom line is that team A out-hustled team B tonight." But surely in sports if there's a literal bottom line, it is reflected in the final score, not in the explanation for the score!

[29] Of course, post-Andersen, accountancy looks rather less hard-headed and legitimate than it did in 1997.

[30] Elkington is co-founder of the consultancy SustainAbility, and played a key role in the production of Shell's 3BL report, "Profits and Principles—does there have to be a choice?" (1998).

companies like Johnson & Johnson, Levis Strauss, Cadbury's, and IKEA. And in the cultures of many smaller or more recent firms, from The Body Shop to your local organic grocer, CSR and green principles have often served as the organisation's very raison d'être.[31] For many of these firms, social and environmental reporting provides an opportunity to display their clean laundry in public, so to speak. They have long sought to improve their social and environmental performance, so they can be confident that reporting these achievements publicly will cause little embarrassment. Indeed, insofar as many of these firms make social responsibility part of their corporate image (hoping to woo the increasingly large pool of consumers and investors who claim to be willing to pay more to support ethical firms), the adoption of 3BL principles and the production of social reports is *consistent with* other strategies of brand management. (This observation is not meant in any way to reduce these efforts to a simple marketing strategy, but just to show why they are a logical step in a direction in which the firm was already traveling.)

The adoption of 3BL rhetoric by a number of very prominent multinationals *without* traditions of support for green and CSR principles is a more curious phenomenon. Perhaps it should not be wholly surprising that prominent on this list are some firms trying to shake off recent reputations for decidedly *irresponsible* business practices or aloof management structures—firms like Shell and BP, British Telecom, AT&T and Dow Chemical. Now we certainly do not wish to cast aspersions on the principled convictions that have been expressed repeatedly in reasoned, and sometimes almost evangelical, fashion by corporate leaders such as BP's Sir John Browne and Shell's Sir Mark Moody-Stuart.[32] Any impartial observer must be impressed with the way these two have been able to make real changes in the cultures of their organisations and to achieve real improvements in terms of human-rights issues and emissions reductions. At the same time, some critics have noted how useful it can be to multinational companies to adopt some of the rhetoric and principles of their critics from the world of the increasingly influential NGOs. David Henderson refers to this as a strategy of "sleeping with the enemy," and Robert Halfon's take is revealed in the two-part, Churchillian title of his report, *Corporate Irresponsibility: Is Business Appeasing Anti-business Activists?*[33] Without similarly casting any aspersions on the integrity of John Elkington, a longstanding critic of capitalism and globalisation, it is noteworthy that he seems to have had nothing but good to say about Shell since he was contracted by them to help prepare their first 3BL report.[34]

And this leads us to the second question we posed at the start of this section: should we be concerned about the use, and propagation of the use, of 3BL jargon that is inherently misleading? From an abstract normative point of view the answer clearly has to be Yes. If the jargon of 3BL implies that there exists a sound methodology for calculating a meaningful and comparable social bottom line, the way there is for the statement of net income, then it is misleading; it is a kind of lie. Even if advocates of 3BL were to issue explicit disclaimers to this effect, and to admit that it was little more than a slogan or shorthand for taking

---

[31] Business for Social Responsibility in the USA has many hundreds of corporate members, most of which are small- to medium-sized enterprises.

[32] See, e.g., John Brown, "International Relations: The New Agenda for Business," Elliott Lecture, St Anthony's College, Oxford, 1998; or Mark Moody-Stuart, "Forward" in *Responsible Business,* London: Financial Times, 2000.

[33] David Henderson, *Misguided Virtue: False Notions of Corporate Social Responsibility,* Wellington, NZ: New Zealand Business Roundtable, 2001; Robert Halfon, *Corporate Irresponsibility: Is Business Appeasing Anti-business Activists?* Social Affairs Unit, Research Report 26, 1998.

[34] See, e.g., Elkington, pp. 10, 48, 125, 176.

social and environmental concerns seriously, there are still reasons for concern. For one thing, words and expressions continue to carry connotations despite official renunciations—including, for new jargon, the misleading connotation that there is something novel about the new concept. But there is another more serious concern that should trouble the most committed supporters of CSR and sustainability principles who have embraced the 3BL.

The concept of a Triple Bottom Line in fact turns out to be a "Good Old-fashioned Single Bottom Line plus Vague Commitments to Social and Environmental Concerns." And it so happens that this is exceedingly easy for almost any firm to embrace. By committing themselves to the principles of the 3BL it sounds like companies are making a *more* concrete, verifiable commitment to CSR and sustainability. And no doubt many are. But it also allows them to make almost no commitment whatsoever. Without any real social or environmental bottom lines to have to calculate, firms do not have to worry about having these "bottom lines" compared to other firms inside or outside of their sector; nor is there likely to be any great worry about the firm being seen to have declining social and environmental "bottom lines" over the years or under the direction of the current CEO. At best, a commitment to 3BL requires merely that the firm report a number of data points of its own choosing that are potentially relevant to different stakeholder groups—typically in the form of a glossy 3BL report full of platitudinous text and soft-focus photos of happy people and colourful flora.[35] From year to year, some of these results will probably improve, and some will probably decline. Comparability over time for one firm is likely to be difficult and time-consuming for anybody without a complete collection of these reports and handy filing system. The firm can also change the indicators it chooses to report on over time, perhaps because it believes the new indicators are more relevant (. . . or perhaps to thwart comparability). And comparability across firms and sectors will often be impossible. At any rate, such comparisons will be on dozens or hundreds of data points, not on any kind of global figure like profit/loss, cash flow, return-on-investment, or earnings-per-share. (For example, company A might have more female directors and fewer industrial accidents than company B; but company B might have more female executives and fewer fatalities than company A; and so on across the various data points, many of which will not even be common to both reports.) In short, because of its inherent emptiness and vagueness, the 3BL paradigm makes it as easy as possible for a cynical firm to appear to be committed to social responsibility and ecological sustainability. Being vague about this commitment hardly seems risky when the principal propagators of the idea are themselves just as vague.

Once again, we do not wish by these remarks to be casting aspersions on any particular firm that has adopted 3BL rhetoric and issued some form of 3BL report. We have tried to emphasize that there can be many non-cynical motivations for doing this. A careful reading of these reports is often sufficient to judge a firm's real level of commitment to the principles.[36] If activists interested in propagating the rhetoric of Triple Bottom Line are not troubled by its inherently misleading nature (perhaps because they feel the ends justify the means), they should at the very least be concerned with the fact that it is

---

[35] It is a bad sign when a report begins with an entirely glossy page used to announce that "This BP Australia Triple Bottom Line Report is printed on environmentally conscious paper." What exactly is "environmentally conscious paper," and how much of it is being used to make this announcement? Fortunately, the report, which was published in November 2001, is rather more specific when it comes to data on social and environmental performance.

[36] Some, but not all, are available on the home pages of 3BL-friendly firms mentioned throughout this article.

potentially counterproductive (that is, a means to ends they do not think are justifiable).

We think it likely that the *future* of firms deciding voluntarily to report on their social performance will end up looking very much like the *history* of firms deciding to bind themselves to a corporate code of ethics. On the one hand, the mere fact that it has produced a social report or a code of ethics tells us very little about a firm's actual commitment to the principles expressed in the documents.[37] It is relatively costless to produce these documents, and—especially if they are relatively vague—they do not generally open up any serious risks for a corporation. On the other hand, both types of documents can play a critical role in a firm's serious strategy to improve its ethical and social performance and to integrate this goal into its corporate culture. It is our belief that clear and meaningful principles are most likely to serve firms of the latter type; and that vague and literally meaningless principles like those implied by the Triple Bottom Line are best only for facilitating hypocrisy.

Appendix 1: Social Performance Indicators[†]

Here is a small sample of the kinds of data that are included in social reports. Such reports typically report dozens of different data points, and often give future targets and comparisons with past performance.

Diversity

- Existence of equal opportunity policies or programmes;
- Percentage of senior executives who are women;
- Percentage of staff who are members of visible minorities;
- Percentage of staff with disabilities.

Unions/Industrial Relations

- Percentage of employees represented by independent trade union organizations or other bona fide employee representatives;
- Percentage of employees covered by collective bargaining agreements;
- Number of grievances from unionized employees.

Health and Safety

- Evidence of substantial compliance with International Labor Organization Guidelines for Occupational Health Management Systems;
- Number of workplace deaths per year;
- Existence of well-being programmes to encourage employees to adopt healthy lifestyles.
- Percentage of employees surveyed who agree that their workplace is safe and comfortable.

---

[37] We now have a couple of decades worth of experience with the widespread use of corporate ethics codes, and a number of studies suggest that most are neglected by corporations and have very little impact on their culture or operations. See, e.g., P. E. Murphy, "Corporate Ethics Statements: Current Status and Future Prospects," *Journal of Business Ethics* 14, 1995: 727–40; and P. M. Lencioni, "Make Your Values Mean Something," *Harvard Business Review*, July 2002.

[†] These representative indicators have been drawn from three sources: *Guided by Values: The VanCity Social Report (1998/99)*, www.vancity.com/downloads/2592_1998socialreport.pdf; Global Reporting Initiative's *Draft 2002 Sustainability Reporting Guidelines*, April 2002; *People, Planet and Profits, The Shell Report 2001* (www.shell.com/shellreport).

Child Labour

- Number of children working.
- Whether contractors are screened (or percentage screened) for use of child labour.

Community

- Percentage of pre-tax earnings donated to the community;
- Involvement and/or contributions to projects with value to the greater community (e.g., support of education and training programs, and humanitarian programs, etc.);
- Existence of a policy encouraging use of local contractors and suppliers.

Source: Wayne Norman and Chris MacDonald, "Getting to the Bottom of 'Triple Bottom Line,'" *Business Ethics Quarterly,* April, 2004.

6. World Wildlife Fund Whistle Blower Policy

Whistle Blower Policy

The whistle blower policy provides a mechanism for the reporting of illegal activity or the misuse of WWF assets while protecting the employees who make such reports from retaliation.

Questionable Conduct This policy is designed to address situations in which an employee suspects another employee has engaged in illegal acts or questionable conduct involving WWF's assets. This conduct might include outright theft (of equipment or cash), fraudulent expense reports, misstatements of any accounts to any manager or to WWF's auditors, or even an employee's conflict of interest that results in financial harm to WWF. WWF encourages staff to report such questionable conduct and has established a system that allows them to do so anonymously.

Making a Report If an employee suspects illegal conduct or conduct involving misuse of WWF assets or in violation of the law, he or she may report it, anonymously if the employee wishes, and will be protected against any form of harassment, intimidation, discrimination or retaliation for making such a report in good faith.

Employees can make a report to any of the following WWF executives at any time: President, General Counsel, Chief Financial Officer, or the Vice President for Human Resources. Their names and contact information are available on the WWF Intranet site and at the end of this policy statement. WWF will promptly conduct an investigation into matters reported, keeping the informant's identity as confidential as possible consistent with our obligation to conduct a full and fair investigation.

Alternatively, employees can make a report by calling a "whistle blower" phone line that will be answered by an outside company. The information provided will be forwarded promptly to WWF for investigation. Callers to the whistle blower line may remain anonymous if they wish. The whistle blower phone line and its hours of operation are listed at the end of this policy statement and on the WWF Intranet site.

Protection of Employees Who Report Misuse of WWF Assets An employee who has made a report of suspicious conduct and who subsequently believes he or she has been subjected to retaliation of any kind by any WWF employee is directed to immediately report it to the Vice President for Human Resources or to the General Counsel.

Reports of retaliation will be investigated promptly in a manner intended to protect confidentiality as much as practicable, consistent with a full and fair investigation. The party conducting the investigation will notify the employee of the results of the investigation.

WWF strongly disapproves of and will not tolerate any form of retaliation against employees who report concerns in good faith regarding WWF's operations. Any employee who engages in such retaliation will be subject to discipline up to and including termination.

Source: www.worldwildlife.org/who/Governance/whistleblowerpolicy.html

7. Society of Professional Journalists Code of Ethics

Preamble

Members of the Society of Professional Journalists believe that public enlightenment is the forerunner of justice and the foundation of democracy. The duty of the journalist is to further those ends by seeking truth and providing a fair and comprehensive account of events and issues. Conscientious journalists from all media and specialties strive to serve the public with thoroughness and honesty. Professional integrity is the cornerstone of a journalist's credibility. Members of the Society share a dedication to ethical behavior and adopt this code to declare the Society's principles and standards of practice.

Seek Truth and Report It

Journalists should be honest, fair and courageous in gathering, reporting and interpreting information.

Journalists should:

- Test the accuracy of information from all sources and exercise care to avoid inadvertent error. Deliberate distortion is never permissible.
- Diligently seek out subjects of news stories to give them the opportunity to respond to allegations of wrongdoing.
- Identify sources whenever feasible. The public is entitled to as much information as possible on sources' reliability.
- Always question sources' motives before promising anonymity. Clarify conditions attached to any promise made in exchange for information. Keep promises.
- Make certain that headlines, news teases and promotional material, photos, video, audio, graphics, sound bites and quotations do not misrepresent. They should not oversimplify or highlight incidents out of context.
- Never distort the content of news photos or video. Image enhancement for technical clarity is always permissible. Label montages and photo illustrations.
- Avoid misleading re-enactments or staged news events. If re-enactment is necessary to tell a story, label it.
- Avoid undercover or other surreptitious methods of gathering information except when traditional open methods will not yield information vital to the public. Use of such methods should be explained as part of the story.
- Never plagiarize.
- Tell the story of the diversity and magnitude of the human experience boldly, even when it is unpopular to do so.
- Examine their own cultural values and avoid imposing those values on others.
- Avoid stereotyping by race, gender, age, religion, ethnicity, geography, sexual orientation, disability, physical appearance or social status.
- Support the open exchange of views, even views they find repugnant.

- Give voice to the voiceless; official and unofficial sources of information can be equally valid.

- Distinguish between advocacy and news reporting. Analysis and commentary should be labeled and not misrepresent fact or context.

- Distinguish news from advertising and shun hybrids that blur the lines between the two.

- Recognize a special obligation to ensure that the public's business is conducted in the open and that government records are open to inspection.

Minimize Harm

Ethical journalists treat sources, subjects and colleagues as human beings deserving of respect.

Journalists should:

- Show compassion for those who may be affected adversely by news coverage. Use special sensitivity when dealing with children and inexperienced sources or subjects.

- Be sensitive when seeking or using interviews or photographs of those affected by tragedy or grief.

- Recognize that gathering and reporting information may cause harm or discomfort. Pursuit of the news is not a license for arrogance.

- Recognize that private people have a greater right to control information about themselves than do public officials and others who seek power, influence or attention. Only an overriding public need can justify intrusion into anyone's privacy.

- Show good taste. Avoid pandering to lurid curiosity.

- Be cautious about identifying juvenile suspects or victims of sex crimes.

- Be judicious about naming criminal suspects before the formal filing of charges.

- Balance a criminal suspect's fair trial rights with the public's right to be informed.

Act Independently

Journalists should be free of obligation to any interest other than the public's right to know.

Journalists should:

- Avoid conflicts of interest, real or perceived.

- Remain free of associations and activities that may compromise integrity or damage credibility.

- Refuse gifts, favors, fees, free travel and special treatment, and shun secondary employment, political involvement, public office and service in community organizations if they compromise journalistic integrity.

- Disclose unavoidable conflicts.

- Be vigilant and courageous about holding those with power accountable.

- Deny favored treatment to advertisers and special interests and resist their pressure to influence news coverage.

- Be wary of sources offering information for favors or money; avoid bidding for news.

Be Accountable

Journalists are accountable to their readers, listeners, viewers and each other. Journalists should:

- Clarify and explain news coverage and invite dialogue with the public over journalistic conduct.
- Encourage the public to voice grievances against the news media.
- Admit mistakes and correct them promptly.
- Expose unethical practices of journalists and the news media.
- Abide by the same high standards to which they hold others.

The SPJ Code of Ethics is voluntarily embraced by thousands of writers, editors and other news professionals. The present version of the code was adopted by the 1996 SPJ National Convention, after months of study and debate among the Society's members.

Source: www.spj.org/ethics_code.asp

8. Association for Computing Machinery (ACM) Code of Ethics and Professional Conduct

Adopted by ACM Council 10/16/92.

Preamble

Commitment to ethical professional conduct is expected of every member (voting members, associate members, and student members) of the Association for Computing Machinery (ACM).

This Code, consisting of 24 imperatives formulated as statements of personal responsibility, identifies the elements of such a commitment. It contains many, but not all, issues professionals are likely to face. Section 1 outlines fundamental ethical considerations, while Section 2 addresses additional, more specific considerations of professional conduct. Statements in Section 3 pertain more specifically to individuals who have a leadership role, whether in the workplace or in a volunteer capacity such as with organizations like ACM. Principles involving compliance with this Code are given in Section 4.

The Code shall be supplemented by a set of Guidelines, which provide explanation to assist members in dealing with the various issues contained in the Code. It is expected that the Guidelines will be changed more frequently than the Code.

The Code and its supplemented Guidelines are intended to serve as a basis for ethical decision making in the conduct of professional work. Secondarily, they may serve as a basis for judging the merit of a formal complaint pertaining to violation of professional ethical standards.

It should be noted that although computing is not mentioned in the imperatives of Section 1, the Code is concerned with how these fundamental imperatives apply to one's conduct as a computing professional. These imperatives are expressed in a general form to emphasize that ethical principles which apply to computer ethics are derived from more general ethical principles.

It is understood that some words and phrases in a code of ethics are subject to varying interpretations, and that any ethical principle may conflict with other ethical principles in specific situations. Questions related to ethical conflicts can best be answered by thoughtful consideration of fundamental principles, rather than reliance on detailed regulations.

Contents & Guidelines

- General Moral Imperatives.
- More Specific Professional Responsibilities.
- Organizational Leadership Imperatives.
- Compliance with the Code.
- Acknowledgments.

As an ACM member I will. . . .

1. General Moral Imperatives

1.1 Contribute to Society and Human Well-Being This principle concerning the quality of life of all people affirms an obligation to protect fundamental human rights and to respect the diversity of all cultures. An essential aim of computing professionals is to minimize negative consequences of computing systems, including threats to health and safety. When designing or implementing systems, computing professionals must attempt to ensure that the products of their efforts will be used in socially responsible ways, will meet social needs, and will avoid harmful effects to health and welfare.

In addition to a safe social environment, human well-being includes a safe natural environment. Therefore, computing professionals who design and develop systems must be alert to, and make others aware of, any potential damage to the local or global environment.

1.2 Avoid Harm to Others "Harm" means injury or negative consequences, such as undesirable loss of information, loss of property, property damage, or unwanted environmental impacts. This principle prohibits use of computing technology in ways that result in harm to any of the following: users, the general public, employees, employers. Harmful actions include intentional destruction or modification of files and programs leading to serious loss of resources or unnecessary expenditure of human resources such as the time and effort required to purge systems of "computer viruses."

Well-intended actions, including those that accomplish assigned duties, may lead to harm unexpectedly. In such an event the responsible person or persons are obligated to undo or mitigate the negative consequences as much as possible. One way to avoid unintentional harm is to carefully consider potential impacts on all those affected by decisions made during design and implementation.

To minimize the possibility of indirectly harming others, computing professionals must minimize malfunctions by following generally accepted standards for system design and testing. Furthermore, it is often necessary to assess the social consequences of systems to project the likelihood of any serious harm to others. If system features are misrepresented to users, co-workers, or supervisors, the individual computing professional is responsible for any resulting injury.

In the work environment the computing professional has the additional obligation to report any signs of system dangers that might result in serious personal or social damage. If one's superiors do not act to curtail or mitigate such dangers, it may be necessary to "blow the whistle" to help correct the problem or reduce the risk. However, capricious or misguided reporting of violations can, itself, be harmful. Before reporting violations, all relevant aspects of the incident must be thoroughly assessed. In particular, the assessment of risk and responsibility must be credible. It is suggested that advice be sought from other computing professionals. See principle 2.5 regarding thorough evaluations.

1.3 Be Honest and Trustworthy Honesty is an essential component of trust. Without trust an organization cannot function effectively. The honest computing professional will not make deliberately false or deceptive claims about a system or system design, but will instead provide full disclosure of all pertinent system limitations and problems.

A computer professional has a duty to be honest about his or her own qualifications, and about any circumstances that might lead to conflicts of interest.

Membership in volunteer organizations such as ACM may at times place individuals in situations where their statements or actions could be interpreted as carrying the "weight" of a larger group of professionals. An ACM member will exercise care to not misrepresent ACM or positions and policies of ACM or any ACM units.

1.4 Be Fair and Take Action Not to Discriminate
The values of equality, tolerance, respect for others, and the principles of equal justice govern this imperative. Discrimination on the basis of race, sex, religion, age, disability, national origin, or other such factors is an explicit violation of ACM policy and will not be tolerated.

Inequities between different groups of people may result from the use or misuse of information and technology. In a fair society, all individuals would have equal opportunity to participate in, or benefit from, the use of computer resources regardless of race, sex, religion, age, disability, national origin or other such similar factors. However, these ideals do not justify unauthorized use of computer resources nor do they provide an adequate basis for violation of any other ethical imperatives of this code.

1.5 Honor Property Rights Including Copyrights and Patents
Violation of copyrights, patents, trade secrets and the terms of license agreements is prohibited by law in most circumstances. Even when software is not so protected, such violations are contrary to professional behavior. Copies of software should be made only with proper authorization. Unauthorized duplication of materials must not be condoned.

1.6 Give Proper Credit for Intellectual Property
Computing professionals are obligated to protect the integrity of intellectual property. Specifically, one must not take credit for other's ideas or work, even in cases where the work has not been explicitly protected by copyright, patent, etc.

1.7 Respect the Privacy of Others
Computing and communication technology enables the collection and exchange of personal information on a scale unprecedented in the history of civilization. Thus there is increased potential for violating the privacy of individuals and groups. It is the responsibility of professionals to maintain the privacy and integrity of data describing individuals. This includes taking precautions to ensure the accuracy of data, as well as protecting it from unauthorized access or accidental disclosure to inappropriate individuals. Furthermore, procedures must be established to allow individuals to review their records and correct inaccuracies.

This imperative implies that only the necessary amount of personal information be collected in a system, that retention and disposal periods for that information be clearly defined and enforced, and that personal information gathered for a specific purpose not be used for other purposes without consent of the individual(s). These principles apply to electronic communications, including electronic mail, and prohibit procedures that capture or monitor electronic user data, including messages, without the permission of users or bona fide authorization related to system operation and maintenance. User data observed during the normal duties of system operation and maintenance must be treated with strictest confidentiality, except in cases where it is evidence for the violation of law, organizational regulations, or this Code. In these cases, the nature or contents of that information must be disclosed only to proper authorities.

1.8 Honor Confidentiality
The principle of honesty extends to issues of confidentiality of information whenever one has made an explicit promise to honor confidentiality or, implicitly, when private information not directly related to the performance of one's duties becomes available. The ethical concern is to respect all obligations of confidentiality to employers, clients, and

users unless discharged from such obligations by requirements of the law or other principles of this Code.

As an ACM computing professional I will . . .

2. More Specific Professional Responsibilities

2.1 Strive to Achieve the Highest Quality, Effectiveness and Dignity in Both the Process and Products of Professional Work Excellence is perhaps the most important obligation of a professional. The computing professional must strive to achieve quality and to be cognizant of the serious negative consequences that may result from poor quality in a system.

2.2 Acquire and Maintain Professional Competence Excellence depends on individuals who take responsibility for acquiring and maintaining professional competence. A professional must participate in setting standards for appropriate levels of competence, and strive to achieve those standards. Upgrading technical knowledge and competence can be achieved in several ways: doing independent study; attending seminars, conferences, or courses; and being involved in professional organizations.

2.3 Know and Respect Existing Laws Pertaining to Professional Work ACM members must obey existing local, state, province, national, and international laws unless there is a compelling ethical basis not to do so. Policies and procedures of the organizations in which one participates must also be obeyed. But compliance must be balanced with the recognition that sometimes existing laws and rules may be immoral or inappropriate and, therefore, must be challenged. Violation of a law or regulation may be ethical when that law or rule has inadequate moral basis or when it conflicts with another law judged to be more important. If one decides to violate a law or rule because it is viewed as unethical, or for any other reason, one must fully accept responsibility for one's actions and for the consequences.

2.4 Accept and Provide Appropriate Professional Review Quality professional work, especially in the computing profession, depends on professional reviewing and critiquing. Whenever appropriate, individual members should seek and utilize peer review as well as provide critical review of the work of others.

2.5 Give Comprehensive and Thorough Evaluations of Computer Systems and Their Impacts, Including Analysis of Possible Risks Computer professionals must strive to be perceptive, thorough, and objective when evaluating, recommending, and presenting system descriptions and alternatives. Computer professionals are in a position of special trust, and therefore have a special responsibility to provide objective, credible evaluations to employers, clients, users, and the public. When providing evaluations the professional must also identify any relevant conflicts of interest, as stated in imperative 1.3.

As noted in the discussion of principle 1.2 on avoiding harm, any signs of danger from systems must be reported to those who have opportunity and/or responsibility to resolve them. See the guidelines for imperative 1.2 for more details concerning harm, including the reporting of professional violations.

2.6 Honor Contracts, Agreements, and Assigned Responsibilities Honoring one's commitments is a matter of integrity and honesty. For the computer professional this includes ensuring that system elements perform as intended. Also, when one contracts for work with another party, one has an obligation to keep that party properly informed about progress toward completing that work.

A computing professional has a responsibility to request a change in any assignment that he or she feels cannot be completed as defined. Only after serious consideration and with full disclosure of risks and concerns to the employer or client, should one accept the assignment. The major underlying principle here is the obligation to accept personal accountability for professional work. On some occasions other ethical principles may take greater priority.

A judgment that a specific assignment should not be performed may not be accepted. Having clearly identified one's concerns and reasons for that judgment, but failing to procure a change in that assignment, one may yet be obligated, by contract or by law, to proceed as directed. The computing professional's ethical judgment should be the final guide in deciding whether or not to proceed. Regardless of the decision, one must accept the responsibility for the consequences.

However, performing assignments "against one's own judgment" does not relieve the professional of responsibility for any negative consequences.

2.7 Improve Public Understanding of Computing and Its Consequences Computing professionals have a responsibility to share technical knowledge with the public by encouraging understanding of computing, including the impacts of computer systems and their limitations. This imperative implies an obligation to counter any false views related to computing.

2.8 Access Computing and Communication Resources Only When Authorized to Do So Theft or destruction of tangible and electronic property is prohibited by imperative 1.2—"Avoid harm to others." Trespassing and unauthorized use of a computer or communication system is addressed by this imperative. Trespassing includes accessing communication networks and computer systems, or accounts and/or files associated with those systems, without explicit authorization to do so. Individuals and organizations have the right to restrict access to their systems so long as they do not violate the discrimination principle (see 1.4). No one should enter or use another's computer system, software, or data files without permission. One must always have appropriate approval before using system resources, including communication ports, file space, other system peripherals, and computer time.

As an ACM member and an organizational leader, I will . . .

3. Organizational Leadership Imperatives

BACKGROUND NOTE: This section draws extensively from the draft IFIP (International Federation for Information Processing) Code of Ethics, especially its sections on organizational ethics and international concerns. The ethical obligations of organizations tend to be neglected in most codes of professional conduct, perhaps because these codes are written from the perspective of the individual member. This dilemma is addressed by stating these imperatives from the perspective of the organizational leader. In this context "leader" is viewed as any organizational member who has leadership or educational responsibilities. These imperatives generally may apply to organizations as well as their leaders. In this context "organizations" are corporations, government agencies, and other "employers," as well as volunteer professional organizations.

3.1 Articulate Social Responsibilities of Members of an Organizational Unit and Encourage Full Acceptance of Those Responsibilities Because organizations of all kinds have impacts on the public, they must accept responsibilities to society. Organizational procedures and attitudes oriented toward quality and the welfare of society will reduce harm to members of the public, thereby serving public interest and fulfilling social responsibility. Therefore, organizational leaders must encourage full participation in meeting social responsibilities as well as quality performance.

3.2 Manage Personnel and Resources to Design and Build Information Systems That Enhance the Quality of Working Life Organizational leaders are responsible for ensuring that computer systems enhance, not degrade, the quality of working life. When implementing a computer system, organizations must consider the personal and professional development, physical safety, and human dignity of all workers. Appropriate human–computer ergonomic standards should be considered in system design and in the workplace.

3.3 Acknowledge and Support Proper and Authorized Uses of an Organization's Computing and Communication Resources Because computer systems can become tools to harm as well as to benefit an organization, the leadership has the responsibility to clearly define appropriate and inappropriate uses of organizational computing resources. While the number and scope of such rules should be minimal, they should be fully enforced when established.

3.4 Ensure That Users and Those Who Will Be Affected by a System Have Their Needs Clearly Articulated during the Assessment and Design of Requirements; Later the System Must Be Validated to Meet Requirements Current system users, potential users and other persons whose lives may be affected by a system must have their needs assessed and incorporated in the statement of requirements. System validation should ensure compliance with those requirements.

3.5 Articulate and Support Policies That Protect the Dignity of Users and Others Affected by a Computing System Designing or implementing systems that deliberately or inadvertently demean individuals or groups is ethically unacceptable. Computer professionals who are in decision-making positions should verify that systems are designed and implemented to protect personal privacy and enhance personal dignity.

3.6 Create Opportunities for Members of the Organization to Learn the Principles and Limitations of Computer Systems This complements the imperative on public understanding (2.7). Educational opportunities are essential to facilitate optimal participation of all organizational members. Opportunities must be available to all members to help them improve their knowledge and skills in computing, including courses that familiarize them with the consequences and limitations of particular types of systems. In particular, professionals must be made aware of the dangers of building systems around oversimplified models, the improbability of anticipating and designing for every possible operating condition, and other issues related to the complexity of this profession.

As an ACM member I will . . .

4. Compliance with the Code

4.1 Uphold and Promote the Principles of this Code The future of the computing profession depends on both technical and ethical excellence. Not only is it important for ACM computing professionals to adhere to the principles expressed in this Code, each member should encourage and support adherence by other members.

4.2 Treat Violations of this Code as Inconsistent with Membership in the ACM Adherence of professionals to a code of ethics is largely a voluntary matter. However, if a member does not follow this code by engaging in gross misconduct, membership in ACM may be terminated.

Source: www.acm.org/constitution/code.html

9. The Institute of Internal Auditors (IIA) Code of Ethics

Introduction

The purpose of The Institute's Code of Ethics is to promote an ethical culture in the profession of internal auditing.

Internal auditing is an independent, objective assurance and consulting activity designed to add value and improve an organization's operations. It helps an organization accomplish its objectives by bringing a systematic, disciplined approach to evaluate and improve the effectiveness of risk management, control, and governance processes.

A code of ethics is necessary and appropriate for the profession of internal auditing, founded as it is on the trust placed in its objective assurance about risk management, control, and governance. The Institute's Code of Ethics extends beyond the definition of internal auditing to include two essential components:

1. Principles that are relevant to the profession and practice of internal auditing;
2. Rules of Conduct that describe behavior norms expected of internal auditors. These rules are an aid to interpreting the Principles into practical applications and are intended to guide the ethical conduct of internal auditors.

The Code of Ethics together with The Institute's Professional Practices Framework and other relevant Institute pronouncements provide guidance to internal auditors serving others. "Internal auditors" refers to Institute members, recipients of or candidates for IIA professional certifications, and those who provide internal auditing services within the definition of internal auditing.

Applicability and Enforcement

This Code of Ethics applies to both individuals and entities that provide internal auditing services.

For Institute members and recipients of or candidates for IIA professional certifications, breaches of the Code of Ethics will be evaluated and administered according to The Institute's Bylaws and Administrative Guidelines. The fact that a particular conduct is not mentioned in the Rules of Conduct does not prevent it from being unacceptable or discreditable, and therefore, the member, certification holder, or candidate can be liable for disciplinary action.

Principles

Internal auditors are expected to apply and uphold the following principles:

- *Integrity.* The integrity of internal auditors establishes trust and thus provides the basis for reliance on their judgment.
- *Objectivity.* Internal auditors exhibit the highest level of professional objectivity in gathering, evaluating, and communicating information about the activity or process being examined. Internal auditors make a balanced assessment of all the relevant circumstances and are not unduly influenced by their own interests or by others in forming judgments.

- *Confidentiality.* Internal auditors respect the value and ownership of information they receive and do not disclose information without appropriate authority unless there is a legal or professional obligation to do so.
- *Competency.* Internal auditors apply the knowledge, skills, and experience needed in the performance of internal auditing services.

Rules of Conduct

1. Integrity Internal auditors:

1.1. Shall perform their work with honesty, diligence, and responsibility.

1.2. Shall observe the law and make disclosures expected by the law and the profession.

1.3. Shall not knowingly be a party to any illegal activity, or engage in acts that are discreditable to the profession of internal auditing or to the organization.

1.4. Shall respect and contribute to the legitimate and ethical objectives of the organization.

2. Objectivity Internal auditors:

2.1. Shall not participate in any activity or relationship that may impair or be presumed to impair their unbiased assessment. This participation includes those activities or relationships that may be in conflict with the interests of the organization.

2.2. Shall not accept anything that may impair or be presumed to impair their professional judgment.

2.3. Shall disclose all material facts known to them that, if not disclosed, may distort the reporting of activities under review.

3. Confidentiality Internal auditors:

3.1. Shall be prudent in the use and protection of information acquired in the course of their duties.

3.2. Shall not use information for any personal gain or in any manner that would be contrary to the law or detrimental to the legitimate and ethical objectives of the organization.

A vast amount of information is freely available to the public and the acquisition and use of this type of information is encouraged. Publicly available information includes information:

found in books and magazines;

available on the internet;

made public by federal, state, or local government agencies;

revealed in legal filings and pleadings;

disclosed or discussed in public places, at conferences or trade shows, or in specialized trade or technical publications;

contained in patent applications or issued patents; and

obtainable from simple observation from the street or another legally permissible location.

While all of this information is publicly available, it is not necessarily widely known. To the degree that this information could have particular relevance to the Company, employees are encouraged to find this information and share it within the Company.

"Trade Secret" Information Generally, information is considered a "trade secret" only if:

> the information is in fact secret, i.e. not generally known to and not readily ascertainable by the public;
>
> the owner has taken reasonable measures to keep the information secret; and
>
> the information has independent economic value because it is not widely known.

In 1996, the U.S. Congress passed the Economic Espionage Act, which makes it a crime to steal trade secrets. More specifically, the Economic Espionage Act prohibits you from acquiring trade secrets of others through improper means, such as deceit or misrepresentation, and prohibits the receipt or use of information illegally acquired by a third party, or from present or former employees who are not authorized to disclose it. The Economic Espionage Act provides for criminal fines for the Company of up to $10 million and criminal fines for an employee of up to $500,000 and up to 15 years imprisonment. Accordingly, an employee should not knowingly:

1. take, carry away, or obtain a third party trade secret without authorization or obtain a third party trade secret by fraud or deception;

2. copy, download, mail, deliver, send, transmit, or communicate a third party trade secret without authorization; or

3. receive, buy, or possess a third party trade secret knowing it has been stolen or obtained without authorization.

Non-Public, Non-"Trade Secret" Information. Certain information is not "public" in the sense that it is not published or widely available to the public, but neither is it a "trade secret." This would include, for example, information about a company that the Company itself made no effort to keep secret. Nothing would bar an employee from obtaining such information in a casual conversation and subsequently reporting or using that information. Accordingly, Company employees are encouraged to obtain, share, and use such non-public, non-trade secret information, *provided* that no improper means are used. If improper means are necessary to obtain information, a good chance exists that the party who would divulge the information knows that he or she should keep the information secret, thus raising the likelihood that the information could be considered a trade secret. "Improper Means" would include:

> lying, engaging in deception, or creating a false impression in order to induce the disclosure of trade secrets;
>
> paying someone to reveal trade secrets;
>
> blackmailing or threatening someone to reveal trade secrets;
>
> paying someone who had already improperly obtained trade secrets to reveal those secrets to you; and
>
> engaging in any activity that is itself illegal (such as theft or computer "hacking") in order to obtain secrets.

The preceding list is not exhaustive. Other types of activity engaged in to obtain trade secrets could be considered "improper." Therefore, if you have any doubts about activities you are thinking of pursuing to obtain information, *do not engage in those activities* until you have first discussed them with the Company's General Counsel. Only if you have first obtained the advice and clearance of the Company's General Counsel may you engage in any activity of a questionable nature to obtain information from others.

4. Competency

Internal auditors:

4.1. Shall engage only in those services for which they have the necessary knowledge, skills, and experience.

4.2. Shall perform internal auditing services in accordance with the International Standards for the Professional Practice of Internal Auditing.

4.3. Shall continually improve their proficiency and the effectiveness and quality of their services.

Source: Adopted by The IIA Board of Directors, June 17, 2000, www.theiia.org/guidance/standards-and-guidance/professional-practices-framework/code-of-ethics/code-of-ethics—-english/

10. American Society of Civil Engineers (ASCE) Code of Ethics[1]

Fundamental Principles[2]

Engineers uphold and advance the integrity, honor and dignity of the engineering profession by:

1. using their knowledge and skill for the enhancement of human welfare and the environment;
2. being honest and impartial and serving with fidelity the public, their employers and clients;
3. striving to increase the competence and prestige of the engineering profession; and
4. supporting the professional and technical societies of their disciplines.

Fundamental Canons

1. *Engineers shall* hold paramount the safety, health and welfare of the public and shall strive to comply with the principles of sustainable development[3] in the performance of their professional duties.
2. *Engineers shall* perform services only in areas of their competence.
3. *Engineers shall* issue public statements only in an objective and truthful manner.
4. *Engineers shall* act in professional matters for each employer or client as faithful agents or trustees, and shall avoid conflicts of interest.
5. *Engineers shall* build their professional reputation on the merit of their services and shall not compete unfairly with others.
6. *Engineers shall* act in such a manner as to uphold and enhance the honor, integrity, and dignity of the engineering profession and shall act with zero-tolerance for bribery, fraud, and corruption.
7. *Engineers shall* continue their professional development throughout their careers, and shall provide opportunities for the professional development of those engineers under their supervision.

Guidelines to Practice under the Fundamental Canons of Ethics

Canon 1 Engineers shall hold paramount the safety, health and welfare of the public and shall strive to comply with the principles of sustainable development in the performance of their professional duties.

---

[1] As adopted September 2, 1914; amended November 10, 1996; and most recently July, 2006.
[2] The American Society of Civil Engineers adopted The Fundamental Principles of the ABET Code of Ethics of Engineers as accepted by the Accreditation Board for Engineering and Technology, Inc. (ABET). (By ASCE Board of Direction action April 12–14, 1975)
[3] In November 1996, the ASCE Board of Direction adopted the following definition of Sustainable Development: "Sustainable Development is the challenge of meeting human needs for natural resources, industrial products, energy, food, transportation, shelter, and effective waste management while conserving and protecting environmental quality and the natural resource base essential for future development."

a. Engineers shall recognize that the lives, safety, health and welfare of the general public are dependent upon engineering judgments, decisions and practices incorporated into structures, machines, products, processes and devices.

b. Engineers shall approve or seal only those design documents, reviewed or prepared by them, which are determined to be safe for public health and welfare in conformity with accepted engineering standards.

c. Engineers whose professional judgment is overruled under circumstances where the safety, health and welfare of the public are endangered, or the principles of sustainable development ignored, shall inform their clients or employers of the possible consequences.

d. Engineers who have knowledge or reason to believe that another person or firm may be in violation of any of the provisions of Canon 1 shall present such information to the proper authority in writing and shall cooperate with the proper authority in furnishing such further information or assistance as may be required.

e. Engineers should seek opportunities to be of constructive service in civic affairs and work for the advancement of the safety, health and well-being of their communities, and the protection of the environment through the practice of sustainable development.

f. Engineers should be committed to improving the environment by adherence to the principles of sustainable development so as to enhance the quality of life of the general public.

Canon 2 Engineers shall perform services only in areas of their competence.

a. Engineers shall undertake to perform engineering assignments only when qualified by education or experience in the technical field of engineering involved.

b. Engineers may accept an assignment requiring education or experience outside of their own fields of competence, provided their services are restricted to those phases of the project in which they are qualified. All other phases of such project shall be performed by qualified associates, consultants, or employees.

c. Engineers shall not affix their signatures or seals to any engineering plan or document dealing with subject matter in which they lack competence by virtue of education or experience or to any such plan or document not reviewed or prepared under their supervisory control.

Canon 3 Engineers shall issue public statements only in an objective and truthful manner.

a. Engineers should endeavor to extend the public knowledge of engineering and sustainable development, and shall not participate in the dissemination of untrue, unfair or exaggerated statements regarding engineering.

b. Engineers shall be objective and truthful in professional reports, statements, or testimony. They shall include all relevant and pertinent information in such reports, statements, or testimony.

c. Engineers, when serving as expert witnesses, shall express an engineering opinion only when it is founded upon adequate knowledge of the facts, upon a background of technical competence, and upon honest conviction.

d. Engineers shall issue no statements, criticisms, or arguments on engineering matters which are inspired or paid for by interested parties, unless they indicate on whose behalf the statements are made.

e. Engineers shall be dignified and modest in explaining their work and merit, and will avoid any act tending to promote their own interests at the expense of the integrity, honor and dignity of the profession.

Canon 4 Engineers shall act in professional matters for each employer or client as faithful agents or trustees, and shall avoid conflicts of interest.

a. Engineers shall avoid all known or potential conflicts of interest with their employers or clients and shall promptly inform their employers or clients of any business association, interests, or circumstances which could influence their judgment or the quality of their services.

b. Engineers shall not accept compensation from more than one party for services on the same project, or for services pertaining to the same project, unless the circumstances are fully disclosed to and agreed to, by all interested parties.

c. Engineers shall not solicit or accept gratuities, directly or indirectly, from contractors, their agents, or other parties dealing with their clients or employers in connection with work for which they are responsible.

d. Engineers in public service as members, advisors, or employees of a governmental body or department shall not participate in considerations or actions with respect to services solicited or provided by them or their organization in private or public engineering practice.

e. Engineers shall advise their employers or clients when, as a result of their studies, they believe a project will not be successful.

f. Engineers shall not use confidential information coming to them in the course of their assignments as a means of making personal profit if such action is adverse to the interests of their clients, employers or the public.

g. Engineers shall not accept professional employment outside of their regular work or interest without the knowledge of their employers.

Canon 5 Engineers shall build their professional reputation on the merit of their services and shall not compete unfairly with others.

a. Engineers shall not give, solicit or receive either directly or indirectly, any political contribution, gratuity, or unlawful consideration in order to secure work, exclusive of securing salaried positions through employment agencies.

b. Engineers should negotiate contracts for professional services fairly and on the basis of demonstrated competence and qualifications for the type of professional service required.

c. Engineers may request, propose or accept professional commissions on a contingent basis only under circumstances in which their professional judgments would not be compromised.

d. Engineers shall not falsify or permit misrepresentation of their academic or professional qualifications or experience.

e. Engineers shall give proper credit for engineering work to those to whom credit is due, and shall recognize the proprietary interests of others. Whenever possible, they shall name the person or persons who may be responsible for designs, inventions, writings or other accomplishments.

f. Engineers may advertise professional services in a way that does not contain misleading language or is in any other manner derogatory to the dignity of the profession. Examples of permissible advertising are as follows:

- Professional cards in recognized, dignified publications, and listings in rosters or directories published by responsible organizations, provided that the cards or listings are consistent in size and content and are in a section of the publication regularly devoted to such professional cards.

- Brochures which factually describe experience, facilities, personnel and capacity to render service, providing they are not misleading with respect to the engineer's participation in projects described.

- Display advertising in recognized dignified business and professional publications, providing it is factual and is not misleading with respect to the engineer's extent of participation in projects described.

- A statement of the engineers' names or the name of the firm and statement of the type of service posted on projects for which they render services.

- Preparation or authorization of descriptive articles for the lay or technical press, which are factual and dignified. Such articles shall not imply anything more than direct participation in the project described.

- Permission by engineers for their names to be used in commercial advertisements, such as may be published by contractors, material suppliers, etc., only by means of a modest, dignified notation acknowledging the engineers' participation in the project described. Such permission shall not include public endorsement of proprietary products.[4]

g. Engineers shall not maliciously or falsely, directly or indirectly, injure the professional reputation, prospects, practice or employment of another engineer or indiscriminately criticize another's work.

h. Engineers shall not use equipment, supplies, laboratory or office facilities of their employers to carry on outside private practice without the consent of their employers.

Canon 6 Engineers shall act in such a manner as to uphold and enhance the honor, integrity, and dignity of the engineering profession and shall act with zero-tolerance for bribery, fraud, and corruption.

a. Engineers shall not knowingly engage in business or professional practices of a fraudulent, dishonest or unethical nature.

b. Engineers shall be scrupulously honest in their control and spending of monies, and promote effective use of resources through open, honest and impartial service with fidelity to the public, employers, associates and clients.

c. Engineers shall act with zero-tolerance for bribery, fraud, and corruption in all engineering or construction activities in which they are engaged.

---

[4] As adopted September 2, 1914; amended November 10, 1996; and most recently amended July 22–23, 2006.

d. Engineers should be especially vigilant to maintain appropriate ethical behavior where payments of gratuities or bribes are institutionalized practices.

e. Engineers should strive for transparency in the procurement and execution of projects. Transparency includes disclosure of names, addresses, purposes, and fees or commissions paid for all agents facilitating projects.

f. Engineers should encourage the use of certifications specifying zero-tolerance for bribery, fraud, and corruption in all contracts.

Canon 7 Engineers shall continue their professional development throughout their careers, and shall provide opportunities for the professional development of those engineers under their supervision.

a. Engineers should keep current in their specialty fields by engaging in professional practice, participating in continuing education courses, reading in the technical literature, and attending professional meetings and seminars.

b. Engineers should encourage their engineering employees to become registered at the earliest possible date.

c. Engineers should encourage engineering employees to attend and present papers at professional and technical society meetings.

d. Engineers shall uphold the principle of mutually satisfying relationships between employers and employees with respect to terms of employment including professional grade descriptions, salary ranges, and fringe benefits.

Source: www.asce.org/inside/codeofethics.cfm.

GLOSSARY

accounting function The function that keeps track of all the company's financial transactions by documenting the money coming in (credits) and money going out (debits) and balancing the accounts at the end of the period (daily, weekly, monthly, quarterly, annually).

altruistic CSR Philanthropic approach in which organizations underwrite specific initiatives to "give back" to the company's local community or to designated national or international programs.

applied ethics The study of how ethical theories are put into practice.

audit committee An operating committee staffed by members of the board of directors plus independent or "outside" directors. The committee is responsible for monitoring the financial policies and procedures of the organization—specifically the accounting policies, internal controls, and hiring of external auditors.

auditing function The certification of an organization's financial statements, or "books," as accurate by an impartial third-party professional. An organization can be large enough to use both internal staff auditors external professionals—typically certified professional accountants and/or auditing specialists.

board of directors A group of individuals hired to oversee governance of an organization. Elected by vote of the shareholders at the annual general meeting (AGM), the true power of the board can vary from institution to institution from a powerful unit that closely monitors the management of the organization, to a placeholder body that rubber-stamps the decisions of the chief executive officer (CEO) and executive team.

business ethics The application of ethical standards to business behavior.

code of ethics A company's written standards of ethical behavior that are designed to guide managers and employees in making the decisions and choices they face every day.

compensation committee An operating committee staffed by members of the board of directors plus independent or outside directors. The committee is responsible for setting the compensation for the CEO and other senior executives. Typically, this compensation will consist of a base salary, performance bonus, stock options, and other perks.

"comply or else" A set of guidelines in which companies abide by a set of operating standards or face stiff financial penalties.

"comply or explain" A set of guidelines in which companies are expected to abide by a set of operating standards or explain why they choose not to.

conflict of interest A situation where one relationship or obligation places you in direct conflict with an existing relationship or obligation.

corporate citizenship An alternative term for corporate social responsibility, implying that the organization is a responsible "citizen" in meeting all its obligations.

corporate conscience An alternative term for corporate social responsibility, implying that the organization is run with an awareness of its obligations to society.

corporate governance The system by which business corporations are directed and controlled.

corporate social responsibility (CSR) The actions of an organization that are targeted toward achieving a social benefit over and above maximizing profits for its shareholders and meeting all its legal obligations.

culpability score (FSGO) The calculation of a degree of blame or guilt that is used as a multiplier of up to four times the base fine. The culpability score can be adjusted according to aggravating or mitigating factors.

culture A particular set of attitudes, beliefs, and practices that characterize a group of individuals.

cyberliability Holding an employer liable for employees' Internet communications to the same degree as if they had written those communications on company letterhead.

death penalty (FSGO) Setting the fine high enough to match all the organization's assets—and basically put the organization out of business. This is warranted where the organization was operating primarily for a criminal purpose.

developed nation Country that enjoys a high standard of living as measured by economic, social, and technological criteria.

DII The Defense Industry Initiatives (1986).

disclosure (FCPA) The FCPA requirement that corporations fully disclose any and all transactions conducted with foreign officials and politicians.

ethical CSR Approach in which organizations pursue a clearly defined sense of social conscience in managing their financial responsibilities to shareholders, their legal responsibilities to their local community and society as a whole, and their ethical responsibilities to "do the right thing" for all their stakeholders.

ethical dilemma A situation in which there is no obvious right or wrong decision, but rather a right or right answer.

ethical reasoning Looking at available information to resolve an ethical dilemma and drawing conclusions based on that information in relation to personal ethical standards.

ethical relativism Ethical principles defined by the traditions of society, personal opinions, and current circumstances.

ethics Living one's life according to a standard of right or wrong behavior—in both how we think and behave toward others and how we would like them to think and behave toward us.

ethics officer A senior executive responsible for monitoring the ethical performance of the organization both internally and externally.

external whistle-blowing When an employee discovers corporate misconduct and chooses to bring it to the attention of law-enforcement agencies and/or the media.

extranet A private piece of a company's Internet network that is made available to customers and/or vendor partners on the basis of secured access by unique password.

facilitation payments (FCPA) Payments that are acceptable provided they expedite or secure the performance of a routine governmental action.

FSGO The U.S. Federal Sentencing Guidelines for Organizations, 1991 (revised 2004).

Foreign Corrupt Practices Act (FCPA) Legislation introduced to control bribery and other less-obvious forms of payment to foreign officials and politicians by American publicly traded companies.

GAAP The generally accepted accounting principles that govern the accounting profession—not a set of laws and established legal precedents, but rather a set of standard operating procedures within the profession.

global code of conduct A general standard of business practice that can be applied equally to all countries over and above their local customs and social norms.

globalization The expansion of international trade to a point where national markets have been overtaken by regional trade blocs (Latin America, Europe, Africa), leading eventually to a global marketplace.

"The Golden Rule" "Do unto others as you would have them do unto you."

instrumental approach The perspective that the only obligation of a corporation is to maximize profits for its shareholders in providing goods and services that meet the needs of its customers.

instrumental value Situation in which the pursuit of a value is a good way to reach another value. For example, money is valued for what it can buy rather than for itself.

internal whistle-blowing When an employee discovers corporate misconduct and brings it to the attention of his or her supervisor, who then follows established procedures to address the misconduct within the organization.

intranet A company's internal Web site, containing information for employee access only.

intrinsic value A value that is a good thing in itself and is pursued for its own sake, whether anything good comes from that pursuit or not.

less-developed nation Country that lacks the economic, social, and technological infrastructure of a developed nation.

multinational corporation A company that operates across multiple national borders in providing and selling products and services.

OECD Guidelines for Multinational Enterprises Governmental initiative endorsed by 30 members of the Organization for Economic Cooperation and Development and 9 nonmembers, promoting principles and standards of behavior in the following areas: human rights, information disclosure, anticorruption, taxation, labor relations, environment, competition, and consumer protection.

organizational culture The values, beliefs, and norms that all of the employees of that organization share.

organizational integrity Situation in which an organization publicly commits and sticks to the highest professional standards.

oxymoron The combination of two contradictory terms, such as "deafening silence" or "jumbo shrimp."

Public Company Accounting Oversight Board (PCAOB) An independent oversight body for auditing companies.

proactive ethical policies A company's clear sense of what it stands for as an ethical organization.

prohibition (FCPA) The wording of the Bank Secrecy Act and the Mail Fraud Act that prohibits the movement of funds overseas for the express purpose of conducting a fraudulent scheme, which the FCPA incorporated.

reactive ethical policies Policies organizations propose that are driven by events and/or a fear of future events.

routine governmental action (FCPA) Any regular administrative process or procedure, excluding any action taken by a foreign official in the decision to award new or continuing business.

social contract approach The perspective that a corporation has an obligation to society over and above the expectations of its shareholders.

society A structured community of people bound together by similar traditions and customs.

SOX Sarbanes-Oxley Act (2002).

stakeholder Someone with a share or interest in a business enterprise.

strategic CSR Philanthropic approach that targets programs that will generate the most positive publicity or goodwill for the organization.

sustainable ethics An ethical culture that persists long after the public scandal or the latest management buzzword.

telecommuting The ability to work outside of an office (from home or anywhere else) and log in to the company network (usually via a secure gateway such as a VPN, virtual private network).

thick consent Consent to a monitoring policy that occurs when jobs are plentiful and the employee would have no difficulty in finding another position—the employee has a realistic alternative if he or she finds the policy to be unacceptable.

thin consent Consent to a formal notification that the company will be monitoring all e-mail and Web activity—either at the time of hire or during employment—when employment with the company is dependent on the employee's agreement to abide by that monitoring.

transparent organization An organization that maintains open and honest communications with all stakeholders.

UN Global Compact A voluntary corporate citizenship initiative endorsing 10 key principles that focus on four key areas of concern: the environment, anticorruption, the welfare of workers around the world, and global human rights.

universal ethics Ethical policy in which actions are taken out of *duty* and *obligation* to a purely moral ideal rather than based on the needs of the situation, since the universal principles are seen to apply to everyone, everywhere, all the time.

utilitarianism Ethical choices that offer the greatest good for the greatest number of people.

value chain The key functional inputs that an organization provides in the transformation of raw materials into a delivered product or service.

value system A set of personal principles formalized into a code of behavior.

vicarious liability A legal concept that means that a party may be held responsible for injury or damage, when in reality he or she was not actively involved in the incident.

virtue ethics A concept of living your life according to a commitment to the achievement of a clear ideal—"*what sort of person would I like to become, and how do I go about becoming that person?*"

whistle-blower An employee who discovers corporate misconduct and chooses to bring it to the attention of others.

whistle-blower hotline A telephone line where employees can leave messages to alert a company of suspected misconduct without revealing their identity.

REFERENCES

Chapter 1

1. Joseph L. Badaracco Jr., *Defining Moments: When Managers Must Choose between Right and Right* (Cambridge, MA: Harvard Business School Press, 1997), pp. 41–42.
2. The Center for Business and Ethics at Loyola Marymount University www.ethicsandbusiness.org/strategy.htm.
3. Arthur Dobrin, *Ethics for Everyone: How to Increase Your Moral Intelligence* (New York: Wiley, 2002), pp. 31–32.
4. Lawrence Kohlberg, *Essays in Moral Development,* Vol. I, *The Philosophy of Moral Development* (New York: Harper & Row, 1981); Lawrence Kohlberg, *Essays in Moral Development,* vol. II, *The Psychology of Moral Development* (New York: Harper & Row, 1984).
5. Randy Cohen, *The Good, the Bad, & the Difference: How to Tell Right from Wrong in Everyday Situations* (New York: Doubleday, 2002), pp. 194–201.
6. Ibid., pp. 134–35.

Chapter 2

1. The Ethics and Compliance Officers Association, www.theecoa.org.
2. ERC, "Creating a Workable Company Code of Ethics", 2003, www.ethics.org.
3. Institute of Global Ethics: www.globalethics.org/bds/reading.html.
4. Gellerman, Saul W., "Why 'Good' Managers Make Bade Ethical Choices," HBR July–August, 1986.

Chapter 3

1. P. Kotler, "Is Marketing Ethics an Oxymoron?" *Marketing Management,* November/December 2004, pp. 30–35.
2. Adapted from A. Pomery, "The Ethics Squeeze," *HR Magazine,* March 2006.
3. M. R. Vickers, "Business Ethics and the HR Role: Past, Present, and Future," *Human Resource Planning* 28, no. 1 (2005).
4. The Institute of Internal Auditors, www.theiia.org.
5. Curtis C. Verschoor, "Ethical Culture: Most Important Barrier to Ethical Misconduct," *Strategic Finance* 87, no. 6 (December 2005), pp. 19.
6. Neil McOstrich, "Crossing the line," *Marketing Magazine, Toronto* 107, no. 45 (November 11, 2002), pp. 24.
7. Brian Steinberg, "Undercover Marketing Is Gaining Ground— Some Promoters Are Doing It—Others Question Its Ethics," *The Wall Street Journal* (Eastern Edition), December 18, 2000, pp. B17.D.

Chapter 4

1. Melanie Merrifield, "Corporate America's Latest Act: Juggling Corporate Social Responsibility," *Baylor Business Review* 2, no. 1 (Fall 2003), pp. 2.
2. Michael E. Porter and Mark R. Kramer, "Strategy and Society: The Link between Competitive Advantage and Corporate Social Responsibility," *Harvard Business Review,* December 2006.
3. Milton Friedman, *Capitalism and Freedom* (Chicago: University of Chicago Press, 1962), pp. 133.
4. Ibid.
5. R. C. Chewning, J. W. Eby, and S. J. Roels, *Business through the Eyes of Faith* (San Francisco: Harper & Row, 1990), pp. 207.
6. Melanie Merrifield, "Corporate America's Latest Act: Juggling Corporate Social Responsibility," *Baylor Business Review* 2, no. 1 (Fall 2003), pp. 2.
7. Melanie Merrifield, "Corporate America's Latest Act: Juggling Corporate Social Responsibility," *Baylor Business Review* 2, no. 1 (Fall 2003), pp. 2.
8. Wayne Norman and Chris MacDonald, "Getting to the Bottom of Triple Bottom Line," *Business Ethics Quarterly,* March 2003.
9. www2.coca-cola.com/ourcompany/citizenship_report.html.
10. Adapted from David Wheeler, Heike Fabig, and Richard Boele, "Paradoxes and Dilemmas for Stakeholder Responsive Firms in the Extractive Sector: Lessons from the Case of Shell and the Ogoni, *Journal of Business Ethics* 39, no. 3 (September 2002), pp. 297.

Chapter 5

1. Organization for Economic Co-operation and Development (OECD) Principles of Corporate Governance, 2004, www.oecd.org/daf/corporate/principles.
2. Cadbury Report on "The Financial Aspects of Corporate Governance," December 1992.
3. "Principles, not Rules," Michael Barrier, Internal Auditor, August 2003, www.theiia.org.
4. "In Pursuit of Good Governance," Tricia Bisoux, *BizEd,* March/April 2004; "What IS Good Governance," Tricia Bisoux, *BizEd,* March/April 2004.
5. "King Report on Corporate Governance for South Africa 2002: What it means to you," Cliffe Dekker, Attorneys, 2003, www.cliffedekker-hofmeyr.com/.
6. Ibid.
7. Breedon, R. C., Report to the Hon. Jeb S. Rakoff, the United States District Court for the Southern District of New York on Corporate Governance for the Future of MCI, Inc., August 2003, Retrieved August 27, 2003 from http://online.wsj.com/documents/RestoringTrust_Final.doc

8. R. P. Gandossy and J. Sonnenfeld, "Reforming Governance," *CEO Magazine*, December 2004, pp. 41–42.
9. "Crisis Prevention: How to Gear Up Your Board," Walter, J. Salmon, *Harvard Business Review*, January–February 1993.
10. "The Irresistible Case for Corporate Governance," International Finance Corporation, World Bank Group, September 2005, www.gcgf.org/.
11. "Giving Ethics Operational Meaning in Corporate Governance," Ronald Berenbeim, *Executive Speeches* 19, no. 5 (April/May 2005), pp. 19.
12. "Corporate Governance Mom: Nell Minow," *The Economist*, April 10, 2003.
13. Cadbury Report on "The Financial Aspects of Corporate Governance," December 1992.
14. Adapted from George O'Brien, "A Matter of Ethics," *BusinessWest* 22, no. 4 (June 13, 2005), pp. 9.

Chapter 6

1. Adapted from Procopio, Cory, Hargreaves, and Savitch, LLP, "Summary of the U.S. Foreign Corrupt Practices Act," www.procopio.com/publications/art_corrupt_en.html.
2. www.fcpaenforcement.com.
3. The 1998 Annual Report, "The Defense Industry Initiative on Business Ethics and Conduct," www.dii.org/annual/1998background.html.
4. K. E. Goodpaster, L. L. Nash, and H-C. de Bettignies, *Business Ethics: Policies and Persons,* 4th Ed., New York: McGraw-Hill, 2006, pp. 97.
5. W. M. Rexroad, T. J. F. Bishop, J. A. Ostrosky, and L. M. Leinicke, "The Federal Sentencing Guidelines for Organizations: Self-Policing Is Central to Minimizing Liability Risk," *The CPA Journal* 69, no. 2 (February 1999); D. R. Dalton, M. B. Metzger, and J. W. Hill, "The New U.S. Sentencing Commission Guidelines: A Wake-Up Call for Corporate America," *The Academy of Management Executive* 8, no. 1 (February 1994), pp. 7.
6. "The Sarbanes-Oxley Act of 2002: Strategies for Meeting New Internal Control Reporting Challenges—A White Paper" Copyright 2002 Price-WaterhouseCoopers, as used in L. P. Hartman, "Perspectives in Ethics," 3rd ed., New York: McGraw-Hill, 2005, pp. 681–683.

Chapter 7

1. Richard T. DeGeorge, *Business Ethics,* 5th ed., Upper Saddle River, NJ: Prentice-Hall, 1999.
2. Mark Taylor, "$73 Million . . . and Counting?" *Modern Healthcare* 49 (December 5, 2005), pp. 18.
3. Neil Weinberg, "The Dark Side of Whistleblowing," *Forbes* 175, no. 5 (March 14, 2005), pp. 90.
4. "What's a Whistle-Blower?" *Maclean's* 118, no 26 (June 27, 2005); "Persons of the Year," *Time* 160, no. 27 (December 30, 2002–Jan. 6, 2003, pp. 32; Richard C. Warren, "Whistleblowing: Subversion or Corporate Citizenship?" (Review), *Journal of Occupational and Organizational Psychology* 71, no. 4 (December 1998), pp. 372; Ann Hayes Peterson, "Inside the WorldCom Fraud," *Credit Union Magazine* 71, no 8 (August 2005), pp. 15.
5. Laura M. Franze, "Corporate Compliance: The Whistleblower Provisions of the Sarbanes-Oxley Act of 2002," *Insights: the Corporate & Securities Law Advisor* 16 (December 2002), pp. 12.
6. Peter Rost, *The Whistleblower: Confessions of a Healthcare Hitman,* Brooklyn, NY: Soft Skull Press, 2006.
7. Adapted from Grant Russell, "The Ethical Dilemma at Northlake," *CMA* 67, no. 2 (March 1993), pp. 13.

Chapter 8

1. Thomas L. Friedman, "The World Is Flat: A Brief History of the Twenty-First Century," Copyright © 2005 by Thomas L. Friedman. Reprinted by permission of Farrar, Straus, and Giroux, LLC.
2. A. Moore, "Employee Monitoring and Computer Technology Evaluative Surveillance v. Privacy," *Business Ethics Quarterly* 10, no. 3 (2000), pp. 697–709.
3. www.letsfixbritain.com/callcentres.htm.
4. www.infoconomy.com.
5. Jerry Adler, "When Email Bites Back," *Newsweek,* November 23, 1998.
6. Richard Mullins, *Rochester Democrat and Chronicle,* October 7, 1999.
7. Andrew Sparrow, *Daily Telegraph,* February 16, 2002.
8. www.michaelhanscom.com.
9. Stanley Holmes, "The Affair That Grounded Stonecipher," *BusinessWeek,* March 7, 2005.
10. www.onlinelawyersource.com.
11. "Cyberliability: An Enterprise White Paper," Elron Software, 2001.
12. "Ten Commandments of Computer Ethics," http://cpsr.org/issues/ethics/cei.
13. www.epic.org/privacy/workplace/.

Chapter 9

1. T. Morrison, W. A. Conaway, "Kiss, Bow, or Shake Hands: How to Do Business in 60 Countries," 2006.
2. www.relojournal.com/sept96/tadpole.htm.
3. L. Thurow, (Aug. 7, 2001) "Third World Must Help Itself," *Boston Globe* F4.
4. R. DeGeorge, "Ethics in Personal Business—A Contradiction in Terms?" 1993 *Business Credit* 102 (8), pp. 45–46.
5. William Greider, "One World, Ready or Not: the Manic Logic of Global Capitalism," New York: Touchstone, 1998, pp. 22.
6. www.unglobalcompact.org/AboutTheGC/index.html.
7. OECD Guidelines for Multinational Enterprises, June 2001, www.oecd.org.
8. Inspired by Alison Maitland, "A Code to Export Better Practice," *Financial Times,* London (UK), January 26, 1999, pp. 14.

Chapter 10

1. William C. Pollard, "The Heart of a Business Ethic: the Hansen-Wessner Memorial Lecture Series," Baltimore, MD: University Press of America, 2005, pp. 197–198.
2. Simon Webley, "Eight Steps for a Company Wishing to Develop Its Own Corporate Ethics Program," www.ibe.org.uk/developing.html.

PHOTO CREDITS

INDEX

Page numbers followed by n refer to notes.